Laurence Echard, John Adams

The Roman History - From the Building of the City to the Perfect Settlement of the Empire

Vol. 4

Laurence Echard, John Adams

The Roman History - From the Building of the City to the Perfect Settlement of the Empire
Vol. 4

ISBN/EAN: 9783337122973

Printed in Europe, USA, Canada, Australia, Japan

Cover: Foto ©ninafisch / pixelio.de

More available books at **www.hansebooks.com**

THE ROMAN HISTORY,

From the Total Failure of the

Weſtern Empire

IN

AUGUSTULUS,

To the Reſtitution of the ſame by

CHARLES the Great.

Containing the Space of 324 *Years*.

VOL. IV.

By the Author of the Third.

Revis'd by *LAURENCE ECHARD*, A. M.
Being a further Continuation of his Hiſtory.

With a Compleat INDEX to the whole.

LONDON,
Printed for *Jacob Tonſon*, within *Grays-Inn* Gate,
next *Grays-Inn* Lane, 1704.

THE
PREFACE.

THE only Reason I can give the Reader for Publishing this Volume, is his favourable Reception of the former, which made me think a farther Continuation of the Roman *History* would not be unacceptable. I have endeavour'd to continue it down to the Erection of a new Empire in the *West*, in the same Method which has been observ'd in the preceding Parts. The Usefulness of this *History* will best appear from the Encouragement it generally meets with in the World; and certainly none can be of greater Use than that of Nations, which sets the Reader, as it were, upon a commodious Eminence, from whence he has a full Survey of Parts remote, and a Prospect beautify'd with the Variety of Men, Cities, Mountains, Vallies, Woods and Desarts; and finds, that tho' Things vary as to Names and Forms, they continue the same in their Nature and Substance; that Men were no better in for-

PREFACE.

mer Times than they are in this Age, and indeed they could not well be worse; that Faction, Pride, Jealousie and Ambition were State Vices as much in Fashion then as now; that the best Princes were envy'd by some, and the worst flatter'd by others; of all which he will meet with several Instances in the following Sheets, which, I hope, are presented to him with as much Perspicuity as the Subject and Materials would admit of. The Affairs of the Church became, by degrees, so inseparably interwoven with those of the State, that I found it impossible to give a just Account of one without treating, in some measure, of the other. I fear, upon the whole, it will appear to be too void of those Excellencies, which are so indispensibly requisite to a Compleat History; and the best that I can pretend to say of it is, that it was well design'd. If, upon Perusal, it appears imperfect, I hope, at least, it will provoke some abler Pen to make the Publick a more valuable Present.

A TABLE

OF THE

EMPEROR S.

A *Naftafius*, 54th Emp. pag. 16 to 45.
Anaftafius II. 66th Emp. p. 355 to 357.
Conftans II. 62d Emp. p. 310 to 326.
Conftantine III. 63d Emp. p. 310 to 326.
Conftantine IV. 68th Emp. p. 370 to 398.
Conftantine V. 71ſt Emp. p. 402 to 411.
Heraclius, 61ſt Emp. p. 279 to 309.
Irene, 72d Emp. p. 412 to 416.
Juftin I. 55th Emp. p. 45 to 57.
Juftin II. 57th Emp. p. 212 to 235.
Juftinian I. 56th Emp. p. 57 to 211.
Juftinian II. 64th Emp. p. 337 to 350.
Leo II. 68th Emp. p. 358 to 369.

Leo

A Table of the Emperors.

Leo III. 70th Emp. p. 398 to 401.
Mauritius, 59th Emp. p. 243 to 268.
Philippicus, 65th Emp. p. 351 to 354.
Phocas, 60th Emp. p. 269 to 278.
Theodosius III. 67th Emp. p. 357 to 358.
Tiberius, 58th Emp. p. 236 to 242.
Zeno, 53d Emp. p. 1 to 15.

THE CONTENTS.

VOL. IV.

FROM the Total Failure of the Weſtern Empire in Auguſtulus, to the Reſtitution of the ſame by Charles the Great ; containing the Space of 324 Years.

CHAP. I.

From the Taking of Rome *by* Odoacer, *to the Reign of* Juſtinian *the Great; containing the Space of* 50 *Years.*   Page 1

CHAP. II.

From the Advancement of Juſtinian *the Great, to the Death of that Prince; containing the Space of* 38 *Years.*   Page 59

CHAP.

The Contents.

CHAP. III.

From the Death of Juftinian *the Great, to the Ufurpation of* Phocas *the Tyrant; containing the Space of* 38 *Years.*   Page 212

CHAP. IV.

From the Beginning of Phocas *his Reign, to to the Death of* Heraclius; *containing about* 37 *Years.*   Page 269

CHAP. V.

From the Death of Heraclius, *to the Reeftablifhment of the Empire in the Weft; containing about* 161 *Years.*   Page 310

ERRATA.

PAGE 33. line 4. dele *of.* p. 36. l. 34. read *Arles.* p. 62. l. 26. for *elfe* r. *lefs.* p. 70. l. 10. dele *fet.* p. 74. l. 19. dele *they.* p. 80. l. 11. f. *brought* r. *got.* p. 136. l. 1. r. *fucceſ-fively.* p. 137. l. 22. f. *'em* r. *it.* p. 151. l. 6. f. *for* r. *to.*

THE
Roman History.

VOL. IV.

From the Total Failure of the Western Empire in Augustulus, *to the Restitution of the same by* Charles *the Great.*

Containing the Space of 324 *Years.*

CHAP. I.

From the Taking of Rome *by* Odoacer, *to the Reign of* Justinian *the Great.*

Containing the Space of 50 *Years.*

I. AS the last Volume began with the Removal of the Imperial Seat from *Rome* to *Byzantium*, or *Constantinople*; so is this to commence with a Translation of the Empire it self thither, at least, so much of it as the

A. D. 476.

Length

Length of Time and Fury of the Barbarians had left; which confifted more in Form than Subftance, and was in reality no other than a Branch of that great ftupendous Body, which for fo many Ages over-fhadow'd the reft of the World. *Italy*, the place of its Nativity, was fubject to the *Heruli*; *Gaul* was feiz'd by the *Franks* and *Burgundians*; *Spain* by the *Goths*; *Britain* was poffefs'd by the *Saxons*, *Scots*, and *Picts*; *Africk* was fubjected to the *Vandals*; and *Pannonia* by fuch Nations, whom Neceflity had driven from home, and who pleaded no other Title to it than what was owing to the Force of Arms. However, it claim'd a Right of Succeffion, and, like fome Heirs of decay'd Families, affum'd the Honour tho' the Eftate was forfeited. The fame Marks of Sovereignty were preferv'd in *Conftantinople*, that had been at firft eftablifh'd in *Rome*; the fame Ceremonies, Titles, and Honorary Employments. And tho' the Empire wa fallen much fhort of what it formerly had been, yet it ftill poffefs'd a fair Inheritance; for, excepting what it loft in the Weft, which indeed was the moft valuable and fubftantial Part, the Dominions were the fame in Extent with what it claim'd in its fulleft Luftre. The Tranfactions that make up the Body of the fucceeding Part of this Hiftory are confin'd to a narrower Sphere, yet we fhall find the fame Viciffitude of Human Affairs; Men acting upon the fame Principles; fome guided by the fober Dictates of Reafon, others tranfported by the Extravagance of fome prevailing Paffion, and all fubfervient in their feveral Stations to the Will and Pleafure of the firft Almighty Mover, who has the fame indifputed Power over Communities, as over private Families and particular Perfons.

About the fame time that the Majefty of the **Weftern Empire** expir'd in the Perfon of *Auguftulus*,

Chap. I.   LIII. Zeno.

stulus, that of the East was insulted by *Basiliscus*; who, as before has been observ'd, taking an Advantage of the publick Distractions, rais'd a Party against *Zeno*, the lawful Prince, and forced him to fly for his Safety into *Isauria*; after which he caus'd himself to be declar'd Emperor, and created his Son *Marcus Cæsar*. He no sooner thought himself establish'd in his Usurpation before he apply'd his Power to the re-establishment of Hereticks, recalling those Bishops who had been formerly banish'd for their Impieties, and by his Edicts condemning the Acts of the Council of *Chalcedon*, proceeding with great Cruelty against those who had the Courage to oppose him. And as these his Practices render'd him odious to the Orthodox Christians, so did his Pride and Avarice expose him to the Hatred and Contempt of the Pretorian Soldiers, who had promis'd themselves great Advantages from the late Revolution, but being defeated in their Hopes became soon weary of the Change; so that according to the Insolence of most Soldiers who are employ'd in the Service of an unlawful Power, they readily listen'd to such Overtures as *Zeno*'s Agents thought fit to make 'em, and were persuaded to destroy him who had no Title to the Authority he enjoy'd, but what he deriv'd from them. Some write that about this time there happen'd a great Earthquake at *Constantinople*, in which a great part of the City was consum'd, especially the Library, containing no less than One hundred and twenty thousand Volumes of all sorts, among which were the Works of *Homer* written in Gold Characters, and cover'd with a Dragon's Skin of a prodigious Length, and that the People attributing these publick Calamities to the Usurpation of *Basiliscus* were more inclinable to restore *Zeno*: But the first Account is founded upon better Authority, and more agreeable to Reason. *Basiliscus* was not so supine and negligent, but he foresaw the Storm they were raising against him, and prepared himself in the best manner he could to encounter it. To the Forces he had already on foot, whose Fidelity he had great reason to suspect, he added such new Levies as the Exigency of his Affairs wou'd permit, and having muster'd his Army committed it to the Conduct of *Harmatius*, or *Armatus*, his near Kinsman; who however, being seduc'd by some Presents sent him by *Zeno*, and allur'd by the Promise he had given him of creating his Son *Cæsar* upon his Restoration, concurr'd with the chief of the Male-contents, and deliver'd up all his Forces to *Zeno*. *Basiliscus* being thus betray'd by his own Soldiers fled once more for Refuge into the great Church, depositing the Imperial Crown upon the Altar. From thence he was forc'd by *Acacius*, Patriarch of *Constantinople*, and being deliver'd into the Hands of *Zeno*, was by him banish'd together with his Wife and Children into *Cappadocia*, where they all perish'd in a short time by Hunger and Cold. Thus ended the Usurpation of *Basiliscus*; who, after he had tyranniz'd for the space of eighteen or twenty Months, receiv'd the just Reward of his Treason and Impiety, and *Zeno* was again saluted Emperor; the People being as zealous in his Restoration, as they had been violent in his Expulsion. At first he appear'd very sensible of the great Services *Armatus* had done him, he advanc'd him to the most profitable Employments of the Court, fed him at his own Table, and according to his Promise created his Son *Cæsar*; but whether he thought he had great reason to suspect him for his Treachery and Ingratitude to *Basiliscus*, or found him aiming at some new Commotions to the Prejudice of his Authority, he shortly after put him to Death, depos'd his Son, and made him be ordain'd

Priest,

A. D. 477.

Zeno restor'd.

Chap. I.   LIII. Zeno.

Prieſt, who ſome time after was choſen Biſhop of *Cyzicus*. This Proceeding of *Zeno* againſt *Armatus* was very grateful to the People of *Conſtantinople*, whom he had highly diſoblig'd, when under *Leo* he had abus'd the Favour and Authority of that Emperor to the gratifying his Cruelty, Avarice and Ambition. *Zeno*, immediately after his Reſtitution, took care by ſeveral Acts of Grace to reconcile himſelf to the Orthodox Chriſtians; he cancell'd all the Edicts that had been publiſh'd by *Baſiliſcus* in Favour of Hereticks, built ſeveral Religious Houſes, and remov'd all thoſe Biſhops that during the late Confuſions had thruſt themſelves into the Church through the Favour or Connivance of the Tyrant; and this he did not ſo much out of any juſt Zeal to the true Religion, as to ſupport himſelf the better by the Intereſt of the Catholick Party, and obtain the good Will of *Simplicius*, Biſhop of *Rome*, whoſe Aſſiſtance would be of great uſe to him in his intended Deſigns againſt *Odoacer*, whom he accounted as no other than an Uſurper, tho' he govern'd in the Weſt with much Prudence and Moderation, reſtoring to the Cities their ancient Privileges, contributing largely to the re-edifying thoſe that had been deſtroy'd by the Fury of the War, and diſtributing Juſtice to all with an impartial Hand; as appears by the Puniſhment he inflicted on *Viator* and *Ovida*, two Commanders, who envying *Nepos* the Tranquility he enjoy'd at *Salone* in *Dalmatia*, whither he had been forc'd to retire after *Oreſtes* had diveſted him of the Imperial Ornaments, and where he liv'd without ever buſying himſelf with the Affairs of State, ſurpriz'd him in his Houſe, and murder'd him.   At the ſame time he gave the People of *Liguria* a Signal Inſtance of his great Mercy and Clemency, in remitting to 'em a heavy Tax

The Death of Nepos.

Tax impos'd upon 'em by *Pelagius*, the *Præfectus Prætorio*, and behav'd himself, in all Respects, with so much Tenderness towards the Catholick Christians, that *Simplicius* could not forbear admiring the great Goodness of God, who after so many strange Convulsions and Revolutions in the State, had at length bless'd the Churches of *Italy* with an universal Repose, tho' under the Government of an Heretick. This made *Odoacer* acceptable to the People in general, it being seldom known, that the Subject calls the Title of the Prince in question, 'till being oppress'd in his private Interest he is provok'd to examine into that of the Publick.

A. D. 481. This general good Will, with which *Odoacer* reign'd in *Italy*, encreas'd *Zeno*'s Aversion to him, and made him more intent upon his Destruction; from the Prosecution of which he was diverted by some Domestick Troubles, occasion'd first by *Theodorich*, a *Scythian*, the Son of *Triarius*, who enter'd *Thrace* with a very powerful Army of *Goths*, and came within Four Miles of *Constantinople*, which he had certainly taken had not his own Men, either out of Envy to his Success, or Fear of the Enemy, over-rul'd and persuaded him to return; shortly after which he was kill'd by a Fall from his Horse.

A. D. 482.

Martian Rebels.

Zeno was scarce recover'd from the Apprehensions of this Invasion, before fresh Troubles of more dangerous Consequence interrupted his Repose; for *Martian*, the Son of *Anthemius*, one of the late *Roman* Emperors, rais'd a Civil War in the Empire, to which he laid Claim in Right of his Wife *Leontia*, the Daughter of *Leo*, who being the younger was Born after her Father had been advanc'd to the Empire, whereas *Zeno*'s Wife was Born whilst he was a private Man. Upon these Pretences he rais'd an Army consisting chiefly of Male-contents, and such whom the Mis-

Chap. I.   LIII. Zeno.

carriages of former Factions had prepar'd for any desperate Attempt; with these he so resolutely attack'd *Zeno*, that he shut him up in his Palace, and had he pursu'd his Design with the same Vigour he begun, he had, in all probability, succeeded; but thinking himself secure of the Emperor, and that it was impossible for him to miscarry in the Attempt, he deferr'd the farther Prosecution of it 'till the next Morning, which gave *Zeno* time to consult his own Safety, and draw off several of the adverse Party to his Interest. These at the next Encounter forsook *Martian*, who was forc'd to fly for Safety into *Cappadocia*, where he led a private Life for some time among the Monks; but being at length discover'd by *Zeno*, he banish'd him into *Tarsus* in *Cilicia*, where he was made a Priest.

This Insurrection was no sooner quell'd before fresh Commotions in the East threw *Zeno* into new Perplexities; for *Leontius*, Governor of *Syria*, at the Instigation of *Verina* the Empress, and Mother-in-Law to *Zeno*, ass'm'd the Imperial Purple; against whom the Emperor immediately dispatch'd *Illus*, the Captain of his Guards, whom *Verina* caress'd, and manag'd with so much Address, that instead of opposing *Leontius* he betray'd his Master, and join'd with the Rebels. This Revolution threaten'd *Zeno* with no less than an utter Ruin, for he knew they were all Persons of great Power in the Empire, and whom he had highly incens'd by his ingrateful Carriage, for they had been of great Service to him in his former Extremities. Wherefore, the better to secure himself against so terrible a Tempest, he address'd himself to *Theodorich Rumal*, King of the *Ostrogoths*, who had for some Years been brought up in the Emperor's Court, where he had formerly been detain'd as an Hostage.

Leontius sets up for himself.

Zeno Courts Theodorich the Goth, to his Party.

stage. He was a Prince, Comely and Couragious, having great part of *Illyricum* under his Dominion, where he kept a powerful Army constantly on Foot the better to secure his Authority. *Zeno* earnestly invited him to *Constantinople*, where being arriv'd he receiv'd him with great Honour, made him many Royal Presents, yielded up to him that Part of *Dacia* and *Mysia* that border'd upon his own Territories, made him General of his Armies, nam'd him Consul for the Year ensuing, adopted him his Son, and promis'd to assist him in driving *Odoacer* out of *Italy*, and Crown him King in his stead; and all this to engage him to undertake the War in *Syria*. This Prince, being of an active aspiring Temper, readily embrac'd such advantagious Conditions, and prepared chearfully for the Expedition.

Tho' *Theodorich* very zealously embrac'd the Service, and march'd into *Syria* with a numerous and well appointed Army, yet the Rebels made a greater Opposition, and maintain'd the War longer than was expected. The People in those Parts were grown weary of the present Government, and generally desirous of a Change, so that for eight Years together *Leontius* disputed it with various Success, 'till at length being defeated in a pitch'd Battel by *Theodorich*, he was constrain'd to fly together with *Illus* into a Castle call'd *Papyrus*, where they were both taken, and their Heads sent to the Emperor at *Constantinople*. *Zeno* was well assur'd *Verina* had been the grand Promoter of the War, for which reason he banish'd her into *Thrace*, where she dy'd in a short time after.

About this time there happen'd very unseasonable Disputes between the Churches of the East and the West, occasion'd chiefly by the indiscreet Obstinacy of *Acacius*, Patriarch of *Alexandria*, and *Felix*, Bishop

Chap. I.   LIII. Zeno.

Bishop of *Rome*; which proceeded so far that *Acacius* openly declar'd himself an Heretick, preferring the great Patrons of Heresie in most Parts of the East, and driving those out of their Sees that stood firm to the Oxthodox Faith; upon which the Pope summon'd a Synod, and Excommunicated him, and *Acacius* on the other Hand did the like by the Pope: And as this was the first open Quarrel between the Eastern and Western Christians, so it brought innumerable Mischiefs upon the Church, to the exceeding Detriment of Christianity. Nor was the State of the Church in a much better Condition in *Africk*, where *Honric* had lately succeeded his Father *Genserich*, who after a victorious Reign of Fifty eight Years dy'd in 'the peaceable Possession of that spacious Country.

His Son *Honric*, as he succeeded his Father in all his Dominions, so he inherited his violent Affection for the *Arian* Heresie, and bitter Spirit of Persecution; he commanded all the great Officers of the Court to embrace the same Profession with himself, otherwise he threaten'd to remove 'em from their Employments; and those who refus'd to comply were banish'd into *Sicily* and *Sardinia*, where they underwent unexpressible Torments with an unshaken Constancy, encourag'd to it by the prevavalent Examples of their Pastors. The better to countenance these his Inhuman Proceedings, he made use of Stratagems unworthy a Prince or Christian, in which, when he saw himself defeated, he banish'd at once, with an Infamous Barbarity, near Seven Thousand Ecclesiasticks into the Desarts of *Africk*, without regard to the Age and Infirmity of several among 'em.

Honric, the Son of Genserich, Tyrannises in Africk.

He took from all the Orthodox the Power of disposing of any thing by Donation, by Testament, or any other way whatsoever, and persisted

so

so obstinately in his Persecution, that his Subjects found themselves under a Necessity of renouncing the Faith, or quitting their Habitations, and embracing a despicable Poverty in a voluntary Exile. The Writers of that Age have recorded several Miracles effected by the Martyrs of those Times, how some upbraided the Tyrant for his Cruelty, even after they had been depriv'd of their Tongues by his Command, the Power of the Holy Ghost wonderfully supplying the Defect of Nature; how others by their extraordinary Piety were able to raise the Dead, and which is almost as miraculous, tir'd their very Executioners by their Constancy and Perseverance; how *Vindemialis*, *Longinus*, and *Eugenius*, three Holy Bishops, by their repeated Miracles confounded their Adversaries, who attempting to delude the People by a Representation of the like, hir'd a poor Man, with a considerable Sum of Mony, to counterfeit Blindness; but as they pretended by their Prayers to Touch and Heal him, he was that instant struck really Blind; and feeling the Hand of God heavy upon him confess'd the Cheat, and apply'd himself to the three Confessors for their Heavenly Consolation, who invoking the Name of the Holy Trinity restor'd him to his Sight; at which the Tyrant was so enrag'd, that he commanded *Longinus* and *Vindemialis* to be put to Death, and banish'd *Eugenius* into a Desart near *Tripoly*.

Nor did he exert his Cruelty only upon a Religious Account, but extended it even to his nearest Relations, for he put his Brother *Theodorich*'s Wife and her Children to Death, the better to secure the Succession to his Son, and proceeded with equal Severity against all such whose Virtue or Interest in the State render'd 'em obnoxious to his Suspicions. I thought fit to mention thus much in this

Chap. I. LIII. Zeno.

this place to give the Reader a better view of the Condition of the Faithful, and of the Difficulties with which Chriftianity was to contend, tho' ftill fupported by an invifible Power, to whom the Wifdom of this World is Foolifhnefs, and who has promis'd his Church that the Gates of Hell fhall never be able to prevail againft it. The Vengeance of God overtook the Tyrant fhortly after in a moft terrible Death, which depriv'd him at once of his Life and Dignity; he was fucceeded in the State by one of his Nephews, notwithftanding all his Precautions, in which he defign'd his Son for his Succeffor.

In the mean time *Zeno*, who began to apprehend no farther Danger from his Enemies, abandon'd himfelf to all manner of Licentioufnefs, in which, as it is ufual, he was follow'd by the reft of his Court: His diffolute Courfe of living threw him upon an Expence that far exceeded his ordinary Revenue, and that forc'd him upon unufual Exactions, in which he burden'd and opprefs'd his People. Among other Methods he had to raife Mony, none render'd him fo odious to his Subjects, as his expofing to Sale all the profitable Offices of the Empire, fo that in a fhort time all the great Pofts of Truft and Honour were fill'd, not by fuch as had Worth enough to deferve, but Mony to purchafe 'em, by which means the Emperor by degrees grew as defpicable to his People in his Officers as his Perfon; whereas Men of Honour and Integrity about their Prince often skreen him from the Contempt of the Publick. *Zeno* had a Son, of whofe Education he took particular Care, defigning him for his Succeffor; but his Father's Example, and that of his Affociates, render'd him fo proud and debauch'd, that he grew infupportable to all Mankind, and his Irregu-

Zeno's Court Debauch'd.

regularities threw him into a dangerous Distemper, which in a short time ended his Days. *Zeno*, being disappointed of his Hopes in his Son, releas'd his Brother *Longinus*, who had been detain'd in Prison, some say by the Emperor's Order, others by that of *Illus*, and had a great Desire to create him *Cæsar*; but he was so notoriously profligate, that all the Men of Worth and Reputation in the Empire oppos'd him, particularly *Pelagius*, a Patrician, and a Person of great Honour and Interest, who was therefore murder'd not long after by the Emperor's express Order.

These Disappointments in his own Family made *Zeno* view *Theodorich* with a suspicious Eye, who not long after return'd with Conquest, and who seem'd to have deserv'd too much from the indigent Emperor, or at least more than he was willing or able to pay. Of this the King of the *Goths* was quickly sensible, and therefore despairing of any Reward at Home, he reminded him of his former Promise, and the Leave he gave him to Conquer *Italy*, which he told him Odoacer *had thus long*

A. D. 489. Theodorich's Expedition into Italy.

Usurp'd in Contempt of the Imperial Majesty; adding, *That if he succeeded in his Design the Honour and Reputation of it would be* Zeno's, *but if he perish'd in the Attempt, then would he be freed from a troublesom Friend, and an expensive Annual Pension;* that it was more reasonable Zeno *should wish to see the Crown of* Italy *on his Head, whom he had adopted for his Son, and bound to his Service by many Acts of Favour and Royal Bounty, than on that of a Tyrant, who detain'd the Senate and People of* Rome *in Slavery.* The Emperor being sensible that this was the ready way to remove a dangerous Neighbour, who taking all his *Goths* with him in his intended Expedition must evacuate *Illyricum*, which by that means would

Chap. I. LIII. Zeno.

would return entire to his Obedience, inclin'd readily to his Demand, and promis'd not only to affift him in his Defign, but put a Crown upon his Head, advifing him to Rule with Clemency, and particularly recommended the Senate and People of *Rome* to his Protection. *Theodorich*, pleas'd with his Succefs, flew with the agreeable News to his *Goths*, whom he animated with the Hopes of being fhortly Mafters of the richeft Country in the World; to which purpofe he order'd 'em to Arm, and Unite themfelves into one Body; and having loaded their Waggons with their Wives, their Children, and whatever of their Subftance was moft valuable, to wait his farther Commands. In the mean time, whilft he was intent upon his Expedition, *Tranfilla*, King of the *Gepides*, (at that time the Inhabitants of *Podolia*) and *Bufa*, King of *Bulgaria*, with united Forces fell upon him; induced to it, either out of Envy to his great Fortune, or at the Inftigation of *Odoacer*, who by that means thought to divert a Storm, which ftood ready to difcharge it felf upon his Head. However *Theodorich* with an undaunted Refolution engag'd and defeated 'em; after which he prepar'd to march with his victorious Army into *Italy*. The Year following he pafs'd the *Drave*, and the *Save*, directing his Courfe immediately for *Italy*, and in a fet Battel overthrew *Odoacer*, who was forced to fly with his broken Troops to *Verona*. Thither *Theodorich* follow'd him, and tho' the King behaved himfelf like a brave experienc'd Commander, he was again routed near the Place, and many of his Soldiers threw themfelves into the *Adige*, where they were all drown'd.

A. D. 490.

The Citizens of *Verona*, aftonifh'd at the Succefs of this warlike Prince, open'd their Gates and receiv'd him into the City. After this he was firnamed

med *Veronensis*, in Memory of the great Victory he obtain'd near *Verona*; and in regard that was the first remarkable City in *Italy* that receiv'd and acknowledg'd him. *Odoacer* engag'd him once more upon the *Adda*, and tho' he was renown'd for his Courage and Discipline, yet was he a third time defeated; after which he march'd with great Precipitation to *Rome*, hoping if he could preserve that City firm to his Interest, he should still maintain himself Master of *Italy*: But the Citizens upon his Approach shut their Gates against him, declaring, that in Obedience to *Zeno*'s Commands they were resolv'd to acknowledge *Theodorich* for their Prince. *Odoacer*, incens'd at this Answer, plunder'd and burnt the Suburbs; after which he march'd towards *Ravenna*, where he met with *Libella*, General of *Theodorich*'s Army, engaged, defeated, and slew him; whereupon he was receiv'd the 10th of *July* into the City.

In the mean time *Theodorich* was advanc'd to *Milan*, which after a short Siege he took by Storm. Whilst he continu'd there several of the *Italian* Soldiers that had deserted from *Odoacer* came and enter'd themselves into his Service, tho' they forsook him again shortly after. *Theodorich* quitting *Milan* march'd with his Army to *Pavia*, where he was well receiv'd, and in which he was besieg'd by *Odoacer*, who having refresh'd and recruited his Forces came and sate down before it; but the *Goths* defended the Place with so much Resolution, and by frequent Sallies so harrass'd the Enemy, that the King found himself obliged to raise the Siege, and retir'd with his Army towards *Ravenna*: *Theodorich* follow'd him with all Expedition, leaving the Wives and Children of his *Goths* behind him in *Pavia*, and recommending 'em to the Protection of *Epiphanius*, the renown'd Bishop of the Place.

Whilst

Chap. I.   LIII. Zeno.

Whilst *Theodorich* was thus pursuing his Fortunes in *Italy*, *Zeno* the Emperor, who in a great measure had given life to the Enterprise, dy'd at *Constantinople*, after he had govern'd the Affairs of the East about eighteen Years, either as Administrator of the Empire, in behalf of his Son *Leo*; or absolute, in himself. The manner of his Death was hinted at in the former Volume; and tho' Authors vary as to the Circumstances of it, yet they all allow it to have been violent, and that his Life and Death were of a piece, shameful and ignominious.

A. D. 491. Zeno dies.

He was a Man void of every Quality requisite to a Prince, in regard either of Church or State; and was so compleat a Monster, that he had not the Art even of Dissimulation, so that the best that can be said of him is, He was no Hypocrite; for he was a profess'd Debauchee, an open Heretick, and a declared Enemy to every thing that favour'd not of the same Brutality with himself. I know, that at the Expulsion of *Basiliscus*, and his own Re-establishment, he for some time appear'd a diligent Asserter of the Orthodox Faith, but his Zeal was of so short a Date, and attended with such Circumstances, as made it visible to the World that Dissimulation was not his Talent. If the Account we have given of his Death upon the Authority of *Zonaras* be true, it seem'd a just Judgment from God upon him, that he who appear'd like one dead amongst the living, should even whilst alive be consorted with the dead.

His Character.

II. Immediately upon *Zeno*'s Death *Longinus* his Brother, and as great a Monster as himself, laid claim to the Empire; but his Vices had render'd him so odious as well to the Senate as the People, that tho' he had obtain'd too great Power during his
Bro-

Brother's Reign, yet *Ariadne*, Widow to the deceas'd Emperor, met with little Opposition in her Designs for *Anastasius*, a Native of *Epidamnus*, and of small Interest or Reputation in the Court 'till his Advancement to the Imperial Dignity, which *Ariadne* effected notwithstanding all the Opposition *Longinus* could make; who was shortly after sent back under a strong Guard to *Isauria*, attended by many more of his Countrymen, who desired Leave to return home.

Anastasius being a Man of mean Condition, the great Zeal *Ariadne* express'd in his Promotion, and her receiving him to her Bed shortly after, made the World quickly conceive, that even in his private State some Familiarities had pass'd between 'em too shameful and scandalous for the Publick View. He was Crown'd on the Ninth of *April*, by *Euphemius* Patriarch of *Constantinople*, who absolutely refus'd to place the Imperial Crown on his Head, before he had oblig'd himself by a solemn Oath to observe the Councils of *Nice* and *Chalcedon*; because, his Uncle and Mother being profess'd Hereticks, there was great reason to believe him no true Friend either to the one or the other. He was too great a Politician not to make a Virtue of Necessity, so that he submitted for the present, tho' he afterwards prov'd a great Persecutor of the Orthodox Christians. He is said in his Youth, and whilst a private Man, to have led a very reserv'd abstemious Life, and to have given great Instances of his extraordinary Piety, going every Morning to Church before it was Day, where he employ'd himself several Hours together in his Devotion, both publick and private; and was so remarkable for his Charity, and other Christian Virtues, that when some time after his Election he appear'd in publick in the *Circus*, the People receiv'd him with a general Joy,

and

Chap. I. LIV. Anastasius.

and unanimously besought him *to govern with that* [*begins his*] *Integrity in which 'till then he had liv'd.* . And in- [*Reign with*] deed he began his Reign with several Acts of Grace, [*the general Approbation of the People.*] abolishing the *Chrysargyrum*, a scandalous Tribute, imposed not only upon the Head of all Persons throughout the Empire, of what Age, Sex or Condition soever, as Harlots, Beggars, Slaves, divorced Women, and the like, but upon Horses, Mules, Dogs, Asses, Oxen, nay Dung it self, and levied every fourth Year with all the Rigour imaginable, which rais'd a general Murmur among the People, who were sometimes hardly restrain'd from breaking out into Rebellion. At the same time he banish'd all Informers out of the City, and put a stop to a great Corruption, countenanc'd and introduc'd by former Emperors, who permitted the publick Offices of State to be expos'd to sale, to the great Corruption of Justice, and Oppression of the Subject.

By these Means *Anastasius* at first render'd himself highly grateful to the People, especially to the Catholick Christians; who began to applaud the Change, effected, as it was generally conceiv'd, by the Artifices of *Ariadne*, who, instead of *Zeno*, a Person corrupt in his Principles of Religion, and infamous in his Behaviour, had now bless'd 'em with a Prince, who seem'd at once to confirm and establish the true Faith by his Edicts, and adorn it by his Example; so that the Church promis'd it self an uninterruped Repose under so propitious an Administration. *Felix*, Bishop of *Rome*, had no sooner heard of his Election, but he congratulated his Advancement by Letters full of Respect, in which he exhorted him *to persevere in the Faith, and put a Stop to the great Progress Heresie had made in the East, through the Authority and Connivance of his Predecessor* Zeno, *and* Acacius, *late Patriarch of* Constantinople. It was a Custom with the most

active

active among the *Arians* to prepossess, as much as they could, every new Prince in favour of their damnable Errors, and represent the Catholick Prelates, as People obstinate and intractable, who labour'd to create and promote Divisions in the Church, to the utter Ruin of that Christian Charity, the great Badge of their Profession. These Practices *Felix* in his Letters took care to obviate, and succeeded so far that *Anastasius* did not break out presently, tho' in time he became a great Plague to the Church.

A. D. 491.

During these Transactions and Changes of State in the East, *Theodorich* pursu'd his Conquests with much Success in the West, he press'd hard upon *Odoacer,* who desired to try his Fortune in another Battel, before he shut himself up within the Walls of *Ravenna,* and was again defeated; so that he was forced to retire into the Town, and make the best Preparations he could for a Siege. It was so well fortified by Art and Nature, and so strongly garrison'd, that *Theodorich* found it impossible to take it by Force, and therefore chose rather to block it up, and reduce it by Famine; to which purpose he order'd a great part of his Army to straiten it both by Sea and Land, and march'd with the rest to conquer those other Towns that still continu'd firm in their Obedience to *Odoacer;* and by degrees grew so strong in *Italy,* through his indefatigable Industry, that *Gondabond,* King of the *Vandals* in *Africk,* surpriz'd at his prodigious Progress, by an express Embassy courted his Alliance, promising to resign *Sicily* up to him, which 'till that time he had grievously molested. *Theodorich* receiv'd the Embassadors with great Civility, and having taken in all the *Italian* Towns that held out against him, except *Cesena,* which he thought not fit to attempt, because he knew it was defended by

Theodorich lays Siege to Ravenna.

a

Chap. I. LIV. Anastasius.

a very numerous Garrison, he return'd to the Siege of *Ravenna*, where *Odoacer* still made a very brave and vigorous Resistance, and by his frequent Sallies greatly incommoded the Besiegers, who however seem'd obstinately resolv'd to take it. The *Goths* had for a long time so straitly beleaguer'd the Town, that the Famine appear'd more terrible within than the Enemy was without the Walls, and render'd the Defendants weak and dispirited. In this Condition *Odoacer* muster'd the best and most resolute of all his Troops, and taking the Advantage of the Night sallied out with such a desperate Courage upon the Enemy, that they first put 'em into Disorder, and after that to Flight; *Theodorich* himself in the general Confusion accompanying his Fugitive Soldiers, 'till at length perceiving his Error he made 'em rally and face the Enemy. Some say, his Mother meeting him in the Rout ask'd him, in imitation of the ancient *Spartan* Matrons, *Whither he was flying?* and bid him *remember he had no Place left to conceal himself, unless he design'd to return into her Womb, there to hide his ignominious Head:* That being nearly touch'd by so seasonable a Reproof he stopp'd, and turn'd against the Besieg'd; who were so far from following the Pursuit, that they were busied in pillaging the Camp, and supplying themselves with Provisions, of which they found great Plenty, and for want of which they were almost famish'd. The *Goths*, taking the Advantage of their Indiscretion, fell with great Fury upon 'em, recover'd that Victory out of their Hands, which had they known how to make a right use of would have been indisputable, and forc'd 'em with great Slaughter back into the City, where a general Want of all Things necessary and convenient imbitter'd the sense of their Defeat. But for as much as on the other Hand the

A. D. 493.

the *Goths* were extreamly weaken'd by the Fatigues of so long and obstinate a Siege, *John*, Bishop of the Place, was upon that Consideration encourag'd to propose some Terms of Accommodation, and succeeded so well in it, that after several Conferen-ces and Intermediations a Treaty was concluded between the two Kings, by virtue of which they were equally to share not only the City of *Ravenna*, but the Kingdom of *Italy*. Accordingly the Siege was rais'd the Twenty seventh of *February*, and on the Fifth of *March* all the People and Clergy went to receive *Theodorich*, who made a publick Entry into the City, and was saluted King with the universal Acclamations of the Inhabitants, being lodged together with *Odoacer* in the Royal Palace, where for some time they lived, and convers'd familiarly together as Friends.

A Peace concluded between the two Kings.

A. D. 493.

In this friendly Correspondence they lived but a very short time, for *Theodorich* being jealous of his Royal Companion, and impatient of a Rival in Empire, invited *Odoacer* to a Banquet, where in the height of his Mirth and Security he order'd him to be assassinated together with his only Son, whom the imprudent Father had brought with him to the bloody Feast. As a Reason for this inhospitable Cruelty *Theodorich* alledg'd, That *Odoacer*, contrary to the late Agreement and Union between 'em, had entertain'd pernicious Counsels against him; and that nothing but the sense of his own Danger had forc'd him to that rigorous Proceeding. From this we may learn, that no Ties of Honour or Humanity are sufficient to restrain Ambitious Princes, and that a Fellowship in Empire is a Notion vain and impracticable.

Odoacer murder'd.

Hereupon *Theodorich* became absolute in *Italy*, where he govern'd above three and thirty Years with much Prudence and Moderation; restoring Order

Theodorich declared King of Italy.

Chap. I. LIV. Anaſtaſius.

Order and Diſcipline, by his peaceable and wholſom Laws, to a Country where the Licence of the preceeding Wars had introduc'd Confuſion and Barbarity; in this he was much aſſiſted by *Caſſiodorus*, his Chief Secretary, a Man of great Learning, Prudence and Application, who ſtudy'd to inure the reſtleſs Minds of the *Goths* to the Arts of Peace, and ſoften 'em with the Delights that attend it. *Theodorich's* firſt Care was to court the Friendſhip of *Anaſtaſius*, which he did in a ſolemn Embaſſy deputed to that purpoſe; and at the ſame time he enter'd into ſuch Treaties and Alliances with the Weſtern Princes that were his Neighbours, as he judg'd would moſt conduce to his own particular Advantage, and the publick Tranquility.

Theodorich's Embaſſadors found *Anaſtaſius* ready to liſten to any Overtures of Peace, not only becauſe it was uſually his Cuſtom to purchaſe it at a high rate from his Enemies, but for that he was now taken up with the *Iſaurian* War rais'd by *Longinus*, the Brother of *Zeno*, who, as we obſerv'd before, was ſuffer'd by *Anaſtaſius* to retire into his own Country, where he preſently began with great Diligence to raiſe ſuch an Army as would enable him to contend upon equal Terms with *Anaſtaſius*. This War, the Particulars of which are not left us in Hiſtory, continu'd with various Succeſs for Six Years together, 'till at length *Anaſtaſius* prevail'd; for having by his Generals defeated *Longinus* in a pitch'd Battel, he took him Priſoner, and brought him to *Conſtantinople*, where, after ſeveral Indignities offer'd his Perſon, he order'd his Head to be ſtruck off, and fix'd upon one of the moſt publick Places in the City. *Conon*, Biſhop of *Apamea*, enter'd into this Quarrel in Behalf of *Longinus*, and being the firſt we meet

meet with in History that quitted the Sacred Function to follow Arms, God thought fit to punish his Presumption with a violent Death.

But whilst Affairs were thus manag'd in *Isauria*, a War of greater Consequence, and more Danger to the Church, continu'd between the Bishop of *Rome* and Patriarch of *Constantinople*, in which the Emperor thought fit to make himself a Party, to such a height were the Disputes aggravated between 'em. *Acacius*, the late Patriarch, dy'd at least a profess'd Favourer of Hereticks, for which reason the Bishop of *Rome* requir'd *Euphemius* to erase his Name out of the *Diptychs*, as it was usual in such Case, and which *Euphemius*, tho' by repeated Admonitions enjoin'd to do it, peremptorily refus'd; tho' at the same time he was so far from Countenancing or Communicating with Hereticks, that at his first Advancement he summon'd a Synod for the Confirmation of the Orthodox Faith, and Condemnation of *Peter* of *Alexandria*, who in a Convocation of his own calling had Condemn'd the Council of *Chalcedon*, and Excommunicated *Euphemius*. Notwithstanding which, *Felix*, at that time Bishop of *Rome*, and his Successor *Gelasius*, were so little satisfy'd with the Conduct of the Patriarch, or rather so ambitious of exerting their Authority over other Sees, that upon that Pretence they refus'd to Communicate with *Euphemius*; from whence a Schism arose, which continu'd with much Animosity for Thirty Years together, tho' the Patriarchs of *Constantinople* were as Orthodox in their Faith as the Bishops of *Rome*, who however would listen to no Accommodation, 'till *Acacius* his Name, together with that of *Flavitas* his Successor, were eras'd, who indeed had but too well deserv'd it. We may here observe how different the Method the Popes at present use in

Chap. I. LIV. Anaſtaſius.

in their Excommunications is from their Proceedings formerly; for then by Excommunication they intended no more, than that they would no longer Communicate with thoſe upon whom they paſs'd the Cenſure; whereas they now not only pretend to deny the Excommunicated Perſon the Benefit of Divine Service, a Participation in the Holy Sacraments, and the Right of Chriſtian Burial, but to Interdict whole Eſtates and Principalities at once, delivering 'em up to the Claim of him that can firſt Conquer 'em.

Anaſtaſius had from the beginning entertain'd a great Prejudice to *Euphemius*, by reaſon he had ſo peremptorily refuſ'd to Crown him 'till he had ſubſcrib'd to the Council of *Chalcedon*: This Averſion was much improv'd by *Euphemius* his firm Adherence to the Orthodox Faith, and inſiſting upon the Obſervation of that Council; whereas the Emperor was equally diſpleaſ'd with ſuch as condemn'd it, as well as thoſe who obſtinately defended it, deſiring the very Memory of it might be aboliſh'd, forbidding the Biſhops to diſpute upon any of the controverted Points, confining thoſe who maintain'd it to ſuch Churches where it had been condemn'd, and baniſhing them that rejected it into thoſe Places where it was moſt vigorouſly aſſerted. Theſe Proceedings of the Emperor encreas'd the Animoſities, which he pretended by his affected Moderation to allay, and raiſ'd a horrible Schiſm in the Churches of the Eaſt, and in *Egypt*: *Anaſtaſius* himſelf in the mean time being as corrupt in his Principles of Religion as the very worſt of 'em, tho' they knew not well in what *Claſſis* or Sect to place him; however they ſeem to be moſt in the right, who make him an Aſſociate of the *Acephali*, or *Hæſitantes*, ſo call'd becauſe they agreed with neither of the contending Parties, nor yet

A. D. 495.

yet were headed by any particular Perſon, by whoſe Name they might diſtinguiſh themſelves from the reſt of the World. The *Iſaurian* War gave him, as he thought, a juſt Opportunity of revenging himſelf upon *Euphemius*, who continu'd ſtill to threaten him with Excommunication, unleſs he put a ſtop to the Perſecution rais'd againſt the Catholicks, and forbore Communicating with the Hereticks. He accus'd him of Countenancing and Aſſiſting the *Iſaurians* in the War againſt him, upon which Pretence he remov'd him from his See, and ſent him into Exile, in which Condition he dy'd, much to be commended for his Conſtancy and Reſolution.

Euphemius baniſh'd.

Anaſtaſius having thus made uſe of his Authority in the Puniſhment of *Euphemius*, thought his Succeſſors, being taught by his Example, would for the future expreſs themſelves with more Compliance and Submiſſion to his Pleaſure, but quickly found the ſame Spirit of Truth animated *Macedonius*, who ſucceeded him, and who was a Learn'd, Pious, and Orthodox Prelate, and who, upon that Account, became as unacceptable as his Predeceſſor had been to the Emperor *Anaſtaſius*; who finding himſelf at laſt deliver'd, by a compleat Victory, from the Danger of the *Iſaurian* War, triumph'd with much Solemnity at *Conſtantinople*, where, being now at Peace at home, he was perſuaded by his Favourites to declare War againſt *Theodorich* in *Italy*, whoſe extraordinary Succeſs and Proſperity in thoſe Parts was no ways acceptable to the Miniſters of State. But *Theodorich*, upon the firſt Intimation of what they were agitating againſt him, ſent to renew the former Alliance, and by that means put a ſtop to a War that might otherwiſe, one Day, have thrown the World into freſh Confuſions; and all this was entirely owing

Chap. I. LIV. Anaſtaſius.

owing to the prudent Management and peaceable Spirit of *Theodorich*, who was univerſally belov'd by his Subjects, and courted and admir'd by the Princes his Neighbours, tho' for no one Quality ſo much as his excellent Juſtice. To the *Rugians*, *Heruli*, and other barbarous Nations, as had been call'd in by *Odoacer*, and had lately poſſeſs'd themſelves of *Pavia*, and ſome other little Towns that adjoin'd to it, he aſſign'd new Poſſeſſions, conferring thoſe they had formerly enjoy'd upon his own Friends and Followers; and was ſo far from expreſſing any Reſentment towards them that had perſiſted in their Faith inviolable towards *Odoacer*, that he not only pardon'd 'em, but preferr'd ſuch as were willing to ſerve him to Places of Truſt, Honour, and Profit, but never receiv'd thoſe into Grace, who contrary to their Faith given to him had revolted to *Odoacer*, and after the Death of that Prince again courted his Favour. He order'd all Suits and Controverſies ariſing among *Goths* to be determin'd by *Gothick* Judges, and thoſe that depended between *Italians* to be decided by *Italians*; but in caſe any Difference aroſe between a *Goth* and an *Italian*, then was the Cauſe to be try'd before Judges of both Nations reſpectively; and accordingly he eſtabliſh'd Magiſtrates in all Cities, the better to bring whatever Controverſies ſhould happen to a ſpeedy Iſſue. As to Religion he was himſelf an *Arian*, but withal ſo favourable and impartial to the Orthodox Chriſtians, that he ſuffer'd none of his Subjects to quit their Principles out of Complaiſance to him, as he made it appear to the World when one of his Chief Favourites, who had been bred up, and 'till then embrac'd the Catholick Profeſſion, made a Complement of his Faith to *Theodorich*, and turn'd *Arian*: *Theodorich* was ſo enrag'd at his Apoſtacy, that he order'd him

Theodorich rich governs with much Prudence in Italy.

A. D. 498.

imme-

immediately to be Beheaded, (some say he Slew him with his own Hands) saying, *How can I expect thou wilt be just and faithful to me, who am but a Man, when thou hast presum'd shamefully to desert the Eternal God?* Nor did he signalize himself for his Justice in this respect alone, but when a Sedition happen'd at *Rome* the Year following upon the Death of *Anastasius*, Bishop of that City, and the Election of a Successor, he show'd himself a Prince more inclinable to heal the Breaches of the Church, than promote the Divisions with which at that time it was most grievously afflicted: For, Four Days after the Death of *Anastasius*, two Persons, by two different Factions, were Elected to succeed him; *Symmachus*, supported by *Faustus* and several others of great Authority in the Senate; and *Laurentius*, protected by *Festus* and *Sabinus*, Men of equal Interest in the same Assembly. The Ambition of the Competitors, and the Obstinacy of their Partisans, rais'd a sort of Civil War in *Rome*, and several on both sides lost their Lives in the Quarrel; at last they were forc'd to have recourse to *Theodorich* for his Decision, who residing then at *Ravenna*, where he usually kept his Court, thither Persons deputed from both Parties went to attend him, and having acquainted him with the Grounds of their Debate he silenc'd their Disputes by Ordaining, That he should be Confirm'd Bishop of *Rome*, who had been first Elected, and was supported by the Majority of Voices; whereupon *Symmachus*, who had been first chosen, and that by a great Majority, was created Bishop; tho' there was a sort of Contention in the Church upon that account, which continu'd three Years together: So obstinately ambitious were the *Roman* Clergy in those Days, that through their Feuds and Animosities the Church was forc'd to have

A Civil War in Rome.

have recourse to the Decisions of an Heretick Prince.

As soon as *Symmachus* was establish'd he acquainted the Emperor *Anastasius* with his Promotion, and adjur'd him at the same time to abandon the Favour and Protection he show'd the Hereticks, to the great Scandal and Affliction of the Faithful. The Emperor was so far from giving Ear to his Exhortations, that he affronted his Messengers, and declar'd himself an open Enemy to those who adher'd to, or favour'd the Council of *Chalcedon*, continuing Deaf to all the Remonstrances of Truth and Reason; but God was so provok'd with this his Obstinacy, that he rais'd the *Bulgarians* against him, who with a numerous Army invaded and destroy'd *Thrace*. Against these Barbarians the Emperor sent *Aristus*, one of his Lieutenants, at the Head of Fifteen Thousand Men, attended by Five Hundred and Twenty Waggons laden with all Things necessary for an Army. *Aristus*, in full Confidence of his own Strength, and Assurance of a Victory, offer'd the Enemy Battel near the River *Zarta*, where above Four Thousand of the Imperialists were Slain, among whom fell some of the most experienc'd Officers of the Empire. The unactive Emperor, instead of raising another Army with speed, and chastising the Barbarians, who were grown Insolent upon their late Advantage, bought an Ignominious Peace with a great Sum of Mony, and so gaining a Respite at present from Foreign Disturbances, he had leisure to apply himself more zealously to encourage Hereticks, and persecute the Faithful, which he did with a most implacable Malice, tho' God visited him the same Year with another Judgment, for a great part of the Country of *Pontus* was destroy'd by an Earthquake.

A.D. 499.

Anastasius *a great Persecutor*.

The Imperial Forces defeated by the Bulgarians.

The

The Troubles and Divisions in *Rome* were so far from being compos'd by *Theodorich*'s Sentence in favour of *Symmachus*, that the Contests were continu'd with great violence in the City, so that on one side and the other infinite Murders were committed; and some say the greatest part of the Clergy, and no small number of the *Roman* Citizens dy'd in the Quarrel; this oblig'd *Theodorich* to take a Journey to *Rome* in Person, and try, by his Presence, to determine so important an Affair. He made his Entry with a Pomp and Magnificence suitable to the Greatness of his Mind, and Affection of his People. *Rome* had not for a long time beheld any thing so Illustrious; it seem'd a Representation of her former Grandure, when her ancient Heroes return'd home with Honour and Conquest; the Citizens were so generally affected with the Sight of their King, that they all striv'd to outvie each other in the sense they had of the publick Prosperity, and their Demonstrations of Joy and Satisfaction. During this Triumph *Fulgentius*, who was at present no more than a Monk, arriv'd at *Rome*, and after having visited such Places as he judg'd proper to quicken and kindle his Devotion, he went to the Amphitheatre, where the King was Addressing himself in a Gracious Speech to the People, and where it might truly be said, all that was Great and Glorious in the World was collected into one Assembly. *Fulgentius* was surpriz'd at so august an Appearance, and with a sort of Exstasie said to those that stood near him, *If earthly* Rome *is so exceeding Glorious, how much more Shining and Majestick must the Heavenly* Jerusalem *be? And if Mortal Men are so delighted with the Pomp and Grandure of this World, what Glory and Satisfaction must the Saints receive in the Contemplation of the Eternal God of Truth?*

Theodorich goes to Rome.

After

Chap. I.   LIV. Anaſtaſius.

After *Theodorich* had viſited the moſt remarkable Parts of the City, and given Order to have thoſe that were decay'd built more magnificent, if poſſible, than they were before, he aſſembled a Synod, in which the Election of *Symmachus* was confirm'd; and having compos'd the Affairs, as well of the Church as State, in the beſt manner he could, he return'd to *Ravenna*.

A. D. 500.

Whilſt *Theodorich* thus employ'd himſelf for the Good of his Subjects in the Weſt, *Anaſtaſius* was following Methods quite contrary in the Eaſt; where he render'd himſelf odious by his Sloth, Wantonneſs, and Cruelty. Whilſt *Longinus* the Brother of *Zeno* liv'd, or any Man in the Empire that had a Power and Inclination to keep that Faction awake, his Fear and Jealouſie reſtrain'd him within ſome Bounds of Modeſty; but being deliver'd from that Fear by the Death of *Longinus* and his Adherents, he then gave way to his Brutal Paſſions, and the Spirit of Perſecution. *Macedonius*, in ſpight of all his Promiſes and Threatnings, ſtood firm to the Council of *Chalcedon*, and was follow'd in the ſame Sentiments by the greateſt Part of the Inhabitants. The Conſtancy of the Patriarch, and the great Number of his Followers, highly incens'd *Anaſtaſius*, and therefore when one day they were aſſembled in the Theatre to behold the publick Shows he maſſacred no leſs than Three thouſand of them, by the Hands of inhuman Ruffians lodged there in ſecret for that purpoſe. This Act of Barbarity, as it render'd him generally hated by his Subjects, ſo it ſeem'd to adminiſter to *Symmachus*, Biſhop of *Rome*, juſt Grounds for his Excommunication, which the Biſhop readily laid hold upon; for beſides the ancient Quarrel of his Predeceſſors, who refus'd to live in Communion with the Patriarchs of *Conſtantinople*, *Symmachus* was

Anaſtaſius his great Cruelty.

perſo-

personally injur'd by *Anastasius*, who had by his Agents privately encourag'd and supported the Faction that was still maintain'd against him, and upon every Opportunity took care to perplex his Affairs. For these Reasons *Symmachus*, by the Advice of his Council, excommunicated the Emperor; and, as we take it, is the first Instance of a Pope who strain'd his Authority so high, and presum'd to direct it against the Person of an Emperor. *Anastasius* being sensibly offended at so signal an Affront declar'd, by a publick Instrument in Writing, That *the Sentence of Excommunication was not, nor ought to be of any Force*; accusing *Symmachus* at the same time of many Crimes, that render'd him unworthy the Dignity he had insolently usurp'd. The Pope found himself oblig'd to make an Apology, in which he justified what he had done, and affirm'd *The Dignity of a Pope was as much above that of an Emperor, as Heaven is higher than the Earth*. This Quarrel between the Pope and the Emperor continu'd during the Pontificate of *Symmachus*, and some time longer; and in all Probability encourag'd *Cabades* King of *Persia* to begin a War upon the Empire.

Excommunicated by the Pope.

That Prince, whether he stood really in need of Mony, or observing the sloathful unactive Temper of *Anastasius*, who whenever he was press'd or threaten'd by a prevailing Enemy bought his Peace, and often at a very extravagant Rate, sent to borrow a considerable Sum of him, and upon a Refusal fell with a great Army into *Armenia*, where he roved up and down with great Licence, destroying the Country round about, and then laid close Siege to *Amida*; which, tho' the chief Town of *Mesopotamia*, had no Garrison nor any Provisions fit for a Defence: However the Inhabitants made a very extraordinary Resistance, and did such Execution from

Amida besieg'd by the Persians.

Chap. I. LIV. Anastasius.

from the Walls, and in their Sallies upon the Enemy, that they much impair'd and dishearten'd the *Persian* Army, insomuch that *Cabades* was once resolv'd to raise the Siege, 'till the Insolence of the Townsmen, who revil'd and affronted him from the Walls, provok'd him to persevere; to which he was encourag'd by the Impudence of some common Prostitutes, who infamously expos'd those Parts to his View, which Nature had intended should be most conceal'd. Hereupon the *Magi* gave him Assurances of an undoubted Success, and that the Inhabitants would e'er long be forc'd to show him all their secret and most darling Treasures. Upon these Suggestions the Siege was continu'd, and some Days after a *Persian* Soldier by chance discover'd an old Vault near one of the Turrets, whose Mouth was cover'd with Stones: This he enter'd alone and in the Night, and the next Morning acquainted the King with his Discovery; who glad of so unexpected an Advantage took the Turret the Night following, by means of this Vault, and shortly after the Town it self, in which he plac'd a *Persian* Garrison, and return'd home with a great Number of Prisoners. *Procopius*, in his Relation of this Siege, gives us a strange Account of one *James* a *Syrian*, who had for many Years led a retired contemplative Life in a Village about a Days Journey from *Amida*, suffering the Extremities of Heat and Cold with a wonderful Patience and Resignation. Some of the *Persians*, in their Excursions, fell accidentally upon his Cottage, and as they prepared to shoot at him, their Hands were on a sudden so benum'd, as with Cold, that they were not able to draw their Bows. Upon their Return to the Camp *Cabades* was soon inform'd of this extraordinary Adventure, and was resolv'd to be an Eye-witness himself of such a

Amida taken.

Miracle.

Miracle. Immediately upon his Arrival he was convinc'd of the Truth of the Report, and having begg'd Pardon for the Insolence of his Soldiers, which he easily obtain'd, he bid him, by way of Return, to demand something from him, imagining he would have ask'd for a great Sum of Mony; but he only desir'd a Privilege of protecting those, whom the Misfortunes of the War should drive thither for their Security: This *Cabades* readily granted, and left him his Letters sign'd with the Royal Signet, to corroborate his Promise.

Anastasius, as soon as he was inform'd that *Amida* was Besieg'd, rais'd an Army, greater, in *Procopius* his Opinion, than ever had 'till then been sent against the *Persians*, and committed it to the Care of *Areobinda*, General of the East, who had marry'd the Daughter of *Olybrius*, one of the late Western Emperors, and who march'd with all Expedition, having Orders from the Emperor to relieve the Place.

As *Areobinda* drew near to the Town with the Forces under his Command he understood *Amida* was taken, and that the *Persians*, after they had reinforc'd it with a good Garrison, and all necessary Provisions, were return'd home. Hereupon the General, being unwilling to lose his Time in a Siege, in which he expected to be obstinately oppos'd, drew off, and made an Impression into the Enemies Country, dividing his Army into several Bodies. Against that which he commanded himself the King of *Persia* advanc'd, and so terrify'd him with his Approach that he fled in a great Consternation to *Constantina*, a Town two Days Journey distant from his Camp, which he left, with all his Baggage, to the Enemy. Encourag'd by this Advantage, *Cabades* march'd with great Expedition against another Party, commanded by *Hypatius* and
Patritius,

Areobinda loseth his Camp.

Chap. I.   LIV. Anastasius.

Patritius, who had lately fallen upon Eighty Hundred of the *Persians* that were advanc'd before the rest of the Army, and kill'd 'em all upon the spot; and not suspecting of any Surprize were, upon the Presumption of their Victory, feasting in great Security. Upon these Men the *Persians* fell with great Fury before they were prepar'd to receive 'em, and did so much Execution that few or none of 'em escap'd. Tho' there was a third Body of the *Romans* that remain'd unbroken, and *Cabades* was forc'd to return home to secure his Northern Borders against the Incursions of the *Hunns*, yet did they little or nothing against the Enemy, but as the Winter drew on sate down before *Amida*, and resolv'd to force it by Famine. Tho' the Besieg'd in a short time found themselves under great Straits for want of Provision, yet they so well conceal'd their Necessities that the *Romans* knew nothing of it, but growing weary of the Service, and imagining the King would in a short time return with his Army, they thought of nothing but raising the Siege. The *Persians*, on the other side, labour'd under more Difficulties, and as many Apprehensions as the *Romans*, but made the best Show they could, and resolv'd to make an honourable and handsom Retreat. In conclusion an Agreement was made, That upon Payment of a considerable Sum of Gold the Town should be surrender'd; the Mony was paid accordingly, and *Amida* deliver'd up to the *Romans*, who were no sooner receiv'd into the Town, but they grew asham'd of their own Weakness and Impatience, for upon Examination they found the Barbarians had not Provisions sufficient for seven Days remaining, tho' they had liv'd during the Siege with much Abstemiousness. Upon this the Generals, who began to repent of the Conditions when it was too late, could not forbear

The Persians defeat another Party of the Romans.

Amida restor'd to the Romans for Mony.

bear reproaching the Soldiers for their Intemperance and Disobedience, who when they had the Town and all the *Persians* that defended it at their Mercy, contrary to the ancient Discipline, made a shameful Bargain with the Barbarians, and bought their own with the *Roman* Treasure. After *Amida* was thus surrender'd a Truce was concluded for Seven Years, between *Anastasius* and the King of *Persia*, who being distress'd by the *Hunns*, a hardy turbulent People, thought it prudent to live in good Terms with the Emperor.

A Truce concluded for Seven Years.

A. D. 507.

Whilst *Anastasius* his Forces were thus employ'd in the Eastern War, the *Bulgarians*, his ancient Enemies, had seiz'd on *Pannonia*, which *Theodorich* claiming as part of his Dominions, and being the Place of his Nativity, he thought himself nearly concern'd to recover it: Accordingly he sent a strong Army, under the Command of *Petra*, one of his Lieutenants, to restrain 'em; and succeeded so well, that he defeated 'em in a set Battel, recover'd *Sirmium* out of their Hands, and drove 'em out of the Country, committing it to the Government of *Colosseus*, a *Roman* by Birth, and one of his chief Commanders. In the mean time he himself was busied in cultivating Peace among his neighbouring Princes and Allies.

Theodorich overthrows the Bulgarians.

Clovis was at that time King of the *Franks* in *Gaul*, between whom and *Alaric*, who commanded the Western *Goths* in *Languedoc* and *Aquitain*, with much Reputation for his Justice and Clemency, there happen'd a Quarrel, occasion'd either for that *Clovis* thought himself affronted by *Alaric*, who he conceiv'd had concern'd himself too much in some late Disputes between the *Franks* and *Burgundians*; or for that, being a *Goth*, he appear'd too zealous an Assertor of the *Arian* Heresie; or rather, out of an Ambition of extending his Dominions,

nions, a Vice too frequent among Princes. Whatever the Inducements were, *Clovis* prepar'd himself very vigorously for the War, which *Theodorich* labour'd earnestly by his Negotiations to prevent. He not only endeavour'd to persuade *Alaric,* who was his Son-in-law, to appease if possible the King of the *Franks,* and so prevent the Danger that threaten'd him, but by his Letters desir'd all the Princes to mediate an Accommodation between the two Kings; at the same time he exhorted *Clovis* by his Embassadors not to begin a War that in all likelihood would prove long, bloody and expensive, and perhaps end in the Ruin of two brave couragions Nations; and told him in the End, that if he persisted in his Resolutions, and would not remit the Differences between 'em to the Decision of their Friends, he was resolv'd to support *Alaric* with all his Power.

Notwithstanding all this, as soon as his Levies were full he muster'd his Army, and having pass'd the *Loire* begun the War, marching directly towards *Poitiers,* where *Alaric* at that time resided. The *Goths* chose rather to hazard a Battel than expect a Siege, so that *Alaric* march'd out at the Head of his Army to encounter *Clovis,* who after an obstinate and bloody Fight defeated the *Goths,* *The* Goths slew the King with his own Hand, and obtain'd *defeated in* an entire Victory: Immediately after which he di- Clovis. spatch'd away his Son *Thierry,* with some of his Troops, to secure *Alby, Rovergne, Quercy* and *Auvergne,* whilst he himself reduc'd all the Towns up to *Bourdeaux*; where *Amalric,* the Son of *Alaric,* tho' young and unexperienc'd, had Courage enough to run the Hazard of a second Battel, which he lost, and found himself oblig'd to fly for Refuge to his Grandfather *Theodorich* in *Italy*; who receiv'd him with much Tenderness, and promis'd

D 2   to

to restore him, tho' at the Expence of his own Life and Fortune. For he was highly concern'd at the great Progress he saw *Clovis* make in *Gaul*, and began to apprehend the Danger his own Dominions would be in, from the Neighbourhood of so victorious a Prince. Tho' no open Acts of Hostility had as yet pass'd between him and *Anastasius*, yet he had great reason to look on him as his Enemy, and one who would rejoice to see him involv'd in any Difficulties, that he might more advantagiously fall upon him. He knew that the Emperor, upon the first News of *Clovis* his Success, had sent an Embassy to him, with very rich Presents, and had enter'd into a secret Alliance with him; that the Coasts of *Italy*, as far as *Tarentum*, had this

A.D. 508.
Year been attack'd and wasted by *Romanus*, who had the Command of a Fleet and Eight Thousand Men, and return'd with a dishonourable Booty to *Anastasius*.

These Considerations, together with the Injuries of his Family, made him resolve to oppose *Clovis*. Hereupon he assembled all the *Goths* that were in *Italy*, in *Gaul*, in *Spain*, in *Sclavonia* and *Dalmatia*; and having by this means rais'd an Army consisting of Fourscore Thousand Men, he committed it to the Charge of *Hibba* or *Ibbas*, who

A.D. 509.
enter'd *Gaul* about the latter end of *June*, the Year following, and reliev'd *Carcasson*, which *Clovis* had closely besieg'd for some Months, and was earnestly desirous to take it, because he was inform'd there were mighty Treasures stored up in it, which *Alaric* had brought thither from the Pillage of *Rome*. From *Carcasson* the *Goths* march'd and rais'd the

Clovis defeated by Theodorich's Forces.
Siege of *Artes*, took in *Tholouse*, *Orange* and *Marseilles*; and having fought *Clovis*, defeated him, and kill'd at least Twenty Thousand of his Men, they recover'd to *Amalric* all *Languedoc* and *Gascogne*,

leaving

leaving *Guyenne, Saintonge, Poitou,* and the Parts adjacent, in the Hands of *Clovis,* whose they became in Right of Conquest.

Nor was *Anastasius* only busied all this time in sowing Divisions among the Western Princes, but in persecuting the Faithful, and fomenting the Divisions of the Church. *Macedonius,* Patriarch of *Constantinople,* had always oppos'd him with an invincible Constancy, for which he was persecuted by the *Eutychians,* who were in greatest Authority with the Emperor; tho' the People in general had a great Veneration for him, which expos'd him more to the Emperor's Displeasure. About this time two Hundred Heretick Monks, under the Conduct of one *Severus,* came and offer'd their Service to *Anastasius,* who receiv'd 'em very graciously, because he knew 'em to be sworn Enemies to *Macedonius,* and encourag'd 'em so far that several Orthodox were prevail'd upon to associate themselves with them: So that the good Prelate had hardly any Assistance to depend upon, but what lay in the Affections of the Inhabitants, who united in his Defence, declaring publickly in the Streets, That *it was a shame for Christians to forsake their Ghostly Father in the Days of Persecution.* By this means the Patriarch found himself secur'd from any forcible Attempts, and *Anastasius* was oblig'd to double the Guards that attended his Person, and prepar'd for an Escape in some Vessels design'd for that purpose, in Case the Sedition continu'd; however he still practis'd secretly against *Macedonius,* and suborn'd some Persons to accuse him of several Enormous Crimes, of which the good Father acquitted himself by undeniable Instances; so that the Emperor finding it impossible to destroy him by due Course of Law, and that the Citizens had united themselves in the Defence

A.D. 511. of his Innocence, he took him by Night forcibly out of his Palace, and sent him under a Guard of Soldiers into Exile. The People, as soon as they understood what had been done, grew implacable, especially when they found *Timotheus*, an Heretick, promoted in his Place, a Man so remarkable for his scandalous dissolute Life, and withal so vile a Hypocrite that he was universally detested by all that knew him; he was no sooner advanc'd but he began to introduce Novelties in the publick Worship, which created so great a Sedition in *Constantinople*, that no less than Ten Thousand Persons are said to have been massacred in the Tumult, and several Houses burnt; the Emperor and Empress being forc'd to shut themselves up in the Palace, whilst the People loaded 'em with many Reproaches, declaring they ought to proceed to the Election of another Prince; and they had certainly dethron'd *Anastasius*, had he not soften'd 'em by a Submission, and Promise to observe, for the future, the Council of *Chalcedon*. Notwithstanding all which he shortly after renew'd the Persecution against the Catholicks, especially the Bishops, Priests and Monks, making use of Threats, Promises, Presents and Preferments, to allure 'em to an Abjuration, being incited to it by *Severus*, of whom mention was made before, and who, not long after, was advanc'd to the See of *Antioch*.

A great Sedition in Constantinople.

A.D. 514. Whilst *Anastasius* thus apply'd his Power to the Ruin of the Church, which he persecuted with an inexorable Cruelty, without any regard had to the Civil Affairs of the Empire, or Condition of his Army, *Vitalianus*, one of his Generals, revolted, urging the Expulsion of *Macedonius*, and the violent Proceedings against the Orthodox, as Reasons for his Rebellion: With such Forces of Horse as he was able to raise in three Days time he seiz'd

Vitalianus Revolts.

on

on *Mysia*, *Scythia* and *Thrace*, having taken *Cyril*, Governor of the last, Prisoner, and peirc'd almost as far as the very Gates of *Constantinople*, being follow'd by an Army of *Hunns* and *Bulgarians*, the inveterate Enemies of the Empire. *Anastasius* in this Extremity had recourse to his usual Artifices; he pacify'd *Vitalianus* with an immense Sum of Mony, and promis'd solemnly by his Embassadors to restore *Macedonius*, and the other exiled Prelates, and call a Council in *Heraclea* to put an end to the Differences in Religion. *Vitalianus*, ensnar'd by the Presents, and deceiv'd by the Emperor's fair Words, drew his Army off from *Constantinople*, dismiss'd his Troops, and sent *Hypatius*, whom he had taken Prisoner, back to his Uncle *Anastasius*; tho' *Vitalianus* found afterwards, by Experience, that the Emperor had no other aim but to deceive him, that he grew as furious a Persecutor as ever, and with the first Opportunity remember'd his Attempts upon him.

During these Contests *Symmachus*, Bishop of *Rome*, dy'd, and was succeeded by *Hormisda*, to whom *Anastasius* directed a Letter, acquainting him with his Intentions of summoning a Council, and desiring him to employ his Interest to heal the Divisions of the Church: This Letter was seconded by another to the same purpose, in which the Emperor complain'd of the Obstinacy of his Predecessors, and, hoping to find him of a more Christian Temper, he besought him to procure, as much as in him lay, an Union among Christians, and appear in the Council, which was to be celebrated at *Heraclea*. In Answer to these Letters the Pope sent his Deputies to the Emperor, sufficiently instructed how to behave themselves as well towards the Emperor as *Timotheus* the Patriarch, commanding 'em to conclude upon nothing relating

ting to the Council 'till the following Articles were agreed unto. 1. That the Emperor should by Letters assure all the Bishops that he receiv'd and approv'd of *Leo*'s Epistle to *Flavian*, and the Council of *Chalcedon*; and that the Bishops should declare each in his own Church, that they likewise acknowledg'd both the Epistle and Council. 2. That they should all Anathematize *Nestorius*, *Eutyches*, *Dioscorus*, &c. together with *Acacius*, and all that adhered to his Communion, and that they should subscribe a Writing to that purpose, which he had sent by *Hilarus* his Notary. 3. That the Cause of the deposed Bishops should be referr'd to the Cognisance of the Apostolick See. As likewise, 4. The Cause of those Bishops that had been Promoters of the Persecution rais'd against the Orthodox. We may observe that these Articles were aim'd chiefly to enhanse the Authority of the *Roman* Bishop, and that by his Instructions to his Deputies he design'd to widen the Breach, rather than compose the Divisions in the Church. The Emperor receiv'd the Legates with much Civility, and told 'em he was ready to consent to every thing contain'd in the Articles, except what related to *Acacius*; he made this Exception because he design'd, by some popular Act, to recommend himself to the People, who he knew were very well affected to the Memory of *Acacius*; and that he might at once thoroughly reconcile himself to 'em, he settl'd a great Sum of Gold upon the Church, to the intent the Priests for the future might exact nothing from the People for Burials. By this means he began to recover the Favour of the Inhabitants, and in the mean time he sooth'd the Legates with plausible Words, tho' the Event show'd he intended nothing less than to be sincere; for he continu'd under-hand to favour the

Here-

Hereticks, supporting those with his Favour and Authority that were most averse to the Catholick Christians.

Having by his Artifices work'd himself into the good Will of the People, and concluding from thence it was no longer in *Vitalianus* his Power to do him any Mischief, he divested him of those Honours and Employments with which, since the Pacification, he had humour'd him, and openly renew'd his Persecution against the Faithful, threatning those with the severest Punishments that adher'd to the Council of *Chalcedon*, or enter'd into Communion with *Hormisda* ; notwithstanding which all the Bishops of *Illyricum* united themselves to the *Latin* Church, whereupon he sent for 'em to *Constantinople*, and finding 'em constant to their Principles he threw 'em into Prison, under the Hardships of which some of 'em languish'd a short time, and dy'd.

A. D. 516.

Anastasius *still a Persecutor.*

These his Prevarications re-kindl'd the People's Indignation against him, especially when they beheld him declaring more openly for the *Eutychian* Heresie than ever, so that they broke out into a furious Sedition, which gave occasion to many Robberies and bloody Murders. During this publick Consternation *Anastasius* appear'd in the *Circus* in the Habit of a Suppliant, without his Imperial Ornaments, and declar'd by his Heralds, *He was ready to sacrifice his private Interest to the publick Tranquility, and resign the Empire to whomsoever they thought worthy of it ; but they ought first to consider who was the most capable to govern, since it was impossible all who aspir'd to it could enjoy it.* These Words, together with the Tears and submissive Behaviour of the aged Emperor, prevail'd so effectually upon the People, that they entreated him to re-assume the Crown, promising him an implicit

A. D. 518.

implicit Obedience for the future. Instead of growing better from the sense of that Danger he so narrowly escap'd, and those terrible Earthquakes which about this time happen'd in *Dardania* and other Places, and seem'd to denounce God's heavy Displeasure against him, he grew more violent and outragious; suspecting some Conspiracy to be forming against him, he put several of the Chief Persons of his Houshold to Death, especially such as he judg'd to be best affected to the Orthodox Religion. *Justin* and *Justinian*, two of the Principal Men in the Empire, and who succeeded him one after the other, were in the heat of the Inquisition ready to be massacred; but a Man, with a furious Aspect, appearing to him in a terrible Vision the Night before, and forbidding him, upon the severest Penalties, to injure those two Persons, stopp'd his bloody Proceedings. The Writers of those Times relate several other strange Passages preceding the Death of *Anastasius*, as how a Man, with the same horrible Aspect, appear'd to him by Night some time after, presenting him with a Book, in which was calculated how long every Person then on the Earth had to live, saying to him, with an angry Countenance; *Behold! for the Perverseness of thy Faith I thus cut off Fourteen Years of thy Life*; that when he acquainted his Chamberlain the next Morning with his Dream, he reply'd, That the very same Night he dreamt a Boar devour'd him in the Presence of the Emperor; and when they both acquainted *Proclus*, that excellent Mathematician, with their several Visions, and desir'd him to inform 'em what was intended by 'em, he reply'd, That they should both of 'em in a very short time come to a violent End. This Report will seem the more probable, if it be true that *Anastasius* was destroy'd by Thunder; tho'

Strange Passages preceding the Death of Anastasius.

we

we are not to give much Credit to it, when we consider he was Eighty Eight Years old when he dy'd; a wonderful Age for an Emperor, without the Addition of Fourteen more to it. The Truth is, Ignorance and Superstition began now to gain Ground among the People, and so prepar'd 'em for an easie Reception of any Miracle, or whatever the Artifice of those, whose Business and Interest it was to deceive 'em, impos'd upon 'em for such; the Church was undermin'd by Heresies, divided by Schisms, and rent asunder by Factions and Contentions; this made way for Envy, Pride and Ambition, of which the most sincere were not absolutely innocent, but sometimes made use of the same Amusements to confirm the Truth, that their Adversaries did to propagate their Errors; whilst the People, who are generally govern'd more by Passion than guided by Reason, readily swallow'd every thing that was offer'd to 'em. It would be tedious and unnecessary to inform the Reader by how many Ways, and how many several Persons the Death of *Anastasius* is said to have been foretold, all which *Baronius* has taken the Pains to insert in his Annals, and that upon the Authority of such fabulous Authors, that the Reader may easily observe how much his Zeal, for the Cause in which he was Embark'd, had blinded his Understanding. They add farther, That *Anastasius* having consulted an Oracle what manner of Death he was to die, was answer'd, He should perish by Fire; and that, to evade it, *Proclus*, at his Request, had contriv'd an odd sort of Lodging for him, into which Fire had no Power to enter; that however the Prediction took place, for he was destroy'd by a Thunderbolt. Certain it is he was found dead in his Chamber on the 11th of *July*, Anastasius and forasmuch as we learn from no Historian that *his Death.*

any

any Marks of Fire were obſerv'd upon him after his Deceaſe, we may impute his End to the Extremities of Age, which frequently produces a ſudden, tho' not a violent Death, without queſtioning the great and juſt Judgments of God, in which he is often terrible, and of which we have the viſible Footſteps in many Reſpects remaining to this Day among us. However we may obſerve how careful Men, eſpecially ſuch as move in high Spheres, ought to behave themſelves whilſt alive, ſince hardly any thing can be reported of a Diſſolute, Tyrannical Prince after his Death, but what, in a great meaſure, will gain Credit with Poſterity. He dy'd, as was before obſerv'd, after he had liv'd Eighty Eight Years, and reign'd upwards of Twenty Seven Years, in the Twenty Fifth Year of *Theodorich*, King of *Italy*, in the Conſulate of *Magnus* and *Florentius*, *Hormiſda* being then Biſhop of *Rome*, *A.D.* 518.

His Character. *Anaſtaſius* was not the firſt Emperor, that from a good propitious Beginning degenerated into a voluptuous, arbitrary Prince; many before him begun as well, but few reign'd worſe, eſpecially if we believe the Eccleſiaſtical Writers of the *Roman* Party, who, ſuppoſing his Diſobedience to the Apoſtolick See the moſt enormous of all his Crimes, think, after that, they can't repreſent him in Colours black enough: We may grant moſt of what they ſay of him to be true, but ſome allowance muſt be given to Paſſion and Intereſt. He oblig'd the State with no one good Office, but is anſwerable to the Church for many ill ones. The Sale of publick Offices was ſo common towards the middle of his Reign, and ſo it continu'd to the very end of it, that the Empire by degrees grew into a ſort of Ariſtocracy. He was ſo covetous of Mony that the Provinces were exhauſted
by

Chap. I.   LV. Juſtin.

by his abominable Exactions, and yet every Motion the Barbarians made againſt him empty'd his Coffers again, not in raiſing Forces to oppoſe 'em, and for the neceſſary Defence and Honour of the Empire, but in bribing 'em to a Forbearance, that he might be the more at leiſure to purſue his Deſigns againſt the Church, in his Enmity to which he exceeded even *Julian* the Apoſtate; ſo that it's no Wonder if his own Name, together with that of his Predeceſſor *Zeno*, were eras'd out of the *Diptychs* after his Deceaſe.

III. *Anaſtaſius* being dead, *Juſtin*, the *Præfectus Prætorio*, was declar'd Emperor by the *Prætorian* Soldiers, who were ſenſible of his Worth, which made 'em hope the Empire would be reſtor'd to its former Vigour under the Conduct of ſo experienc'd a Commander, and ſome Remedy be found for the diſtracted Condition of the Church. He was by Original a *Thracian* of obſcure Birth, and employ'd in his Youth to look after Cattle, but being at length receiv'd into the Army, he quickly became remarkable for his Valour and conſtant Adherence to the Catholick Faith. From a private Soldier he was made a Tribune, after that *Præfectus Prætorio*, and from thence he was advanc'd to the Imperial Dignity; but by what Means he obtain'd it is not eaſily determin'd. *Anaſtaſius* had ſeveral Relations living, who were of great Intereſt and Authority in the Empire, and thought themſelves highly injur'd in the unexpected Promotion of *Juſtin*, for which reaſon they enter'd into a Conſpiracy againſt him, but being diſcover'd before they had time to put their Deſigns in Execution they were put to Death, together with *Amantius* and *Theocritus*. *Amantius* was great Chamberlain of the Houſhold, a cruel Perſecutor of the

JUSTIN.

Ca-

Catholick Christians, and in great Power whilst *Anastasius* liv'd, through whose Favour he heap'd up Wealth enough to have purchas'd the Soldiers Votes for himself, had he not been an Eunuch, and consequently incapable of the Imperial Purple; for which Reason *Evagrius* saith he employ'd all his Wealth and Authority in Favour of his Friend *Theocritus*, and for that Purpose entrusted *Justin* to distribute his Mony among the Guards to obtain his Election; but *Justin* made use of the Mony to his own Advantage, and having by the Influence of that secur'd the Army to his Interest, he was accordingly declar'd Emperor. If this Account be true, it's no wonder he took care upon the first Provocation to dispatch 'em out of the way, as soon as he had the Power in his Hands: But, upon the whole, this ill agrees with those Letters said to be written by *Justin* to the Pope, immediately after his Advancement, wherein he tells him he was Elected against his Will by the Senate and the Army. By what Means soever he attain'd the Purple, his first Care, after his Election, was to ingratiate himself with the People, by removing several Corruptions that had prevail'd in his Predecessor's Reign, and obliging the Inhabitants by some peculiar Acts of Grace. His Wife's Name was *Lupicina*, which, because it sounded something disagreeably, he chang'd into that of *Euphemia*, a Martyr, whose Memory was very dear and much reverenc'd by the People.

Marginal note: Justin very agreeable to the People.

But above all Things *Justin* express'd a great Zeal for the Peace and Welfare of the Church: Some short time after his Advancement *Timotheus*, the unworthy Patriarch of *Constantinople*, dy'd, in whose Place *John*, sirnamed the *Cappadocian*, a pious Orthodox Prelate, was by an universal Approbation Elected. Four Days after his Election he

Chap. I.   LV. Juſtin.

he ſummon'd a Synod, in which all the Catholick Biſhops were reſtor'd, and the ſound Doctrine and good Diſcipline of the Church carefully eſtabliſh'd, to the great Joy of all the Orthodox Prelates, who following ſo good an Example, ſummon'd Synods in their reſpective Dioceſſes, where the like wholſome Acts were agreed to and eſtabliſh'd. At the ſame time *Juſtin* writ to *Hormiſda*, Biſhop of *Rome*, conjuring him to propoſe ſome Means of a Re-union between the Churches of the Eaſt and Weſt; and the Emperor acted ſo vigorouſly in that Affair, that tho' *Hormiſda* expreſs'd much Pride, Obſtinacy and Ambition in the Courſe of it, yet the Thing was at laſt effected, to the great Honour and Reputation of *Juſtin*; who, by theſe and many other worthy Actions, gave the People ſuch a general Satisfaction in his Government, that they ſoon forgot the ſiniſter Practices, if they were ſuch, by which he obtain'd the Empire, and the Obſcurity of his Birth.

Tho' *Juſtin* had, at his firſt Advancement, taken care to remove all ſuch as he thought had been his Competitors, or were willing and able to diſpute his Right, yet he began this Year to apprehend new Diſturbances from *Vitalianus*, of whom mention was made before in the Reign of *Anaſtaſius*. *Vitalianus* was by Birth a *Scythian*, and being a Man of great Spirit and Reſolution had rais'd himſelf to a conſiderable Authority in the State, inſomuch that he had the Courage to aim at the Imperial Dignity it ſelf. During the Reign of *Anaſtaſius*, who was the profeſs'd Patron of Hereticks, he eſpous'd the Catholick Cauſe, for no other Reaſon, as *Baronius* will have it, but to render himſelf popular, and oppoſe the Emperor; he ſo far ſucceeded in his Deſigns that he brought his Maſter to Terms of Compoſition, *Anaſtaſius* being glad to pur-

A. D. 519.

purchase his good Will at a very high rate. So soon as *Justin* was advanc'd to the Empire there follow'd a Turn of Affairs in the Church, whereupon *Vitalianus* quitted his former Interest and revolted to the *Eutychians*, as if he thought it a worthy thing still to protect the declining Party. He was at this time in *Thrace*, where he behav'd himself more like a Male-content, than one affected to the present Government. *Justin* was not ignorant of his Practices against his Predecessor, and found now by his Apostacy that Religion was not the Ground of his Quarrel; he knew him to be a brave experienc'd General, and for that Reason in good Esteem with the Soldiers; he likewise knew him to be arrogant and ambitious, and therefore ready to promote any Innovations: To proceed with open Force against him he judg'd dangerous and unseasonable, so that he conceiv'd the only way to suppress him was to circumvent him; to which purpose he invited him by an honourable Message to Court, where he made him Captain of his Guards, and design'd him Consul for the Year ensuing. But as on the one hand the Emperor conferr'd all these Favours upon him with no other intent but to destroy him, so on the other *Vitalianus* grew more presumptuous upon his Exaltation, for which Reason he was murder'd in the Palace, in the Seventh Month of his Consulate, by the Order of *Justin*.

Vitalianus Slain.

Justin having thus eas'd himself of his Fears, in the Death of *Vitalianus*, met with no Interruptions from the State that were able to divert him from his Inspection and great Care for the Prosperity of the Church, and the Maintenance of the true Religion, which he express'd in several Edicts directed for the Suppression of Heresie, and Punishment of obstinate Hereticks. Out of Respect to *Theodorich*,

King

King of the *Goths* in *Italy*, he for a long time abstain'd from molesting the *Goths*, and most of his Prosecutions exempted the *Arians*, who upon that Account became more insolent, and propagated their Errors with a greater Licence; which when the Emperor observ'd, and that the Catholick Christians were scandalised at his Temporising, he at length by a new Edict depriv'd the *Arians* of all their Churches in his Dominions: At the same time *Elderic*, King of the *Vandals* in *Africk*, and Son of *Trasimund* and *Valentinian*'s Daughter, relinquish'd the Errors of his Fathers, and embrac'd the Catholick Faith. In this Conjuncture the *Arians* apply'd themselves to *Theodorich*, who being of the same Profession zealously espous'd their Cause, and therefore writ very pressing Letters in their Favour to the Emperor; but finding the Emperor to persist still in his Proceedings, and that his Application had not the desir'd Effect, he resolv'd to assure him, in a solemn Embassy, that the Catholicks should meet with the same Rigour in the West, which he express'd towards the *Arians* in the East; and to render his Intercession the more efficacious, he made *John*, at that time Bishop of *Rome*, Chief of the Embassy, joining with him in the same Commission Men of the greatest Quality in the City. *Boetius*, that great Man, who was lately fallen into Disgrace, notwithstanding he had deserv'd more from *Theodorich* than any Subject in his Dominions, and lay at this time in Prison, gives another Reason for this Embassy; he saith, The *Roman* Senate were accus'd of High-Treason against the King; who complain'd that the Principal among them had been corrupted by the Emperor, with whom they held secret Intelligence, in Prejudice to the Alliance between 'em, and of which these Persons were sent to complain at *Constantinople*. *Boetius*

A. D. 524.

Boetius *in Disgrace with Theodorich.*

being

being a Man too conversant with the Transactions of those Times to be mistaken, it's very probable that both the one and the other were the Subject of their Embassy. Whatever the Design of it was, the *Roman* Writers have taken care to signalize it with several remarkable Miracles: *Gregory* the Great *Pretended* tells us, That when *John* arriv'd at *Corinth*, in his *Miracles.* way to *Constantinople*, great Enquiry was made after a gentle Horse for *John* to ride upon, of which when a Nobleman of that City was inform'd, he sent him one that for its exceeding Temper was reserv'd for the Use of his Lady; that after *John* had travell'd upon it as far as he at first propos'd he return'd it to the right Owner, but the next time the Lady thought to mount the Beast as usual, she found him proud, and impatient of so mean a Burden, after the Honour he had receiv'd in carrying the Successor of St. *Peter*; whereupon the Gentleman sent it back to the Pope, and desir'd him to accept of that which was now become of no Use to any but himself. To this Miracle *Gregory* thought fit to add another, and saith, That whilst the Pope was making his publick Entry into *Constantinople* he restor'd a blind Man to his Sight, by laying his Hand upon his Eyes. These Miracles, as they are absurd in themselves, so is it as absurd to imagine God would so visibly at that time exert his Power in the Person of one who was sent as an Embassador from an Heretick Prince, in behalf of those who deny'd the very Fundamentals of Christianity. The greatest thing to be wonder'd at, during his Stay at *Constantinople*, was his Pride and Arrogance, which is sufficiently hinted at by such as write of that Embassy; in which he behav'd himself so ill, and displeas'd *Theodorich* John, *the* to that Degree, that at his Return he was thrown *Pope, dy'd* *in Prison.* into Prison, where he dy'd not long after. It must indeed

indeed be allow'd, that *Theodorich*, being now grown old and jealous, was no more that excellent Prince which for a long time had shin'd with so much Lustre in the West. Hitherto he had govern'd himself and his People with so much Prudence, Valour, Magnificence, Bounty, Justice, Equity, and Moderation, that he worthily deserv'd to be set forth as a Pattern for other Princes; but now the Infirmities of old Age, that increas'd daily upon him, came attended with the Vices of it too. Some late Affronts put upon him in the Person of his Sister by the *African Vandals*, and the little Power he had to revenge the Injury as he desir'd, together with some Disappointments he met with in his private Affairs very much discompos'd that Sweetness of Temper, of which 'till now he had been absolute Master. Of this some, who for a long time had been Enemies to the great Merits of *Boetius*, and that excellent Senator *Symmachus*, his Father-in-law, were no sooner sensible, but they miss-led him to the Ruin of those worthy Persons, whom they accus'd of having conspir'd against the Life and Dignity of *Theodorich*, and suborn'd Witnesses to make good the Accusation; in conclusion, *Theodorich*, whether privy to their Villany, or persuaded of their Guilt, commanded 'em both to be Beheaded, which Sentence was executed upon 'em accordingly. But how undeservedly they both suffer'd will best appear by the too late Repentance of *Theodorich*, whose Sorrow for their Deaths equall'd if not exceeded the Injustice of their Punishment. A short time after their Execution the Head of a large Fish was serv'd up to Table, whilst he was at Supper; this Head, which was of an unusual Bigness, *Theodorich* fancy'd to be that of *Symmachus*, upbraiding him as it were with a threatning ghastly Countenance for his Cruelty against him. The

A. D. 526. Boetius *and* Symmachus *put to Death.*

Sight

Sight of it wrought so much upon his Imagination that he was immediately seiz'd with Horror and Amazement, and carry'd from the Table into his Chamber, where he was seiz'd by a violent Feaver, *Theodorich dies.* of which he dy'd in a few Days, after he had liv'd Seventy two Years and reign'd something more than Thirty three.

His Character. He may be said to have been almost the only Person who obtain'd a Kingdom by Force and Violence, that knew how to preserve it with Calmness and Sweetness, which eminently appear'd in all his Actions and Councils; and *Italy*, contrary to the Fate which usually attends conquer'd Kingdoms, enjoy'd as much Serenity, Peace, Pleasure, and Security, under his Government, as ever she did in the Height of her Greatness and Authority. This his prudent, paternal Administration, as it made him belov'd at home, so it render'd him terrible to his Enemies; it being certain, a Prince's Strength does not so much consist in Foreign Treaties and Alliances as the Love and Affections of his Subjects, which upon all Occasions *Theodorich* took care to cultivate. It has been usually observ'd, that no People are so tyrannical, uncharitable and inhuman as Hereticks, when once they have the Power in their Hands; but this Unchristian Temper was what *Theodorich*, though an *Arian*, was totally a Stranger to, for he show'd himself a common Father to all his Subjects, and extended his Protection to all Parties with an equal Indulgence. *Rome* it self was much oblig'd to him for his Bounty towards her, in repairing her Walls, supplying her with several convenient Fountains, and beautifying her with many magnificent Buildings; and the State in general ow'd no less to him for the many wholsome Laws with which he strengthen'd and enrich'd it. In a word, setting aside his Heresie,

with

with which from his Birth he had been infected, and so, in some measure, may be imputed rather to the force of his Education than the Perverseness of his Mind, and except his last Acts of Cruelty, to excuse which he may plead the Weakness and Infirmities of old Age, he may be justly reckon'd one of the most excellent and accomplish'd Princes that 'till then had appear'd in the World.

Theodorich, some time before his Death, summon'd the Chief of his Nobility to attend him at Court, where he declar'd *Athalaric*, his Grandson by his Daughter *Amalasont*, his Successor, desiring them to ratifie his Choice, to be dutiful to the young Prince, to be affectionate to the Senate and People of *Rome*, and court the good Will and Friendship of the Emperor, to all which Particulars he made 'em take a solemn Oath.

Athalaric, at his Grandfather's Death, was no more than Eight Years of Age, for which reason his Mother *Amalasont* was declar'd Regent of the Realm, a Trust, of which no Person living was more worthy than her self. She was a Princess Beautiful and Majestick, well skill'd in the *Greek* and *Latin* Tongues, and knew well how to insinuate her self into the Affections of the People, being Mistress of a Prudence and Courage greater than what is usually found in the most extraordinary of her Sex. From the Moment she undertook the Administration, she govern'd with so much Justice and Sagacity, that *Italy* promiss'd it self all manner of Happiness under her propitious Conduct. She restor'd to the Children of *Boetius* and *Symmachus* all their Fathers Inheritance, and made the best Amends she could for the Injustice her Father had done 'em. She confirm'd a Peace with *Amalric*, King of the Western *Goths* in *Spain*, who, being her Sister's Son, had succeeded his Father

Athalaric succeeds him.

Alaric

Alaric after his Defeat by *Clovis*, and restor'd to him all that Tract of Land that lyes between the *Rhône* and the *Alps*, committing it to the Government of *Patricius Liberius*. On the other Hand she resign'd up to the King of *France* such Countries as had been contested between them and her Father, and by that means depriv'd 'em of the least Pretence for a Quarrel; but, above all, she was sollicitous for the Education of her Son, well knowing that upon that depended his own Honour and Welfare, as well as the Prosperity of his People. How she succeeded in this her pious Care, and what Difficulties she met with in the Administration, we shall find hereafter in the Reign of *Justinian*, when the Divisions among the *Goths* call'd for his Arms into *Italy*.

In the mean time we are to return back to *Justin*, whom we find wholly employ'd in Affairs relating to the State of the Church, 'till some Overtures from *Persia* suspended his Application. About this time *Cabades*, King of *Persia*, was grown old and infirm, and much perplex'd about the Succession, which he was afraid would create such Disputes, after his Decease, as would prove very prejudicial to his Family. With his eldest Son, who had a Legal Claim, he was offended beyond a Reconciliation; his second Son, call'd *Zances*, having lost one of his Eyes, was, according to the Constitutions of the Country, incapable of Reigning; but being an active, valiant Prince, an experienc'd Soldier, and withal a very virtuous Person, he was afraid lest the Favour of the People should encourage him to attempt any thing against *Chosroes*, who was his third Son, the best belov'd, and to whom he was very desirous to secure the Succession. He thought, if some way could be found to engage the Emperor *Justin* to his Interest, his Desires

fires would be the more easily effected. Whereupon he sent his Embassadors to him, and in his Letters reminded him of *the Injuries the* Persians *had receiv'd at several times from the* Romans, *for which, however, he declin'd to demand any Reparation, because he was earnestly desirous an inviolable and perpetual Peace might be establish'd between the two Nations; as a Pledge whereof, and of their future Friendship, he wish'd the Emperor would Adopt his Son* Chosroes, *whom he design'd for his Successor in the Kingdom, and who, by Virtue of so near a Relation to the* Roman *Emperor, would be the better able to support his Pretensions.* This Proposal, at first, was readily embrac'd by *Justin,* and all the Chief Ministers, except *Proclus,* the great Treasurer of the Empire, who represented to the Emperor *the Danger of such Novelties, what Design* Cabades *might possibly have in his Request; that to desire* Justin *to Adopt* Chosroes *for his Son, was, in effect, to desire he might be declar'd Heir to the* Roman *Empire; that a Peace with the* Persians *was highly requisite, and that Embassadors ought to be dispatch'd with all Diligence to negotiate it, with Orders to decline all Motions relating to the Adoption*: Accordingly Embassadors from both Princes met upon the Frontiers, but return'd more dissatisfy'd than ever, so that a War seem'd unavoidable. *Cabades* was at the present diverted from expressing his Resentments as he thought it became him, tho' in this Emperor's Time there were on one side and the other some Encounters and Incursions, the Preludes of a War, which broke out with greater Violence in the Reign of *Justinian.*

After this we meet with no considerable Transactions during the Reign of *Justin,* who from his first Advancement was chiefly busied in Matters relating to Ecclesiastical Affairs; and indeed the Monks

Monks of those Times began to grow so troublesom, and invented so many new *Chimæras* in Religious Matters, the pure Effects of Ignorance or Idleness, that it was a very difficult matter to keep 'em within the Bounds of Decency and Order; notwithstanding which the Church flourish'd exceedingly in his Days, for the Orthodox Faith was not only re-establish'd in *Africk*, but the Pale of the Church was enlarg'd by the Conversion of the *Lazians* to Christianity, which the whole Nation embrac'd at once, after the Example of *Zathus* their Prince, who, coming to *Constantinople*, was Baptiz'd by the Patriarch, gratify'd with many Presents, honour'd with a Royal Crown, and marry'd to a Lady of one of the best Families in the Empire. At this *Cabades*, the King of *Persia*, was highly offended, and complain'd, *For that* Justin *had enter'd into an Alliance with a Nation, that, being his Tributaries, were broken out into open Hostilities and Rebellion against him.* The Emperor reply'd, in his own Justification, *That his Transactions with them had no relation to their Temporal Interest and Engagements, but their Spiritual; that he was oblig'd by his Profession and Dignity to encourage and assist them in their Conversion, upon which the Salvation of so many Souls depended.* With this Answer *Cabades* was satisfy'd for the present, tho' he objected it afterwards to the Emperor, when the Adoption we before mention'd was in Agitation.

A. D. 526.
A terrible Earthquake at Antioch.

Sometime before the Death of this Emperor so terrible an Earthquake happen'd at *Antioch*, which was attended by as dreadful a Fire, that the greatest part of that beautiful and capacious City was bury'd in Ruins. At the same time the Cities of *Dyrrachium*, *Corinth*, *Anazarbo* in *Cilicia*, and *Edessa*, were almost destroy'd by Earthquakes. The

The Monks, who never fail to abuse the Judgments, as well as Mercies of God, which in themselves are often wonderfully stupendous, with some pretended Miracles, have not been wanting, upon this Occasion, to insert some in their Legends as egregiously ridiculous, as they are abominably false; but the Emperor *Justin* made a better use of it, for as soon as he heard of the miserable Condition *Antioch* was in he pull'd off his Imperial Ornaments, and by all the Actions of a Christian Humiliation study'd to appease the Divine Wrath. The same Year the *Lombards*, a Northern Nation, left their Dwellings, and enter'd *Hungary*, where, having expell'd the *Ostrogoths*, they continu'd Two and Forty Years, and then erected a Kingdom in *Italy*, where in the Course of our History we shall find 'em.

Justin, finding himself broken with Age, and unable to live much longer, like a most prudent virtuous Prince, summon'd the Senate together, to consult with them about the Choice of a Successor, having himself no Children to succeed him; by whose united Advice and Consent, *Justinian*, his Sister's Son, about Forty Five Years of Age, was declar'd *Cæsar*, to the great Joy and Satisfaction of the People; and some time after *Justin* perceiving his End to be near at Hand, he put the Imperial Crown upon *Justinian*'s Head, in the Presence of the Patriarch, and the Grandees of the Empire, after which he was Crown'd publickly in the Theatre, and his Wife *Theodora* proclaim'd *Augusta*; so that from this time forward, 'till the Death of *Justin*, which happen'd shortly after, he reign'd jointly with him: Tho' *Justin* was Seventy Seven Years old when he dy'd, yet an old Wound he had formerly receiv'd in his Thigh is said to have been the occasion of his Death, after

JUSTINIAN.

Justin *dies*.

he

he had reign'd Nine Years and Two or Three Months, in the single Consulate of *Movortius*, *An. Dom.* 527. for the Dignity, as well as Power of Consul, began now to decline, and to be little regarded, which show'd the Expiration of it to be at Hand.

His Character.

Thus have we seen *Justin*, a Man of obscure Parantage, simple and unlearn'd, hold the Reins of the Empire with more Honour, and leave it with greater Reputation than many of his Predecessors, who by Birth, Fortune, and Education, seem'd destin'd for the Sovereignty. He is said to have been so very illiterate, that he could neither Write nor Read, a thing the *Romans* never met with in any of the Emperors before, so that he was forc'd to make use of a peculiar Mark or Stamp in the Authorising any Imperial Edicts, or publick Ordinances, and yet he was as Just, Prudent, Temperate and Sagacious, as the most knowing among the Philosophers, so that he seem'd endow'd by Nature with those Beauties of Mind which others had acquir'd by Art. If we add to all this his great Zeal for the Christian Religion, and his continu'd Labours for the Peace and Prosperity of the Church, we must upon the whole allow him to have been a Prince that in many things deserv'd to be imitated, in few or none to be reprehended.

CHAP.

CHAP. II.

From the Advancement of Justinian the Great, to the Death of that Prince.

Containing the Space of 38 Years.

I. WE are now entering upon a Reign long and active, in which the *Roman* Genius seem'd once more to exalt her venerable Head, and, like the returning Spring, infpir'd with frefh Vigour the aged Body of the Empire; thofe Provinces which the Mifcarriages of former Reigns, and the fuccefsful Arms of the Barbarians had torn from her, fhe again claim'd by Right of Inheritance, and gave the World a lively Idea of her former Majefty.

A. D. 527.

Juftinian, being a Prince of great Defigns, and ambitious of fecuring as much of the Empire as had been left him by his Anceftors, and recovering what had been loft by his Predeceffors, took, at his firft Eftablifhment, the beft Method to obtain his Defires; for, knowing all his Endeavours would be ineffectual without the Divine Affiftance, he prepar'd himfelf for it by fuch Works of Chriftan Piety and Charity, as he thought moft likely to draw down the Bleffing of God upon his Defigns, which tended all to the Profperity of the Church, and reftoring the *Roman* Empire to its ancient Splendor and Authority.

His firft Care was to preferve his Dominions from the Infults and Incurfions of the Barbarians, to which purpofe *Belifarius*, his General, a Perfon that is to make a noble Figure in the fucceeding Courfe

The beginning of the firft Perfian War.

Course of this History, had Orders to build a Fort at *Mindon*, a Place seated on the Frontiers near *Nisibis*; who so vigorously pursu'd his Instructions, that the Work was considerably advanc'd when the *Persians*, who were much offended at it, commanded him, with many Menaces, to desist; and finding he still proceeded to execute the Emperor's Orders, they rais'd an Army and demolish'd the Building, notwithstanding the Assistance *Justinian* had sent to support him. This Action, together with some other Provocations the *Persians* pretended to have receiv'd in the former Reign, gave a Beginning to that War, which was afterwards carry'd on with much Violence between the two Crowns.

Cabades, of whom frequent mention has been made already, was at this time King of *Persia*, but, after a Reign of near Thirty Years, was grown very infirm and unfit for Publick Business, yet he was by Nature Warlike and Ambitious; he had from his Youth encounter'd with many Difficulties, and overcame 'em all by his Courage and Dexterity; he was afraid of the Factions with which he imagin'd his Kingdom would be distracted at his Death; and when he beheld a Prince vigilant and sagacious, as *Justinian* appear'd to be, upon the Imperial Throne, his Apprehensions were encreas'd. Since therefore he had fail'd by Treaties to persuade the *Romans* to listen to such Terms as he desir'd, he was resolv'd, if possible, to gain his Ends by a War, which for that reason he intended to begin, but was prevented by *Justinian*, who, besides the Affront he had receiv'd in his General, for which he requir'd Reparation, demanded several Places belonging of Right to him, but at that time in the Hands of the *Persians*; upon

Refusal

Refusal he declar'd War against him, and sent a strong Army into *Mesopotamia* under the Command of *Belisarius*, who was made General of the East. *Belisarius* met the *Persians*, under the Conduct of *Myrrhanes*, near *Daras*, where he engag'd with him, and defeated him. This was the first Victory the *Romans* had for many Years obtain'd against the *Persians*, who fought with much Obstinacy, and, in all probability, had defeated the *Romans*, whom they almost doubl'd in number, had not a Reserve of the *Heruli* advanc'd seasonably to their Assistance. The *Romans* kill'd above Five Thousand of the Enemy, and might perhaps have done more Execution, had not the General prudently sounded a Retreat, lest the *Persians* should rally upon 'em, and make their Advantage of a disorderly Pursuit. *The Persians defeated.*

This Victory, which Crown'd the Arms of *Justinian* in *Mesopotamia*, was seconded by another in *Armenia*, whither *Cabades* had sent another Army under the Conduct of *Mermeroes*, who was surpriz'd by *Cittas*, General of the *Roman* Forces, who kill'd a great number of his Men, and rifl'd his Camp; and having in a second Engagement routed 'em, and forc'd 'em to march in a disorderly manner home, he took in several Towns in *Persarmenia*, together with the two Forts of *Bolus* and *Pharangium*, which had the Command of the Royal Mines.

These Advantages, on the part of the *Romans*, made way for a Treaty, which being ineffectual, the *Persians* early in the Spring invaded the *Roman* Territories, being accompany'd by *Alamundarus*, King of the *Saracens*, who brought a considerable Body of his Subjects to the Assistance of the *Persians*. *Alamundarus* was an old experienc'd Soldier, having for the space of Fifty Years together *The Persians and Saracens at once Invade the Roman Empire.*

been

been at Enmity with the *Romans*; he knew better than any the manner of their Discipline, as well in the Camp as the Field, and where, and in what manner to attack 'em with the best Advantage; 'twas he encourag'd *Cabades* to this Expedition, and advis'd him to break into the *Roman* Territories, not as they usually did by the way of *Osroene*, but to pierce directly into *Syria*, where they would meet with no fortify'd Town, nor any considerable Forces to resist 'em; and that consequently *Antioch*, the Capital of the East, in which there was no Garrison, and the Inhabitants whereof were taken up in Festivals and wanton Diversions, must of necessity fall into their Hands, which they might rifle, and carry off all the Wealth of the Place, before the Army in *Mesopotamia* could move to relieve it.

A.D. 530.
With this Assistance, and these Instructions, the Army began to march, but, before they were enter'd into *Syria*, *Belisarius*, who was inform'd of their Design, having left convenient Garrisons for the Defence of *Mesopotamia*, was ready upon the Frontiers to dispute their Passage. This unexpected Expedition in the *Roman* General very much surpriz'd and perplex'd the *Persians*, who, 'till now, had thought of nothing else than the Pillage of *Antioch*. They thought it dangerous and unseasonable to hazard a Battel, and therefore prepar'd for an orderly Retreat. On the other side *Belisarius* concluded he had done his part in preserving the Country, and that it was imprudent to provoke a flying Enemy much stronger than himself. But his Men were of another Opinion; they upbraided their General, as *if he deny'd 'em the Honour of a Victory, and chose rather to prolong the War by his cautious Proceedings, that favour'd of Cowardice, than put an end to it by suffering 'em*

'em to lay hold of an Advantage Fortune had thrown into their Hands. His Army confifted of fome *Veterane* Troops, whom their late Succeffes had made rafh and defperate, and fuch Recruits of the *Ifauri* and *Lycaonians* as he could levy in his March, who being for the moft part taken from the Plow knew not what a Battel meant, and yet were the moft forward for an Engagement. *Belifarius*, inftead of punifhing 'em as they deferv'd, fubmitted to Neceffity, and led 'em on againft the Enemy. The *Perfians*, feeing it would unavoidably come to a general Engagement, turn'd head, and drawing themfelves up into Battel, ftood ready to recive 'em. The Difpute was obftinate on both Sides, and the Fortune of the Day for a long time continu'd very doubful, 'till at laft a Body of the moft refolute among the *Perfians* charg'd the Right Wing of the *Roman* Army, where *Arethas* commanded fome mercenary *Saracens*, who at the firft Onfet fled, perhaps with a Defign refolv'd upon before to betray *Belifarius*. The *Roman* Horfe being by this time weary, weaken'd and difhearten'd, quitted the Field, whilft *Belifarius* with a few, that were afham'd to forfake him, defended himfelf with fo much Courage and Succefs, that the *Perfian* Cavalry, finding it impoffible to break in upon him, return'd towards Night with the reft of their Army to the Camp. The next Day, when they came to plunder the Field, and compute the Numbers that were loft on both Sides, they found they had no great reafon to boaft of the Victory; and the King himfelf was afham'd of the Enterprize, when he faw his General return with a broken inglorious Army, that had neither taken *Antioch*, nor any other Place that could anfwer his Expectation, or the Expence of the Expedition.

The Romans fighting contrary to the Opinion of their General, are overthrown

Tho'

Tho' the Loss the *Romans* receiv'd was not very considerable, yet *Justinian*, who began now to cast his Eyes upon the *Vandals* in *Africk*, sent his Embassadors into *Persia* to treat of a Peace, but at the same time prepar'd vigorously for the War; and the better to strengthen himself against so powerful an Enemy enter'd into an Alliance with the *Æthiopians*, *Homerites* and *Nabatheans*, who promis'd his Embassadors mighty things but perform'd nothing. Nor had his Negotiations in *Persia* any better Success; for *Cabades*, being enrag'd at the late Losses he had receiv'd, would give Ear to no Offers of Accommodation; so that with a fresh Army, under the Command of new Generals, the *Persians* once more enter'd into *Mesopotamia*, where meeting with no Forces strong enough to oppose 'em, they went and laid Siege to *Martyropolis*, a City about thirty Miles North of *Amida*, situate upon the River *Nymphius*, that parted the *Roman* Dominions from those of *Persia*. The Town wanted all manner of Provision, and was in no way prepar'd for a Siege; *Belisarius* was sent for home to command the Emperor's Forces in *Africk*; and *Sittas*, who succeeded him in the Government of the East, had not Strength sufficient to relieve it. At the same time *Cabades* had hir'd the *Massagetes* to advance into *Persia*, and from thence invade the *Roman* Territories. Of this the Emperor being inform'd by a *Persian* Spy, in whom he had great reason to confide, he persuaded him to go and report to the Army lying before *Martyropolis*, that these *Massagetes* were in the Emperor's Pay, and that they were moving with a great Body of Men to raise the Siege. The *Persians*, who believ'd all the Spy reported, were in great doubt what Measures to take, when in the mean time News was brought that *Cabades* was dead, which put an end to their Consultations;

Martyropolis besieg'd by the Persians.

tations; for being ignorant in what Condition the
Affairs of their own Country stood, and being apprehensive of the *Massagetes,* who, as they thought,
were marching against them, they listen'd to *Sittas*
and *Hermogenes,* who press'd 'em to a Cessation of
Arms, which shortly after was follow'd by a Conclusion of the Peace. For tho' *Chosroes* was ordain'd Successor by his Father's last Will, and declar'd such by the great Officers of the Kingdom,
yet he knew not how the People stood affected to
his elder Brother, who had the juster Title, and
therefore thought it prudent to secure all at home,
before he engag'd himself in any Wars with his
Neighbours.

A. D.
531.

The Siege rais'd.

Sometime before the Confirmation of this Peace
such a Mutiny happen'd at *Constantinople,* as, perhaps, has not been equall'd in any Age before or
since, if consider'd either in its Beginning, its Progress, or Conclusion. Tho' *Marcellinus,* and some
others with him, say it was first rais'd by *Hypatius,*
Pompeius and *Probus,* Nephews to the late Emperor
Anastasius, yet *Procopius* traces it a little higher;
and in his Account of it gives us a terrible Idea of
an enrag'd head-strong Multitude.

A great Mutiny at Constantinople.

As in most other Cities at that time, so especially in *Constantinople,* it was customary with the Citizens to divide themselves into several Factions, in
favour of the several Charioteers that ran the Races in the *Circus;* and these Factions were denoted
by some peculiar Colour, by which they each distinguish'd themselves from the rest. This Custom
was of an ancient standing in *Rome,* where the
Contests in behalf of the contending Parties proceeded often so high that much Blood has been shed
upon that account, the Emperors themselves frequently espousing this or that Side. Of these Factions
there were no less than Four in number, the *Pra-*
sina

F

sina or *Green*, the *Russata* or *Russet*, the *Albata* or *White*, and the *Veneta* or *Blue*; tho' the *Green* and *Blue* grew at length to be the most popular. It is not to be imagin'd with what Zeal the People embrac'd these Factions, the very Women themselves engaging in the Disputes, and the Men wasting their Estates in the Support of their respective Party.

It happen'd at this time that the Officers of Justice were leading some of these Antagonists out to Execution, whereupon both Parties, tho' at other times irreconcileable, united in great Numbers with a Design at first only to rescue the Malefactors, but proceeding with an irresistable Fury, they first broke open all the Prisons in the City, and then kill'd the Officers of Justice. Those who were of neither Faction, amaz'd at so sudden an Uproar, fled over into the opposite Continent, abandoning the City as to an enrag'd Enemy, whilst the Mutineers set Fire to it in every Quarter. The Emperor from the first Beginning of the Tumult had shut himself up in the Palace, together with the Empress and some of the Senate, among whom were *John* the *Præfectus Prætorio*, and *Trebonian* the Treasurer. These two had render'd themselves extreamly odious to the People by their Avarice and Oppression, whom therefore the Emperor dismiss'd from their Employments, hoping to appease the Tumult by so seasonable a piece of Justice. But tho' they rail'd openly against 'em in the Beginning of the Mutiny, and seem'd to aim at nothing but their Destruction, yet now they would not be satisfy'd with so mean a Sacrifice, but threaten'd a thorow Alteration of the Government. *Hypatius* and *Pompeius* were among the Senators that were shut up with the Emperor in the Palace, but, contrary to their earnest and repeated Desires, had Orders from him to retire to their own Houses;

they

they told him they were afraid the People, in that general Confusion, would force 'em to accept of the Empire, to prevent which it would be safer for 'em to continue in his Presence, protesting at the same time they were ready to defend his Person at the certain Hazard of their own Lives. The Emperor, who thought he had just Reason to distrust 'em, was deaf to all they could offer, and so without any farther Consideration drove 'em out of the Palace; but how much his Fears at that time were too strong for his Reason evidently appear'd from what follow'd, for the Multitude ran the next Morning to *Hypatius,* and saluting him Emperor conducted him to the *Forum,* there to invest him with the Government, whilst his Wife *Maria,* a sober discreet Lady, hung upon him, protesting they were leading him forth to Destruction, nor would she be persuaded to quit him 'till they forc'd him from her. Whilst the Mutineers were busied in this tumultuous Solemnity, the Emperor was consulting whether he had best stay or make his Escape by Sea, for all the Senators that were not with him in the Palace had now join'd with the Multitude, who by this time threaten'd to pull him out of the Palace. Whilst they were deliberating what was best to be done in so great an Extremity, *Theodora,* with a Masculine Courage, persuaded him to stem the Tide, concluding all with that old Saying, *How brave a Sepulchre is a Kingdom!* Hereupon they consider'd how they might best defend themselves. The Soldiers that then lay quarter'd in the Town declar'd neither for the Emperor nor the Mutineers, but waited to see the Event; all the Emperor's Hopes were in *Belisarius,* who being lately recall'd from the *Persian* War came timely to his Assistance, with a good Body of Forces under his Command; at the same time

Mundus, having been sent for out of *Illyricum*, where he commanded as General for the Emperor, arriv'd with a Troop of the *Heruli*: With these Forces the two Captains quickly quell'd the Tumult, *Hypatius* and *Pompeius* were Beheaded, and *John* and *Trebonian* restor'd to their former Dignities. This Insurrection, call'd *Nica*, being the Word the Mutineers gave, continu'd for several Days together, during which there were near Thirty Thousand Persons murder'd, many publick Buildings as well as private Edifices burnt; and had not the Hand of God visibly interpos'd, it is not to be doubted but the whole City had been laid in Ruins; so much was he in the right, who compar'd the Fury of the People to the Raging of the Sea.

Quell'd by Belisarius.

This Tumult being thus appeas'd, and a Peace concluded with *Persia*, *Justinian* began to apply himself in good earnest to the War in *Africk*. *Hilderick*, King of the *Vandals*, was now in the Seventh Year of his Reign; he was a Prince of a mild and gentle Disposition, and withal a great Friend to the Church, encouraging upon all Occasions the Catholick Christians: He had been lately worsted in some Engagements with the *Moors*, which made him the less respected by his *Vandals*. Having no Children of his own, *Gelimer*, a near Relation, being the next in Years, was, according to the Constitution of that Country, to succeed him in the Kingdom. This *Gelimer* was a warlike, valiant, and sagacious Prince, but withal he was haughty and ambitious: *Hilderick* had resign'd up to him the absolute Management of Affairs, but he was impatient to govern in his own Right, and could no longer endure to be the Substitute of another; hereupon he rais'd a Party against him, and accus'd him to the *Vandals*, *as an unactive effeminate Prince, and one who endeavour'd to betray the State to the*

The Reasons of the War in Africk.

Chap. II.   LVI. Justinian.

Emperor, and to take from him the Right of Succession; for these Reasons he persuaded 'em to depose him, and told 'em, *The State would never be secure 'till they had done so.* To this, after a short Deliberation, the *Vandals* consented, so the unfortunate Prince was shut up in a Prison with his two Brothers, *Amer* and *Evagenes,* and *Gelimer* declar'd King in his stead.

Upon this *Justinian* sent his Embassadors into *Africk,* who, according to their Instructions, represented to *Gelimer* the Heinousness of the Crime, and exhorted him *patiently to wait for a Succession, to which he had so just a Title, and not chuse to be a Tyrant, rather than a lawful Prince.* Gelimer dismiss'd the Embassadors without any Satisfaction, pull'd out *Amer*'s Eyes, and put *Hilderick* and *Evagenes* under a more severe Confinement. This oblig'd *Justinian* to send him a second Embassy, in which he was more urgent than the former, desiring him, in conclusion, *to send* Hilderick *and his Brothers to* Constantinople; *threatning to Treat with him as with an Enemy, if he refus'd it.* To this *Gelimer* return'd Answer, *That he had neither forcibly seiz'd upon the Kingdom, nor stain'd his Hands in Blood; that the* Vandals *had depos'd* Hilderick *for his Practices against the House of* Genserich; *that he claim'd the Kingdom by Right of Eldership, and would defend it to the utmost; as he should find, if, in breach of the Oath sworn by* Zeno, *he presum'd to invade it.* These Transactions happen'd whilst *Justinian* was engag'd in the *Persian* War, which made him more desirous of a Peace with *Cabades,* as thinking a more Honourable Cause call'd for his Arms into *Africk.* Having therefore concluded a Peace with *Chosroes,* he muster'd Ten Thousand Foot, and Five Thousand Horse, and appointed Five Hundred Vessels for their Transportation.

A. D. 533.   As a necessary Introduction to so great an Undertaking, *Justinian* publish'd several Laws against Hereticks, especially the *Nestorians*, repair'd such Churches as wanted it, and gave Order for the Building several new ones. He suffer'd no Person whatsoever to be entertain'd in his Army that was not a Christian; and when the Fleet was ready to set Sail the Patriarch of *Constantinople* gave it his Benediction, according to the Custom of those Times. *Belisarius*, who was attended by his Wife in the Expedition, took care to have an exact Discipline observ'd on Board, and put two *Massagetes* to Death for murdering a Man that laugh'd at 'em when they were Drunk. Having weigh'd Anchor he arriv'd upon the *Sicilian* Coasts, about the latter end of *August*, but had suffer'd much in his Passage through the Avarice of *John* the *Cappadocian*, who supply'd the Army with such unwholsom Provisions, that a great number of the Soldiers dy'd at *Methone*, whilst they lay there Wind-bound. He staid upon these Coasts 'till he could get such Intelligence as was necessary for his future Conduct, then proceeding on his Voyage he landed at a Place call'd *Caputuada*, about Five Days Journey from *Carthage*. It was a barren sandy Soil, without any Water, of which the Army stood very much in need, for what they had a-board stunk, and was corrupted; but, as they were digging their Entrenchments, the Labourers discover'd a Spring, which prov'd a seasonable Relief, and supply'd both Men and Beasts with wholsom fresh Water, a thing never heard of before in that dry Tract of *Byzacium*, which made *Belisarius* consider it as a Pledge of his future Success. From *Caputuada*

Belisarius lands with the Army in Africk.

he

he design'd to march directly for *Carthage*, from whence he understood *Gelimer* was remov'd, after he had put *Hilderick*, and several others that were in Prison with him, to Death. The General's chief Care was to establish such good Order among his Troops, that the Country might not suffer in their March, but that they might pay for what ever they had, as justly as if they were in their own Country, behaving themselves with an equal regard to the *Africans*, as if they had been *Romans*; this made the Imperial Army be supply'd by the Country in great abundance, and drew several of the Natives into their Party. The Governor of *Tripolis* had from the very first declar'd for the Emperor, and the Orthodox Christians, who for a long time had been oppress'd by the *Arian Vandals*, fled to the *Romans* as to their Deliverers. The Army, under the Command of *Belisarius*, arriv'd at *Carthage* on the 25th of *September*, being the *Vigil* to the Feast of St. *Cyprian*, who heretofore had been Bishop of that Place. This animated the *Africans* who had join'd themselves with the Imperialists so much, that they immediately attack'd the *Vandals* that had secur'd themselves in the Church dedicated to that Martyr, and forc'd them out, after which they celebrated the Feast with a Joy and Magnificence suitable to their Success. *Procopius* saith, That *Belisarius* in his March was attack'd first by *Amatas*, the Brother of *Gelimer*, whom he defeated and slew, and after that by *Gelimer* himself, who fell so couragiously upon his Rear, that the *Romans* were put into great Confusion; and had not *Gelimer*, upon the News he heard of his Brother's Death, desisted, and drawn back his Forces, in all probability he had that Day obtain'd an entire Victory; but the Sense of his Brother's Misfortune, which

Gelimer *defeated.*

depress'd

depress'd and dispirited him, inspir'd fresh Courage into the *Romans,* who set boldly upon the Enemy, slew a great number upon the Place, and forc'd *Gelimer* to fly for his Safety into the Plains of *Bule,* whilst *Belisarius* proceeded in his March to *Carthage,* where he was receiv'd without any Opposition; for he took Care to have his Orders so exactly observ'd, that the Citizens follow'd their several Imployments with as much Security as in the Times of Peace. The same Day the Fleet arriv'd in the Bay, about Five Miles from the City, and the Men were commanded on Shore by the General, who was lodg'd in *Gelimer*'s Palace, seated upon his Throne, serv'd by his Servants, and din'd with his Officers upon those Provisions that had been prepar'd for *Gelimer*; who, upon the first Motions of the *Romans* against him, had sent his Brother *Tzazon,* or *Zanzon,* into *Sardinia,* to secure that Island from the Practices of *Godas,* one of his own Servants, who declar'd for the Emperor.

Belisarius enters Carthage.

Zanzon obey'd his Orders with so much Courage and Success, that he restor'd the Island to his Brother's Obedience, having first overthrown *Godas,* who was Slain in the Engagement. *Gelimer,* under the present Necessity of his Affairs, stood much in need of his Brother's Amity and Assistance, who therefore came and join'd him, whilst he lay encamp'd upon the Plains of *Bule,* but their Meeting was such as suited with the distracted Condition of their Family. However, after some reasonable time for their Refreshment, and that the first Transports of their Grief were over, *Gelimer* advanc'd with the whole Army towards *Carthage,* where, when he was arriv'd, he cut off the Aquæduct, a piece of admirable Workmanship, and extraordinary use to the City. After he had rested
some

some time near it, and when he found none of the Enemy thought fit to sally out upon him, he retir'd, and dispos'd his Army in the Towns adjacent, intending to block up the City. His Men expected the *Carthaginians*, who they imagin'd had no great Friendship for the *Romans*, would deliver it up into their Hands, and that such of the *Romans* as were *Arians*, would, upon the Account of Religion, declare for them. Besides, they had by large Promises invited the Chief Officers of the *Hunns* or *Massagetes* to their Party; they knew they were very averse to the *Romans*, and that they had enter'd unwillingly, and by Compulsion into the Service; so that they readily agreed to the Proposals the *Vandals* made 'em, and promis'd, when they came to Fight, that they would turn against the *Romans*. But a Matter of that Consequence could not be transacted so secretly, but *Belisarius* must have some Information of it; he first Crucify'd *Laurus*, a *Carthaginian*, after he had been regularly convicted of Treason, and wrought so effectually with the *Massagetes* by his artful Address and obliging Carriage, that they reveal'd and confess'd the whole Matter to him; and at the same time they assur'd him that two Particulars very much cool'd their Zeal for the Emperor's Service: The first, a Jealousie they had, that after the Reduction of *Africk* they should not be permitted to return home, but be worn out there: The other, that tho' they were dismiss'd into their own Country, their Booty would be taken from 'em. He on the one side gave 'em all Security imaginable to the contrary, and on the other oblig'd them by Oath to assist him with all Diligence and Alacrity. After this *Belisarius* exhorted his Army, in a very Pathetick Speech, not to suffer themselves to lose a Conquest of which they were already, in a great

measure,

measure, assur'd; and then commanded *John*, the *Armenian*, his Lieutenant, to advance against the Enemy with a great Part of the Horse, whilst he prepar'd to follow the next Day with the rest of the Army; tho' the *Massagetes* had promis'd him all Assistance and Obedience for the future, yet they resolv'd so to behave themselves with both Parties, as to expect the Event, and join with the Conquerors. The *Roman* Army came up with the *Vandals* at *Tricomar*, Seventeen Miles from *Carthage*, and encamp'd at some distance from them. At Midnight some of 'em were much surpriz'd at the sight of a great Prodigy, for they beheld Fire upon the Heads of their Spears, the Points appearing on a sudden red, and glowing hot. The same thing they observ'd afterwards in *Italy*, but, being better instructed from Experience, they beheld it not with that Surprize and Amazement they did here, but consider'd it as an infallible Sign of Victory.

The next Morning *Gelimer* plac'd the Women and Children, with all their Wealth, in the midst of his Camp, and then, having endeavour'd to animate his Men by such Arguments as were drawn from the present Condition they were in, he advanc'd about Noon towards the *Romans*, and after both Armies had for some time fac'd each other, the Fight began on both sides. *Zanzon* was one of the first that fell, after he had behav'd himself like an Officer of Courage and Experience: In him the *The Van-* *Vandals* may be said to have lost all their Hopes *dals routed.* and Resolution, for immediately upon his Death they gave Ground, and the *Hunns*, according to their former Resolution, join'd with the *Romans* in the Chace, which lasted not long, for the *Vandals* soon recover'd their Camp, and secur'd themselves in their Entrenchments; whereupon the *Romans*

mans retir'd back in an orderly manner to their own, having loft but Fifty Men on their fide, whereas the *Vandals* loft upwards of Eight Hundred. *Belifarius* being join'd in the Evening by a ftrong Body of his Infantry, thought fit to compleat his Victory, and fo march'd, with his whole Army, to the Camp of the *Vandals*. Upon his Approach *Gelimer*, attended by a few of his neareft Friends and moft faithful Servants, withdrew privately out of the Camp, and fled, with great Precipitation, into *Numidia*; of which, as foon as the *Vandals* were inform'd, and when they difcover'd the *Roman* Batallions in Motion towards 'em, every Man provided for his own Safety, without any Regard had for the Defence of their Wives and Children, whom they left behind to the Mercy of the infulting Conquerors, by whom they were all taken Captive. The Purfuit lafted all Night, during which the *Romans* flew great Numbers of their Enemies, and found fo great a Mafs of Treafure in their Camp, as never had been feen in any other; for the *Vandals* having no Place of Security in which they might lodge their Wealth, remov'd it up and down with them, and were now, in a Moment, depriv'd of all they had been fcraping up for Ninety Five Years together.

Gelimer flies.

The Spoil was fo great, and the *Romans* became Mafters of it fo unexpectedly, that they were intoxicated with their good Fortune, and obferv'd fo little Order and Caution, that had the *Vandals* rally'd back upon 'em, they had, with eafe, taken that Victory out of their Hands, which they took fuch little Care to fecure. But *Belifarius* having, with much Difficulty, reduc'd them into fome Order, fent *John*, with a confiderable Body of Horfe, to purfue *Gelimer*. *John*, after a March of Five Days, came up to *Gelimer*, and, in all probability, had

had taken him, had not one of his own Officers shot him accidentally in the Neck, of which he instantly dy'd, and by that means gave *Gelimer* an Opportunity of escaping to the Rocks in the Mountains near *Hippo Regia,* a Maritime City in *Numidia,* whither *Belisarius,* having left a sufficient Garrison in *Carthage,* came in Pursuit of him; and finding he had secur'd himself in *Madenos,* one of the strongest Cities upon the Mountains, he left *Pharas,* a valiant and prudent Commander, with sufficient Forces to Besiege it, whilst he return'd back with the rest of the Forces to *Carthage,* there to settle the Affairs of the Province, which, after it had been so long under the Usurpation of the *Vandals,* was, in less than Four Months time, recover'd back to the Empire. The General, in his Return, had all *Gelimer*'s Treasure deliver'd up to him; for having order'd it to be transported into *Spain,* whither the King himself intended to follow, it was forc'd back, by contrary Winds, into the Haven of *Hippo,* and there seiz'd for the use of the Emperor. *Belisarius* being come to *Carthage,* took in such Places as remain'd in the Possession of the *Vandals;* had the Island of *Majorca* and *Minorca* deliver'd up to him; secur'd *Tripolis* against the Attempts of the *Moors;* reduc'd *Sardinia* and *Corsica,* and omitted nothing that could contribute to the Security of the Province, and make the Conquest compleat.

Gelimer besieg'd by Pharas.

A. D. 534.

In the mean time *Gelimer* was so closely press'd by *Pharas* in the Mountains, that he was reduc'd to the last Extremities; from a soft luxurious Life, to which he, as well as the rest of the *Vandals,* had, from the time they became Masters of *Africk,* continually accustom'd themselves, he was now forc'd to the greatest Hardships, and labour'd under Necessities, with which he never 'till then had been

been acquainted. *Pharas* had once or twice attempted by Force to take the City, but being repuls'd with Loss he resolv'd to block it up. He knew what Distress *Gelimer* was in, and therefore in a Letter advis'd him *to consider with himself whether it were not better for him to submit, and upon his Submission enjoy the Dignity of a Patrician, with large Revenues by the Emperor's Favour, than undergo such Hardships, and live in the Misery with which he knew he was then afflicted.* *Gelimer* wept at sight of the Letter, and in his Answer complain'd bitterly of the Emperor, *for labouring as he did to ruin a Prince, from whom he never receiv'd any Injury*; and in Conclusion desir'd *Pharas* to send him an Harp, a Loaf of Bread, and a Sponge. *Pharas* knew not what Interpretation to put upon so odd a Request, 'till the Messenger inform'd him that *the King long'd to see a Bak'd Loaf, because it was a thing he had not so much as beheld since he came into the Mountains, that he wanted a Sponge to dry up his Tears, and a Harp to comfort him up in his present Calamity.*

Pharas, touch'd with a sense of his Misery, and the Vicissitude of Human Affairs, sent him what he desir'd, but block'd him up closer than ever, which at length forc'd *Gelimer* to yield, upon such Conditions as *Belisarius* undertook to make for him with the Emperor; accordingly he was conducted by *Pharas* to *Carthage*, where the General receiv'd him very favourably, and *Gelimer*, when he was presented to him, is said to have burst out into a Laughter, which made those who were unacquainted with him think him distracted through the Excess of his Misery; but his Friends, who better knew the Temper of his Mind, imputed it to the View he had, from his present Condition, of the Inconstancy of Fortune, which in so short a time had,

Gelimer surrenders himself.

had, from a great and powerful Prince, render'd him a despicable indigent Slave: And indeed it was something amazing, that a Handful of Strangers, as they were no more in comparison, should, in the Space of Six Months, subvert a large and flourishing Kingdom, where at their first Arrival they had not room to drop an Anchor. But we are to consider, that the Course the *Vandals* took for their Security, upon their first Settlement in *Africk*, turn'd now very much to their Prejudice; for *Genserich*, the better to restrain the *Africans*, who might otherwise be ready to start out into Rebellion, if they had any strong Holds to which they could retire, demolish'd all the Forts and wall'd Towns in the Country, *Carthage* only excepted: Which, tho' it might be of Service against the Inhabitants, was very pernicious Counsel in case of an Invasion; for by this means *Belisarius* render'd himself Master of the whole Province, with little or no Resistance.

Belisarius his happy Success abroad, in finishing a War of so great Importance in so short a Time, expos'd him to the Envy of some People at home, who are too often ready to injure, and, if possible, ruin those they judge to be more deserving than themselves. These Persons represented *Belisarius* to the Emperor, as one whose Ambition made him inclinable to usurp; that he was a dangerous Man before, but that his late Victories would make him insupportable, unless Care was taken to prevent his Designs. The Emperor, either because he despis'd these malicious Suggestions, or for that he chose rather to conceal his Suspicions, gave *Belisarius* leave either to come to Court, or continue in *Africk*, when he sent him an Account of his Success, and desir'd Liberty to come with his Prisoners to *Constantinople*. But having discover'd the

Practices

Practices they were then forming against him, he was more earnest to appear at Court, where he might clear himself of the Imputation, and punish his Accusers. Being arriv'd at *Constantinople*, he was thought worthy of those ancient Honours which the *Romans* of old conferr'd upon their favourite Heroes after some extraordinary Atchievements, and which had now been discontinu'd for Six Hundred Years, except when their Emperors, *Titus*, *Trajan*, and some few more, had in Person led their Armies forth, and subdu'd some Barbarous Nations. Among the Spoil, which consisted of infinite Treasure and Royal Furniture, were some Monuments of the *Jews*, which having been brought to *Rome* from *Jerusalem* by *Titus*, were carry'd afterwards into *Africk* by *Genserich*, and were now, by *Justinian*'s Order, restor'd to *Jerusalem*. Among the *Vandals* that were reserv'd to be led in Triumph, for the Talness and Beauty of their Persons, appear'd *Gelimer*, more conspicuous for his Stature than the rest, and cloth'd in a Purple Robe, as an Instance of the Inconstancy of Human Affairs; who being brought into the *Hippodrome*, and beholding the Emperor seated on the Imperial Throne, surrounded on all sides by great Numbers of Spectators, and himself the publick Scorn of the People, he express'd himself in no other Lamentations but that Sentence of the Preacher, which he often repeated, *Vanity of Vanities all is Vanity*. The lively sense of his Calamities touch'd the Emperor so nearly, that instead of putting him to Death, as he deserv'd, he granted him and his Relations several Possessions in *Galatia*, at the Intercession of *Belisarius*; and had he not continu'd obstinate in the *Arian* Heresie, he had created him a Patrician.

Belisarius Triumphs at Constantinople.

The Emperor at the same time made a liberal Provision for the Subsistence of *Hilderich*'s Children, as the Descendants from *Valentinian*; and *Belisarius* had such Honours decreed him as had been formerly us'd in ancient Triumphs, for being created Consul the Year following he was born on the Shoulders of Captives, and drawn in a Chariot, from which he distributed among the People Part of the Spoils taken in the *African* War; the Inhabitants being pleas'd, not so much for what they by that means brought of the Royal Treasure, but for that they beheld the Ceremonies of their Ancestors reviv'd, which gave 'em a pleasant Idea of their former Greatness, and a Prospect of their present Felicity.

New Troubles in Africk.

Belisarius, upon his Departure for *Constantinople*, had left *Salomon*, an Eunuch, and his Lieutenant, to command in *Africk*; who, whilst the Triumph was celebrating with great Solemnity in the City, was busily employ'd in quelling some new Commotions rais'd in his Absence. The *Moors*, upon the first News of the Emperor's intended Expedition into *Africk*, consulted their Old Women, whose Answers were esteem'd as so many Oracles, what Share they were to have in the Success of the War. These Prophetesses foretold an Army from the Waters, and the Destruction both of *Vandals* and *Moors*, when the *Romans* should be led against them under the Command of a Beardless General. Hereupon they renounc'd all Friendship with the *Vandals*, and enter'd into League with *Belisarius*; but so soon as the *Vandals* were subdu'd they sent their Spies into the *Roman* Army, to know if they had any General among 'em without a Beard, but finding they were all plentifully supply'd in those Parts, they thought the Prophecy no way concern'd them, but related to their Posterity,

so

so that they had a great Desire to break the League, but were afraid to venture whilst *Belisarius* continu'd in the Army; but when they heard he was embark'd for *Constantinople*, and that the Soldiers lay dispers'd in Garrisons upon the Borders, they fell upon the defenceless *Africans*, whom they kill'd, and then pillag'd their Houses and their Fields, after which they surpriz'd the Garrison in *Byzacium*, and destroy'd the adjacent Country.

Salomon, who then lay in *Carthage*, try'd first by Letters to convince them of their Folly, but finding them obstinate, and that they continu'd to harass the Country, he march'd against 'em; and tho' at the first Onset the *Roman* Cavalry were disorder'd by the Enemies Camels, yet *Salomon* falling with Five Hundred Horse upon them kill'd Two Hundred of those Camels, which so disorder'd the *Moors* that they fled in great Amazement up to the Mountains, and were pursu'd by the *Romans*, who kill'd Ten Thousand of 'em, and took the Women Prisoners, after which he return'd to *Carthage*; where he was scarce arriv'd before the Barbarians made an universal Invasion, and overrun the Country of *Byzacium*, where they committed unspeakable Mischiefs, after which they encamp'd upon the Mountain *Burgaon*; from whence they were forc'd with much Difficulty by *Salomon*, who, according to the Report of their own Countrymen who surviv'd the Defeat, destroy'd Fifty Thousand of 'em, the rest recollecting with great Sorrow the Truth of the Oracle, that foretold their Nation was to be destroy'd by a Beardless Man. *Salomon*, after this, met with little Disturbance from the *Moors*, who were very much weaken'd by their late Misfortunes. And now, according to the Course of Time, we are to attend the Emperor's Arms into *Italy*, but forasmuch as

A. D. 536.

The Moors *defeated by* Salomon.

G there

there were after this several remarkable Transactions in *Africk*, by which the whole Country was in a great measure endanger'd, and which, for that Reason, deserve a place in this History, we'll suspend the Narration of the *Gothick* Wars in *Italy*, 'till, with *Procopius*, we have finish'd that of the *Vandals* here in *Africk*.

The Lands of the conquer'd *Vandals* were, by a publick Edict, confiscated to the Emperor's Use, but the Soldiers were permitted to marry the Wives and Daughters of those they had overthrown; and claim'd a Right to those Lands in behalf of their Wives, and upon a Repulse became discontented and mutinous. The Emperor at the same time had publish'd some severe Edicts against the *Arians*, of which there were no less than a Thousand in the Army, whereby he interdicted 'em the free Use of the Sacraments or Churches, and would not suffer 'em to baptize their Children at the Feast of *Easter*, nor exercise any other publick Acts of Devotion. Add to all this, that he had rais'd Five Troops of Horse out of the *Vandals* that *Belisarius* brought with him to *Constantinople*, which he intended to settle in Garrisons in the East, there to spend the rest of their Days in the Wars against the *Persians*. Four Hundred of these Soldiers being shipp'd off for that purpose watch'd their Opportunity, forc'd the Seamen to put first into *Peloponnesus*, and from thence they set Sail for *Africk*, where when they were landed they march'd directly to the Mountain *Aurasium*, and the most inaccessible Parts of *Mauritania*. The News of this so encourag'd the Mutineers, that they resolv'd instantly to put their Designs in Practice, and agreed first of all to murder *Salomon* in the Church on *A Mutiny Easter-Day*, where they met accordingly at the *in Africk.* Time appointed; but whether seiz'd with a sudden

Hor-

Horror at the Villainy of the Fact, or aw'd by the Presence of the Governor, or rather prevented by an over-ruling Providence, they separated without perpetrating their Design; and tho' they met a second time with the same Intent, yet they mov'd no farther in it than they did at the first. However, having proceeded thus far, they conceiv'd it impossible for the Thing not to be discover'd, so most of 'em drew out of *Carthage*, and falling upon the *Africans* pillag'd their Towns.

Salomon endeavour'd to persuade those who were left behind to continue stedfast in their Obedience to the Emperor; but they were so far from giving ear to his Advice, that they chose another Governor in his stead, and rifled the Town, in spight of all he could do to reduce 'em. By the Assistance therefore of *Theodorus*, whom the Ring-leaders of the Mutiny had chosen to succeed him, he got a Ship provided for him in the Harbour, in which he embark'd with *Procopius* the Historian and some others, and sail'd to *Belisarius*, who lay then at *Syracuse*, whom he acquainted with the Condition of Affairs in *Africk*, and desir'd his Assistance against the Mutineers; who, in the mean time, having plunder'd *Carthage*, muster'd themselves, to the number of Nine Thousand, in the Plains of *Bule*, and chose *Stotzas*, one of the Guards, for their General. *Stotzas* was a bold industrious Soldier, and led 'em on with great Resolution to the Walls of *Carthage*, where he summon'd those within to yield immediately to him, but they, disliking their Proceedings, return'd Answer by a Messenger of their own, that they held the Place for the Emperor. *Stotzas* put the unfortunate Messenger to Death, and prepar'd vigorously for a Siege, which they press'd on with so much Expedition, that the Town was just upon the point of surrendring when *Beli-*

sarius

farius arriv'd with *Salomon*, and no more than an Hundred of his Life-gurrd; upon notice of whose Arrival the Besiegers, who judg'd themselves sure of the Town before, rais'd the Siege early in the Morning, and broke up in great Disorder. *Belisarius* reduc'd Two Thousand of 'em by fair Persuasions, the rest he overtook at *Membrissæ*, a Town distant from *Carthage* Three and Forty Miles, where the Rebels waited for him with great Resolution, for they depended upon their Numbers, tho' he despis'd 'em as an headstrong undisciplin'd Rabble.

<small>Belisarius engages with the Mutineers,</small>
When they came to engage a strong Wind blew full in the Faces of the Mutineers, which made 'em wheel about; for they thought the Imperialists would do so too, and thereby give them the Advantage: But in Wheeling they were forc'd to break their Ranks and fall into some Disorder, which *Belisarius* observing, he charg'd 'em sooner than they expected, <small>and defeats 'em.</small> and put 'em into so great a Disorder that they were forc'd to fly with Precipitation into *Numidia*. *Belisarius*, whose Army was but small, thought not fit to pursue 'em very far, but gave their Camp up to the Discretion of his Soldiers, who found a great deal of Treasure in it, together with the *Vandal* Women, who had been the Occasion of the War. After which, having taken the best care he could to restore things to a peaceable Condition in *Africk*, he return'd into *Sicily*; whither he was likewise call'd by a Mutiny of the Army in that Island.

After his Departure *Stotzas* so prevail'd upon the Troops under the Command of *Marcellus*, Governor of *Numidia*, that they all deserted to him, upon which their Officers fled into the next Church for Refuge; thither he went to Besiege 'em, and tho' he had giv'n 'em a Promise to save their Lives, if they would surrender themselves up to him, yet he no sooner had 'em in his Power, but he perfidiously murder'd 'em. These Proceedings in *Africk* oblig'd the Emperor to send his Cousin *Germanus*, the Patrician, with others of the Chief Officers in his Court into *Africk*. *Germanus*, as soon as he arriv'd at *Carthage*, muster'd the Army, and found that two Thirds had revolted, and the rest were employ'd in the necessary Defence of that Place, and the Towns adjoining. Seeing therefore it was impossible for him to deal with open Strength against the Rebels, he so far prevail'd upon 'em with fair Words and great Promises, especially an Assurance of full Pay from the time they had been in Rebellion, that he recover'd great Numbers of 'em to their Duty; by which means he got such an Army together as equall'd that of the Rebels, and so he was resolv'd to Fight 'em.

Stotzas finding his Men desert a-pace, thought it his Interest to bring it to a Battel as soon as he could, and therefore encamp'd with the rest of his Forces within Four Miles of *Carthage*, hoping, by his Neighbourhood to that Place, to allure some of his Fugitive Companions back again; but their Minds were so well settl'd by the prudent Management of *Germanus*, that there was not a Soldier among 'em, but what was ready to swear Obedience to the General; which, when the Mutineers observ'd, they drew off with great Fear towards *Numidia*; but being overtaken by the Imperialists they were forc'd to an Engagement, in which at first they had the Advantage, 'till *Germanus*, who run a great hazard in his own Person, encourag'd his Troops by his Example, *The Mutineers again defeated.* and so routed the Enemy. Many were Slain on both sides in the Pursuit, for using the same Language

guage and Arms, and being clothed after the same manner, the Pursuers destroy'd their own Friends, 'till *Germanus* order'd his Men to demand the Word. The Enemy's Camp was taken with much Difficulty, and plunder'd by the Soldiers. The Mutineers, after this Defeat, were so thoroughly broken, that they never were able to gather to an Head again, tho' some farther Attempts were made that way, but happily prevented by the seasonable Circumspection of *Germanus*; who, some time after, was recall'd home, and *Salomon* restor'd to his former Employment by the Emperor, who gave him another Army.

Salomon, immediately upon his Arrival, endeavour'd to confirm that Peace to which the Province was, in a great measure, restor'd; he took Care to reform the Army, in which he establish'd an exact Discipline; he privately remov'd all such as he knew to be of a seditious Temper, sending 'em, upon some plausible Pretence or other, either to *Constantinople*, or to *Belisarius*, who then commanded the Emperor's Forces in *Italy*, filling their Places up with others of a more tractable Disposition, and banishing those *Vandals* that were left in the Country, as well the Women as the Men; after this he turn'd his Care to the *Moors*, who had committed some Disorders in the Province, and were become very considerable in their Numbers, being join'd by *Antalas*, a great Man with the *Moors*, who had continu'd very faithful to the *Romans*, 'till *Salomon* had provok'd him to revolt, by withdrawing from him the Emperor's Allowance, and putting his Brother to Death for raising some Commotions among the *Byzaceni*. In this Contest *Salomon* unfortunately lost his Life, to the great Prejudice, and almost utter Ruin of the Emperor's Interest in *Africk*.

Salo-

Salomon was succeeded in his Command by *Sergius*, one of his Nephews, whose Incapacity render'd his Uncle's Loss the more deplorable; for being young, fiery and insolent, all the General Officers in the Province were much discontented at his Advancement, whilst the Soldiers consider'd him as a Coward, and slighted him accordingly. The *Africans* hated him for his abominable Avarice and Lust, and for that reason declin'd to serve against the *Moors*, whose Forces were augmented daily. *Antalas* invited *Stotzas* out of *Mauritania*, tho' at the same time he sent to the Emperor, and offer'd to be obedient, as became him, provided a worthy Governor was sent to Command in *Africk*. The Emperor at first, out of Respect to the great Merits of his Uncle *Salomon*, was very unwilling to remove him; but finding what great Cruelties the *Moors*, under the Conduct of *Antalas* and *Stotzas*, to whom several *Roman* Soldiers join'd themselves, committed daily in the Province; how none oppos'd 'em, but that they grew more and more formidable; without divesting him of his Command, he at first join'd *Areobindus* in Commission with him, 'till he was convinc'd how destructive two Generals of equal Power in the same Province were to his Affairs, and then he sent *Sergius* into *Italy*, committing the entire Government of *Africk* to *Areobindus*, who was a Senator, and a very honest Man, but never bred up a Soldier, which encourag'd *Gontharis*, who had the Command of the Forces in *Numidia*, to revolt, and attempt the Sovereignty. To this purpose he persuaded the *Moors* to march against *Carthage*, and held private Correspondence with *Antalas* and *John*, whom the Mutineers had chosen for their General in the room of *Stotzas*, to whom he discover'd what secret Measures the Governor took in order to suppress 'em.

Tho'

Tho' *Areobindus* was inform'd of *Gontharis* his Treason, and Designs upon him, yet he refus'd to proceed openly against him, 'till he had sent for him, and heard what he had to say in his own Behalf, tho' he was advis'd to begin first, and so put a stop to any farther Mischief. *Gontharis*, instead of vindicating himself, or denying his Designs, publickly own'd his Usurpation, and then *Areobindus* was prevail'd upon to go out and Fight him, follow'd by *Artabanes*, the *Armenian*, who, being of the Race of the *Arsacidæ*, had, together with his Brother who was kill'd in a late Engagement with the *Moors*, enter'd into the Emperor's Service, and Commanded some of his Countrymen that came over with *Areobindus*. Tho' the Usurper had endeavour'd to possess the Soldiers with a Belief of *Areobindus* his Cowardice, and persuade 'em he intended to Defraud 'em of their Pay, yet the greatest Part continuing firm in their Duty, issu'd out of their several Quarters; and had, in all likelihood, destroy'd the Tyrant and his Adherents, had not *Areobindus*, who was not us'd to see Men cut and destroy each other, fled like a Madman, and taken Sanctuary in a Monastery, within the Walls of *Carthage*; after which *Artabanes* retir'd with the rest, and left *Gontharis* Master of the City, the Palace and the Haven. *Areobindus* was, by means of *Reparatus*, Bishop of *Carthage*, persuaded to come to *Gontharis*, before whom he behav'd himself with a Submission more becoming a Slave than a *Roman* Senator and General: *Gontharis* gave him a great many Fair Words, but had him murder'd the same Night, and sent his Head to *Antalas*, who was asham'd and affronted at the Treason and Perjury of the Tyrant; and therefore resolv'd to submit to the Emperor, with whom he was not mortally offended, rather than

Gontharis Usurps in Africk.

than truſt to an Uſurper, who would neither keep his Faith with him, nor any one elſe; accordingly he drew off from the Mutineers, who, together with *John* their Commander, revolted to *Gontharis*. *Artabanes* likewiſe, upon aſſurance of Safety, came to Court with his *Armenians*, profeſſing an implicit Obedience to the Uſurper, tho', being of a great and generous Spirit, he reſolv'd from the very firſt, if poſſible, to ruin him, but conceal'd his Deſigns by readily eſpouſing his Service. The better to attain his Ends, he advis'd the Tyrant to march in Perſon againſt *Antalas*, who grew dangerous, and made him very unſecure in his Uſurpation. *Gontharis* prepar'd accordingly for the Expedition, leaving a ſtrong Garriſon in *Carthage*, under the Command of *Paſiphilus* his Chief Miniſter, who had been a Ringleader in the Mutiny of *Byzacium*, and a great Promoter of *Gontharis* his Uſurpation. Him he order'd to deſtroy all the *Greeks* in his Abſence, and, the Night before his Departure, invited his Friends to Supper, which *Artabanes* judg'd a fit Opportunity to execute his Deſign: Having communicated it before to *Gregorius*, his Nephew, and *Artaſiris*, one of his Guard. *Gregorius* was to bring ſome of the ſtouteſt *Armenians* to the Palace arm'd with their Swords, and, upon a pretended Suſpicion that their Captain was invited out of no true Affection to his Perſon, they were to deſire to ſtand among the Guards of *Gontharis*. *Artaſiris* was to watch the moſt convenient time, and then kill the Tyrant; but he deſir'd *Artabanes* to do as much by him if he ſaw he had not mortally wounded him, leſt he ſhould be forc'd, by Torture, to diſcover him, and, together with himſelf, ruin his Captain. All things being thus concerted and agreed upon, *Gregorius* and *Artaſiris* ſtood behind *Gontharis* at Supper,

whilſt

whilst the rest of the *Armenians* continu'd, according to their Instructions, with the Tyrant's Guards without, and were not to stir 'till they heard the Cry within, and then they were to do as they had been directed. In the midst of the Feast, and when the Tyrant grew heated with Wine, *Artasiris*, upon some Pretence, went out, for he found he could not draw his Scimiter without being observ'd in the Room; but returning presently after with it drawn, and hid under his Robe, he stepp'd up to *Gontharis*, as to whisper something to him in private; at that Instant one of the Waiters discover'd the Scimiter, and thrusting in between him cry'd out, upon which, as the Tyrant was turning about, *Artasiris* cut off part of his Skull, and *Artabanes*, who sate by him, stabb'd him into the Side, whereupon he fell down dead; after which the *Armenians*, who heard the Noise, rush'd in, and kill'd the *Vandals*, and such other of the Usurper's Friends as were seated upon other Couches in the same Room at Supper. Thus did the Courage and Loyalty of a few Strangers recover *Africk* to the Emperor's Obedience, and punish an Usurper with a Death he too well deserv'd, on the Thirty Fifth Day of his Usurpation; and *Africk*, after a long and bloody War, to which the Emperor was forc'd by the Inhumanity of *Gelimer*, enjoy'd at length some Repose, tho' much broken and impoverish'd. After this the Emperor had more leisure to attend the War that was carry'd on with great heat in *Italy*, occasion'd likewise by the Parricide of a Barbarian; and as both in the one, and the other, *Justinian*'s Cause was just, so was it Crown'd with the Success it deserv'd.

Gontharis kill'd.

The beginning of the Wars in Italy.

II. Tho' *Theodorich* at his Death had declar'd *Athalarick*, his Grandson, King of *Italy*, and he was

was acknowledg'd as such by the Nobility and People; yet the young Prince's Mother, *Amalasont*, had the sole Management of Affairs during her Son's Minority, and discharg'd her Trust with so much Honour and Integrity, that she was belov'd and esteem'd by all, but such as preferr'd their private Interest and Ambition to the publick Prosperity. She took Care to have her Son educated after the manner of the *Roman* Princes, committing him to the Care of such Governors as were renown'd for their Prudence and Learning. This the *Goths* dislik'd, and declar'd it was an Education unfit for their Prince, who was to be Active and Warlike, not Soft and Effeminate; and when his Mother once struck him upon some just Provocation, he went out weeping into another Room, where some of the Principal among the *Goths* were met together, who took occasion from thence to complain more loudly of the Queen, as if she design'd to remove her Son, and Reign, in her own Right, both over the *Goths* and *Italians*. They exclaim'd against Learning, as an Enemy to a valiant Spirit, corrupting the Mind with Baseness and Cowardice; they reminded her of her Father, who tho' he was utterly ignorant of Letters, yet he was a warlike, victorious Prince, and concluded that her Son must be bred up in the same Studies, if he would be attended with the same Fortune; and therefore they desir'd her to dismiss his Pedants, and associate him with Companions of his own Age, who by their Conversation might make the Customs of their own Nation familiar to him, and incline him to govern according to their own Laws. This they demanded with so much Warmth and Importunity, that she was forc'd, out of Fear, to comply with 'em; so that from that time forward her Son was attended by such as taught him the
ill

ill Use of Wine, and unlawful Love of Women, to which, by degrees, he became so much addicted, that the very Footsteps of Virtue were defac'd in him; and, to render a Reformation impossible, they taught him to be stubborn and undutiful, so that he unnaturally deserted his Mother in a Faction that had the Arrogance to command her to retire from Court; however she behav'd her self with a masculin, undaunted Spirit, and confin'd two or three of the most forward severally to the remotest Parts of *Italy*, under a Pretence of securing the Borders against the Enemy. These Persons, being thus remov'd from Court, through their Correspondence with their Friends and Relations, maintain'd and exasperated the same malevolent Spirit against her, so that not being able to contend with the general Dislike of the People, that were cheated and miss-led into the Faction, she desir'd leave of *Justinian* to retire to *Constantinople* when ever she found it dangerous to continue longer in *Italy*. To this the Emperor, who was glad of the Opportunity, return'd her a very favourable Answer, and dealt so effectually by his Embassadors with her, that they found her inclinable to deliver *Italy* into his Hands; for her Son was by this time fall'n into a Consumption, occasion'd by his intemperate living, and she found her self vigorously oppos'd in all her Affairs by her Nephew *Theodatus*, who, being Lord of many Towns in *Tuscany*, grievously oppress'd the Inhabitants, of which she being inform'd, endeavour'd to restrain him by her Authority, and thereby made him her implacable Enemy. Being thus divided between themselves, both of 'em endeavour'd to support their particular Interest by the Emperor's Friendship: *Theodatus* profer'd to betray *Tuscany* into his Hands, upon Payment of a good Sum of Mony, and Dignity of a

Senator,

Senator, at the same time that *Amalasont* propos'd to deliver all *Italy* up to him. These Divisions the Emperor endeavour'd to husband to the best Advantage, when the Death of *Athalarick*, which happen'd during these Negotiations, after he had reign'd Eight Years, threw *Amalasont* into new Difficulties. She was not yet prepar'd to make good her Promise to the Emperor, and she found that her Interest, which was declining in her Son's Life time, grew every Day weaker with the *Goths*, the Principal among whom she had, during her Administration, very much offended. She perceiv'd 'em earnestly desirous of a King, and thought if she had Power enough left to raise one to the Throne, she hop'd the Person so advanc'd by her Favour would be contented with the Title, and in Gratitude re-establish her in the Authority. With these Considerations she cast her Eyes upon *Theodatus*, and forgetting how much she had incens'd him against her, or thinking at least so signal a Service would appease and reconcile him to her, she offer'd him the Title, on condition he would continue her in the Power. He still resenting her former Usage swore solemnly to whatever she demanded, but with an intent never to perform it; for being in Possession of the Kingdom, he quickly made it appear he was irreconcileable; and, in spite of his Oath, confin'd her to an Island on the Lake *Ulsinus* in *Tuscany*. And fearing the Displeasure of the Emperor, who he knew had always maintain'd a secret Correspondence, and was in strict Amity with her, he forc'd her to write to him, and commend her Nephew for his great Civility and Respect towards her. These Letters he sent in a Dispatch with his own, in which he complain'd of the many Injuries he had receiv'd from

A. D. 534.

Athalarick *Dies.*

Theodatus *made King.*

the

the Queen, and made the Senate at the same time write to the same purpose.

The Emperor was so far from giving Credit to what *Theodatus* endeavour'd to urge against her, that he openly espous'd her Cause, and sent her Letters by his Embassadors full of Comfort, and his Resolutions to protect her. But before his Embassadors could reach *Italy Amalasont* was murder'd, by the Relations of some whom in the late Factions she had upon just Provocations put to Death. As this Murder was highly resented by the most sober and discerning Party among the *Goths*, who deservedly admir'd her for the Excellency of her Virtues, so was *Justinian* extreamly enrag'd against *Theodatus* for so horrible a Cruelty committed upon his Aunt and Queen, whose Person ought to have been Sacred, and whose Life, in Nature and Gratitude, he ought to have defended at the Hazard of his own. *Theodatus* endeavour'd to clear himself, and charge the Murder upon the *Goths*, who were too headstrong to be restrain'd by him. How little Truth and Sincerity there was in this Excuse appear'd from his Carriage towards the Murderers, whom he was so far from punishing as the Heinousness of their Crime deserv'd, that he countenanc'd and advanc'd 'em; which made it evident to the World that the Murder was committed by his Procurement. *Procopius* saith he was incited to it by the secret Sollicitations of the Empress *Theodora*, who knew her Husband design'd to send for her to *Constantinople*, where she was afraid of being eclips'd by *Amalasont*'s great Virtues and most excellent Qualities. This execrable Act of *Theodatus* gave the Emperor a just Provocation to declare War against him; and 'tis very probable *Justinian* was glad of so favourable an Opportunity of entring

who Murders Amalasont.

tring into *Italy*, which he earnestly desir'd to reunite to the Empire.

Justinian having, with the Advice of his Council, resolv'd upon a War, made choice of *Mundus* and *Belisarius* for his Generals. *Mundus*, being General of *Illyricum*, was commanded to march into *Dalmatia*, subject at that time to the *Goths*, and attempt *Salonæ*, the better to open a Passage into *Italy*. The *Goths* readily offer'd him a Battel, which, after a hot Dispute on both Sides, they lost, and *Salonæ*, the Fruit of the Victory, fell into his Hands. *Belisarius* was order'd to make a Descent into *Sicily*, having a good Fleet ready, on Board of which were Four Thousand Legionary Soldiers and Confederates, Three Thousand *Isaurians*, Two Hundred Auxiliary *Hunns*, and Three Hundred *Moors*, besides his own Life-guard. *Belisarius* was made General with absolute Authority; and his Instructions were, to pretend a Voyage to *Carthage*, but to attempt *Sicily*; which, if it might be effected with Ease, he was to subdue and secure, otherwise to sail directly for *Africk*, without discovering his Instructions. The Island was reduc'd with more Expedition than the General himself expected, for he took all the chief Towns without any Opposition, only he met with some Resistance at *Syracuse*, which the *Goths* defended with great Resolution, depending upon the Strength of the Place; which indeed by Land was impregnable, but attacking it furiously by Sea it was surrender'd upon Articles, and he enter'd into it on the Last of *December*, concluding that Consulate with a Victory which he begun with a Triumph; for he was the sole Consul of that Year, at the Beginning of which he Triumph'd at *Constantinople* for his late Success in *Africk*.

A.D. 535.

Sicily reduced by Belisarius.

In

In the mean time *Juſtinian*, who knew the Kings of *France* were of the ſame Faith with himſelf, and allow'd the *Arians* no Toleration in their Dominions, endeavour'd to perſuade him by many Preſents to join with him in the War againſt *Theodatus*, the profeſs'd Enemy of the Catholick Faith. Of which *Theodatus* being ſenſible, as likewiſe terrify'd at the Succeſs of the Emperor's Forces both in *Sicily* and *Dalmatia*, he began to liſten to the Imperial Embaſſador, who perſuded him to a Submiſſion, and in a ſecret Conference agreed to renounce all Pretenſions to the Iſland of *Sicily*; to ſend the Emperor yearly a Crown of Gold in token of Submiſſion; and to raiſe Three Thouſand Men for his Service, when ever he ſhould require them: He oblig'd himſelf likewiſe never to put to Death or confiſcate the Goods of any Prieſt or Senator, without the Emperor's Conſent, nor advance any to the Degree of a Patrician or Senator contrary to his Approbation; in all Acclamations *Juſtinian*'s Name was to be firſt mention'd; and whenever *Theodatus* had his Statue erected, the Emperor was to have another plac'd on the Right Hand: Condeſcentions unworthy a Prince, and which ſhow'd the Poorneſs of his Spirit. And yet, left the Emperor ſhould not be ſatisfy'd with theſe Terms, but reſolve upon the War, which he extreamly abhorr'd, and apprehended with Diſtraction, he recall'd the Embaſſador, that was on his Journey homewards as far as *Albania*; who, obſerving the great Terror he was in, took the Advantage of his Cowardice, and perſuaded him to reſign the Kingdom to *Juſtinian*, and content himſelf with a Penſion ſuitable to his Quality, to be paid him out of the Emperor's own Patrimony. This Reſignation in *Theodatus* his Name was to be made to *Juſtinian*, in caſe he rejected the firſt Conditions: But by a ſolemn

A.D. 536.

Oath

Oath he bound *Peter*, the Emperor's Embassador, and *Agapetus*, Bishop of *Rome*, who was sent on Behalf of *Theodatus*, not to make mention of it 'till they found the Emperor resolv'd against any Terms more moderate. The first Capitulations were so far from pleasing *Justinian*, that the very mention of 'em enrag'd him; but upon sight of the second he was so overjoy'd that he immediately sent his Embassadors to conclude and establish the Agreement, and order'd *Belisarius*, as soon as he had settled Affairs in *Sicily*, to pass over into *Italy*, and take Possession of the Country in his Name. But before these things could be put in execution, *Theodatus*, who being naturally a Coward was consequently of an irresolute inconstant Temper, grew as haughty and presumptuous as he had before been humble and complying; which was chiefly owing to an accidental Advantage the *Goths* had obtain'd over the Emperor's Forces in *Dalmatia*: For as *Mauritius*, the Son of *Mundus*, went with a few others out of *Salona*, to view the Condition and Number of the Enemy, they were all cut off by an advanc'd Party, wherewith his Father was so enrag'd, that he engag'd the whole Body with more Courage than Discretion; however he defeated 'em; but out of a Thirst of Revenge he pursu'd 'em so far before his Troops that a *Goth*, who fled from him, turn'd back and slew him, before any of his own Men could come up to his Assistance. At the same time *Belisarius* was call'd by *Salomon* out of *Sicily* into *Africk*, to quell the Mutiny we had occasion to mention before. Upon which Considerations *Theodatus* grew so elevated, that when the Emperor's Embassadors objected to him the Breach of Faith he put a Guard upon 'em, and declared resolutely for the War. *Justinian* being justly offended at these his Proceedings sent *Constantianus* with fresh

Mundus and his Son slain in Dalmatia.

H   Forces

Forces into *Dalmatia*, who drove the *Goths* out of the Country, and put strong Garrisons into all the defensible Towns, at the same time that *Belisarius*, who was return'd out of *Africk*, made a Descent into *Italy*. *Theodatus* had rais'd a strong Army for his Defence, and made *Ebremudas*, who had marry'd his Daughter, General; who, tho' he lay under all Obligations imaginable to be faithful to his Benefactor, deserted his Command, and fled over to *Belisarius*, whilst he was embarking his Forces in *Sicily*, who sent him to *Constantinople*, where he discover'd all *Theodatus* his Intrigues to *Justinian*, by whom he was kindly receiv'd, and dignify'd with the Honour of Patrician; tho' not so much to reward him for his Treason, as to allure the *Goths* by his Clemency and Bounty.

Belisarius lands with an Army in Italy. From *Messina Belisarius* transported his Army, and landed without any Opposition at *Rhegium*. All the Towns in the *Abruzzo* and *Lucania* open'd their Gates to him, induc'd to it either through Fear, or for that being grown weary of the *Gothick* Government they were willing to receive him. Passing up the Country into *Campania* his Army encreas'd every Day by such as came to join with him, so that when he sate down before *Naples* it was much stronger than at his first Landing. *Theodatus* had taken care to put a good Garrison of *Goths* into the City, and they were resolv'd to defend it to the utmost. The Eyes of the whole World were fix'd upon this Siege, upon the Success of which the Event of the War in a great measure depended: For if the Defendants were able to make it good against the Emperor's Forces, it would turn much to the Discredit of *Belisarius*, and dishearten his Soldiers; and, on the other side, if he carry'd it, the King would unavoidably lose the small Reputation he was in with his Subjects, and the

He besieges Naples.

the *Goths* be afraid afterwards to make head against a victorious Army. Of this *Belisarius* was very sensible, and therefore endeavour'd first to win 'em by a Treaty, in which he urg'd many Arguments drawn from Self-preservation; and when he found they would give ear to no Accommodation, he made several Assaults, but was as often repuls'd with great Loss, the Walls, by reason of the Steepness of the Ground and the Advantage of the Sea, being inaccessible. He cut the great Aquæduct that supply'd the City with Water, to remedy which they dug Wells that serv'd their Turns as well. This made him imagine the Siege would continue longer than he at first propos'd, and so force him to set upon *Rome* and *Theodatus* in the Winter: Hereupon he resolv'd to rise, and gave Orders for his Army to dislodge, when an *Isaurian*, who was viewing the Structure of the Aquæduct with a Curiosity more than ordinary, observ'd, that if the Passage which was cut through a Rock for the Conveyance of the Water was enlarg'd, a Body of Forces might easily get through, and surprize the City. He inform'd the General of the Observation he had made, who joyfully entertain'd the Overture, and having widen'd the Passage once more summon'd the Besieg'd to surrender, who defy'd him from the Walls, and declar'd they would hold out to the last Extremity: The next Night therefore he order'd Six Hundred Men to enter the Vault, who took some Lights and two Trumpets with them, as well to terrifie the City as to give the General Notice of their Success. These Men with much Difficulty got into the Town, and hav- *and takes* ing kill'd the Guards open'd the Gates for the rest *it.* of the Army to enter, who slew all those they found in Arms, and pillag'd the City. *Belisarius* is much commended by *Procopius* for his great Clemency towards

wards the Citizens, whilft others, tho' of lefs Authority, condemn him for his Barbarity. The Garrifon, confifting of Eight Hundred Men, were taken into the Emperor's Pay; and *Belifarius* continu'd a few Days at *Naples*, as well to refresh his Army as provide for the Security of that and the Towns adjacent, which, following her Fortune, had declar'd for the Emperor.

The *Goths* throughout all *Italy* were much alarm'd at the General's Succefs, and no lefs amaz'd at the Stupidity of their Prince, who made no Preparation to ftop the Progrefs of the Enemy by a Battel, but feem'd inclinable to betray the Country upon the Profpect of an unactive retir'd Life. He was hated by fome for his Cruelty to *Amalafont*, defpis'd by others for his Inactivity, and fufpected by all to correfpond privately with *Juftinian*, fince his Son-in-law was fo much in that Emperor's Favour. Whereupon the moft leading Men of the Nation met at a Place about Five and Thirty Miles from *Rome*, and, after a ferious Confultation, proclaim'd *Vitiges* King of the *Goths*. *Vitiges* was a Perfon of no confiderable Family, but had behav'd himfelf with much Honour and Reputation in the Wars under *Theodorich*, for which Reafon he was very acceptable to that Martial Nation. *Theodatus*, who lay then at *Rome*, fled towards *Ravenna* upon the firft Intimation of their Proceedings, but was flain before he could reach to that City by Order from the New King, who at the fame time put his Son into Prifon, and there had him murder'd. After this he writ a very handfom Circular Letter, to be found amongft the reft in *Caffiodorus*, wherein he exhorted all the *Goths* to exert their ancient Courage, and to preferve and maintain their Conquefts againft all thofe that dar'd difturb 'em in the Poffeffion of them. Being of Opinion he was not

Theodatus depos'd, and Vitiges proclaim'd King;

ftrong

strong enough to defend *Rome* against *Belisarius*, who was marching towards it, nor able as yet to meet him in the Field, he resolv'd to remove to *Ravenna*, where he might more conveniently reinforce his Army, and be the better able to face the Enemy; and this he was the more inclin'd to because he was apprehensive of the *French*, who were in Confederacy with the Emperor, and of whose Friendship notwithstanding he did not totally despair: He therefore left Four Thousand *Goths* in *Rome* for the Defence of the City, took an Oath of Fidelity from the Senate and the Pope, and carry'd several of the Senators with him to *Ravenna* as Hostages for the rest; and to preserve the good Will and Affection of the *Goths*, he marry'd *Matasuntha*, the beautiful Daughter of *Amalasont*; and seizing upon the Treasure of his Predecessors, bestow'd it upon such as he thought were faithful, and could be the most serviceable to him. At *Ravenna* he summon'd the *Goths* from all Parts together, and put 'em into a posture of Defence; and considering how easie it was for the *Franks* to break into *Italy*, whilst he march'd with his Army towards *Rome*, and how impossible it was for him to contend at once with them and the *Romans*, in a general Council he persuaded his Officers to send some Embassadors to Treat of an Alliance between 'em, and draw 'em over to their Interest by giving 'em a considerable Sum of Mony, and resigning up that Part of *Gaul* which had hitherto been under the Dominion of *Theodorich* and his Successors, and which *Theodorich* had promis'd to deliver to 'em before his Death. The Princes of the *Franks* divided the Mony and the Country between 'em, and, entering into a Confederacy, promis'd to assist the *Goths*; tho', being at the same time in Alliance with the Emperor, they could not openly enter into

who goes to Ravenna.

into a War against him, and therefore the Aid they sent *Vitiges* into *Italy* consisted not of *Franks*, but such Nations as were subject to 'em, having learnt the Art of evading the Intent of a Treaty, tho' they had adher'd to the Letter of it. About this time, as *Procopius* observes, the Kings of *France* began to Coin Mony with their own Image impress'd upon it, and not that of the Emperor, or King of *Italy*, which show'd 'em Soveraigns independant of the one or the other.

In the mean time *Belisarius*, having Garrison'd all the Places of Consequence in *Campania*, prepar'd to march with his Army to *Rome*, whilst *Vitiges* was more employ'd in confirming himself in his new Authority, than prepar'd to defend the City. The taking of *Naples*, which was esteem'd a very strong and well fortify'd Town, and the barbarous Usage the Inhabitants were said to have receiv'd from the insulting Soldiers, together with the Reputation of their Victorious General, so aw'd and terrify'd the Citizens of *Rome*, that when they heard of his Approach they were resolv'd to make no Opposition, but open the Gates and receive him into the City; they therefore sent and invited him thither, and so order'd it, that the *Goths*, who found it in vain to contend, sally'd out at one Gate, whilst *Belisarius* was entering at another, who accordingly took Possession of *Rome* in the Emperor's Name, and so reunited it to the Empire, Sixty Years after it had been taken by the *Heruli*, *An. Dom.* 536. the Year after the Consulate of *Belisarius*.

Belisarius enters Rome.

A. D. 536.

III. *Rome* being thus recover'd out of the Hands of Barbarians, became a Member of that Empire, of which heretofore she had been the Head. She had worn the Yoke of Captivity too long not to retain the Marks of it; for as under the *Goths* she was

was us'd as a Slave, so was she still a Servant, guided by the Councils of Foreign Powers, and depending on the Fortunes of another City.

The Keys of the City, together with *Leuderis*, the Governor, who chose rather to be taken, than fly with those who had not the Courage to wait his Commands, *Belisarius* sent to *Constantinople*, and then apply'd himself, with great Skill and Industry, to the Reparation of the Walls; in which he extreamly disoblig'd the Inhabitants, who wonder'd he should prepare against a Siege in a City, that was neither situated on the Sea, nor had Walls capable of a Defence, but expos'd without any natural Fortifications in an open Champion, liable to all Assaults. Notwithstanding which *Belisarius* vigoroufly prepar'd for a Siege, sending for great Quantities of Corn out of *Sicily*, which he stor'd up in the publick Granaries, and compelling the *Romans* to bring in all the Grain their Farms afforded, with what ever else was necessary for the Subsistance of Human Life.

Nor was this the only thing in which *Belisarius* offended the Citizens, for not long after he depos'd *Sylverius* their Bishop, and substituted *Vigilius* in his Place, wherewith they were the more affronted, because, 'till then, the Choice of their Bishops resided solely in their own Clergy. A fuller Account of this Matter will give the Reader a little Insight into the Affairs of the Church in those Days.

Theodora, the Empress, was grievously infected with the *Eutychian* Heresie; and tho' *Justinian* himself firmly adher'd to the Orthodox Faith, yet he had not Power enough over the intractable Humour of his Wife to make her abjure her Errors, but on the contrary was often miss-led by her, to the great prejudice as well of the Church as State. *The State of the Church about that time.*

Upon

Upon the Death of *Epiphanius Syncellus*, Patriarch of *Constantinople, An. Dom.* 535. *Theodora*, contrary to the Forms and Canons of the Church, forc'd *Anthimus*, Bishop of *Trebisond*, into the See. *Anthimus* was a crafty factious Priest, who tho' he made an outward Profession of the Catholick Faith, yet in his Heart he was devoted to the Doctrines of *Eutyches*. At the same time the Empress, who apply'd all her Interest and Authority to the Support and Encouragement of the *Eutychians*, preferr'd *Theodosius*, a Priest of that Faction, to the See of *Alexandria*; with which the Citizens and Monks were so little pleas'd, that they chose another of the same Opinion, call'd *Gaian*, who in less than three Months was driven into Exile by *Narses*, whom the Empress had sent on purpose to *Alexandria* to support *Theodosius*. He held the Chair no longer than one Year and four Months, during which time the City was divided into *Theodosians* and *Gaianites*, who were likewise call'd the *Incorruptibles*, because they maintain'd, *That, after the Union of the two Natures in Jesus Christ, his Body was incorruptible, and that it was subject to none of the Infirmities incident to Human Nature, such as Grief, Pain, and the like*; which manifestly overthrew the Verity of the Human Nature in our Saviour, and destroy'd the Mystery of our Redemption. So fruitful is Error, that the *Eutychians* themselves were divided into no less than Five or Six Parties, such as the *Severians*, the *Gaianites*, the *Theodosians*, the *Themistians*, the *Jacobins*, and *Barsanians*, who tho' they all agreed in rejecting the Council of *Chalcedon*, yet did they disagree among themselves in some particular Points, by which it plainly appear'd that they had broken the Bond of Unity, when once they had renounc'd the Spirit of Truth.

Anthimus,

LVI. Justinian.

Anthimus, being thus introduc'd into the Patriarchal See by the Credit of the Empress, profess'd himself a Catholick 'till his Establishment, tho' the Poison was rooted deep in his Heart; but when the Emperor and Clergy desir'd him to make a sincere Confession of his Faith, he deluded 'em by his Stratagems, and daily countenanc'd and preferr'd the *Eutychians*. About this time *Agapetus*, Bishop of *Rome*, was arriv'd at *Constantinople*, in Quality of *Theodatus* his Embassador, and at his Arrival found the Process drawn up, and Judgment ready to pass upon *Anthimus*, who was shortly after depos'd, and *Menas* consecrated in his room, to the great Indignation of *Theodora*, who labour'd earnestly with *Agapetus* for his Restoration, and after his Death address'd her self to *Vigilius* his Deacon, who she knew to be of an haughty ambitions Temper. She promis'd to make him Bishop of *Rome*, upon Condition he revoked the late Synod of *Constantinople*, wherein *Anthimus*, *Severus*, and *Theodosius* were condemn'd as Hereticks, and that in a Letter to 'em he would approve and confirm their Faith. *Vigilius* readily undertook to do what ever she desir'd, and so return'd into *Italy* loaden with Gold, and with Letters directed from the Empress to *Belisarius*, wherein she enjoin'd him to expel *Sylverius*, chosen Pope upon the Death of *Agapetus*, and procure the Election of *Vigilius*. *Sylverius* having first refus'd to comply with her in behalf of *Anthimus*, *Vigilius* promis'd *Belisarius* Two Hundred Marks of Gold upon his Promotion. *Belisarius* being then at *Rome* sent for *Sylverius* to Court, where he reproach'd him for holding Intelligence with the *Goths*, to whom he had a Design of betraying the City, and forg'd Letters were produc'd to make good the Allegation. *Belisarius*, who knew very well that the

A. D. 537.

Accu-

Accusation was false, endeavour'd privately to persuade the Pope to condemn the Council of *Chalcedon*, and *Sylverius* demanded some Advocates to consult with them what was proper to be done; but being got out of the Palace betook himself to a Church as to a Place of Safety, for he apprehended they would offer him some Violence. *Belisarius* sent and entreated him to come again to Court, promising, upon Oath, that he should return in Safety. Whereupon, contrary to the Advice of his Friends, he went to the Palace, and was suffer'd to go back again that Night to the Church. Some time after *Belisarius* sent for him again, and being come to Court was carry'd into an inner Apartment, where he was divested of his Episcopal Habits, and made a Monk; after which *Vigilius* was created Pope by the sole Power and Authority of *Belisarius*, who banish'd *Sylverius* into *Lycia*. *Justinian* being inform'd of these infamous Proceedings, commanded *Sylverius* to be recall'd into *Italy*, where if it appear'd he was Author of the Letters produc'd against him, then he should have Liberty to Reside any where but in *Rome*, and if he was innocent, he order'd him to be restor'd to his See. Tho' the Empress us'd all her Arts and Authority to oppose this, yet *Justinian* continu'd unalterable, and so *Sylverius* return'd into *Italy*; of which when *Vigilius* was inform'd, and fearing to be himself expell'd, he told *Belisarius*, *That unless* Sylverius *was deliver'd up into his Hands, he should not be able to make good his Promise of paying the Sum of Mony they had at first agreed upon the Payment of*, and which *Vigilius*, either out of Covetousness, or Fear of offending the *Romans*, had hitherto declin'd. Upon this *Sylverius* was deliver'd to those *Vigilius* had sent for him, and hurry'd into the Isle of *Palmaria*, where

he

he dy'd of Famine under their Hands. *Vigilius*, in pursuance of his Promise to the Empress, writ to the Principal among the *Eutychians*, declaring that he had always been of the same Faith with them, which however he desir'd might be kept secret, and that in their great Wisdom they would openly appear distrustful of him, 'till he had accomplish'd the great Things he had undertaken; at the same time he express'd his Confession in these Words, *We deny two distinct Natures to be in Jesus Christ, who is one sole Son, one sole Christ, one sole Lord, compos'd of the two Natures*; and Anathematis'd those that were of a different Sentiment.

This Action of *Vigilius* appear'd so heinous in the Eyes of *Baronius*, that he exclaim'd against him with all the Bitterness the sense of so Sacrilegious a Villany could suggest; and yet afterwards, when upon the Death of *Sylverius*, whom he may justly be said to have murder'd, he was confirm'd Pope without a Competitor; this Wolf, this Antichrist, is by a strange Metamorphosis become the most Holy Vicar of Christ; so full of wonderful Virtues is the Papal Chair, that, in his Opinion, it's able to turn Black into White, and transform a Child of Darkness into an Angel of Light.

Whilst *Belisarius* was thus preparing for the Defence of *Rome*, he sent *Constantianus* in the mean time to take in the Towns in *Tuscany*. The Inhabitants of *Calabria* and *Apulia* had submitted to the General, so that both the Mediterranean and Maritime Coasts were restor'd to the Obedience of the Empire; for at the same time that part of *Samnium*, that borders upon the Sea, was surrender'd by *Pitzas*, a *Goth*, who, without regard to the publick Interest of his Nation, chearfully embrac'd the Cause that promis'd the greatest Success. In the

A. D. 538.
The Progress of the Emperor's Wars in Italy.

the mean while *Vitiges* lay not idly at *Ravenna*, but having rais'd an Army of One Hundred and Fifty Thousand Men, most of 'em good Soldiers, and well arm'd, he prepar'd to march directly for *Rome*, which he was sorry he ever quitted; and in Contempt of *Belisarius* his little Army, he imagin'd he should instantly recover. Indeed the General, being inform'd how strong the Enemy was, drew as many of the Forces, as could well be spar'd, out of the Garrisons to *Rome*: If he evacuated all the Places in *Tuscany*, the *Goths*, by possessing themselves of it, might, in a great measure, block up the City; he therefore sent Orders to *Bassas* and *Constantianus* to leave competent Garrisons in all the defensible Towns, and then make haste to join him. *Bassas*, tho' by Nation a *Goth*, had embrac'd the Emperor's Service, and was a brave experienc'd Commander; he had lately recover'd *Narnia*, a City standing upon a high Hill near the *Nar*, about Forty Miles distant from *Rome*; and staying there some time to settle it, and put it into a posture of Defence, he fell in accidentally with the advanc'd Guards of the *Goths*, of whom he kill'd and routed a great number, but being press'd upon by their Multitudes he retir'd into *Narnia*, where he left a sufficient Garrison, and then hasten'd to *Rome* to acquaint *Belisarius* with the Approach of the Enemy. *Vitiges* march'd with as much Expedition as possible towards *Rome*, without staying before any of the Towns in *Tuscany*, which he knew were well provided for a Defence, and would give *Belisarius* an Opportunity of running away, a thing he very much fear'd; and was extreamly pleas'd when he found he fortify'd himself in *Rome*, where he intended to expect his coming, and was indeed so far from avoiding, that he was resolv'd to maintain his Conquests at the hazard of his Life.

Belisarius

Chap. II. LVI. Juſtinian.

Beliſarius had built two Forts upon a Bridge about a Mile from *Rome*, and ſupply'd 'em with a good Body of his Troops, who were to diſpute the Paſſage with the Enemy, 'till the *Romans* had brought in all their Proviſions, and thoſe additional Forces and Supplies he daily expected from the Emperor had join'd him: For he concluded, if the *Goths* receiv'd a Repulſe there they could not paſs by any other Bridge in Twenty Days, and to form a Bridge of Boats would require a longer time. Beſides thoſe two Forts he deſign'd to lodge ſome Troops near the *Tiber*, who were to diſpute the Paſſage with the Enemy, and make ſome Trial of their Courage: But they who had the Guard of the Bridge were ſeiz'd with ſuch a Pannick Fear, that without any Oppoſition they quitted their Poſts, and left the Paſſage clear to *Vitiges*, who had paſs'd over a great Part of his Army before *Beliſarius* had the leaſt Apprehenſion of it; for he march'd out the next Morning with a Thouſand Horſe to view the Ground near the Bridge, where he might moſt commodiouſly plant his Soldiers, and was ſurpriz'd when he beheld *Vitiges* his Troops marching up againſt him.

Beliſarius had, in all former Engagements, behav'd himſelf with that Caution and Conduct that became a General, but now imagining that thoſe who were plac'd in the Forts for the Defence of the Bridge had been deſtroy'd, he was tranſported beyond his uſual Diſcretion; and ventur'd farther than the Nature of his Place and the preſent Poſture of Affairs requir'd, fighting in great Danger at the Head of his Men; who, following the Example of their General, bore down with great Fury upon the Enemy. *Beliſarius* his Perſon was diſcover'd by ſome Fugitives to the *Goths*, who therefore directed their whole Force againſt him, and aſſaulted him

A ſtrange Encounter near Rome.

him with their Swords and Lances; which made his own Men more follicitous to preserve and defend him than annoy the Enemy: So that the whole Controversie for some time was only about his Person. In conclusion the *Goths* were defeated, and forc'd back to their Camp, where being supported by their Foot, who were fresh and unbroken, they turn'd head against the *Romans*, who pursu'd the Chace with more Vigour than Order. By this time *Vitiges* had order'd another Party of Horse to assist and relieve those who had been engag'd from the Beginning, by whom the *Romans* were not only repuls'd, but closely follow'd to the very Gates of the City; where when they were come, the Guard, who had been inform'd by some Fugitives that *Belisarius* was slain in the Conflict, refus'd to admit 'em, lest the *Goths*, taking the Advantage of so sudden a Confusion, should enter with 'em, and without a Siege become Masters of the City. Tho' the General himself call'd earnestly out to 'em, and commanded 'em to open the Gates, yet Night approaching, and his Face being so disfigur'd with Blood and Dust that they could not discern him, they refus'd to obey. This reduc'd him to a greater Extremity than he was in before, for he was driven up into a narrower Compass, and they charg'd upon him as furiously as ever. In this Exigency he had Recourse to a bold and dangerous Resolution; he persuaded and encourag'd his Men to turn head, and charge the *Goths* with fresh Vigour, whilst they were disorder'd in the Pursuit; which Orders they so effectually executed, that the Barbarians, who little expected so furious an Onset from a conquer'd Enemy, imagin'd fresh Troops were sallying out upon 'em from the City, and ran with great Expedition back towards their Camp; so that *Belisarius*, who

would

would not suffer his Soldiers to pursue 'em far, had time to get into the City, where he was known and receiv'd with great Joy, and where he had leisure to reflect upon his great Deliverance. His Horse and Armour were almost cover'd with Arrows, of whom not one touch'd his Flesh, which was esteem'd little less than a Miracle by those who had been Witnesses of the Danger to which he had been that Day expos'd.

Vitiges, having wasted the Fields lying about *Rome,* came, a Day or two after, and sate down before it; he divided his numerous Army into Six Camps, who lying extended on both Sides the *Milvian* Bridge had thereby free Access, and could direct their Attacks towards what Part they pleas'd. Nor was *Belisarius* less vigilant within than the Enemy was without; the useless Multitude he sent out of the City, some into *Campania,* others into *Sicily,* and elsewhere; the Walls of the City being of great Extent, and the Soldiers too few to defend every Part against such Numbers of Assailants, he lifted the poor Artificers, who had no means of Subsistence left 'em, and incorporating them with his Troops allow'd 'em constant Pay, by which means he provided for the Necessities of the Indigent, recruited his Army, and reliev'd the Sick and Wounded who were unfit for Duty. The Enemy having cut the Aquæducts, being Fourteen in number, he found out other Means to convey Water into the Town; and lest any of the Inhabitants, who were averse to the Siege, should have a Design by Night upon the Gates, he broke the Keys twice a Month, chang'd the Sentinels every Night, together with the Officers that walk'd the Rounds; caus'd Musicians to play all Night upon the Ramparts, and employ'd *Moors* constantly to lye with Dogs about

Rome Besieg'd by Vitiges.

the

the Ditch, to discover such as approach'd the Walls; in all which he made it appear that he was firmly resolv'd to hold out to the last Extremity; Upon which the Citizens, unacquainted with Want and Hardship, assembled together in a tumultuous manner, railing at *Belisarius, as one who, without any Regard to the publick Calamities, obstinately presum'd to defend a Place, by Nature indefensible, only for the sake of his own Reputation.* These Murmurs *Vitiges* endeavour'd, by Messengers from the Camp, to exasperate, and drive 'em, if possible, into a perfect Mutiny. The Messengers, in Presence of the Senate and Chief Officers of the Army, arrogantly upbraided the General with Temerity and Presumption; and, extolling much the Power and Bounty of their King, offer'd a safe Retreat for him and his Army, and assur'd the City of their Master's Favour and Protection. Tho' the Citizens were very ready to lay hold of this Act of Grace, yet the Awe and Authority of *Belisarius* effectually restrain'd 'em, so that the Messengers were dismiss'd with no other Answer, but that *the General was not to be won or frighted with Words:* Whereupon *Vitiges* prepar'd for the Assault, and the Siege was carry'd on with great Obstinacy on both Sides, in the Management of which *Vitiges* behav'd himself like a compleat Soldier, both in Contrivance of his Engines, and Disposition of the Attacks; so that the Defendants stood in great need of a General so wary and experienc'd as *Belisarius*, who never suffer'd the Enemy to rest, but sally'd forth upon such Advantages, and receiv'd 'em whenever they assaulted him with so much Conduct, that in seven Months time *Vitiges* is said to have lost above Forty Thousand of his *Goths*, at which he was so enrag'd, that out of Indignation to be thus unexpectedly oppos'd he slew all the Senators, whom at the Beginning of
the

Chap. II. LVI. Justinian.

the War he had carry'd with him to *Ravenna*. The *Romans*, on the other side, grew elevated and presumptuous, and having lately receiv'd a Supply from the Emperor of Fifteen Hundred Horse, they scorn'd to act any longer by Sallies and Surprise, and declar'd for a more open and generous Management of the War, which they were for determining at once by a general Battel.

Belisarius, who well knew if ever it came to that what great Odds he should have against him, oppos'd it with all the Arguments his Reason and Experience, together with the present Circumstances of Things, could suggest; but being weary'd with the Importunities both of the Citizens and Soldiers, he at length resolv'd upon Battle, which he was desirous to bring on by slight Skirmishes and outwardly casual Excursions, rather than an Engagement form'd and premeditated on both Sides; but when he found his Attempts that way ineffectual, he then determin'd to fight openly; of which when the *Goths* were inform'd they were extreamly pleas'd, for they dreaded his Stratagems, which had cost 'em so many Men, and concluded he could have no Opportunity to circumvent 'em in a pitch'd Battel. *Belisarius*, having with great Care and Prudence prepar'd for the Engagement, and encourag'd his Men to render that Course fortunate by their Valour which he had been forc'd upon by their Forwardness, led his Army out at two of the City Gates, and fell in two Parties so warmly upon the *Goths*, that the *Romans* at first promis'd themselves an assured Victory, but being overborn by Numbers they confess'd, when it was too late, that their Courage was far inferior to the Wisdom and Foresight of their General; so that after a great Slaughter on both sides they were glad to retire back to- *The Romans, obstinate to fight, are defeated.*

I wards

wards the City, which with great Difficulty they enter'd, leaving *Vitiges* to boast of a Victory that cost him a great many good Soldiers, and was entirely owing to his Superiority in Numbers. Among the *Romans* a great many brave Men were lost, particularly *Principius*, one of the General's own Guard, and *Tarmutus*, Captain of the *Isaurians*. *Principius* was cut in pieces in the Rout, and *Tarmutus*, rescu'd by his Brother *Ennes*, fell down in a Swoon at the Gates, from whence he was carry'd on a Target to his Quarters, where he dy'd of his Wounds two Days after, leaving behind him an immortal Honour, for his great Courage, Zeal and Fidelity to the Emperor, whose Service receiv'd a considerable Loss in his Death.

The *Romans*, being instructed by this Lesson of Experience what they refus'd to learn from the Precepts of their General, were now contented to skirmish, as formerly, sallying out in Parties of Horse, lin'd with Foot that march'd by their Saddles Skirts, and 'had always the Advantage over the Barbarians. In these Skirmishes several of *Belisarius* his own Guard did Wonders, to the great Amazement of the *Goths*, who imagin'd the ancient *Roman* Valour, so much renown'd by Antiquity, was reviv'd to oppose them, and that the Genius of the Empire inspir'd new Courage into those, who generously undertook to defend the Place of her Nativity.

In this manner *Belisarius* weary'd out the Assailants, 'till he receiv'd Advice that a Supply of Mony to pay the Army was already landed in *Italy*, which how to get undiscover'd into the City was his principal Care. He march'd out at the Head of his Army, as if he had resolv'd to try the Fortune of a second Battel; this he did to amuse the *Goths*, who uniting themselves into one Body the better

Chap. II. LVI. Justinian.

better to receive him, had by that Diversion deserted the Place through which he had appointed the Treasure with its Convoy to pass, by which Means it got safe into the City. By this Stratagem he successfully remov'd one Evil, yet he still labour'd under others more fatal and pernicious. The City was grievously oppress'd with Famine, and the Plague rag'd furiously in it; and had he not with great Assurance persuaded 'em that he expected sudden Supplies from the Emperor, that a vast Army was approaching, and a Fleet already arriv'd, greater than any *Roman* Eye had ever yet beheld, they had forc'd him to another Battel; so far was the Sense of their present Sufferings more prevalent than the Reflections upon their former Miscarriage. The better to support their drooping Spirits, and add a greater Authority to what he had promis'd 'em, he sent away *Procopius* the Historian to *Naples*, who had Orders to command the Soldiers, to freight the Ships with Corn, and conduct 'em under a sufficient Convey to *Ostia*. Upon these Encouragements he not only reinforc'd his own Garrison, but by seizing on the adjoining Forts and the several Avenues about the Town he cut off the Enemies Provisions, and so in some measure besieg'd the Besiegers.

In the mean time a sufficient Supply of Men arriv'd at *Naples, Otranto*, and other convenient Ports from *Constantinople*, and a little before this some hundreds had already reach'd *Rome* by the way of *Samnium*. In their March through *Campania* they were join'd by Five Hundred Men newly levy'd in that Country, and coasted along the Shoar, having many Waggons with them, as well to fortifie themselves upon Occasion, as for the Covenience of carrying Corn and other Provisions. *Belisarius* having receiv'd Intelligence of their Motions, was afraid

Fresh Supplies from the Emperor arrive in Italy.

afraid left the *Goths*, who detach'd frequent Parties from their numerous Army, should meet and cut 'em off, and therefore had Recourse to his usual Stratagems, in which he seldom fail'd. Finding, at the Beginning of the War, that the *Flaminian* Gate was unserviceable for Sallies, and fearing the Enemy should take the Advantage of that weak Place and force the City, he took care to have it ramm'd up with Stones, which were now order'd to be remov'd with great Secresie, and having cautiously plac'd the greatest Part of his Army near the Gate, he order'd a Body of Forces to issue out at another, who, after a slight Skirmish, were to counterfeit a Flight, and draw the *Goths* down to that Gate, from whence he unexpectedly fell upon 'em with great Execution, and gave the Supplies an Opportunity of entring without any Loss or Opposition. The *Goths* were so thoroughly broken by these Disasters, that they had lost all their Courage and Resolution; the Hopes they had conceiv'd at the beginning, of Mastering the City, were turn'd into so many Reflections upon their own Misfortunes. Tho' they had for many Months press'd the Town with a strong and powerful Army, yet they lay under greater Hardships than the Besieg'd themselves; they were in more want of Provision, and no less afflicted with the Plague, so that the Famine and Pestilence had exceedingly reduc'd 'em: At another time, and upon other Occasions, Numbers might prevail, but they had now to deal with a General, who in Valour, Sagacity and Contrivance out-weigh'd Multitudes. These Considerations made 'em all weary of the Service, but more especially when they were inform'd of the Forces arriv'd from *Constantinople*, the Strength and Power of which, as it is usual in such cases, were represented to 'em greater than they really were,

were, then they thought of nothing but retreating upon the best Terms they could obtain. Accordingly they deputed three Commissioners into the City, who were to insist upon the Injustice of this Invasion on the Emperor's part, *Since by Virtue of* Zeno's *Assignment to* Theodorich, *they had a lawful Hereditary Claim to the Kingdom of* Italy: *They boasted that the Laws and Liberties of the Commonwealth were as tenderly regarded, and preserv'd under them, as they had heretofore been under the Emperors*; *that neither* Theodorich, *nor any of his Successors, had ordain'd any new Laws, either written or unwritten*; *that they had not deny'd the* Italians *a Liberty of Conscience in Religious Matters, nor infring'd the Immunities of the* Roman *Churches; in a Word, that all Preferments had been enjoy'd by* Romans, *no* Goth *having been preferr'd to any Place of Reputation*; *particularly, they had suffer'd the Consulship to be conferr'd yearly on* Romans, *by the Emperor's peculiar Designation.* Belisarius, instead of acknowledging that *Zeno* had conferr'd the Sovereignty of *Italy* upon *Theodorich,* accus'd that Prince of Ingratitude and Injustice, *who, like an Usurper, arrogantly seiz'd on that Country himself, out of which he had been Commissioned by* Zeno *to remove an Usurper*; *and bid the Commissioners never to think he would upon any Terms be persuaded to part with the Emperor's Provinces.* They then offer'd to quit *Sicily* to the Empire, which they said *he knew would serve as a Check upon* Africk; in Answer to which he told 'em, *The Emperor had quitted* Britain *to them, an Island of far greater Extent than* Sicily. And to other Offers and Demands, tending much to the same purpose, he return'd such Answers as might assure 'em, *They were to expect nothing from him which lay in his Power to deny.* At last they desir'd a Cessation of Arms for three Months, in which they might have leisure to send to the Emperor himself; which, after several Meetings on both sides, was in conclusion agreed upon.

A Truce agreed upon.

During this Negotiation the *Romans* found an Opportunity of receiving in the Supplies of Men, Mony and Provision lately mention'd; by which means *Belisarius* having first furnish'd *Rome* with a sufficient number of Soldiers, he sent the Supernumeraries out into the Country, where they form'd themselves into a Flying Camp, watching all Opportunities of incommoding the Besiegers, or seizing on such Places as they could conveniently attempt. This Detachment prov'd very serviceable to the Emperor's Affairs, and hasten'd the raising the Siege, which had already cost *Vitiges* so many Men, Time and Treasure; however he was still intent upon it, and form'd Designs against the City, tho' the Truce was not yet expir'd. He let some Soldiers down into one of the Aquæducts, to discover if a Passage could be forc'd through it into the Town; they, upon Trial, found a Way direct up into the midst of the City; but *Belisarius* having, at the beginning of the Siege, providently rais'd a Work to damn up the Cave, and prevent a Surprize, when they found they could go no farther they return'd to inform *Vitiges* of what they had seen and observ'd. In their Passage to and fro one of the Sentinels perceiv'd a Light through a breach in the Arch, which tho' he and some of his Companions, to whom he related his Observation, regarded as a Matter of no moment, yet when it accidentally came to the General's Ear, he was too sagacious to slight a Hint that might prove of so great a Consequence; he therefore order'd some of his Men to enter the Aquæduct, who quickly found, by some pieces of Lamps, and several droppings of Torches, that it was a thing not to be despis'd;

Vitiges his Stratagems defeated.

despis'd; whereupon *Belisarius* plac'd a strong Guard upon the Aquæduct, which, when the *Goths* observ'd, they desisted from any farther Attempts of that Nature, and prepar'd for a general Assault, in which they were discover'd through the Vigilancy of the Officer, who commanded the Watch, and repuls'd with Disgrace. This Disappointment made *Vitiges* apply himself to another Stratagem; he corrupted two *Romans* to intoxicate with a sleepy Potion, infus'd into some Wine, the Sentinels that kept Guard upon the Wall towards the *Tiber*, which part of the City was the least secur'd, because the Inhabitants trusted to the natural Fortifications of the River. So soon as the Infusion began to work, which was design'd to be about Midnight, they were to give a Signal to the *Goths* on the opposite Shore, who were to pass over and scale the Walls; and *Vitiges* had prepar'd the whole Army for a pretended Storm, the better to favour their Undertaking. But this Design being discover'd by one of the Conspirators, the other, who had the Drug about him, was first tortur'd, after which they cut off his Nose and Ears, and then sent him upon an Ass into the Camp of the *Goths*, who acknowledg'd the Hand of God was against 'em in this Discovery of all their Designs form'd against the City, and were for that reason inclinable to raise the Siege, which they found themselves oblig'd to do not long after for the Preservation of *Ravenna*; for those Troops *Belisarius* had some time before detach'd from *Rome*, under the Command of *John*, the Marshal of his Army, had wasted all *Picenum*, kill'd *Ulitheus*, Uncle to *Vitiges*, and seiz'd on *Rimini*; the loss of which, being but a Days Journey from *Ravenna*, threaten'd that Place with the like Fortune, unless some Care was taken for the Security of it; whereupon the *Goths*, startled

startled at the Report, and in great want of Provisions, after they had lain above a Year before *Rome*, during which time the Flower of their Army was, in a great measure, destroy'd, burnt their Huts, and rais'd the Siege; which could not be done so secretly, but *Belisarius*, having notice of it, charg'd them so warmly in their Retreat, that great numbers of 'em were destroy'd by the *Romans* Swords, and as many perish'd in the River, into which, as they press'd and crowded to escape, they fell, and sunk with their heavy Armour upon 'em.

The Goths raise the Siege.

IV. And so with Shame, Dishonour, and Diminution of his Power, *Vitiges* return'd towards *Ravenna*, putting strong Garrisons into all the Places in his Passage, and directing his March to *Rimini*, which being a Town of such great Consequence, he was resolv'd to force out of the Enemy's Hands, and so prepar'd to Besiege it. *Belisarius*, who was not ignorant of his Design, took care to have such Supplies put into the City, as could well be spar'd, and his Orders were executed with so much Expedition, that *Ildeger* and *Martinus*, two *Roman* Officers, threw themselves into the Town with a competent Body of Foot, which they had drawn out of *Ancona*, a City standing upon the *Ionian* Gulph, two Days Journey from *Rimini*. *John*, a brave experienc'd Commander, and one who had been of great Service to the Emperor in his Wars, was already in the Town, where he commanded in Chief, tho' he had receiv'd Orders from *Belisarius* to rise with the Horse from thence, for he concluded he might do more Service at the Head of the Cavalry abroad, than in the Town; however *John* would not forsake the Place, but resolv'd to defend it in Person, at which *Belisarius* was highly displeas'd;

displeas'd; and this, among other Matters, gave a beginning to the Jealousies that shortly after broke out between him and *Narses*.

Vitiges at first thought to carry the Town by main Force, and accordingly, as soon as he sate down before it, began to batter it with his Rams, and other warlike Engines, in the Invention of which he was very fortunate; but *John* manag'd the Defence with so much Industry and Experience, that he found it almost impossible to take it by Storm, and therefore resolv'd to starve out the Enemy, who he knew were in great want of all manner of Provision, and in no probability of being reliev'd; and so the Siege was protracted longer than either he intended, or the *Romans* expected.

Vitiges Be-sieges Rimini;

In the mean time *Belisarius* was busied in another Quarter of *Italy*, for he detach'd a Thousand Men from his Forces, who, under the Command of *Mundilas*, had Orders to March towards *Milan*, which City he hop'd they would reduce, at least he intended by it to transfer the War into the Enemy's Country. *Mundilas* took *Milan* without any Opposition, and in a short time made himself Master of all *Liguria*, being now the Territories of the State of *Genoa*, to the no small Mortification of *Vitiges*, who sent *Uraiah*, his Nephew, at the Head of a powerful Army, to recover it out of the Hands of the *Romans*. *Uraiah*, with the Assistance of Ten Thousand *Burgundians*, sent him by *Theodebert*, King of the *Franks*, so straitly Besieg'd *Milan*, that the *Romans*, in a short time, were reduc'd to the last Extremity, which, together with the Misunderstanding between *Belisarius* and *Narses*, occasion'd the Loss of the City, as we shall see hereafter.

and Uraiah, Milan.

For

A.D. 540.
Narses sent into Italy.

For the Summer following, whilst *Vitiges* continu'd still before *Rimini*, and his Nepew, *Uraiah*, before *Milan*, the Emperor sent fresh Supplies of Men and Mony into *Italy*, under the Conduct of this *Narses*, who was a Man of great Authority both in the Camp and Court, for he was a good Soldier, and an experienc'd Statesman. At *Firmum*, a City standing on the Adriatick, both Armies join'd, and a Council of War was immediately call'd, wherein they deliberated what Course was best to be taken for the Emperor's Service. *Auximum*, a strong well fortify'd Town, was still Garrison'd by the Enemy, who from thence might fall upon the Backs of the Imperialists, and harass the Country inhabited by the *Romans*, should they move from thence to the Relief of *Rimini*. On the other Hand, it was thought unreasonable to suffer the Besieg'd to perish for want of Assistance; tho' most of the Officers were incens'd against *John*, who had unadvisedly thrust himself into such imminent Danger out of a thirst of Wealth, and disobey'd the General's Orders; however *Narses*, who had a very great Respect for him, earnestly press'd to have the Army march to *Rimini*, from whence Letters arriv'd in the very Crisis, wherein *John* declar'd, *That unless he was reliev'd within Seven Days, he must of necessity deliver up the Place.*

Belisarius found it no easie thing to contend with so many Difficulties; he was unwilling to lose *Rimini*, and as unwilling to leave the Country about *Auximum* to the Mercy of the *Goths*, who would, without fail, endeavour to destroy it, and thereby endanger his Army in case of a Battel. To provide therefore the best he could against both Inconveniences, he left a Thousand Men under the Command of *Aratius* by the Sea side, who were to keep the Garrison of *Auximum* in awe, and sent some Forces by Sea with Orders to sail directly to *Rimini*, and to land near the Foot, which *Martinus* was directed to conduct along the Shore; when they approach'd the Enemy he commanded 'em to make great Fires, the better to terrifie the *Goths* with a false Apprehension of their Numbers, whilst he, with *Narses*, and the rest of the Army, march'd at a distance from the Sea by the way of the Mountains, with a Resolution not to hazard a Battel, both because the Enemy were superior in Number, and render'd desperate by their late Misfortunes. This Division of his Forces, and his Stratagems had the Effect he desir'd; for some of the *Goths* that were straggling abroad fell by chance upon a Party of his Men, and observing the main Body appear upon the Mountains, they hasten'd back to the Camp, where they reported the *Romans* were Marching with an innumerable Army to the Relief of the City. Whereupon *Vitiges* prepar'd for a Battel, apprehending no Danger but from the North, and the Tops of the Mountains; but when the Night following he observ'd the Fires kindl'd by *Martinus* to the East of the City, he immediately concluded he should be unavoidably surrounded by the Enemy, especially when in the Morning he beheld the Fleet, which was bearing down directly towards him; this struck him with so much Consternation, that he grew incapable of Counsel, and his whole Army was seiz'd with so much Terror, that, regardless of all Command, every Man grew intent upon his own Safety, and thought of nothing but securing himself in *Ravenna*; they fled away in so much haste, that they left the greatest part of their Baggage behind 'em; and had not the Besieg'd been feeble and heartless, for want of Sustenance, they might easily have cut

Rimini Releiv'd by Belisarius.

cut 'em off in the diforderly Retreat, and made an end of the War at once.

After this Succefs the Jealoufies that appear'd before between the two Generals were improv'd to an open Rupture. *Narfes*, tho' for the moſt part he was a Perfon of a juſt and generous Temper, yet kept his Ears too open to the Infinuations of his flattering Dependants, who extoll'd his Power and Parts, and perfuaded him that it was beneath his Worth to be accountable to the Authority of any other General whatfoever. *Belifarius*, who was foon made fenfible of thefe pernicious Practices, endeavour'd to divert that malignant Humour by Action, and therefore in a Council of War propos'd, *That part of the Army fhould march towards* Milan, *which was clofely befieg'd by* Uraiah, *who held all* Liguria *at his Devotion, whilſt the reſt march'd to* Auximum, *where the Goths had a great and gallant Army, and held feveral other Places as far as* Urbiventum, *a City not far from* Rome, *each of which were able to contend with the whole Power of the Emperor.* Narfes excepted againſt this with much Heat, and the Difpute was carry'd on between 'em fo long 'till *Belifarius* produc'd the Emperor's Letters, wherein he declar'd, *He had not fent* Narfes *into* Italy *to Command his Forces, but, together with the reſt of his Officers, be fubfervient to* Belifarius, *and obferve his Orders in all things that related to his Service, and the good of the State;* thefe laſt Words *Narfes* infiſted upon, and endeavour'd to prove, *Obedience was due to* Belifarius *no longer than it appear'd his Actions concurr'd with the common Intereſt of the Empire.*

Thefe Difputes and Animofities rais'd fuch a Divifion among the General Officers, as very much retarded the Progrefs of the Emperor's Affairs; for *Belifarius* having detach'd *Peranius* with part of
the

the Forces to besiege *Urbiventum*, he march'd with the rest against *Urbinum*, distant about a Days Journey from *Rimini*, situate upon an Hill, and render'd strong as well by Art as Nature. *Narses* and *John* follow'd in the Rear, but encamp'd at a distance from him, and were of so little Service in the Siege, that before the Rams were apply'd, or any Attack prepar'd, they withdrew by Night, and return'd with Part of the Army to *Rimini*, notwithstanding all Motives, Entreaties and Persuasions the General could use to the contrary; for *John* having been formerly baffled before the Place, they pretended the Town was impregnable, and that *Belisarius* at once show'd his Obstinacy and Temerity, in his Attempt upon it. The Departure of so many Men greatly discourag'd those that continu'd behind, and strengthen'd the Resolution of the Defendants: Notwithstanding which *Belisarius* proceeded with great Constancy of Mind, and prepar'd for an Assault; but as the Assailants were ready to approach the Besieg'd hung out a Flag, and upon a Promise of Indemnity surrender'd. The *Romans* were much elated at this unexpected Submission, for at first they thought it entirely owing to the Terror of their Arms, tho' it appear'd afterwards to proceed from another Cause more prevalent; for the only Fountain the *Goths* had in the City dry'd up of it self, by which unforeseen Accident they were forc'd to drink thick, unwholsom Water, which bred a Sickness among 'em.

Narses, who lay idle in *Rimini*, was amaz'd at this sudden Success, and being sensible that what he had done had subjected him to the publick Censure, endeavour'd by Action to redeem his Reputation, and therefore sent *John* out against *Cesina*, a City built upon the Banks of the *Rubicon*; before which being repuls'd he surpriz'd the ancient City

of

of *Forum Cornelii*, in the same District, and call'd at present *Imola*, and shortly after recover'd all *Æmilia*; for the *Roman* Arms were grown so terrible to the *Goths*, through the continu'd Success of this War, that they had not the Courage to stand an Engagement with them.

All this while *Milan* was closely press'd by *Uraiah* and the *Burgundians*; *Mundilas* commanded the Garrison in the Town, and took care to send for timely Assistance to *Belisarius*, who immediately dismiss'd *Martinus* and *Uliaris* with a strong Body of Forces to relieve the City. These Generals, advancing as far as the *Po*, a Day's Journey from *Milan*, encamp'd upon the Banks of that River; and tho' earnestly sollicited by the Besieg'd to hasten their Assistance, they excus'd themselves by Letters to the General, pretending *the Goths were too powerful for 'em in* Liguria, *and therefore they were afraid to proceed farther 'till they were join'd by more Forces*. Hereupon *John* receiv'd Orders from *Belisarius* to join *Martinus* with all Expedition, which *John* peremptorily refus'd to do unless he receiv'd the like Orders from *Narses*, to whom *Belisarius* writ upon that Subject, *beseeching him not to cause the Emperor's Affairs to suffer through their unseasonable Emulation*. Tho' *Narses* was convinc'd of the Reasonableness of this Remonstrance, and by Letters commanded *John* to obey the General's Orders, yet these Negotiations took up so long time, *Milan surrender'd to the Goths.* that *Mundilas* was forc'd by his Soldiers to submit to the Conditions offer'd by the *Goths*, who promis'd to indemnifie the *Romans*, but vow'd to destroy all the *Ligurians*; the City was accordingly surrender'd, and *Mundilas* and the Garrison made Prisoners of War, in breach of the Articles agreed *Their Barbarity.* upon: The City was demolish'd, and the Inhabitants, to the Number of Three Hundred Thousand, were murder'd; the Senators, Priests, and other Ecclesiasticks, that had taken Sanctuary in the Churches, were butcher'd before the Altars; the Women ravish'd, and made Slaves to the *Burgundians*; *Reparatus*, a Præfect, was cut in pieces, and cast to the Dogs; *Dacius*, the renown'd Bishop of the Place, escap'd with the melancholy News to *Constantinople*; and *Martinus* and *Uliaris* return'd with Shame and Dishonour towards *Rome*, whilst the *Goths*, in confidence of their Success, pursu'd their good Fortune, and speedily reduc'd all *Liguria*.

 The Monks that write of those Times have attributed several Miracles to this *Dacius*, and other *Italian* Bishops, his Contemporaries; which are for the most part so absurd in their Circumstances, and so trivially design'd, that the greatest Wonder is how they could so impudently presume to impose upon the World.

 During the Fury of these Wars the Earth was left uncultivated, which occasion'd a most horrible Famine almost throughout all *Italy*. In some Places they were forc'd to make Bread of Acorns, which engender'd several Distempers, mortal to those that fed upon it. No less than Fifty Thousand Persons are said to have been starv'd in the *Picentin*: Several Persons, by a voluntary Death, prevented the Torments of a lingring Famine: Some Mothers, in the Bitterness of Hunger, murder'd and devour'd their own Infants: Several that stoop'd to eat Grass, being unable to pluck it up, fell upon their Heads, and dy'd with some of it in their Mouths. There was no care had of Burials, those that surviv'd being unable to provide for or protect the deceas'd, whom however the Birds of Prey refus'd to approach, there being no Flesh left upon the Corps to gratifie their Appetites. Two Women living in an House accustom'd to entertain

A grievous Famine.

Passen-

Passengers, kill'd Seventeen while they slept; as they came, one after another, to lodge with them, and devour'd 'em; but the Eighteenth, who was inform'd of their Barbarity, pretended himself a Guest; and in the dead of Night dispatch'd 'em both.

Belisarius, as soon as he was inform'd of the Loss of *Milan*, and the great Misfortunes that attended it, banish'd *Uliaris* from his Presence, and gave the Emperor an impartial Account of the whole Matter. *Justinian*, being unwilling to offend any of his Generals, for whom he had now so much Business, without calling any Man to an Account contented himself with sending for *Narses* home, and thereby prevent the Mischiefs arising from the unhappy Contentions between him and *Belisarius*, whom he confirm'd in the absolute Command over his Arms in *Italy*. *Vitiges*, who promis'd himself mighty Advantages from the Disagreement between the Generals, found his Hopes defeated by this prudent Conduct of the Emperor, and grew more in fear of *Belisarius*, who he knew was preparing with all his Forces to besiege him, the Spring following, in *Ravenna*: He knew the *Romans* were grown hardy and couragious by their repeated Victories, by which the *Goths*, on the other side, were quite broken and dishearten'd.

At first, therefore, he endeavour'd to engage *Varis*, King of the *Lombards*, in his Quarrel; but finding him firm to his Alliance concluded lately with the Emperor, he persuaded *Chosroes*, King of *Persia*, to invade the *Roman* Territories, concluding that such an Enemy was able to give *Justinian* a powerful Diversion, and make him recal *Belisarius*, and give over any farther Care for the Dominions of the Empire in the West, since the Security and Defence of the Eastern Territories were of a far greater

Vitiges engages Chosroes in his Quarrel.

greater Consequence to his Interest and Reputation. *Chosroes*, who had agreed to the Peace before mention'd, more out of regard to his own Security than any Affection to the Emperor, repented of what he had done, when he beheld the great Prosperity of the Emperor's Affairs in *Africk*, and thought it chiefly owing to the late Treaty between the two Crowns; however being terrify'd by some Conspiracies which he about that time discover'd against his own Person and Dignity, he thought it safe to quit still; and demanded only, in a merry Embassy, his Share in the *Vandal* Spoils, since by the Peace he had contributed so largely to the Conquest. *Justinian*, who thought it unadvisable to disoblige him, return'd a friendly Answer, and a considerable Present in Mony. For the Peace was at that time seasonable to the Emperor's Affairs, not only in respect of the *African* War, but because *John*, a Soldier in the Garrison of *Daras*, had just then revolted, and set up for himself. This Usurpation had undoubtedly been of very ill Consequence to the Empire, had *Chosroes* made use of the Opportunity, and supported the Usurper; but *Justinian*'s Ministers so well temporis'd with that Prince, that he refus'd to assist the Rebels, so that *John* was easily suppress'd, and slain a few Days after his Usurpation. But tho' *Chosroes* could so easily digest the Conquest of *Africk*, yet he consider'd the Reduction of *Italy* with Thoughts fuller of Apprehension, and conceiv'd it a Member too considerable to be re-united to the Empire; which would, by such an Accession, be restor'd to her former Vigour, and recover her native Sovereignty. For these Reasons he watch'd all Opportunities for a Quarrel, and when *Vitiges* his Embassadors arriv'd, and in a set Speech persuaded him, *That if he sate*
neuter, and beheld them destroy'd, he would unavoi-
dably

dably be undone himself; without considering how much Interest they had in the Counsels they gave him, he resolv'd upon a Rupture, to the great Satisfaction of *Vitiges*; who however receiv'd little or no Advantage from it, tho' it put a stop to the Progress of *Justinian*'s Arms in *Italy*, out of which he was forc'd to call *Belisarius*, tho' not 'till he had fully settled his Authority in those Parts.

Auximum Besieg'd by Belisarius. For pursuing the course of his Fortunes he sat down with Eleven Thousand Men before *Auximum*, the Metropolis of *Picenia*, standing within Ten Miles of the *Adriatick*, and something more than Three Days Journey from *Ravenna*, strongly situated, and provided with a very good Garrison; at the same time he sent another Party, under the Command of *Cyprian*, one of his Lieutenants, to besiege *Fesula*, a Place in the *Apennine* Straights, and which, together with *Auximum*, open'd a Passage to *Ravenna*, whither *Belisarius* resolv'd to follow *Vitiges*.

A. D. 539.
The Franks invade Italy.
Whilst *Belisarius* was busy'd in the Siege of *Auximum*, and *Vitiges* by frequent Messages from the Besieg'd sollicited to relieve it, the *Franks*, concluding both Nations sufficiently weaken'd by their mutual Hostilities, invaded *Italy* with an Army of One Hundred Thousand Men, under the Conduct of *Theodebert*; who, in Violation of his late Oaths made, as well to the *Goths* as the Emperor, resolv'd to attack both, and so put an end to the Controversie, by seizing on that for which both Parties with so much Earnestness contended. The *Goths* were highly pleas'd when they beheld the *Franks* marching over the *Alps* into *Liguria*, certainly concluding that they were moving to their Assistance; and this Opinion was confirm'd by the *Franks*, who abstain'd from any hostile Act, whilst they continu'd in that Country, moving directly towards the *Po*,

Po, their Passage over which would be much facilitated, if they administer'd no Grounds of Jealousie to the Inhabitants: And herein they succeeded so well, that they receiv'd frequent Assistance in their March from the *Goths*, who permitted 'em to pass the River near *Pavia* without any Opposition. But having by this means secur'd the Bridge and Passage, they seiz'd upon the *Gothick* Women and Children, as the first Fruits of the War; at which the *Goths* were so terrify'd that they fled with great Consternation into the Town, whilst the *Franks* pass'd on to the Camp, where, through the same Mistake, they were kindly receiv'd, 'till by their barbarous Behaviour they declar'd themselves their Enemies, whereupon they fled by the *Roman* Camp into *Ravenna*. The *Romans*, who were encamp'd over-against them, observing the Rout, thought they had been defeated by *Belisarius*, with whom they resolv'd to join in the Chace; but being as cruelly treated as the *Goths* had been, and unable to recover their Camp, they fled into *Tuscany*, and sent their General an Account of their Misfortune. Thus both Camps fell into the Hands of the *Franks*, in which they found Provisions sufficient for their present Supply, and they had done wisely if they had retreated with their Booty; but piercing on into a desolate exhausted Country, destitute both of Corn and Wine, they were forc'd to feed upon Beef, their only Nourishment, and drink unwholsome Water, and that being unable to digest their Food threw 'em into a Dysentery, of which above a Third of their Army is said to have perish'd, and the rest were become unable to proceed farther. *Belisarius* reproach'd *Theodebert*, in his Letters, for Breach of Faith to the Emperor, *Since he had been so far from assisting him, in pursuance of his Treaty, that he had set upon and de-*

and seize the Gothick and Roman Camps.

feated

feated his Troops; an Action unworth[y]
and so great a Prince: Telling him,
That the Emperor's Affairs were not [in a]
Condition, but that he should be abl[e to]
egregious an Affront at a time conveni[ent.]
this Prince was terrify'd at the Let[ter, re-]
pented of what he had done, or to [avoid the]
Reproaches of his Subjects, who mu[st see]
he had brought 'em to die like Dog[s in an]
impoverish'd Country, or call'd hom[e by Do-]
mestick Commotions, he rose up [and left,]
leaving behind him terrible Instance[s of cruel-]
ty throughout *Liguria*, for he destro[y'd]
several other adjacent Places.

In the mean time the two Garriso[ns of]
and *Fesulæ* held out with great Resol[ution, and]
struggled with many Difficulties, an[d had no]
Support but *Vitiges* his Promise of [speedy]
Relief. *Fesulæ* was so closely block[ed up]
an that no Provisions could possibly [be brought]
to the Town, so that the Besieg'd, [in ex-]
pectation of being succour'd, wer[e forc'd to]
render; and *Cyprian*, leaving a Par[ty in]
the Town, brought the Inhabitant[s to Au-]
mum, where *Belisarius* show'd 'em [Vitiges,]
and gave 'em thereby an Opportun[ity of see-]
ing what they were to expect, and [how]
the King was to relieve them. [Those who]
were before weaken'd with Famine, [the sight]
of *Fesulæ* had now so much opera[tion on their]
Minds, that they were contented to [yield the]
Town, on condition they might en[joy Life]
and Substance. This the General [was willing]
to grant, but the Soldiers oppos'd i[t, since the]
Wealth of the City was deservedly th[eir Repa-]
ration of their Wounds and Labours. [At last it]
was agreed on both Sides that the

Chap. II.   LVI. Justinian.

have half, and that the other half should be continu'd to the Besieg'd, who were to take the Oath of Allegiance to the Emperor; accordingly *Belisa-* *rius* was receiv'd with the *Romans* into the City, *Auximum surrender'd* from whence he march'd with the whole Army towards *Ravenna*, and proceeded with so much forwardness and success in the Siege, that the Kings of *France*, particularly *Theodebert*, knowing in what extremity *Vitiges* was, and disdaining to suffer the *Romans* to recover their Dominions in *Italy*, by their Embassadors offer'd him a powerful Assistance, consisting of no less than Five Hundred Thousand Men, on Condition they might have a share in the Country with him. *Belisarius*, being inform'd of this Negotiation, sent and represented to *Vitiges* on one side the Valour of the *Romans, which was not to be overpower'd by Numbers*; on the other he reminded him of the Perfidy of the *Franks, who had given him a bloody Instance of it in their last Year's Expedition; and that consequently it was safer for him to embrace the Freindship of the* Romans, *who were ready to admit him upon Terms very just and honourable.* *Vitiges*, upon a serious Deliberation in Council, dismiss'd the Embassadors with a Refusal, and grew inclinable to an Accommodation with the Emperor, who, being inform'd how Affairs stood in *Italy*, sent two Senators, who offer'd *Vitiges*, on *Justinian*'s part, half the Revenue, and the Dominion of the Country on this side the *Po*; and the Proposals were so acceptable to *Vitiges*, that he readily embrac'd 'em; but when the matter was fully concerted on both sides, *Belisarius* refus'd, at first, to sign the Treaty, and still press'd the *Goths* so closely, that they found it impossible to hold out any longer; notwithstanding which, and tho' they were grown weary of *Vitiges*, yet they were unwilling to submit to the Emperor, for fear they should

A.D. 540.

should be transported to *Constantinople*, and forc'd to settle in *Thrace*; whereupon the *Gothick* Nobility agreed among themselves to declare *Belisarius* Emperor of the West, and accordingly sent their Agents privately to him, who had Commission to assure him they were ready, and willing to swear Allegiance to him. Tho' *Belisarius*, in regard of his Oath formerly made to *Justinian*, was resolv'd never to attempt any Innovation during the Life of that Emperor, yet he outwardly seem'd to accept of the Offer, the better to facilitate his Design upon the City, and confirm his Master's Authority; accordingly he negotiated so successfully with them, that at their own Request he was receiv'd into *Ravenna*, which he enter'd in a Triumphant manner at the Head of his Army, which appear'd so inconsiderable for its Numbers, that the *Gothick* Women could not forbear spitting in their Husbands Faces at the sight of 'em; for they had pretended to 'em that the *Romans* were more numerous, that they were stout in their Persons, and for their Courage invincible. *Procopius*, who beheld this Entry, gives it as an Instance that Human Affairs are not conducted by Multitudes, nor does Success depend upon Force or Valour, but that all our Actions are influenc'd and directed by some superior, invisible Power, who governs all things by his own irresistible Will.

Belisarius, being by these means become Master of *Ravenna*, secur'd the rest of the Towns thereabouts, which readily surrender'd, and so all *Italy* was, in a great measure, restor'd to the Emperor's Obedience; however, he behav'd himself with much Moderation towards the *Goths*, for he suffer'd the Soldiers to plunder none of the Inhabitants, but seiz'd on the Royal Treasure, which, together with *Vitiges*, whom he kept in honourable Restraint, he

The Goths propose to declare Belisarius Emperor of the West.

A. D. 540.

Belisarius receiv'd into Ravenna.

he intended to carrry with him to *Conſtantinople*, whither he was recall'd by the Emperor to take upon him the Management of the *Perſian* War, which requir'd a General of his Capacity; tho' it has been upon good Grounds conjectur'd, that ſome Jealouſies the Emperor had, at the Inſtigation of his Court Sycophants, entertain'd concerning him, were the chief Motives for his Revocation. Indeed he was Maſter of thoſe extraordinary Virtues, which uſually attract the Envy of ſuch as are unable imitate 'em, ſo that it's no wonder if they took care to render him ſuſpected to his Maſter, whom they were angry any one was better able or willing to ſerve than themſelves, tho' he never appear'd, in the leaſt reſpect, fond of any Innovation, but, on the contrary, continu'd deaf to the repeated Remonſtrances of the *Goths*, who earneſtly ſollicited him to accept of the Crown. However, he was receiv'd at *Conſtantinople* with a Reſpect due to his extraordinary Merit, the People beholding him with Eſteem and Admiration, as one that had highly deſerv'd of his Country, which he had enrich'd with the Treaſure of two Potent Princes, *Genſerich* and *Theodorich*, and honour'd with the Preſence of two Royal Captives, *Gelimer* and *Vitiges*. The Emperor receiv'd him without the leaſt Tokens of a Diſtruſt, and with great Demonſtrations of his Royal Favour; he treated *Vitiges* with a Reſpect anſwerable to his Birth and Dignity, confer'd on him the Honour of a Patrician, and ſent him to Command his Troops Quarter'd upon the Frontiers of *Perſia*.

He is recall'd out of Italy.

V. This Year, as it was famous for *Beliſarius* his Triumphant Return to *Conſtantinople*, ſo was it no leſs remarkable, for that it was the laſt in which any Perſon exercis'd the Office of Conſul;

A. D. 541.

which

which Dignity, after it had been succesfully executed for the space of One Thousand and Forty Seven Years, determin'd this Year in *Basilius*, the last that ever bore that Honour; it being abolish'd by the Advice of *Trebonian*, for no other Reason, but because he never had Interest enough to be advanc'd to it. It's true, that after the Sovereign Power resided in the Persons of the Emperors, the Consulate was in reality no other than an honorary Title, and faint Resemblance of the ancient Power of the *Roman* Consuls, who heretofore made the Earth to tremble; from henceforward the Years were computed, at first, by the First, Second, &c. after the Consulate of *Basilius*, but shortly after they began to reckon by the Years of the Emperor's Reign, who usually declar'd himself Consul the First Day of his Empire, and *Justinian* enter'd upon the Fifteenth of his, the First of *August*, this present Year.

The Consulate ends.

In the mean time the War waxed very hot in the East, where the *Persians* had gain'd very considerable Advantages against the *Romans*, before *Belisarius* could arrive out of *Italy* to take the Command of the Army upon him. It was preceded by an amazing Comet, appearing about that time in *Capricorn*, at first seemingly about a Man's length in extent, afterwards much longer, with its Tail pointed towards the East; and by another Irruption of the *Hunns*, who, tho' formerly they had been very outragious, never did so much Mischief as at this time. For having pass'd the *Ister*, they wasted all the Country up as far as *Constantinople*, took Thirty two Castles in *Illyricum*, destroy'd *Cassandria*, call'd anciently *Potidæa*, after which they return'd home loaden with Spoils, and One Hundred and Thirty Thousand Captives. These Calamities, and a Presumption that *Justinian* was

An amazing Comet.

grown

grown jealous of *Belifarius*, whom he would no longer truft with an abfolute Command in his Wars, together with fome Advantages the rebellious *Armenians* had obtain'd over the *Romans*, encourag'd *Chofroes*, at the Inftigation of *Vitiges*, to proceed to an open Rupture; accordingly, in the Thirteenth Year of *Juftinian*, he invaded the Roman Territories with a very powerful Army, directing his Courfe towards *Syria* and *Cilicia*, burning and deftroying all before him, whilft *Buzes*, who commanded in the Eaft, inftead of providing for the Defence of the Provinces, fhamefully deferted his Poft, and withdrew no one knew whither, leaving *Chofroes* at liberty to make what Conditions he thought fit with *Berrhæa*, *Hierapolis*, and the adjacent Cities, from whom he exacted moft unreafonable Contributions; after which he went and befieg'd *Antioch*, which, after a fhort Refiftance, he mafter'd. Tho' the City had often felt the weight of Divine Vengeance in preceding Times, yet it never was pour'd out in fo heavy a meafure upon 'em before; the *Perfians*, in the heat of their Conqueft, fparing neither Age nor Sex; and thofe, who furviv'd the firft Fury, were made Slaves by the King's Command, who gave the Town up for a Spoil to his Soldiers. He himfelf feiz'd on the immenfe Treafure of the Church, and commanded the greateft Rarities of the City to be taken down, and tranfported into *Perfia*, after which he fet Fire to the Town, and deftroy'd it. Thus perifh'd the largeft, the richeft, the moft populous, beautiful, and happy City of the Eaft, by the Hands of the moft impious Man of that Age, who was the Inftrument of God's Vengeance upon a luxurious, ungrateful, ftubborn, and rebellious People.

Chofroes Invades the Roman Territories,

and takes Antioch,

and deftroys it.

Justinian complain'd loudly by his Embassadors against these Proceedings, charging *Chosroes* with Perfidy and Barbarity; in Answer to which *Chosroes* suggested many specious Pretences, which show'd him more influenc'd to a Rupture by his own Ambition, than urg'd to it by any Provocation; however, after many Recriminations on both sides a Truce was agreed upon, and *Chosroes,* in Consideration of a great Sum of Mony, promis'd to return into his own Country, where new Embassadors were to be sent from the Emperor, who were to change the Truce into a firm and lasting Peace. Accordingly *Chosroes* march'd back, but, in Defiance of the Treaty, robb'd all the Cities as he pass'd, and, crossing the River *Euphrates,* rifled *Mesopotamia* in his Passage. He had a great Desire to make himself Master of *Edessa,* the Metropolis of *Osrhoene,* for no reason more than to elude a certain Tradition then in Request among the Christians of those Parts, by which they were confident it never was to be taken by an Enemy, for that it was render'd impregnable by a Letter our Saviour is said to have sent to *Agbarus,* at that time Governor of the Country, in which he promis'd the City should never be subject to Barbarians; which Letter, *Procopius* affirms, but upon what Authority is not easily determin'd, the Inhabitants had engrav'd upon the Gates of the City for the better Security of the Place. Whether that or some other Reason restrain'd him he attempted nothing against the City, but satisfy'd himself with a Sum of Mony, which preserv'd that and the Neighbouring Towns and Villages.

These Actions of *Chosroes* highly provok'd *Justinian,* who declar'd that he had broken the Peace, and therefore refus'd to stand to the Ratification; so that Preparations were made for a War on both sides, fides, especially upon *Belisarius* his Arrival at *Constantinople*, where he was declar'd General by the Emperor against the *Persians*, and prepar'd to take the Field the Spring following. In the mean time the *Persians* so effectually tamper'd with the *Lazians*, that they withdrew themselves from the Emperor's Obedience, and declar'd for *Chosroes*. These were Inhabitants of *Colchus*, who, without receiving either Mony or Soldiers from the *Romans*, defended the Marshes from the Incursions of the *Hunns*, in Consideration of which Service they had Liberty to Trade with the Emperor's Subjects in *Pontus*. In the Reign of *Justin* the *Romans* were oblig'd to send some Forces into *Lazica*, upon the account of the unruly *Iberians*, which administer'd to 'em the first Grounds of Discontent; and about this time *John Tribus*, a Man of a mean Condition, but of a tyrannical, rapacious Temper, who, by building a Fort, as a Curb to the *Lazians*, and exacting extravagant Contributions for the Payment of his Soldiers, so far provok'd the Inhabitants, who were otherwise well affected to the Empire, that they threw themselves into the Protection of *Chosroes*, who wanted little or no Persuasions to make him incline to their Proposals; and these Matters were so secretly transacted, that *Chosroes* was got with a powerful Army into the midst of the Country, where the King did him Homage, and deliver'd the Palace and the most important Places of the Kingdom up into his Hands, before the Emperor had any notice of it. In the mean time *Belisarius*, who was persuaded that all *Chosroes*'s Preparations were against the *Hunns*, and no way related to the *Romans*, had enter'd *Persia* at the Head of a considerable Army, and having fac'd *Nisibis*, he took the Fort of *Sisibranum*, and harass'd *Assyria*; after which, the

The Lazians revolt to the Persians.

Belisarius enters Persia.

Heats

Heats encreasing, and *Syria* being threaten'd by the *Saracens*, it was resolv'd, in a Council of War, speedily to retreat, whilst *Chosroes*, upon the News of *Belisarius* his Invasion, at the same time march'd back into his own Dominions. Thus ended this Year's Campaign, more remarkable for the sudden Retreat of both Parties, than any considerable Action it produc'd.

A. D. 542. *Chosroes second Invasion.* The Spring following *Chosroes* again invaded the *Roman* Territories with a great Army, and marching through *Comagena*, a Country bordering Eastward upon the *Euphrates*, and from thence call'd *Euphratesia* by the *Romans*, he neither staid to plunder the Country, nor take in any of the Towns, but march'd directly for *Palestine*, which he heard was a Province very fertile, and well inhabited; he therefore already imagin'd himself Master of the Spoils of it, and of the great Treasures in *Jerusalem*, especially when he found the *Romans* gave him no Opposition in his Passage, but thought it sufficient to secure their own Garrisons. *Justinian*, upon the first News of this Invasion, immediately sent away *Belisarius*, who rode Post into *Comagena*, and at *Europus*, a Town situate upon the *Euphrates*, begun to levy an Army some time after *Chosroes* with his had pass'd that River; at this the *Persians* were so alarm'd, for they were now far within the *Roman* Territories, and dreaded an Enemy at their Backs, that they were glad to retire, and, after an expensive, fruitless Expedition, return home with Shame and Dishonour, much to the Reputation of *Belisarius*, who, with a handful of Men, and his prudent couragious Conduct, was able to stop the Progress of a powerful inveterate Enemy, and drive him out of the midst of the Country, and that at a time when the rest of the *Romans* hid their fearful Heads in their strong Holds and Garrisons.

After

LVI. Justinian.

After this great Piece of Service *Belisarius* return'd to Court, and forasmuch as he was never after employ'd in the *Persian* Wars, we must follow him into *Italy*, whither he was sent some time after by the Emperor, and where we shall find his Fortunes, together with that of the Empire, decline, and give way to the prevailing Arms of the Barbarians.

Nor did the Sword alone rage at this Time, to the great Destruction of Mankind, but the World was visited with a Plague, which prov'd more destructive than War it self, and appear'd to be the immediate Finger of God: For it was neither restrain'd to one Part of the World, nor confin'd to this or that particular Season of the Year, but seiz'd on all Men alike, of different Climates, Diet, Complexions and Inclinations. It took its Flight from *Pelusium* in *Egypt*, and extended its infectious Wings to the utmost Bounds of the World. Into whatever Nation it pierc'd it began first at the Sea-Coast, and pass'd from thence up into the in-land Country; visiting all Parts alike with equal Fury where Mankind inhabited, sparing neither Islands, Caves, nor the Tops of Mountains. About the Middle of the Spring, in the second Year of its Tyranny, it visited *Constantinople*, where Apparitions of Spirits appear'd to many, who were thereupon immediately struck with the Distemper. At first when they met them they thought to fright 'em by the Repetition of Divine Names, and fled into the Churches for Sanctuary, but to no purpose. Some beheld such imaginary Sights in their Dreams, others fancy'd they heard a Voice telling them they were enroll'd in the Number of those that were appointed to die; whereupon great Swellings arose that Evening, or the Day following, in their Groin generally, the preceding Symptoms of the

A Plague.

Procop.

Disease.

Disease. Some were seiz'd with a Deadness upon their Spirits, and an Inclination to Sleep, insomuch that they grew forgetful of all things, and unless Care was taken to feed 'em they starv'd themselves to Death. Others grew distracted, and in their Fits were vex'd with Apparitions, who, as they imagin'd, were going to kill them. Some immediately receiv'd the Poison upon their Approach to those that were infected, others continu'd sound and untouch'd, tho' they were continually employ'd in attending the sick, and burying the dead. A great many receiv'd Benefit by Bathing, and to others in the same Condition it prov'd immediate Death. Many, whom the most experienc'd Physicians had given over for lost, miraculously recover'd; and others, whom they judg'd to be past all Danger, unexpectedly dy'd. Some perish'd for want of Care, whilst others escap'd without it. In a Word, it was not in the Power of Art to find out a Means to prevent or remove the Disease; for as no Reason appear'd, by any precedent Disposition, why the Patient fell sick, so could they find out no Method for his Recovery. A great many that escap'd had their Tongues so much diminish'd that they were unable to pronounce any Articulate Sound ever after. This Pestilence rag'd with great Fury for Four Months in *Constantinople*, in which, at first, Five, but by degrees Ten Thousand and upwards dy'd every Day; and, according to *Evagrius*, who, together with his Family, had been visited by it, continu'd for Fifty Years together in one Corner of the World or another, so that the greatest Part of Mankind then living may be said to have been destroy'd by it. In some Things he saith it resembled the Plague of *Athens*, in others he instances how much it was unlike it. Indeed it appears, upon all Accounts, to have been so extraordinary,

Chap. II.   LVI. Justinian.

traordinary, that it may be thought to have deserv'd a larger Description than either he or *Procopius* has left us of it.

However these immediate Judgments from Heaven put no Stop to the Fury of the Wars in *Italy*, where the Emperor's Arms met with many Defeats after the Departure of *Belisarius*.

For the *Goths*, when they found he persisted to reject the Offer they had made him of the Empire, apply'd themselves first to *Uraiah*, *Vitiges* his Nephew, desiring him to take the Government upon him; but he prudently declin'd the Burden, as well because he apprehended his Uncle's Misfortunes would redound to his Dishonour, as because he thought it unnatural in him to assume the Title whilst he was living. Whereupon, by *Uraiah*'s Advice, they made Choice of *Ildebald*, at that time Governor of *Verona*, and Nephew to *Theudis*, King of the *Visigoths*, who they hop'd by that means would be induc'd to espouse their Quarrel. *Ildebald* was a Man of great Accomplishments being both valiant and of much Experience. He was no sooner proclaim'd King, but he advis'd the *Goths* once more to remind *Belisarius*, before his Departure for *Constantinople*, of what he had engag'd himself to do before *Ravenna*, and urge him to the Performance of his Promise; which if he did they would be ready to proclaim him King of the *Goths* and *Italians*, but if he refus'd then *Ildebald* advis'd 'em immediately to enter upon Action.

When he found *Belisarius* stedfastly resolv'd to obey the Emperor's Summons, and that he was set out accordingly for *Constantinople*, he instantly undertook the publick Management of Affairs, and undertook no less than the Re-establishment of the *Gothick* Dominion in *Italy*. He was at first Lord

The Progress of the Goths in Italy.

Ildebald chosen King

of

of no more than a Thousand Men, and one single Town in *Picenum*; but by degrees the *Goths* that had lain dispers'd up and down the Country united themselves to him, and he was at the same time strengthen'd by no inconsiderable Numbers of discontented *Romans*. For *Alexander*, an Auditor of *Constantinople*, who, for his penurious Temper, and clipping the Coin, was nick-nam'd *Forsicula*, was sent by the Emperor into *Italy*, after the Departure of *Belisarius*, to state the Accounts of the Army; which Office he manag'd with so much Rigour and Extortion, that both the *Italians* and the Soldiers became very ill affected to *Justinian*; and were by degrees so indispos'd to their Duty, that they refus'd to embark themselves in any Enterprize of Consequence to the Emperor's Service. At the same time the Officers left behind by *Belisarius* for the Defence of those Parts, disagreeing among themselves, serv'd to advance *Ildebald*'s Affairs, who having defeated *Vitalis*, commanding for the Emperor in *Venetia*, near *Tervisio*, very much strengthen'd his Interest and Reputation, tho' he liv'd not long to enjoy the Fruits of his Victory: For some Female Contests arising betwixt his Queen and *Uraiah*'s Wife he indiscreetly concern'd himself in the Quarrel, and having accus'd *Uraiah* of an intended Revolt, he very treacherously and ungratefully procur'd him to be murder'd, and by that means expos'd himself to the Displeasure of the whole Nation; which encourag'd *Vilas*, one of the Guard, upon some Personal Disgust to murder *and murder'd*. him, whilst he was feasting the Nobility. The *Goths* were much amaz'd and discourag'd at the Murder, for they look'd on *Ildebald* as a Man able to recover the Dominion of *Italy*, notwithstanding his late Misdemeanour. After some Deliberation upon the Necessity of their Affairs, and Choice of

King to succeed him, the Election fell upon E-*rarick*, a Man of good Reputation among 'em, who however was not able to satisfie them long, but follow'd the Fate of his Predecessor: For *Balduillas*, Nephew of *Ildebald*, and surnam'd *Totilas*, being Commander of the *Goths* in *Tervisio*, sent, upon the News of his Uncle's Death, to *Constantine*, who govern'd then for the Emperor in *Ravenna*, and promis'd, upon an Assurance of Indemnity, to deliver up the Place, and the Men he had in Garrison in it. *Constantine* readily embrac'd the Overture, and gave Oath for Performance of the Articles; but before the Day appointed for the Surrender came, the *Goths*, grown weary of *Erarick*'s Government, made *Totilas* an Offer of the Crown, not only in respect of his Birth but his great Deserts. *Totilas* frankly acquainted 'em with his Engagements to *Constantine*, but promis'd, if they dispatch'd *Erarick* before the Day he had promis'd to surrender the Garrison, he would accept of their Offer, and comply with all their Desires. In the mean time *Erarick* persuaded the *Goths* to send Embassadors to *Constantinople* with Proposals of a Peace, upon condition they had the same Terms granted them that had been formerly offer'd to *Vitiges*; but he secretly instructed the Embassadors to bargain with the Emperor in his Behalf, for a good Sum of Mony, and the Dignity of a Patrician, in consideration of which he undertook to deliver all *Italy* up into his Hands. But before these Things could be transacted as he desir'd at *Constantinople*, the *Goths*, in compliance with *Totilas* his Demands, treacherously murder'd *Erarick*, after he had reign'd five Months; and *Totilas* was unanimously declar'd King by the whole Nation, who expected great Matters from him, and indeed he prov'd a great Support to that Nation during his Reign in *Italy*.

Erarick chosen King

and kill'd.

Totilas elected.

L The

The Emperor being inform'd of his Promotion, and the Distraction of his Affairs in *Italy*, sharply reprehended his Officers commanding there, whose ill Conduct had notoriously contributed to it. It was therefore agreed in a Council of War held at *Ravenna*, first to besiege *Verona*, after the Reduction of which City they concluded to march against *Totilas*, who was at the Head of a small Body in *Picenum*. Accordingly the Army, consisting of about Twelve Thousand Men, had Orders to march under the Command of Eleven Officers,

The Emperor's Officers, disagreeing among themselves, ruin his Affairs.

who by their selfish, unseasonable Disputes, render'd the Design ineffectual, tho' it had been wisely propos'd, and as luckily concerted. *Marcianus*, a Person of great Interest in the Country, and well affected to the Emperor's Service, had procur'd a Citizen of *Verona* to betray the Place; a Watchman was to open one of the Gates by Night to such as should be sent by the *Romans* to that Purpose, whilst the rest of the Army follow'd at their leisure. This Service was look'd upon to be of great Danger, for there was a good Garrison within the Town, and if the Watchman prov'd a Traitor the whole Party would infallibly be cut off: For this Reason all the Commanders refus'd the Service, except *Artabanes*, an *Armenian*, who had the Command of those *Persians*, who having deserted or been taken Prisoners by *Belisarius* in the War in the East, he had sent to the Emperor, and were now employ'd by him in *Italy*. *Artabanes* therefore, at the Head of One Hundred Men, had the Gate open'd to him, and was receiv'd into the City, out of which the *Goths* fled at another Gate, and secur'd themselves upon a Rock not far from the Walls, where they had not only a fair Prospect of the Country round about, but had a full View of all the Streets in *Verona*, and in the Morning discover

scover'd to what a Handful of Men they had, in the Heat of their Surprize, abandon'd the City. For the rest of the *Roman* Army, instead of marching on to assist thier Fellows, were detain'd by a shameful Contention between their Officers, who spent the Night in Quarrels about the Plunder of the City, so that the Day was far advanc'd before they could agree to share the Wealth of *Verona* among themselves; and the *Goths*, viewing the Army at that Distance, return'd back with great Expedition into the City, whilst the *Romans*, being unable to make it good against so great an Inequality, fled to the Battlements, where they defended themselves with great Resolution, and did Wonders. By this time the *Romans* were come up, but when they found the Gates shut against 'em they scandalously retreated, and forsook their Companions, who earnestly call'd out for their Assistance. *Artabanes*, and those of his Followers that were still alive, when they saw themselves thus barbarously betray'd, leap'd down from the Walls; he, with a few more that pitch'd upon plain Ground, got safe to the *Roman* Camp, where he severely upbraided the Officers for their ill Conduct; but the rest, who fell on the Stones, were destroy'd.

The *Romans*, after this Disappointment, pass'd the *Po*, and march'd to *Faventia*; whilst *Totilas*, who was inform'd of their Miscarriage, drew most of the Garrison out of *Verona*, and march'd against the Enemy with his whole Strength, which consisted of no more than Five Thousand Men. The *Roman* Generals, upon Notice of his Motions, call'd a Council of War, at which *Artabanes* advis'd 'em *to act with Caution against the Goths, who by their former Misfortunes, and present Advantages, were become desperate and presumptuous;* and propos'd to engage 'em when they were half pass'd the River, ra-

ther

ther than wait 'till their whole Body was come up. Instead of following this wholsome Counsel they spent their Debates in contradicting one another, as it is usual among Men who have an Equality of Command, and so sate still without doing any thing at all; whilst *Totilas*, after he had encourag'd his Men by a seasonable Exhortation, order'd Three Hundred of 'em to pass the River at some Distance below, that they might get behind the Enemy, and, when they perceiv'd the Fight begun, gaul 'em in the Rear. These Orders were carefully executed, and prov'd of great Advantage to the *Goths* in the Engagement: *Totilas*, with the rest of his Forces, without any Opposition, went over at the Place where they had lain encamp'd, and so both Armies began to face each other. Whilst they were drawing up in Order of Battel, *Valiaris*, a hardy robust *Goth*, advanc'd beyond the Ranks, and boldly challeng'd any *Roman* to a single Combat; which was readily accepted by the valiant *Artabanes*, who in the first Encounter ran his Lance into his Right Side, and gave him a mortal Wound, so that the *Goth* sunk backward and rested upon his Lance, which hardly kept him from falling. *Artabanes*, who thought the Wound he had given him had not been mortal, unfortunately charg'd him a second time, and wounded him in the Belly, at the same time that the Head of *Valiaris* his Lance lighted upon his Neck, and cut an Artery; notwithstanding which, *Artabanes*, who was acknowledg'd Conqueror, gallop'd back to the Army, and left his Adversary dead upon the Place. At first he felt no Pain, nor apprehended any Danger, but the Flux of Blood prov'd so great that it was impossible to be stopp'd, so that he dy'd three Days after, much lamented by all those who wish'd well to the Emperor's Affairs, which receiv'd an exceed-

A single Combat, in which both are destroy'd.

ing great Loss in his Death. He was remov'd out of Danger of the Enemy's Shot, where all Care was taken to attend him; and in the mean while both Armies join'd Battel, and the *Romans* were entirely defeated; for the Three Hundred *Goths* before mention'd, in pursuance of their Instructions, fell in the heat of the Engagement upon the Backs of the *Romans*, who, apprehending their Numbers to be greater than they were, immediately gave Ground, and fled away in great Confusion; the Enemy, who follow'd close at their Heels, took a great many Prisoners in the Pursuit, and all their Ensigns, whilst the Commanders shifted the best they could for themselves, and got, with a few of their Followers, into the Towns next adjoining.

Totilas, after this Victory, which prov'd of great Advantage to his Affairs, made use of his good Fortune, and sate down before *Florence*, from whence however he was forc'd to rise, and remove to *Micale*, a Town about a Day's Journey distant from it, whither the *Romans* prepar'd to follow him, intending with part of the Forces under the Command of *John*, Governor of *Florence*, to set suddenly upon the Enemy, whilst the rest march'd slowly after; but here again some untimely Disputes among the Officers frustrated all their Designs; for upon a Disagreement among 'em, *John* was forc'd to engage with no more than his own Guards, and, after a sharp Dispute, was worsted; for as the rest of the Army was at last marching up to his Assistance, a false Report that he was kill'd by one of his own Life-guard threw 'em into such a Consternation, that they all dispers'd themselves in great Confusion, and left *Totilas* absolute Master of the Field of Battel. He us'd his Victory with so much Moderation, and treated his

A. D. 542.

The Romans routed.

Prisoners with so much Humanity, that many of 'em enter'd into his Service against the Emperor.

A. D. 543.

The Spring following he took in several Places that had been Garrison'd by the *Romans*, which readily surrender'd, so that in a short time he became Master of the greatest part of *Tuscany*, *Campania*, and *Samnium*; after which he march'd with the main Strength of his Army to Besiege *Naples*, reducing *Brutia*, *Lucania*, *Apulia* and *Calabria*; and having seiz'd on the Publick Revenue, as well as private Rents, he behav'd himself like a Prince absolute in *Italy*, in which his Power and Authority encreas'd every Day, whereas the Emperor's on the other side was daily declining. For having no Mony to pay his Army, he contracted a vast Debt in the Country, and the Soldiers grew Licentious, and Disobedient to their Officers, whilst the Inhabitants themselves were miserably harass'd and impoverish'd by the contending Parties. To remove these Difficulties *Justinian* Mann'd out a good Fleet, and rais'd a considerable Army, both which he committed to the Conduct of *Maximinus*, with the Title of *Præfectus Prætorio* of *Italy*, joining with him, as his Lieutenant, *Demetrius*, who had formerly been General of the Foot under *Belisarius*. *Maximinus* was a Man of a weak, cowardly Spirit, and altogether a Stranger to Military Affairs, nor was *Demetrius* much better qualify'd for the Service, being a Person of little or no Conduct, and very ill belov'd by the Soldiers. Whilst *Maximinus* loiter'd upon the Coasts of *Epirus*, *Demetrius* undertook to relieve *Naples*, closely Besieg'd by the *Goths*, by whom it was reduc'd to the last Extremity; but having very few Forces with him, he fraited a good Number of Ships with Corn and other Provisions in *Sicily*, intending

to

to terrifie the Enemy, who would conclude that so considerable a Navy must have an Army proportionable on Board. He had undoubtedly succeeded had he sail'd directly for *Naples;* but being too fearful of his own Strength he rather chose to go first for *Rome,* where he hop'd for raise Soldiers to reinforce his Army, but found, upon trial, they had lately been so beaten by the *Goths,* that they refus'd to march against *Totilas,* so that he was necessitated either to sit still there, or undertake the Expedition with no more than those he had brought with him; the last Expedient he thought the most advisable, and *Totilas,* upon notice of his Design, Mann'd out a Fleet of light Pinnaces to Encounter him, who, bearing up to him unawares, quickly terrify'd and defeated him. Every Ship he had was taken or sunk, together with all his Men, except a few, that following his Example sav'd themselves in the long Boats. This Disaster sadly discourag'd the Besieg'd, and animated the Assailants with fresh Vigour, so that *Conon,* who commanded for the Emperor in *Naples,* dispatch'd a Messenger with an Account of his Condition to *Maximinus,* who, being advanc'd as far as *Sicily,* lay carelesly at *Syracuse,* like one who was afraid to Embark himself in the War; and tho' the *Romans* in *Naples,* by repeated Messages, demanded his Assistance, and he was threaten'd with the Emperor's heavy Displeasure, he refus'd to hazard his own Person, and therefore dismiss'd the Army to *Naples* under the Command of other Officers. The Fleet set Sail in the midst of Winter, and by that time they drew near the Coast of *Campania,* so violent a Storm arose, as render'd all the Care and Skill of the Seamen ineffectual, so that they were all driven a-shore near the Enemy's Camp, who, with much ease, sunk what Ships, and kill'd as many Men as they pleas'd.

The Romans overthrown at Sea.

Demetrius, who after his late Defeat was got aboard the Fleet, happen'd to be among them that were taken, and was led, with a Rope about his Neck, to the Town Wall, where *Totilas* compell'd him to persuade the Inhabitants to surrender, by assuring 'em that all hopes of Relief was lost with the Navy; so that *Conon*, sensible of the Necessity he lay under, and the ill Condition of the Emperor's Affairs, surrender'd the City upon Honourable Conditions, which *Totilas* punctually observ'd, and thereby endear'd himself very much to the Inhabitants. He was sensible his Nation had been infamous for their Dissoluteness and Barbarity, which Character he endeavour'd to obliterate by establishing an exact Discipline in his Army, and giving the World severe Instances of his Justice by the Punishments he inflicted on the Offenders. One of his own Guard, having Ravish'd the Daughter of a *Roman* Gentleman in *Calabria*, he sentenc'd to Death; and tho' he was otherwise a valiant deserving Soldier, and the Chief Officers of the Army petition'd for him, he was executed accordingly, and his Estate conferr'd upon the injur'd Lady. These Courses render'd him and his Followers by degrees grateful to the *Italians*, who on the other side were insolently abus'd by the Imperialists; for the Officers themselves liv'd in all Debauchery with their Mistresses, and suffer'd the licentious Soldiers to follow their Examples, so that Men of all Conditions, but especially the Peasant, had great reason to complain, for the *Goths* seiz'd upon his Land, and the *Romans* wasted and devour'd his Goods.

Naples surrender'd to Totilas.

Totilas his prudent Conduct.

A. D. 544.

By this time the Emperor had but few Places remaining firm to his Obedience, *Constantianus* commanded in *Ravenna*, *John* govern'd in *Rome*, *Bessus* in *Spoletum*, *Justin* and *Cyprian* in *Florence* and

only Towns almoſt of conſequence
nder the Dominion of the *Goths*.
ow Maſter of *Naples*, and all the
thoſe Parts, began to turn his
ds *Rome*, and ſent a Letter to the
e earneſtly deſir'd to draw over to
x'd 'em in very civil Terms with
to the Goths, by whom they had
ſure been oblig'd; he advis'd and
return to their Allegiance, from
unworthily departed for the ſake of
em more like Slaves than Subjects,
uch Outrages upon 'em, as he al-
his Power to protect 'em from; he
only way they had left to remove
nder which they labour'd, was to re-
ty, in which Caſe he aſſur'd 'em of
Protection, which ſhould extend not
ite but the People. *John*, who
?*ome* for the Emperor, forbad the
this Letter, or to receive any more
no however privately convey'd ſe-
rs into *Rome* by unknown Hands,
the Night to Poſt 'em up in the
Places of the City. The *Arian*
pected to have been Inſtrumental
for that Reaſon expell'd. This
nuch affronted *Totilas*, who for
olv'd to proceed after another man-
ſent part of his Army into *Cala-*
Otranto, he march'd with the reſt
vns lying about *Rome*, and having
the Treachery of ſome of the
put all to the Sword, thereby
izens of *Rome* what they were to
had refus'd to accept of his Grace

VI. The

VI. The Emperor being deeply concern'd and perplex'd at the ill News which he daily receiv'd out of *Italy*, which was in Danger entirely to be lost without some speedy Prevention, and knowing by Experience he had no Man in his Empire whom he could so implicitely trust as *Belisarius*, he recall'd him out of *Persia*, and commanded him to prepare to pass with all Expedition into the West. In his way through *Illyricum* he rais'd with his own Mony what Forces he could, and at *Salona* muster'd about Four Thousand Men. From thence he dismiss'd *Vitalius*, or *Valentin*, General of those Parts, with Part of his Army to raise the Siege of *Otranto*, where he arriv'd just Four Days before the Besieg'd had promis'd to surrender, in case no Succours were sent in the mean time: Hereupon the Siege was rais'd, and the Town re-inforc'd with fresh Supplies of Men and Provision. *Belisarius* being arriv'd in *Italy* inform'd the Emperor of the Condition he found the Country in, telling him that he was destitute both of Men, Arms and Mony, without which it was impossible for him to prosecute the War. The few Soldiers he had rais'd in his Passage through *Illyricum* were raw and undisciplin'd, those upon the Place were cowardly and mutinous, for having been so often defeated by the *Goths* they were terrify'd at their very Names, and having been so long unpaid he was cautious of commanding them upon any Service for fear of being disobey'd; that he dar'd not raise any Contributions from the Inhabitants, lest they should be thereby provok'd to revolt to the Enemy; concluding in these Terms, *If your Majesty's Design was only to send me into* Italy *I have follow'd your Orders, and am now in it*; *but if you expect I should serve you against the Enemy I ought to be furnish'd with*

A.D. 545.
Belisarius *sends the Emperor an Account of the Affairs in* Italy.

Chap. II. LVI. Juſtinian.

with *Materials proper for that Deſign, without which I am in no Condition of propoſing a Peace, or continuing the War.* Theſe Letters he committed to *John,* the Son of *Vitalian,* with Orders to deliver them forthwith to the Emperor, and ſollicite Supplies for the Service in *Italy.* But *John,* being arriv'd at *Conſtantinople,* inſtead of obeying his Orders, minded nothing for ſome time but his own private Affairs, and got himſelf marry'd with much Pomp and Solemnity to the Daughter of *Germanus,* the Emperor's Nephew. By theſe Delays *Totilas* had an Opportunity of purſuing his good Fortune, and wreſting thoſe Places that remain'd firm to their Obedience out of the Emperor's Hands. He made himſelf Maſter of *Fermo, Aſcoli, Spole.o,* and *Peruſa,* and took ſeveral other Towns of Conſequence, in which he met with little or no Oppoſition. *Procopius* tells us, that a certain poor Biſhop of *Tuſcany,* call'd *Cerbonius,* having about this Time hid ſome *Roman* Soldiers in his Houſe, thereby to ſecure 'em from the Cruelty of the *Goths, Totilas* was ſo enrag'd, when he was inform'd of it, that he commanded the good Biſhop to be expos'd to a wild Boar, which was let looſe upon him; but the Animal, tho' by Hunger made furious and implacable, inſtead of devouring his Prey fell offenceleſs down at the Prelate's Feet, and fawn'd friendly upon him: The People, amaz'd at the Miracle, importun'd *Totilas* to pardon *Cerbonius,* which he readily granted, being aſham'd of his Indignation expreſs'd againſt a Perſon whom God had ſo miraculouſly protected. This Account is no ways contradictory to the true Deſign and Nature of Miracles, whereas another related upon the ſame Occaſion, by *Gregory* the Firſt, ſounds too much like a Fable to be inſerted in this Hiſtory.

Totilas being thus become Master of the greatest Part of *Italy* commanded the Husbandmen to till and cultivate the Fields, and expresly forbid his Soldiers, upon the severest Penalties, to impeach or molest them. This civil Treatment wrought so effectually upon the Inhabitants of the *Parmesan*, which is a fruitful, profitable Soil, that they voluntarily surrender'd themselves to *Totilas*, who was directing his chief Designs against the City of *Rome*, which he block'd up so closely that he suffer'd no Provisions to be imported either by Sea or Land, by which Means the City was reduc'd to the last Extremity; for the Famine rag'd so furiously within the Walls, that the Inhabitants were forc'd to feed upon Things the most filthy and unwholsome, not sparing their own Excrement. They flock'd in great Multitudes to *Bessas*, who commanded for the Emperor, desiring *either Food for their Subsistance, or Leave to go out of the unfortunate City, otherwise that he would dispatch 'em out of the way*. *Bessas* reply'd, *That to supply them with Food was impossible, to let 'em go was unsafe, and to kill 'em impious:* And that was all the Comfort they receiv'd from him, who had undertaken their Protection. All the Support they met with was from *Pelagius*, a Deacon of the Church, who having been a great Favourite of *Justinian*'s, in whose Court he had a long time resided, was grown Master of much Wealth, which he, being at this time in *Rome*, distributed with a generous Hand to the Necessities of the People, and for some time mightily supported 'em.

Belisarius, at his first Arrival into *Italy*, finding the Coasts of *Calabria* and *Campania* secur'd by the *Goths*, so that it was impossible to land at any Place near *Rome*, disembark'd at *Ravenna*, where he was inform'd of the Difficulties the Garrison labour'd under,

<small>Rome closely besieg'd by Totilas.</small>

<small>Belisarius lands at Ravenna.</small>

Chap. II.   LVI. *Justinian.*   157

under, and quickly found how hard a Matter it would be to relieve 'em. By repeated Messengers he demanded fresh Supplies from the Emperor, notwithstanding which it was a considerable time e'er *John* return'd with a little Army, consisting partly of *Romans* and partly of Barbarians: At the same time *Narses*, the Eunuch, arriv'd with some Auxiliary Troops of the *Heruli*, who in their March defeated a great Body of the *Sclavi*, whom *Totilas* had bought to assist him, and who, passing the *Ister*, had wasted the Country, plunder'd the Cities, and taken vast Numbers of Prisoners. *Belisarius*, having committed the Care of *Ravenna* to *Justin*, march'd through *Dalmatia* to *Epidamnus*, or *Durazzo* in *Albania*, where joining the Supplies he order'd *John* to march through *Calabria*, and, having driven the *Goths* out of those Parts, to meet him, with the rest of the Forces, near *Rome*, towards which he set sail, and landed at *Portus*. *John*, being advanc'd as far as *Capua*, and having done some Execution in his Passage, durst not attempt that City, tho' garrison'd by no more than Three Hundred Men, and tho' he himself was follow'd by the choicest of the *Roman* Army. This gave *Belisarius* just Grounds to fear lest the Besieg'd in *Rome*, who were almost starv'd, would listen to *Totilas*, who persuaded 'em earnestly to surrender. He knew himself unable by main Force to relieve the City, and therefore endeavour'd by some means to victual it. *Totilas* had built a Bridge cross the *Tiber*, where it was narrowest, about Eleven Miles from *Rome*, on either Side of which he rais'd wooden Towers, and put good Garrisons into 'em, the better to hinder any Vessels loaden with Provisions from passing by into the Town: *Belisarius* therefore fasten'd two Barks together, and rais'd a Tower which was higher than those the Enemy had at the Bridge,

His Endeavour to relieve Rome

and

and the same time he man'd out two hundred Pinnaces, which were full of Port-holes to shoot at the Enemy; on board of these he put Corn and other Provisions, and posted a good Body of Horse and Foot on either Side the Bank, for the better Security of *Portus*, which he garrison'd, and committed to the Care of *Isaac*, one of his Lieutenants, with express Order not to quit his Post, tho' he heard *Belisarius* had miscarry'd and was slain; for all the other Forts in the Country being in the Enemies Hands, he reserv'd that as a Place of Retreat for the Army upon any unfortunate Accident. He himself conducted the Pinnaces, and tow'd the Bark after, putting a Cock-boat upon it loaden with combustible Materials; and that his Stratagems might have the better Success upon the Enemy, he order'd *Bessas* to make a general Sally, and alarm their Camp. *Bessas*, who drove a very beneficial Trade with the Corn that had been stor'd up for the Use of the Garrison, selling it to the People at an exorbitant Price, desir'd the Siege might be prolong'd, and therefore neglected these and several other precedent Orders from *Belisarius*, who was as desirous to raise it.

By that time *Belisarius* was got near the Bridge with his Pinnaces he found an Iron Chain lying cross the River, which, with no small Slaughter of the *Goths* who were plac'd there to secure it, he easily remov'd, after which he resolutely attack'd the Bridge, and order'd the Barks to attempt one of the Towers, out of which the *Goths* did great Execution upon the *Romans*, 'till it was set on Fire by the Cock-boat, which consum'd that, and Two Hundred of the Enemy in it; so that they might easily have master'd the Bridge, and pass'd on without any Opposition into *Rome*, had not Fortune fought against them, or rather Providence, which
often

often eludes all Human Precaution. For the good Success the *Romans* met with at the Bridge was unluckily carry'd to *Portus* before the Service was perfected, whereupon *Isaac* the Governor, who was resolv'd to have his share in the Honour of the Action, in Breach of the Orders and Trust he had receiv'd from the General, went with an Hundred Horse and charg'd the Enemies Quarters on the other Side the River, in which *Roderick*, an experienc'd and resolute Captain, commanded for *Totilas*: *Roderick* was wounded in the first Onset, together with several more of the *Goths*, who either suspecting that Party was follow'd by other Forces, or designing to draw the *Romans* into farther Danger, quitted their Post, but seeing *Isaac* enter the Trenches and amuse himself with the Pillage, they return'd briskly upon him, and took him with most of his Followers Prisoners. *defeated*

Belisarius, who knew nothing of these Transactions, being inform'd that *Isaac* was in the Enemies Hands, concluded *Portus*, in which he had left his Wife and all his Equipage, was taken, whereby all Hopes of a Retreat were cut off unless he could speedily recover the Town; whereupon he drew back his Forces, with an Intent to charge the Enemy before they could be prepar'd to receive him: But when upon his Return he found how *Isaac* by his Rashness and Disobedience had ruin'd all, he took it so to Heart that he fell into a Feaver, which very much endanger'd his Life, and perplex'd the Affairs of the Empire. *Roderick* dy'd of his Wounds shortly after the Action, at which *Totilas* was so incens'd that he put *Isaac* to death.

The *Romans* that were within the Walls were so disharten'd with these Disappointments, and pinch'd with Hunger and Necessity, that they grew negligent and tumultuous, whilst *Bessas*, who was wholly

A. D. 547.

ly intent upon his own Profit, neglected his Charge, and suffer'd the Soldiers to live at Discretion. This Remissness, as well in the Governor as the Garrison, encourag'd Four *Isaurians*, posted as Sentinels near the *Porta Asinaria*, to make Proposals to *Totilas* of receiving his Forces into the Town. *Totilas* readily embrac'd the Overture, and, upon repeated Assurances of their Sincerity, led his Troops in the silence of the Night near the Gate, which was, according to their Agreement, open'd to him by the *Isaurians*. Upon the first Alarm, *Bessas*, who perceiv'd the Town was betray'd, fled out at another Gate with such as were able to follow him, so that there were not above Five Hundred Soldiers who fled for Sanctuary into the Churches, of which no more than Five and Twenty were kill'd, together with Sixty of the Inhabitants; for as *Totilas* was going in the Morning to St. *Peter*'s Church to Prayer, *Pelagius* the Deacon met him, and throwing himself at his Feet, with the Gospels extended in his Hands, implor'd him to pardon and spare the Inhabitants, which, after much Importunity, he obtain'd; for *Totilas* forbad his Soldiers to kill any more, or to offer Violence to the Women, but gave 'em leave to pillage the City, reserving the choicest of the Spoils to his own use. The Houses of the Patricians abounded in Wealth, but the most considerable of all was that of *Bessas*, who by his Exactions had hoarded up immense Treasures for the use of *Totilas*. The Goths spent several Days together in stripping the Inhabitants, the most wealthy of whom were reduc'd to so much Poverty, that many of the Senators, and *Rusticiana*, *Boetius* his Widdow, and Daughter of *Symmachus*, a Matron of most exemplary Charity, went begging their Bread from Door to Door. The *Goths* had a great

Rome taken and pillag'd.

Desire

Desire to put this Lady to Death, because, as they said, she hir'd the *Roman* Officers to pull down the Images of *Theodorich*, for his Injustice and Cruelty to her Husband and Father; but *Totilas* preserv'd her, and the rest of the Women, from the Insolence of the Soldiers, to his great Honour and Reputation. Thus *Rome* fell into the Hands of the *Goths*, in the Second Year of the Siege, and Twelfth of the War, *An. Dom.* 547.

VII. *Totilas* being now Master of the Capital City of the Universe, manag'd his Fortune with much Moderation. At first he reproach'd the *Roman* Senators for their Ingratitude to the *Goths*, and threaten'd, in the Heat of Passion, to make 'em his Slaves, but pardon'd them presently after at the Intercession of *Pelagius*, whom he sent with *Theodorus*, a *Roman* Orator, as his Embassadors to the Emperor, with Letters full of Respect, in which he desir'd to live in Amity with him, as *Theodorich* had done with *Anastasius*; upon which Consideration he promis'd to reverence him as his Father, and assist him against all his Enemies whomsoever: But if *Justinian* rejected the Offer of Peace, he threaten'd to level *Rome* flat with the Ground, to kill all the Senate, and carry the War into *Illyricum*. The Emperor return'd no other Answer than that *he had constituted* Belisarius *his Vice-gerent in the West, who accordingly had full Power relating to all Things of that nature in those Parts.* Totilas was so provok'd at this Answer, that he resolv'd to continue the War, and demolish *Rome*, in which he said he would not leave one Stone upon another. Accordingly he threw down a Third Part of the Wall, and was ready to set Fire to the most beautiful Buildings in the City, when he receiv'd Letters from *Belisarius*, dissuading him from his Pur-

Totilas sends an Embassy to the Emperor.

pose: He told him, *If he continu'd Conqueror he ought to preserve a City which would be his own by right of Conquest, and was the most beautiful of all his Dominions; that it would be to his own Loss if he destroy'd it, and would redound much to his Dishonour:* For Rome *having been rais'd to her Majesty and Grandeur by the Virtue and Industry of former Ages, Posterity would consider him as a common Enemy to Mankind, in depriving 'em of an Example and living Representation of the Worth and Magnanimity of their Ancestors.* On the other hand, *if in the Course of the War he should prove unfortunate, he told him he would highly oblige the Emperor in the Preservation of that beloved City, and who therefore would be more inclinable to grant him easy Terms; whereas, in the Ruin of it, he could expect no Mercy from an incens'd Conqueror.* Totilas having seriously consider'd the Substance of these Letters, and how much Reason they contain'd, proceeded no farther in his Designs against the City. After this he march'd with his Army into *Lucania*, and other Parts of *Italy*, where the *Goths* through their Presumption and ill Management had lately been worsted.

Belisarius being in the mean time re-inforc'd with some fresh Troops from *Constantinople*, retook *Tarentum* and *Spoleto*, and seeing *Totilas* had quitted *Rome*, in which he left no Garrison for its Defence, for having demolish'd so much of the Walls he thought it was in no Man's Power to defend it against him, but that he might return at his Pleasure, he was earnestly desirous to recover that City once more to the Emperor; and therefore leaving a competent Garrison in *Portus*, he march'd thither with the rest of his Army, and resolv'd to hold it. Accordingly he dug a large Ditch round it, repair'd the Walls with as much Diligence and in the best

Belisarius regains Rome, and fortifies it.

Manner he could, provided it with Necessaries, and recall'd such of the Inhabitants as had fled from the Fury of the *Goths*, restoring to every Man his own House and Possession, and promising an Immunity from Taxes to such as would settle themselves there. Upon this News *Totilas* return'd back instantly to *Rome*, not doubting but to have it yielded up at his first Appearance; but he met with a greater Resistance than before, and quickly found how much Difference there was betwixt *Bessas* and *Belisarius*: After several Assaults, in which he was beaten back with great Loss, he was forc'd to draw off, and retir'd to *Tibur*, the Castle of which he re-built, and continu'd for some time quietly in it. Here he first experimented how much some People are influenc'd in their Duty and Obedience by Fortune; the *Goths*, that hitherto had caress'd and extoll'd him, like a God ador'd him, and follow'd him as their Deliverer, began now to be weary of their Allegiance, and reproach'd him for his ill Conduct, in suffering *Rome*, which had cost them so much Time and Labour, to be so easily recover'd by the Imperialists: And this ill Humour towards him made 'em so refractory, that when he repar'd to march to the Siege of *Perusia*, which held out against him for the Emperor, they refus'd to obey his Orders, 'till in a set Speech he made an Apology to 'em.

Totilas, after he had taken *Rome*, confin'd several of the *Roman* Senators with their Wives in *Campania*, but in his Absence they were set at Liberty by *John*, who routed a strong Party of *Goths* near *Capua*: Hereupon he resolv'd to be reveng'd upon him for the Disgrace, and march'd immediately in quest of him. *John* had encamp'd himself in *Apulia*, and had undoubtedly been destroy'd with all his Forces, if *Totilas* had made a right Use of the

Advantage his Diligence in the Expedition had put into his Hands; for the *Goths* exceeded the *Romans* ten to one in Number, and might easily have surrounded them, if *Totilas* could have waited with Patience 'till the Morning, but he fell unadvisedly upon them in the Night, and the *Romans* upon the first Alarm escap'd by the Benefit of the Darkness, with the Loss of no more than a Hundred of their Men, into *Otranto*. After this there was very little Action on either Side for some time, both Parties seeming careful to preserve what they were in Possession of, and to despair of wresting any more out of their Enemies Hands, especially the *Romans*, who shortly after lost their chief Strength in the Person of *Belisarius*, who was recall'd by the Emperor to *Constantinople*, which City was this Year more terrify'd than hurt by an Earthquake; which, together with the taking a prodigious Whale, and the overflowing of the *Nile*, administer'd to the Inhabitants many Speculations. This Whale was call'd *Porphyrion*, and had for the Space of Fifty Years, very much infested the Seas in those Parts, drowning Ships, and driving the Sailers, who study'd to avoid her, into great Inconveniencies; *Justinian* had many ways attempted to destroy her, but still to no Purpose, 'till now pursuing a great Number of Dolphins she came so near the Shoar that she struck upon the Mud, where the Country People hew'd her with great Axes but were unable to kill her, so that they were forc'd to drag her with great Ropes a-shore, and upon measuring found her to be thirty Cubits long and ten broad.

A Conspiracy against the Emperor.

Before *Belisarius* his Arrival at *Constantinople* a Conspiracy, form'd against the Emperor, was luckily discover'd. The chief Person concern'd in it was *Artabanes*, who slew the Tyrant *Gontharis* in *Africa*

Chap. II. LVI. Juſtinian.

Africk, as has been obſerv'd before; for this Service the Emperor made him his General in that Province, but being in Love with *Projecta*, *Juſtinian*'s Neece, and *Areobindus*'s Widdow, whom he earneſtly deſir'd to Marry, he was, upon his own Requeſt, recall'd to *Conſtantinople*, where he hop'd to effect the Match, the Lady her ſelf being very inclinable to it. Upon his Return to Court the Emperor receiv'd him very graciouſly, made him General of his Forces in *Conſtantinople*, and gave him the Command of all the Confederates in thoſe Parts, ſo that nothing was wanting now to compleat his Happineſs but the eſpouſing *Projecta*; but as he was preparing himſelf, with much Satisfaction for the Nuptials, a former Wife, whom upon ſome ſmall Diſcontents he had deſerted, appear'd, and forbad the Banes, whereupon *Projecta* was marry'd to another. *Artabanes*, enrag'd to find he had not Intereſt enough, after all his Services, to Divorce himſelf from a diſcarded Wife for the ſake of another, grew ſo diſaffected to the Emperor, that he immediately reſolv'd upon his Ruin, uniting himſelf to *Arſaces*, an *Armenian*, his near Relation, and other dangerous Male-contents. *Arſaces* had lately been convicted of corresponding ſecretly with the King of *Perſia*, and conſpiring with him againſt the Emperor, for which however he receiv'd no other Puniſhment than a few Stripes upon his Back, and being led through the City upon a Camel; for *Juſtinian* ſtill continu'd him in his Employments, and ſuffer'd him to appear at Court as formerly, notwithſtanding which he grew ſo diſcontented that he vow'd to be reveng'd. *Juſtinian* had lately diſoblig'd his Nephew *Germanus*, and his Sons, by with-holding from 'em an Eſtate had been left 'em, which *Artabanes* and *Arſaces* thought Provocation ſufficient to make 'em join with them in their Designs against him; upon which Consideration they discover'd themselves to *Justinus, Germanus* his eldest Son, who, tho' but young, was valiant and wary; they propos'd to kill *Justinian* one Night as he sate up late with some old Priests, with whom he frequently convers'd without his Guards, and declare *Germanus* Emperor: The Execution was to be deferr'd 'till *Belisarius* his Arrival, who otherwise, upon notice of what was done, might levy an Army in his Passage through *Thrace*, and oppose the new Emperor; for which Reason they resolv'd to dispatch him at the same time, together with *Marcellus*, Captain of the *Palatine* Soldiers. *Justinus* listen'd patiently to what they propos'd, but was so far from joining with them, that he immediately reveal'd it to his Father, who made a *discover'd.* Discovery of it to *Marcellus*; and he, upon a full Assurance that the Conspirators were in earnest, reported it to the Emperor, who order'd 'em all to be seiz'd, examin'd, and committed to Prison, which was the only Punishment inflicted upon 'em.

A. D. 548.

Whilst the Emperor's Person was thus in Danger the Empire it self was threaten'd with almost a total Dissolution by her Enemies, who began to Invade her on every part; the *French*, taking the Advantage of the Wars in *Italy*, seiz'd on the greatest part of *Venetia*; for as on one side the *Romans* were unable to resist 'em, so the *Goths* on the other found it impossible to contend with both Parties at once. About the same time the *Heruli* broke into *Illyricum* and *Thrace*, spoiling the Country and destroying the Inhabitants; whilst the *Gepidæ* seiz'd on *Sirmium*, and the greatest part of *Dacia*, which *Justinian* had lately recover'd from the *Goths*. These Calamities were attended by a Mutiny in the Garrison *Belisarius* had left in *Rome*;

for

for being offended at *Conon* their Governor, who had juftly provok'd them by his Avarice, they kill'd him, and arrogantly fent to the Emperor to excufe the Matter, threatning, that unlefs he pardon'd 'em, they would revolt, and deliver up the City to *Totilas*; who, taking the Advantage of this Mutiny, and the Abfence of *Belifarius*, march'd with a powerful Army againft it, and, after feveral Sallies and Affaults, was receiv'd into it by the Treachery of fome *Ifaurians*, who following the Example of their Countrymen, and offended for that they had not receiv'd their Arrears, open'd one of the Gates and let him in, the Inhabitants, who dreaded his Fury, fhifting for themfelves in the beft manner they could. He now behav'd himfelf with more Moderation than before, for inftead of deftroying the Walls he repair'd the Breaches, added new Fortifications, replanted the City with *Goths* and *Romans*, provided it with all manner of Neceffaries, recall'd the Senators, celebrated the *Circenfian* Games, and omitted nothing that he thought proper to fecure it to his Obedience, and ingratiate himfelf with the *Italians*. And indeed he was oblig'd both in Honour and Intereft to preferve *Rome*, for having fome time before fent to demand from the King of the *Franks* his Daughter in Marriage, the King reply'd, He would never beftow her on a Man who was not, nor never could be King of *Italy*, fo long as he was unable to preferve the Capital City, which, after he had taken, he improvidently difmantl'd, and abandon'd to the Enemy. Being thus once more Mafter of *Rome*, he fent and defir'd a Truce from the Emperor, who was fo far from condefcending to it, that he would not fo much as fee the Meffenger, for which Reafon *Totilas* refolv'd to purfue the War with more Vigour than ever,

A. D. 550.
Rome a-*gain taken by* Totilas.

and laid Siege to *Centumcella*, call'd at present *Civita-vecchia*, which *Diogenes*, the Governor of it, defended with so much Courage, that he was forc'd to raise the Siege, and pass'd with his Army into *Sicily*, which he extreamly wasted; and to drive him from whence *Justinian* sent *Artabanes*, whom he had pardon'd for his late Treason against his Person, and made him General of his Forces in *Thrace*. At the same time he nam'd *Germanus*, his Nephew, General against the *Goths* in *Italy*. *Germanus* his late Services in *Africk* had acquir'd him great Reputation, which he was ambitious to improve by the Glory of recovering *Italy*. He had newly marry'd *Metasuntha*, the Daughter of *Amalasont*, and Widdow of *Vitiges*, lately deceas'd, whom he intended to carry with him into *Italy*, concluding the *Goths* would be asham'd to lift up their Hands against the Grand-Daughter of *Theodorich*; and *Totilas* himself was not without fear that they would receive him for their lawful Prince in Respect of his Wife: He was a Man generally belov'd by the Soldiers, whom he had frequently oblig'd by his Liberality, so that in his Passage through *Thrace* he quickly rais'd a very powerful Army, many who by their frequent Defeats in *Italy* had been dispers'd, and withdrawn themselves from the Service, coming in to him; and the Barbarians inhabiting about the *Danube*, allur'd by his Fame, join'd themselves with him, and brought him Presents of Mony and Provisions.

On the other Hand the *Goths* were exceedingly dispirited, especially when they consider'd they were to make War against the Posterity of *Theodorich*, and to Encounter with a General of consummated Experience, and universally belov'd by the Soldiers; so that the Emperor's Affairs began to put

Germanus declar'd General in Italy.

LVI. Justinian.

on a new Face, and the Eyes of the whole Empire were fix'd upon *Germanus*, who, as a Prelude to his future Success, in his Passage through *Thrace* drove the *Sclavi* out of it. These People, observing the Emperor's Forces wholly employ'd in the *Persian* and *Italian* Wars, had pass'd the *Danube* to the Number of Three Thousand Men, and having divided themselves into two Bodies wasted all *Thrace* and *Illyricum*, roving about the Country, and committing unheard of Cruelties, 'till hearing of *Germanus* his Approach, who, they conceiv'd, was sent General against them, terrify'd at the Apprehension of so renown'd a Commander, they relinquish'd their former Designs upon *Thessalonica*, and the Towns adjacent, and departed in a precipitate March over the Mountains of *Illyricum* into *Dalmatia*; whereupon *Germanus* order'd his Army to be ready within three Days to march into *Italy*, where a good Number of *Roman* Soldiers, collected into one Body, were ready to receive him. But the Hand of Fate, which now lay heavy upon the *Roman* Empire, had otherwise dispos'd of Affairs; for *Germanus* was suddenly seiz'd with a violent Distemper, which put an end to all his great Designs, and Life together. He dy'd universally lamented by all sorts of People, being a Person of as great Excellencies as any in the Empire, for he was a good Man, a brave Soldier, and experienc'd General, just in Peace, active in War, grave and severe in the Court, but facetious and obliging at his Table; so free from lawless Ambition, or factious Contention, that tho' he was offer'd the Empire by *Artabanes* and his Accomplices, as we observ'd before, who he knew were able to make good their Offer, and tho' the Emperor had in many Respects disoblig'd him, yet he gave the World ample Proofs

A. D. 551.

Germanus dies.

of

of his Integrity, in rejecting the Purple, and discovering the Treason.

Upon his Death the *Sclavi* took fresh Courage, and made another Irruption into the *Roman* Provinces, whether induc'd to it by their own rapacious Inclinations, or hir'd by *Totilas*, who was alarm'd at the Emperor's Preparations against him, and which therefore he was willing to divert another way. They proceeded up as far as *Greece*, which they cruelly wasted, and having defeated a Party sent against 'em near *Adrianople*, they seem'd to threaten the Imperial City it self, 'till by degrees grown careless and licentious, they were at length routed, and glad to repass the *Danube* with what Booty they could carry off.

Totilas his Progress in Sicily.

In the mean time *Totilas* prevail'd wonderfully in *Sicily*, which he entirely conquer'd and ransack'd; for tho' the Emperor had sent *Liberius*, a Citizen of *Rome*, into that Island the Year before, and order'd *Artabanes* to follow him; and tho' *Liberius* forc'd his Way into *Syracuse* with the Fleet under his Command, and reliev'd the City, which was closely Besieg'd by the *Goths*, yet this Year he was starv'd out of it by the Enemy, who exceeded him in Numbers, and forc'd to retire to *Palermo*, whilst *Artabanes* his Squadron met with a greater Disaster, for it was dispers'd by a furious Storm, which drove him upon the Island of *Malta*, where, with much Difficulty, he sav'd himself. Whereupon *Totilas*, finding no Person in *Sicily* able to oppose him, left Four sufficient Garrisons in it for the Security of the Island, and return'd back into *Italy*, whither the Emperor had sent *Justin* to Command in the room of his Father *Germanus*, and and appointed *John*, the Son of *Vitalian*, and *Germanus* his Son-in-Law, to be his Lieutenant; but before these Generals could arrive in *Italy*, where

Chap. II. LVI. Juſtinian.

the *Goths* prevail'd with their accuſtom'd Succeſs, the Emperor chang'd his Reſolution, and declar'd *Narſes*, the Eunuch, Generaliſſimo of all his Forces in thoſe Parts. Theſe Variations in the Emperor's Councils very much retarded his Affairs at the preſent, tho' *Narſes* prov'd afterwards a very fortunate Commander, and drove the *Goths* out of *Italy*. He was by Nation a *Perſian*, but had been long in the Service of *Juſtinian*, who made him Pay-Maſter of the Army, and a Patrician, which Honour and Truſt he very well deſerv'd, for he was a Perſon of great Capacity, and well acquainted with all Political and Military Virtues. *Evagrius* tells us he was ſo regular in his Devotion, and apply'd himſelf ſo frequently in his Prayers to God, that the Virgin *Mary* appear'd to him, and preſcrib'd him the Seaſons proper for him to engage the Enemy, with whom he never encounter'd before he had firſt receiv'd a Sign from Heav'n; tho' this Account favours ſomething of a Fable, yet it ſuffices to ſhow how requiſite a regular and exemplary Devotion is to the Office and Duty of a General. But before we attend him into *Italy*, it will be convenient to take a ſhort view of Affairs in the Eaſt, at leaſt ſo much of 'em as are interwoven with thoſe of the Empire.

A. D. 552. Narſes declar'd General in Italy.

Choſroes being frighten'd into a Retreat by *Beliſarius*, after a long and expenſive Expedition, advanc'd Northward as far as *Ardabigara*, a Town in *Aſſyria*, where he began to reflect upon his Ignominious Flight, as he then term'd it, and reſolv'd once more to Invade the *Roman* Territories, being encourag'd to it by his *Perſian* Prieſts, and a ſhameful Overthrow of Thirty Thouſand *Romans*, who taking the Advantage of the Difficulties *Choſroes* then labour'd under (for his Territories were grievouſly viſited by the Plague before mention'd, and his Son had conſpir'd againſt him) invaded *Perſarmenia*,

The Romans defeated by the Perſians.

menia, and were defeated by *Nabades,* who drew 'em first into an Ambush, and after that entirely defeated 'em. The *Romans* fled with so much Precipitation, that they destroy'd all their Horses in the Flight, and lost such a great quantity of Arms, and all their Baggage, that the whole State of *Persia* appear'd visibly enrich'd by so important and unexpected a Victory. Upon this Success *Chosroes* made an Inroad into *Mesopotamia*, where, in the Opinion of *Evagrius* and *Procopius,* he seem'd to War against God rather than Man, and therefore met with a Success suitable to his Irreligion and Impiety. In his first Invasion he had been forc'd to retire from before *Edessa*, without performing any thing against that City, and grew very much incens'd to think he should be thus shamefully overcome by the God of the Christians, for which reason he threaten'd now to make the Inhabitants Slaves in spight of the Deity that protected them, and turn their City into a Pasture for Cattle; but notwithstanding these presumptious Menaces, he receiv'd such a Repulse upon his first Attempt, that he was willing the Citizens should buy their Safety with a round Sum of Mony, for he apprehended a second Disgrace before the Town and his Apprehensions were improv'd by several Dreams, and other superstitious Observations. Hereupon a Conference was procur'd, wherein he demanded all the Treasure in the City, which the Besieg'd, with much Indignation, refus'd, and he in great Fury commanded the Works to be carry'd on. He rais'd a prodigious Machine, which over look'd the Walls of *Edessa*, from whence he play'd without Intermission upon the Town, easily defeating those who appear'd in its Defence. The *Romans* on the other side drew a Mine, which they continu'd 'till they came under the middle of the Machine, but then finding the *Persians* had discover'd

Chosroes Besieges Edessa;

discover'd and were countermining 'em, they stopped the Work, and dug a hollow Vault hard by, filling it with dry Logs steep'd in the Oil of Cedar, and *Assyrian* Pitch; to this they set Fire, which prevailing at length forc'd the *Persians* to abandon the Work.

Chosroes, perceiving his Machine was disabled, and that his Labour and Expence had been hitherto unsuccessful, sate still in his Trenches for several Days, thinking to lull the Inhabitants into a fatal Security, and then fall unexpectedly upon 'em. In this Design he had unavoidably succeeded, had not a Peasant awaken'd the Watch, and warn'd 'em of the Enemy's Approach. The *Romans*, being thus alarm'd, receiv'd the Assailants with so much Vigour that they drove the *Persians* with great Slaughter back to their Camp, and seiz'd on their Ladders which they had us'd in the Assault. This Attempt was follow'd by two or three more, in all which the *Persians* miscarry'd, and *Chosroes* was so discourag'd, that upon some very reasonable Conditions he agreed to raise the Siege, and never more infest *but raises the Siege.* the *Roman* Territories; accordingly he demolish'd his Works, and return'd with his Army into *Persia*.

The Christian Reader will readily ascribe the Safety of this City to the immediate Assistance of God Almighty, whose Power and Protection visibly appear'd in the Preservation of it, without attributing it to the efficacious Virtue of a pretended Image of our Saviour, thrown, in their Extremity, by the Besieg'd into the Vault, which, setting Fire to the Wood pil'd up in it, consum'd the Machine, render'd the Flame unquenchable, and constrain'd *Chosroes* to raise the Siege. However we may observe from this Account, that the Use of Images began first in those Days to prevail in the Church,

Church, as did likewſe the Veneration of Relicks; tho' as yet no outward Adoration or Religious Worſhip was paid to either, but was a Novelty, not properly ſaid to be eſtabliſh'd and confirm'd 'till the Eighth Century, as we may have Occaſion to obſerve hereafter.

Choſroes, tho' ſhamefully diſappointed in his laſt Attempts, and tho' he had conſented to a Truce for Five Years with *Juſtinian*, could not continue idle at home, but apply'd himſelf to ſome new Projects. *His Deſigns upon Lazica.* The *Lazians*, who had revolted from the *Romans*, and embrac'd the Protection of the *Perſians*, grew weary of their new Maſters; at the ſame time that *Choſroes* earneſtly deſir'd to gain an abſolute Poſſeſſion of the whole Country, which he knew lay very commodious for the reſt of his Dominions; for being once Maſter there he could curb the *Iberians*, reſtrain the *Hunns* from their Incurſions into the *Perſian* Provinces, and favour 'em in any Deſigns they had upon the *Roman* Territories; for *Lazica* was the only Barrier againſt the Barbarians of Mount *Caucaſus*: It would open the *Perſians* a Paſſage into the *Euxine* Sea, facilitate the Conqueſt of *Capadocia*, *Galatia* and *Bithynia*, and lead 'em up to the very Gates of *Conſtantinople* it ſelf. He knew the *Lazians* were no way pleas'd with their late Change, but very averſe to the Humour and Diſpoſition, as well as Religion of the *Perſians*, and therefore the more likely to effect an Alteration, which he was reſolv'd, if poſſible, to prevent; the beſt Expedient for which he thought was to murder *Gubazes* their King, to tranſport the Natives, and people the Country with *Perſians* and others, who would be well affected to his Intereſt. Theſe his Deſigns were diſcover'd to *Gubazes*, by ſome whom the King of *Perſia* had employ'd to effect 'em, and by *Gubazes* to the Emperor, from whom

he

he begg'd Pardon, in the Name of his Subjects, for what was pass'd, and his Assistance and Protection for the future. The Emperor readily embrac'd the Opportunity, and sent him Eight Thousand Men under the Command of *Dagisthæus*, a young unexperienc'd Officer, uncapable of any Warlike Undertaking.

However, having join'd his Forces with those of the *Lazians*, he sat down before *Petra*, which was garrison'd by the *Persians*, and stor'd with all manner of Provisions. *Chosroes*, alarm'd at this sudden Revolution, sent a great Army of Horse and Foot, under the Conduct of *Mermeroes*, his High Chamberlain, to the Relief of the Place; of which *Gubazes* being advis'd, he by his Letters desir'd *Dagisthæus* to detach Part of his Forces to secure the Passage beyond the *Phasis*, and with the rest push on the Siege 'till he was Master of the Town; whilst he march'd with his own Army to the Borders of *Lazica*, for the Security of another Passage, and hir'd some *Alans* to defend those Parts. But *Dagisthæus*, instead of sending Forces sufficient to make good the Passage, and appearing in Person at the Action, detach'd no more than Two Hundred of his Men, and with the rest did little or nothing against *Petra*, which he had often an Opportunity of taking, and which he as often neglected. By this means he gave *Mermeroes* an Opportunity of obtaining the Pass with the Loss of no more than a Thousand *Persians*, whereupon *Dagisthæus* rais'd the Siege, and fled in a great Consternation toward the *Phasis*, leaving his Camp to be rifled by the Garrison. *Mermeroes* proceeded at the Head of his Army to *Petra*, the Garrison of which Place consisted at first of Fifteen Hundred Men, but were now reduc'd to Three Hundred and Fifty, Two Hundred of which were disabled and

unfit

unfit for Service. At his Arrival he could not but admire and commend the Courage, Fidelity and Self-denyal of the Defendants, who rather than cast the dead Bodies from the Walls, and thereby let the Besiegers know how much their Numbers were weaken'd, chose to keep 'em within the City, and suffer themselves to be almost stifled with the Stench. He repair'd the Breaches in the best manner he could, and garrison'd the Town with Three Thousand Men, after which he return'd with the rest of his Army into *Persarmenia*: For he was unable to distress *Lazica*, tho' he had forc'd the Passage, because he had no Ships to pass the River, which rising out of the *Armenian* Mountains runs through the whole Country, and is navigable for Ships of Burden eighteen Miles from the Sea. Besides, he knew *Justinian* was preparing to assist *Gubazes* with Supplies, as well of Mony as of a strong Army, under the Conduct of *Recithangus*, a *Thracian* by Birth, who had been bred up in the Wars from his Infancy, and was an experienc'd General.

The Persians defeated in Lazica.
At his Departure he left a Body of Five Thousand Men, under the Command of *Fabrozas* and other Commanders, who had Orders to Coast upon the Confines of *Lazica*; to get what Provisions they could, and transport all they were able to spare to *Petra*, for the Preservation of which Place he was very sollicitous. Of this when *Gubazes* was inform'd he join'd himself with *Dagisthæus*, and both together fell first upon a Thousand of the *Persians*, who had been sent out as a flying Guard to gain Intelligence, and secure the Camp from any Surprize: Of this Party not one escap'd, but were all either slain or taken Prisoners. Encourag'd by this Success, and being inform'd by the Captives of the Condition of the Camp, they unexpectedly set upon the main Body of the *Persian*

Chap. II. LVI. Juſtinian.

ans in the Dead of Night, and eaſily defeated 'em; purſuing 'em with much Execution up into *Iberia*, and cutting off ſeveral other *Perſian* Troops they met with in the Purſuit, who were conveying ſome Meal and other Proviſions into *Petra*, all the Avenues to which they now ſeiz'd upon, and ſo block'd up all Acceſs to the Town. In this Action the *Romans* became Maſters of the Enemies Camp, with all their Enſigns and Baggage, together with great Quantities of Arms, Mules, and Horſes.

When *Choſroes* was inform'd of this Overthrow he ſent *Corianes*, an old experienc'd Commander, at the Head of a conſiderable Army, conſiſting of *Alans* as well as *Perſians*, into *Lazica*, which he was willing to conquer, whatever it coſt him. For tho' he had often invaded the *Roman* Territories, and done unexpreſſible Miſchiefs to the Empire, yet he always return'd with much Loſs, which render'd him very ungrateful to the People, who call'd him *The Deſtroyer of their Nation*; but now he hop'd, by getting this Country into his Power, to obliterate the Memory of all his former Miſcarriages. *Corianes* advanc'd with his Army to the River *Hippus*, the greateſt in the whole Country of *Colchis*, where *Gubazes* and *Dagiſthæus* fell upon him, ſlew him, and overthrew his Army. The *Perſians* loſt the Camp, and the beſt of their Officers, together with a great Number of common Soldiers; they that ſurviv'd return'd home with a melancholy Account of the Invaſion.

In the mean time *Dagiſthæus*, whoſe Succeſs was owing more to Fortune and the Courage of *Gubazes* than his own Conduct, was, upon ſome Complaints preferr'd againſt him, recall'd; and *Beſſas*, the late Governor of *Rome*, was ſent in his ſtead, with expreſs Orders to recover *Petra* out of the Hands of the *Perſians*, who for a long time defended

Beſſas ſent General againſt the Perſians.

ed it with much Courage and Resolution. *Bessas* never behav'd himself with more Conduct and Gallantry than in this Service; he was an old Man, upwards of Seventy Years of Age, and encourag'd his Soldiers by the most powerful Exhortations, Examples of his own Valour. He mounted the scaling Ladder himself, and tho' he once fell from it, to the exceeding great Hazard of his Life, he return'd with an obstinate Bravery, which made the *Romans* push on with an invincible Constancy, and gain by Inches upon the *Persians*, who were as obstinate in the Defence. The Besieg'd had rais'd a great wooden Tower, from which they discharg'd Balls of Fire upon the *Roman* Rams, and at first put 'em into great Confusion, 'till part of the Tower took Fire, by means of a strong Southerly Wind which drove full upon it, and consum'd the miserable *Persians* that were in it, before they had time to shift for themselves. In the mean while *John Gazes* an *Armenian*, follow'd by several of his Countrymen, mounted a Rock where the City was thought impregnable, and which was said to have given Name to it, whilst both the *Romans* and *Persians* were engag'd on other Parts of the Wall; so that this, together with the unfortunate Accident of the Tower, open'd an easie Passage to the *Romans*, who by this means enter'd the Town, and took all the *Persians*, except Five Hundred who retir'd into the Castle, which, notwithstanding all the Threats and Persuasions *Bessas* could use, made it good against him 'till he set it on Fire, and then they perish'd in the Flames together with it. They that were taken were Seven Hundred and Thirty in Number, being all that were left of Two Thousand Three Hundred, and of whom no more than Eighteen were unwounded; so desperately obstinate were they in the Defence of a Place, which

Petra taken by the Romans.

the King of *Persia* judg'd to be of the last Consequence, as sufficiently appears by placing the choicest of his Men in it, and supplying it with so large a Provision of Arms and Victuals; for the *Romans* found in the Town Five Mens Furniture for every Soldier, and as much Corn and Salted Meat as would have supply'd a Siege of Five Years Continuance.

Bessas demolish'd the Walls of *Petra*, and sent all the Prisoners he had taken to *Justinian*, who highly commended him for his Valour and Conduct, which in some measure had made an Atonement for his ill Administration at *Rome*, and silenc'd the Murmurs of the People, who complain'd loudly against the Emperor for committing the Conduct of the Eastern War to a decrepit old Man, who had so notoriously ruin'd the *Roman* Interest by his Management in the West. And indeed that Success, which was chiefly owing to his Courage and Conduct, was shortly after ruin'd by his Precipitancy and Avarice. Had he, after the Reduction of *Petra*, fortify'd the Passes between *Iberia* and *Lazica*, he might have prevented the *Persians* from entring into the Country; but instead of this he retir'd into *Pontus* and *Armenia*, his own Government, there to scrape up what Riches he could, without engaging himself any farther in the Fatigues of War, and so in a manner quitted *Lazica* to the Enemy, for he left no more than Twelve Thousand Men in the Country, Three Thousand of which were garrison'd in *Archæopolis*, the chief City of all *Lazica*, the rest lay encamp'd near the *Phasis*, under the Command of *Odonachus*, with Orders to succour any Place that wanted their Assistance. *Mermeroes* hearing *Petra* was lost, and which as soon as the Season would permit he was preparing to relieve, march'd towards *Archæopolis*; but being inform'd of the

Disposition of the *Roman* Army, and unwilling to leave the Enemy at his Back, fac'd about, and directed his Course towards *Odonachus*; who, tho' he was a faithful and experienc'd Commander, finding himself unable to contend with *Mermeroes*, who far exceeded him in Numbers of Men, embark'd his Army in some Vessels riding at Anchor near his Camp, and carry'd with him all the Baggage he could get on Board, and cast the rest into the River, and so left an empty Camp to *Mermeroes*; who arriving shortly after, in a great Rage to be thus deluded of his expected Booty, set it on Fire, after which he return'd to *Archæopolis*, with an earnest Desire to get the Place; before which he receiv'd a remarkable Defeat, in a Sally made by the Defendants, which oblig'd him to raise the Siege, and employ his Army in taking in other Forts in the Country, in which he grew more powerful every Day, especially after another Truce was agreed upon between both the Crowns for Five Years longer.

For all this while the King of *Persia* was negotiating a Peace by his Embassadors at *Constantinople*, where they manag'd their Business with so much Address, that the Emperor at length consented to buy a Cessation with an immense Sum of Mony; which looking more like a Tribute than the Result of an honourable Agreement, rais'd great Discontents among the People, who complain'd that the *Persians* had now gain'd their Ends by virtue of a Treaty, which they never could obtain in the Field; that their main Ambition for a long time had been to make the *Romans* their Tributaries, which they had now effected under colour of a Cessation of Arms. Indeed this Truce contributed very much to the total Loss of *Lazica*, which was solely owing to that, and a Misunderstanding

that

that unseasonably arose between *Gubazes* and the Officers sent into that Country by the Emperor; of which we shall hear more hereafter.

VIII. But tho' Fortune seem'd to retard the Progress of the Emperor's Affairs in the East, she appear'd more favourable to him in *Italy*, whither *Narses* was sent to command his Armies, as has been observ'd before. Tho' *Narses* undertook the Service with much Chearfulness, and was a Person of approv'd Fidelity to the Emperor, yet the necessary Preparations, requisite for his Expedition, met with so many Obstacles, that *Totilas* grew exceedingly elevated, and scorning to confine himself and his Arms to *Italy*, he Mann'd out a Fleet consisting of Three Hundred Sail, which made a Descent into *Greece*, and pillaging the Isle of *Corfu*, sail'd up into the *Peloponnesus*, where several Vessels of the *Romans* fell into their Hands, among whom were some of the Transport Ships loaden with Provisions for *Narses* and his Army. In the mean time *Totilas*, who continu'd in *Italy*, had block'd up *Ancona* by Sea and Land, the only Town upon that Coast remaining to the Emperor. *Valerianus* was then at *Ravenna*, but being too weak to relieve it, he sent an Account of the Condition the Place was in to *John*, who had been sent by the Emperor to Command in *Italy*, as we observ'd before; but, Wintering with his Forces at *Salonæ*, was, by fresh Instructions, order'd to wait there for the Arrival of *Narses*. Tho' he paid a great Respect to the Emperor's Commands, yet, considering the Importance of *Ancona*, and the Extremity to which it was reduc'd, he ventur'd to disobey his Orders; and having Shipp'd the best of his Men in Forty Vessels he appear'd before *Ancona*, where *Valerianus* join'd him with a Squadron

The Goths *beaten at Sea.*

of Twelve more. Againſt theſe the *Goths* Mann'd out Forty Seven of their beſt Ships, and Engag'd them; but being unexperienc'd in Sea Fights, and unable to govern their Veſſels, they were eaſily defeated, and loſt all but Eleven of their Ships, which they themſelves ſet on Fire after they were landed, to prevent their falling into the Enemy's Hands. The *Goths* which lay before *Ancona*, hearing their Fleet was loſt, broke up in great haſte, and left the Camp to the *Roman* Generals, who, having reinforc'd the Garriſon, ſail'd away, *Valerianus* to *Ravenna*, and *John* to *Salonæ*. This Defeat very much impair'd the Intereſt of *Totilas*, and dejected his Followers, eſpecially when they were inform'd that *Artabanes* had recover'd all the Caſtles from the *Goths* in *Sicily*, from whence he ſent a powerful Aſſiſtance of Men and Ammunition to the *Romans* Beſieg'd in *Crotona*, which forc'd the *Goths* to raiſe the Siege, and at the ſame time they abandon'd *Tarentum*, which was immediately ſecur'd for the Emperor. This ſudden turn of Fortune, that began to frown upon the *Goths*, affected no one more than *Totilas* himſelf; having often apply'd to the Emperor by his Ambaſſadors, he knew he was reſolv'd againſt an Accommodation upon any Terms whatever, and that he hated the very Name of a *Goth*; and tho' at firſt he ſeem'd regardleſs of the War, yet he found that now he appear'd in earneſt. *Narſes* drew near with a very gallant Army, and Mony to pay off all the Arrears due to the Forces in *Italy*. He was attended not only by ſuch Troops as at a very great Expence he had been raiſing himſelf, which for Numbers of Men, and Proviſions of Arms, and all other Neceſſaries, appear'd like an Army worthy the Ancient Grandure of the *Roman* Majeſty, but by great Bodies of Auxiliaries, who chearfully follow'd

Chap. II. LVI. Justinian.

low'd his Ensigns; the *Gepidæ, Heruli, Hunns, Lombards,* and several Fugitive *Persians* rang'd themselves under his Banners, a great many old *Roman* Officers, with their Independant Companies, serv'd under him, and nothing was wanting that might advance his Honour, or add a Terror to his Enemies.

Being advanc'd as far as the Confines of *Venetia,* where several of the *Franks* had plac'd themselves, as we observ'd before, they resolutely deny'd him Passage, so that by the Advice of *John,* who was perfectly acquainted with those Parts, he pass'd along the Sea-Coast, and got safe with his whole Army to *Ravenna,* where he was join'd by *Valerianus* and *Justin,* to the great Confusion of *Totilas,* who thought it very improbable he would attempt to march that Way, by reason of the many Rivers that discharg'd themselves into the Sea, and therefore had posted *Teias,* his Successor in the Kingdom, a valiant Captain, with the choicest of his Army at *Verona,* where they had render'd all the Passages very Incommodious, and were prepar'd to fight the *Romans* if they advanc'd on that side, as they expected. *Narses arrives at Ravenna.*

Having staid a few Days in *Ravenna* to refresh his Army he took the Field, and directed his Course towards *Rome;* passing the *Rubicon* near *Ariminum,* or *Rimini,* he kill'd the Governor of the Garrison, plac'd there by *Totilas,* who sally'd out with a Design to surprize him: Without staying before that City, which was much dishearten'd by the Death of the Governor, he proceeded onward, and encamp'd upon the *Apennine* near that Place, which was memorable for the Defeat the *Gauls* receiv'd from *Camillus,* the *Roman* Dictator, and was call'd *Busta Gallorum,* because they that were slain were bury'd in it; to this Place *Totilas* was
like-

likewise advanc'd with a Resolution of fighting the *Romans* upon the first Advantage. Here *Narses* sent to *Totilas*, advising him *to listen to peaceable Councils, and not contend with the whole Strength of the* Roman *Empire*; but he order'd the Messengers to bid him appoint a Day for a pitch'd Battel, in case they found him resolv'd for War. *Totilas* receiv'd 'em with an undaunted Resolution, declar'd loudly for the War, and bade 'em inform *Narses, That Eight Days after he would not fail to meet him*. *Narses*, suspecting some Design in this Delay, prepar'd as if he was to fight the Day following, in which he did very wisely, for *Totilas* advanc'd with his whole Army in Order of Battel. There was a little Hill which stood near both Camps, and both had a Desire to gain it for Advantage of upper Ground. *Narses* by Night sent Fifty Men, who seiz'd it without any Opposition, and, being supported by fresh Supplies, maintain'd their Post so well that *Totilas* could not dislodge 'em, tho' he attempted it three times together.

Before the Fight began, *Cocas*, a bold and valiant *Goth*, advanc'd before the Ranks, and challeng'd any one on the *Roman* side to a single Combat; the Challenge was readily accepted by an *Armenian*, who kill'd his Adversary, and therein gave the *Romans* a Pledge of their future Victory. *Totilas* had all that Day expected to be join'd by Two Thousand Horse, who being near at Hand, he endeavour'd to delay the Fight 'till their Arrival; accordingly he sent an Offer of a Parly to *Narses*, and spun out the Time so long 'till they were come up to the rest of the Army; after which he drew the Army off, and commanded his Men to Dine, then shifting his Armour he led 'em out suddenly against the Enemy, thinking to surprize 'em; but *Narses*, who was apprehensive of his

his Troops to ſtir from the ſpot,
them to take a Morſel as they
ve a watchful Eye upon the Ene-
ho' otherwiſe an experienc'd and
in, committed a great Overſight
h in a great meaſure contributed to
; for he commanded his Men to
n their Lances, call'd *Pili*, where-
'em very much inferior in their
ons to the *Romans*, who us'd both
nces, and ſuch other Weapons as
he Courſe of Battel requir'd, fight-
Horſeback, or on Foot, ſometimes
at others ſurrounding the Enemy.
, together with that great Alacrity
which aroſe from their late Suc-
oſperous Condition of their Affairs   A. D.
with ſo much Courage, that the   553.
ken at the firſt Onſet, and at laſt *The* Goths
after they had loſt Six Thouſand *defeated.*
who were kill'd upon the Spot, be-
: fell in the Purſuit. The King
the Day irrecoverably loſt, fled
Followers in the Dark, and was pur-
mander of the *Gepidæ*, call'd *Aſ-*
ithout knowing who he was, gave
Wound with his Lance, of which
after, and was bury'd by his Sub- Totilas
called *Capræ*, after he had reign'd *ſlain.*
ven Years, with much Honour and
his Valour, Prudence, Juſtice and
pon his firſt Advancement to the
d the Affairs of the *Goths* in a ve-
Condition, which however proſper'd
is Adminiſtration, that he recover'd
men almoſt the entire Dominion of
Captive twice the Capital City of
the

the Universe. And indeed his Nation receiv'd a fatal stroke in his Death, for after him their Power and Sovereignty declin'd apace, so that in a short time after the very Name of that People was lost in *Italy*, at least they were so blended in Blood and Interest with the Native *Italians*, that they grew into one Nation.

The *Romans*, who knew nothing of the King's Death, continu'd in a full Pursuit after him, 'till a *Gothick* Woman assur'd 'em of his Death, and show'd 'em where he was bury'd: They look'd upon his Death, and the Certainty of it to be of so great consequence, that they would not believe the Report 'till they had digg'd up the Coffin; and when upon Examination they found it true, they reinterr'd it, and hasten'd with an Account of all to *Narses*, who immediately return'd Thanks to God Almighty for so important a Victory, and dismiss'd the *Lombards*, who were grown infinitely unruly, burning Houses, and ravishing Women, tho' they had taken Sanctuary in the Churches.

The *Goths* that escap'd the Swords of the *Romans* fled over the *Po*, and assembling themselves in the *Picentin*, they there made choice of *Teias* for their King, who was esteem'd the most valiant Man of their Nation, and had signaliz'd himself upon several Occasions in the Reign of *Totilas*. His first Care was to secure his Predecessor's Treasure, with which he endeavour'd to draw the *Franks* into his Assistance, doing every thing for the Advantage of his Subjects, that became a valiant and careful Commander; in the mean time *Narses*, making a right use of his Victory, commanded *Valerianus* to observe the Motions of the Enemy, and prevent their uniting themselves about the *Po*, whilst he, with the rest of the Army, march'd towards *Rome*, taking in several Towns in his way.

Teias chosen King.

Totilas,

Chap. II. LVI. Justinian.

Totilas, before *Narses* his Arrival in *Italy*, having burnt most of *Rome*, and considering he had not Men enough to guard the whole Circuit of the Town, had surrounded the strongest and most defensible Part of it, near *Adrian*'s Tomb, with a new Wall, and form'd it into the Nature of a Castle, which the *Goths* now took Care to Man with the best of their Nation, neglecting the other Parts. By this means they found themselves able to oppose the *Romans* for some time, but were in the issue forc'd to give Place to the prevailing Power of their Enemies; and, after having lost the Town, surrender'd the Castle upon assurance of their Lives, and *Narses* sent the Keys of the City to *Constantinople*. Thus was *Rome*, once more recover'd to the Obedience of *Justinian*, forc'd still, like a Sycophant, to follow the Interest of the most fortunate. This Victory, which prov'd of great Consequence to the Emperor's Affairs, was however very prejudicial to the *Roman* Senate; for the *Goths*, who now despair'd of the Dominion of *Italy*, kill'd all the Senators that fell into their Hands; such of them as *Totilas* had confin'd to *Campania*, and who, upon the Report that *Rome* was recover'd by *Narses*, were returning to the City, were miserably murder'd by the *Goths* Quarter'd upon the Road, who left not one Patrician alive. Three Hundred young Gentlemen, Sons of the Principal *Romans*, had been sent by *Totilas* beyond the *Po*, as Hostages, upon his first setting out against *Narses*, and were now all kill'd by *Teias*; so fatal was this Victory to many private Persons, which prov'd of so much Advantage to the Publick.

Teias, during the Siege of *Rome*, had dispos'd the best part of the Royal Treasure in the Castle of *Cuma*, and secur'd it with a strong Garrison,

A.D. 554.

upon

upon Notice whereof *Narses* detach'd a strong Party to Besiege the Castle, and another to Attempt *Centumcellæ*, whilst he himself staid behind to repair the Breaches of the Wall, and Ruins of the City. *Teias*, who knew of what Consequence the Loss of *Cuma* would prove, prepar'd to prevent it by a Battel, and march'd accordingly with the Strength of all his Forces to cover it, which, when *Narses* understood, he sent some Troops to intercept his Passage through *Tuscany*, but he fetching a large Compass by the Sea-Coast, declin'd the direct Road, and so got into *Campania*, whereupon *Narses* remanded his Forces, and march'd thither with his whole Army in order to fight him. *Teias* encamp'd on one side the River *Draco*, near the City *Nuceria*, and *Narses* on the other; the *Goths* being first in the Field, had seiz'd the Bridge, on which they built several Forts, and so had the Command of the River, and being Masters at Sea, seem'd to have the better of their Enemies. But *Narses* found means to have their Ships betray'd to him, and being reinforc'd by several Vessels out of *Sicily*, he thereby constrain'd the *Goths*, through want of Provisions, to betake themselves to the Fastnesses of the Mountains, where they soon repented of their Change, for they labour'd there under greater Difficulties than before: Wherefore chusing rather to die like Men in Battel, than perish by Famine, they descended suddenly, and fell resolutely upon the *Romans*, whom they took unprovided to receive them, and thereby gave a beginning to a very bloody Fight. The *Goths* were grown desperate, and resolv'd to venture all, and the *Romans* chose to die on the spot, rather than yield shamefully to their vanquish'd Enemies; the Obstinacy of the Combatants, and the Blood that was spilt on both sides, made this Battel,

A second Battel, wherein the Goths are worsted.

el, in *Procopius* his Opinion, as remarkable as any that had been fought formerly by the great Heroes of Antiquity, tho' he confesses it was remarkable for nothing so much as the conspicuous Valour of *Teias;* he, knowing the Fate of *Italy* depended upon the Fortune of that Day, stood in the first Rank holding out his Shield, and shaking his Lance in Defiance of his Enemies. The *Romans,* who had discover'd his Person, and knew his Death would put an End to the Controversie, directed their whole Force against him, some thrusting at him with their Spears, and others plying him with their Darts, which he receiv'd on his Shield, and kill'd many of the Assailants, who with all their strength were not able to drive him out of the Rank, nor force him to quit one Inch of Ground, or bend back upon his Target, 'till having shifted his Shield three times that Day, which was as often loaden with the Darts of the *Romans,* in the third Change he left his Breast expos'd naked, and was that Moment wounded by a Javelin, of which *Teias slain.* he instantly dy'd, and with him the Hopes of the *Goths,* who however gave not over the Fight 'till the Night parted them: Both Parties lay in their Armour 'till the Morning, and then they began again with fresh Appetite, nor would their savage Courage suffer 'em to give over 'till the second Night, their Hatred to each other carrying 'em through all Difficulties; for the *Goths* knew they were now contending for their last Stake, and the *Romans* scorn'd to defer their Fortune to a second Trial. At length the *Goths* were oblig'd to yield to the prevailing Numbers of the *Romans,* and consented to lay down their Arms, upon Condition they might be suffer'd to enjoy their Goods and Possessions without Molestation, paying a certain Tribute to the Emperor. This was agreed to by
Narses,

Narses, and the Benefit of the Agreement extended to all the rest of the *Goths* in *Italy* that voluntarily surrender'd themselves.

In the mean time, notwithstanding the Terror of this Victory, and the favourable Condescensions granted by *Narses,* *Cumæ* held out against the *Romans,* which *Teias* had committed to the Charge of *Aligern,* his Brother, who upon this Occasion gave great Proofs of his Strength and Activity. He depended much upon the Assistance of the *Franks*

The Franks and *Germans,* who, to the Number of Sixty Thouand Ger- sand Men and upwards, Subjects of *Theudebald,* or mans *move* *Tibaud,* Son of *Theodebert* King of *Mets,* were en-
to the Assi- ter'd *Italy*; the *Germans* were commanded by *Leu-*
stance of *tharis,* and the *Franks* by *Butelinus,* two Brothers,
the Goths. *Germans* by Nation, but in such great Credit with *Theudebald,* a weak unactive Prince, averse to any Military Attempts, that by their sole Authority they got the Proposals of the *Goths* to be embrac'd and were the Life of the Expedition, which they outwardly pretended was undertaken for the Assistance of the *Goths,* who promis'd to chuse *Bucelin* for their King, tho' in effect they intended nothing less than to make themselves absolute in *Italy.* *Narses* march'd with his Army into *Tuscany,* and sent a Detachment before to oppose the *Franks,* whilst he took in several Towns that still continu'd possess'd by the *Goths* in those Parts; most of 'em voluntarily surrender'd, *Luca* only continu'd obstinate, and gave him an Opportunity of manifesting not so much the Strength of his Arms as the noble Temper of his Mind. The Citizens had promis'd *Narses* to surrender, if they were not reliev'd by a certain Time, and had deliver'd up their Hostages accordingly; but tho' the Day was elaps'd before any Relief appear'd, they still continu'd obstinate, and refus'd to open their Gates. *Narses,* tho' much

offended

offended at this Affront, bore it with much Moderation, tho' the Hostages were in his Power, by which means he had his Revenge in his own Hands. However, he found a Way to frighten the Defendants, and by a feign'd Execution let 'em know what they had deserv'd; for having rais'd a Scaffold at a just Distance from the Walls he presented the Hostages to the View of the Inhabitants as prepar'd for Death, and by the Behaviour of the Executioners, the feign'd Consternation of the Attendants, and the Motion of the Axes, made 'em believe he had punish'd their Perfidy by a real Tragedy, tho' it was no more than an artificial Representation of it. The Relations of the Hostages, being thus deluded by their Senses, in loud Cries and Lamentations revil'd *Narses* for his cruel and impious Resentment: He answer'd, *He had done no more than their Treachery had deserv'd*; however he promis'd 'em *to work a Miracle for their sakes if by a speedy Repentance they could deserve it*, assuring 'em *that upon their Submission he would present all the Hostages alive into their Hands.* They laugh'd at his Presumption, in pretending to raise the Dead, yet made a scornful Promise to open the Gates so soon as they should find their Friends were safe; thinking, at the same time, that the Impossibility of the Condition would necessarily release them from the Performance of the Bargain: But they no sooner beheld their Relations alive, tho' not out of Danger, before they return'd to their old Obstinacy, and refus'd to yield the City. Then did *Narses* give the World a remarkable Instance of a truly *Roman* Magnanimity, for he dismiss'd the Hostages without any Ransom, sending 'em back into the Town with this Message, *That it was beneath him to flatter any with vain Hopes, and unworthy in them thus to impose upon him*; assuring 'em,

that

that unless they speedily submitted his Sword should force 'em to surrender, without the Help of their Hostages. These Men being thus discharg'd, and receiv'd into the City, highly extoll'd the Magnanimity, Justice and Clemency of *Narses*; and their loud Encomiums upon his Virtue prov'd more effectual than all his battering Rams and Engines, for the most forward and refractory among 'em were consenting to yield, when News came that the Army he had sent to the *Po*, to stop the Irruptions of the *Franks*, was entirely defeated through the Temerity of *Fulcaris*, Captain of the *Hunns*; who being an Officer of more Courage than Discretion, contrary to the Orders of *Narses*, had made an Excursion up to the Gates of *Parma*, where he was slain, and his Men routed; whereupon the rest of the Officers, who were posted in those Parts to serve as a Rampart against the *Franks*, retir'd in great Haste to *Faventia*. This Accident alter'd the Measures of the Besieg'd, who grew more confident of Relief than ever, and *Narses* found his Affairs much entangled by it; but accommodating himself to the present Exigency in the best manner he could, he encourag'd his desponding Soldiers in a chearful Speech, and prevail'd with the Officers lying at *Faventia* to return to their former Quarters in the *Parmesan*; and all this was done with the greatest Expedition imaginable, after which *Narses* block'd up *Luca* more closely than ever, for he was much affronted at their unhandsome Carriage towards him; but when the Besieg'd saw the Rams approaching, and all Things prepar'd for an Assault, they suffer'd themselves to be prevail'd upon *Luca deli-* by the Hostages, and after a Three Months Siege *ver'd to* deliver'd up the City to *Narses*, who accordingly *Narses*; took Possession of it in behalf of the Emperor.

By

By this time *Aligern*, who had call'd in the *Franks* to his Affiftance, confidering how readily they embrac'd his Caufe, conceiv'd, upon good Grounds, that what they did was not for his fake but their own; and that, if they drove *Narfes* out of *Italy*, they would fecure it for themfelves inftead of reinftating the *Goths*; he therefore judg'd it more reafonable to refign it up into the Poffeffion of the firft Owners, than fuffer it to be enjoy'd by Strangers: Accordingly he went and deliver'd *Narfes* the Keys of *Cumæ*, making him Mafter at *and* Cumæ. once of the Town and the Treafure of the *Goths*. *Narfes* receiv'd him very favourably, and entertain'd him in the Emperor's Service, which he readily embrac'd. The *Franks* in the mean while were advanc'd far into the Country, having divided themfelves into two Bodies; for *Bucelin*, coafting along the *Tyrrhenian* Shoar, had wafted all *Campania* and *Lucania*, as far as the Straights of *Rhegium*, on the one Side, whilft *Leutharis* pierc'd through *Apulia* and *Calabria*, on the other. The *French*, conducted by *Bucelin*, being Chriftians, abftain'd from the Violation of the Churches, and Things confecrated; whereas *Leutharis* and the *Germans*, who were for the moft part Pagans, committed all manner of Sacrilege, by which Means having exceedingly enrich'd his Army, *Leutharis* was defirous to return homeward: But *Bucelin*, who ftill flatter'd himfelf with Hopes of the Crown promis'd him by the *Goths*, and had therefore made an Oath to affift 'em with all his Power againft the *Romans*, was refolv'd to purfue his Fortunes. So that *Leutharis* returning by eafie Marches encamp'd with his Forces near *Fano*, a City in the Ma,fhes of *Ancona*, and not far from *Pifaro*, where *Artabanes*, and *Uldac*, an *Hunn* by Nation, were quarter'd with fome Troops of *Romans*, who briskly ly charg'd a Body of *Goths* that were join'd with the *Germans,* and entirely defeated them, which struck such a Terror into *Leutharis* his Soldiers that they thought of nothing but a Retreat, or rather a Flight, for they left all their Booty and Prisoners, together with the greatest part of their Baggage behind them; and in their Passage through *Lombardy* *A Plague* the Plague rag'd with so much Fury among 'em that *in the German Army.* they almost all dy'd of it, *Leutharis* himself was seiz'd among the rest, and dy'd in a raving Frenzy, tearing his Flesh from off his Bones, and sucking his own Blood, being thus deservedly punish'd by Divine Vengeance for his Sacrilege and Impiety.

In the mean time *Bucilinus,* having wasted all the Country as far as *Rhegium,* was returning toward Rome through *Campania,* and hearing *Narses* was marching with the main Strength of his Army against him he encamp'd near *Capua.* He had not as yet heard of the Misfortune arriv'd to his Brother, and being Thirty Thousand strong he thought himself able to encounter the *Romans,* and was very earnest to bring it to a Battel before his Army was diminish'd by a Dysentery, occasion'd by their eating new Raisins, which they devour'd with too much Greediness and Excess. Some *Heruli,* who had deserted to him from the *Romans,* inform'd him that there was a Misunderstanding between *Narses* and those of their Nation, who were for that Reason ready upon the first Onset to declare for him; upon which Encouragement he march'd out of his Entrenchments to attack the *Romans,* *The French defeated.* who receiv'd him so warmly, that, after a long and obstinate Fight, they were all cut off, with the Loss of no more than Eighty Men on the other Side. As this Action was remarkable for the great Loss the Barbarians sustain'd, of whom no more than Five Men are said to have escap'd, so was no less memorable for the Courage and Bravery of the *Roman* Officers, among whom *Aligern* the *Goth* did eminent Service.

Tho' this Victory seem'd to compleat the Reduction of *Italy*, yet there were still remaining Seven Thousand *Goths*, who, under the Conduct of one *Regnares*, had seiz'd upon a Fort near *Capua*, call'd *Cassin*, strongly situated, and environ'd by inaccessible Mountains, and which they furnish'd with all manner of Ammunition, and Provisions for several Months. *Regnares* was an *Hunn* by Nation, and being a Soldier of Fortune had animated 'em to this desperate Course, and persuaded them to submit upon no Terms, hoping in the end to make the better Bargain for himself. *Narses*, finding upon Trial the Place was not to be taken by Storm, resolv'd to block it up, and starve 'em out. And thus the Winter pass'd over without much Action on either side, and when the Spring came *Regnares* demanded a Conference of *Narses* in behalf of the Besieg'd, and insisted upon such unreasonable Demands that the General, who perceiv'd his Ambition, sent him back with much Indignation, which he took so heinously that having gain'd a Hill near the Walls he let fly an Arrow at *Narses*, with an Intent to kill him; in which, tho' he fail'd of his Design, the General's Guards were so provok'd, that they sent a Shower of Darts after him, wherewith being mortally wounded he dy'd in the Castle two Days after: Whereupon the Besieg'd yielded upon Promise of Pardon, and were sent by *Narses* to *Constantinople*, to prevent any farther Trouble they might hereafter create in the Country.

Thus was the Kingdom of the *Goths* extinguish'd in *Italy*, by the Valour and Conduct of *Belisarius* and *Narses*, two of the bravest Generals that ever serv'd the Eastern Emperors, after they had reign'd there

there for the Space of Seventy two Years, or thereabouts; during which for the moſt part *Italy* was the Stage whereon the greateſt and moſt bloody Feats of War were acted, in all which *Rome*, the Metropolis, had the largeſt Share. With the Kingdom of the *Goths* fell likewiſe the Hereſie of *Arius* in thoſe Parts, to the great Eaſe and Comfort of the Church, which however was at this time diſtracted by different Intereſts, occaſion'd chiefly by the finiſter Practices of *Vigilius*, Biſhop of *Rome* and *Theodora* the Empreſs, who during the whole Courſe of her Life appear'd a zealous Aſſerter of the *Eutychian* Hereſie; yet this muſt be allow'd to the Honour and Reputation of the then *Roman* Church that tho' ſhe was aſſaulted by Hereticks from without, and divided by Diſputes within, ſhe ſtood a thoſe Trials of her Faith with an exemplary Integrity, turning aſide or inclining to no Opinion whatever which was not warranted by the Holy Scriptures, and authoris'd by the concurring Teſtmonies of Antiquity. In the midſt of all thoſe Storms, in which her very Foundations were almoſt rooted up, her Doctrine continu'd pure and undefiled; and thoſe Errors with which ſhe now abounds, to the great Scandal of Chriſtianity, were the Product of after Ages, whilſt one Part of the World lay bury'd in Ignorance, and the other was kept awake by a reſtleſs Ambition.

A.D. 556.

IX. After *Narſes* had thus deliver'd *Italy* from the Arms of the *Goths* and *French*, he took care for the Security of the Borders, and taking the Advantages of a Rebellion rais'd by *Sindualdus*, whom he had created King of the *Heruli*, he drove that Nation out of the Habitations aſſign'd 'em by *Theodorich* near the *Alps*, after the Death of *Odoacer* their King; hanging their King for an Example of

Terror to others, if any were still remaining that aim'd at Innovations. When this was done he endeavour'd to establish Peace, and a regular Course of Justice throughout the Country, which he earnestly labour'd to restore to its former Lustre and Felicity, repairing the Cities, and beautifying it with new and magnificent Buildings, and other publick Works, and governing it, by Commission from *Justinian*, as a Province of the Eastern Empire.

The Satisfaction *Justinian* took by putting a happy End to so important a War, was sensibly abated by the Success of the *Persians* in *Lazica*, who, about this time, took from the *Romans* the strong Castle of *Telepsis*, wherein *Martinus* was Governor for the Emperor. *Mermeroes*, the *Persian* General, had often attempted to take it by Assault, but was still defeated by the Care and Circumspection of the Garrison, as well as the natural Strength of the Place, whereupon he had recourse to a Stratagem; for feigning himself sick, he at length order'd it to be reported abroad that he was dead, to the great Affliction of the Besiegers, who now despair'd of Success. Upon Presumption of his Death the *Romans* grew remiss and careless, and suffer'd the *Persians* to gain so insensibly upon 'em, that it was in *Mermeroes* his Power to master the Fort, before they were sensible of their Error, whereupon they fairly forsook it, and fled, in great Consternation, with *Mermeroes* at their Heels, to the *Roman* Army, which lay encamp'd not far off, and who were so alarm'd at the Accident, that they ran all away, in great Confusion, to an Island an Hundred and Fifty Furlongs off, whither *Mermeroes* thought not fit to pursue 'em; but making a Bridge over the *Phasis*, he return'd for want of Provision to the Frontiers, where he dy'd of extream Age shortly after, much lamented by *Chosroes* for his Personal Valour and Extraordinary Conduct.

Gubazes, King of *Lazica*, was much offended at the Behaviour of the *Roman* Officers. *Bessa* had in a manner ruin'd all by his Covetousness, and *Martinus* had now quitted to the *Persians* a most important Fortress by his Cowardice. Upon a Complaint to *Justinian* he turn'd *Bessas* out of Command, but tho' *Martinus* was equally culpable for his Negligence, as the other had been for his Covetousness, the Emperor, by an impardonable Oversight, continu'd him in his Employment to the utter Destruction of *Gubazes*, and great Detriment to the Affairs of the Empire; so careful ought Princes to be in examining into the Miscarriages of their Ministers, and punishing the Offenders, especially upon any Complaints on reasonable Grounds preferr'd against them. *Martinus*, who was before but ill affected to *Gubazes*, grew now his implacable Enemy, joining himself with *Rusticus*, a Quæstor in the Army, who having behav'd himself with much Corruption in his Office, was as earnest to have him remov'd out of the way as *Martinus*. They sent *John*, the Brother of *Rusticus*, to *Constantinople*, where he accus'd him of Treachery, and private Correspondence with the *Persians*, and obtain'd an Order from the Emperor, the sense of which they so wrested, as at least to make it excuse and challenge a Connivance at what ever they should practise against him; tho' *Justinian* design'd nothing less in his Instructions to 'em, provided he continu'd firm in his Alliance and Engagements with the *Roman*: for he knew the Enmity that was between them, and therefore gave little Credit to the Accusation. Upon the Authority of these Orders they requir'd him

him to join with them in some Service against the *Persians*, which, tho' he was ready to enter upon, he first expostulated with them for having, by their late Cowardice and Negligence, made that Service necessary; this they would have interpreted as a Demonstration of his Revolt to the Enemy, and immediately murder'd him, and thereby endanger'd the Loss of the whole Country; for on the one Hand the *Lazians* were so highly offended at this Barbarity, that they were about to throw themselves into the Hands of the *Persians*; and on the other, so great a Misunderstanding arose between the *Rigicides*, and the rest of the Officers that had been Strangers to their pernicious Councils, and abominated that most execrable Act, that the whole Army had like to have been destroy'd. At length a Commission was sent from *Constantinople* to Try the Offenders, who, upon a fair Hearing, were sentenc'd to be Beheaded, which Sentence was executed upon 'em accordindly; and *Gubazes* his Brother, being by the Emperor's Consent appointed his Successor, the Minds of the People were in a great measure appeas'd, and the Army once more in a Condition to make Head against the *Persians*, who, to the Number of Sixty Thousand Men, under the Command of *Nachoragan*, *Mermeroes*'s Successor, threaten'd no less than an entire Conquest. But this new General, after the loss of Twelve Thousand of his Soldiers, fled away, and gave so ill an Account of his Conduct at Court, that he was flay'd alive, at his Return, by the Command of *Chosroes*; who finding, by fatal Experience, how little he was like to get by the War, sent his Embassadors to *Constantinople* with Proposals for a Peace, where, after some Disputes and Alterations, a Cessation was in the end *A Truce* concluded, 'till a more solemn Peace could be con- *with* Persia. firm'd

200   *The Roman History*

firm'd between the Princes, equall[y]
the Cares and Viciſſitudes of War.

A. D. 557. *A great Earthquake.*

The Inhabitants of *Constantino*[ple]
finiſh'd their Publick Feſtivals for [the]
and the Concluſion of the War in [the]
City was viſited by a moſt terri[ble]
which, beginning in the dead of [Night shook?]
the whole World at one Inſtant,
Darkneſs adding to the Terrors o[f it.]
At firſt moſt diſmal Groans were [heard be-]
neath, after which enſu'd ſuch vio[lent]
Hurricanes as exceeded all Belief; [lasting]
ſeveral Days together, during whi[ch many]
publick Buildings were ſwallow'd [up. A]
Number of Churches, together w[ith the]
Conditions, who in that publick C[alamity fl]
ed into 'em. The like Calamity [raged]
about the ſame time, where the Inh[abitants]
more from the Fury of the Ea[rthquake]
from the Inſolence of their moſt [barbarous?]
victorious Enemies. And as if [one Plague]
was order'd by Providence to follo[w a-]
nother, the Plague return'd again [now,]
and ſwept off an infinite Multitud[e; which]
was no ſooner remov'd, before an [Army of]
Hunns threaten'd the City with gr[eater harm]
than it had ſuffer'd in either of t[he Visi-]
tations.

Juſtinian, being now grown C[onval]e[ſc]ent of Noiſe and Action, had taken [measures]
to prevent the Incurſions of the [Nati-]
ons, and eaſe himſelf of an exp[ence]
which he had hitherto born thro[ugh the]
Courſe of his Reign. According [to what is]
in *Tacitus*, by his Emiſſaries, wh[om he used]
for that purpoſe, he ſet the Barba[rians one]
againſt another, and ſow'd Jealouſ[ies]

ons among 'em, by which means he found so much Employment for 'em at home, that they had neither Time nor Opportunity to molest him. These subtle Measures he thought would prove so effectual, that he concluded for the future he should have but little Employment for Military Men, great Numbers of whom had before this been dismiss'd, and the Fortifications upon the Frontiers lay neglected; nor was any Care taken to recruit the Legions, which lay dispers'd throughout the Empire; hereupon the several Armies of the State grew in time to be diminish'd, that whereas, by the Historian's Computation, the standing Forces of the ancient Emperors consisted usually of Six Hundred Forty Five Thousand Men, they now hardly amounted to an Hundred and Fifty Thousand, some of which lay in *Italy*, others in *Egypt*, and the rest were dispers'd through *Africk*, *Spain*, and *Lazica*. These Considerations, and the Advantage of the Frost, which facilitated their Passage over the *Ister*, encourag'd the *Hunns* to Invade the Empire; accordingly they march'd in two Bodies directly for *Constantinople*, cruelly wasting the Country as they pass'd, and sparing neither Sex, Age, or Condition. The Forts that had been built formerly for the Defence of the Royal City, lay now naked and defenceless, the Mony that was oginally assign'd to maintain 'em being squander'd away upon Women, Chariot-Drivers, and other Extravagancies, so that the *Hunns* approach'd, without the least Opposition, within an Hundred and Fifty Furlongs of the City, where an universal Consternation had seiz'd the Inhabitants. In this Extremity *Belisarius*, grown old in Years and Honours, almost unable to hold a Shield, or brandish a Sword, was sent against 'em. His whole Army consisted of Three Hundred old Soldiers that had

The Hunns *Invade the Empire.*

serv'd

serv'd under him in the late Wars, and had hitherto follow'd his Fortunes; the rest were a rude undisciplin'd Multitude, without Skill or Courage, bred up in the Imperial Guards, where he who had the most Gold was enroll'd a Soldier, and not such who for their former Services in the Field deserv'd to be preferr'd to those Honourable Employments. In his March he was join'd by such Peasants, who had been driven from their Habitations by the *Hunns*, and who were ready, by their Terror and Amazement, to weaken and dispirit, rather than strengthen the Party they had embrac'd; notwithstanding which he march'd forward, and encamp'd as near as conveniently he might to the Enemy. He planted Two Hundred of his Men in a Wood, with Orders, at a Signal given, to fall upon Two Thousand of the *Hunns*, who he heard were marching against him. This done he commanded the Peasants to make as great a Noise, and raise as much Dust as they could, whilst he with the rest fell upon the Enemy, who, imagining the *Romans* to be more in Number than they were, began to turn back; when they from the Wood fell upon their Rear, and behav'd themselves with so much Courage, that the *Hunns* were glad to fly to their Camp, after they had lost near Five Hundred of their Men. By these Stratagems of *Belisarius* they were so much weaken'd, that they offer'd to return home if the Emperor would Ransom the Prisoners they had taken, threatning otherwise to cut their Throats before they stirr'd. The Conditions were readily accepted by *Justinian*, tho', had *Belisarius* pursu'd his good Fortune, and fallen upon 'em whilst they were generally seiz'd with a Panick Fear, 'tis very likely they had been all cut off; but he was recall'd on a sudden, at the Instigation of some who envy'd him the Honour

Belisarius envy'd at Court.

of

of this last good Service to his Country; the great Favour he was in with the People, who admir'd his Conduct and Valour, and compar'd him with the most renown'd Heroes of Antiquity, made his Enemies represent him as a Person dangerous to the Emperor, whose Jealousies encreas'd with his Years, and taught him to be barbarously ungrateful to the most deserving of all his Servants, one who had been the Support of the Empire, and Restorer of her ancient Military Glory. Shortly after this *Ablavius, Marcellus,* and *Sergius,* Men of great Wealth and Interest in the Empire, conspir'd against *Justinian,* and had agreed to kill him by Night in his Chamber; whether urg'd to it by his Ingratitude to *Belisarius,* or upon some other Provocations occasion'd by the Infirmities of Age, is uncertain. The thing was discover'd by some whom *Ablavius* had acquainted with their Conspiracy, and invited 'em to be Associates in it; whereupon they were all seiz'd with their Swords about 'em, but *Marcellus,* before he could be persuaded to surrender his to the Officer, who had the Charge of him, drew it out and stabb'd himself. When they were brought severally to Examination, *Sergius* accus'd *Belisarius* as privy to the Design, for which Reason the Emperor, to whom his great Virtues and Deserts had already render'd him obnoxious, immediately depriv'd him of all his Employments, confiscated his Estate, and threw him into Prison; tho' he was releas'd the Year following, and upon a Re-examination of his Case, restor'd to all his Employments, which he enjoy'd, without any farther Disgrace, 'till his Death. Such is the Account we have of the latter End of this Great Man, which we have drawn from the most Authentick Writers of that Age, and which seems more agreeable to Truth, than what has since been

A Conspiracy against the Emperor discover'd.

im-

impos'd upon the World by the Partizans of the Papacy, who tell us *Justinian* did not only strip him of all he had, but pluck'd out his Eyes, and reduc'd him to such extream Poverty, that he was forc'd to beg his Bread from Door to Door through the Streets of *Constantinople*; and that God had inflicted this just Punishment upon him for his unjust and violent Proceedings against *Sylverius*, Bishop of *Rome*, in Complaisance to *Theodora* the Empress. Whether the one Account or the other be true, he is set before us as an Example of all Human Honour and Greatness, and may teach us to pursue something more substantial and immutable.

Tho' *Justinian* was continually at War in one Part of the World or another, during the greatest part of his Reign, yet he manag'd that by his Lieutenants abroad, whilst he busied himself at home in Religious Disputes, and Buildings, as well of whole Cities and capacious Castles, as of Churches and Hospitals. His Buildings, which were almost without Number, were great and magnificent; and tho' they were vastly expensive, and burdensom to the Subject, yet they seem'd the Product of a Spirit highly Noble. The Church of *Sophia* in *Constantinople* has been the Wonder of all succeeding Generations, said by some to have excell'd the celebrated Temple of *Solomon*; besides which he rais'd so many more throughout the Empire so stately and beautiful, that *Procopius* saith, a just Survey of any one of 'em would make the Spectator imagine he had employ'd his whole Time and Care in that single Building, and yet as there was hardly a City in his Dominions in which he did not erect a Church, so was there scarce a Province throughout the Empire wherein he did not build or repair some City, Fort or Castle, so that

Justinian much addicted to Building.

that he is reported to have restor'd no fewer than an Hundred and Fifty Cities, which he found entirely ruin'd or very much decay'd, embellishing 'em with beautiful Houses, as well private as publick, securing 'em with substantial Walls, and adorning 'em with Churches lofty and capacious.

As from the Beginning of his Reign he had us'd himself to the Conversation of the most Learned Prelates of his Time, sitting up late every Night, and discoursing with them in his Closet upon some controverted Points of Christian Religion; so towards the latter End of it, when the Infirmities of Age had weaken'd his Reason, and impair'd his Judgment, he fell into some dangerous Errors, which occasion'd great Troubles in the Church. We observ'd before that there were some in *Alexandria* who maintain'd, that the Body of Jesus Christ was Incorruptible, that is, that it was not subject to the Natural Necessities and Infirmities of other Men; from whence sprung insensibly the Error of the *Eutychians*, who held, that there was but one Nature in him. This Opinion *Justinian* was perswaded to espouse by the Artifices of *Theodorus*, Bishop of *Cæsarea*, who, being an *Eutychian* in his Heart, had a great Influence over the Emperor, and at length impos'd so far upon his Credulity, that he openly profess'd his Belief was that the Body of Jesus Christ had never been subject either to Hunger or Thirst, to Pain, Death, or any other Inconveniences naturally incident to the rest of Mankind; that he was nourish'd in the same manner before his Passion as he was after his Resurrection, which effected no Change upon his Body, but that it retain'd the same Qualities it receiv'd at his Conception. He was not content himself to maintain this absurd and impious Heresie, but by an Edict publish'd to that Purpose would oblige all the

He embraces some Heretical Opinions;

A. D. 563.

the Bishops of the East to subscribe to it, and teach it in their several Churches. They at first excus'd themselves by alledging they could do nothing in it, without the Advice and Approbation of *Anastasius*, Patriarch of *Antioch*, first obtain'd to that Purpose. *Anastasius* was a Prelate renown'd for his great Learning, Orthodox Doctrine, and most exemplary Life; so that when the Emperor made use of all his Artifices to gain him to his Party, the good Bishop answer'd him with so much Presence of Mind and Solidity of Judgment, that *Justinian* despairing to obtain his Wishes that way had Recourse to Violence, and declar'd all those Bishops depriv'd who refus'd to submit to the Imperial Edict. *Anastasius*, fearing lest some of 'em might be terrify'd by the Emperor into a shameful Submission, sent his Circular Letters throughout his Diocess, in which he earnestly exhorted the Clergy, and the Flock committed to their Care, to continue stedfast in the Truth and Profession of the Catholick Faith. *Justinian*, who grew more obstinate when he saw the Opposition that was made against him, and was resolv'd to make all the Bishops in his Dominions swallow down his Heresie, began first with *Eutychius*, Patriarch of *Constantinople*, thinking that if he could once prevail with him others would more easily be brought to follow his Example; but *Eutychius*, instead of complying with the Emperor's Pleasure, writ against the Opinions he would have him embrace, proving by the Authority of Scripture and the Fathers that they were Heretical: At which *Justinian* was so much provok'd that he depriv'd him of his Episcopal Function, and confin'd him to a Monastery in *Chalcedon*; where, in a Synod consisting of such Bishops as had obey'd the Edict, and subscrib'd to the Heresie, several frivolous and ridiculous

were preferr'd againſt him, where-
y Prelates depos'd him from his
John, who reſided then at Con-
ent for the Church of *Antioch*,
l himſelf up to follow the Empe-
as eſtabliſh'd in his Place. The
thus depos'd excommunicated all
at had ſubſcrib'd his Depoſition,
y to exaſperate them the more a-
being ſupported by the Imperial *which cre-*
firſt confin'd him to a barren I- *ates great Troubles in*
ch they remov'd him to *Apamea*, *theChurch.*
, where they ſhut him up into a
own Foúnding. All this he bore
ignation, and by his Chriſtian Ex-
the reſt of the Biſhops againſt
nperor deſign'd againſt 'em, conti-
eſtraint 'till the Death of the U-
appen'd Twelve Years after in the
, at which time he was reſtor'd by
t the general and importunate Re-
ple. *Juſtinian*, at the Inſtigation
as proceeding with equal Violence
of the Biſhops, eſpecially *Anaſtaſi-*
Antioch, when thoſe and all his o-
ere interrupted by Death, which *Juſtinian*
nly away, to the great Benefit of *Dies.*
10, 'till the Evening of his Reign
nament and Support to it, after he
irty Eight Years and Seven Months.
ler, if, during ſo long an Admini- *His Cha-*
rs, and a Reign ſo active, this Em- *racter.*
'd himſelf, in ſome Particulars, to
n of thoſe, who often enquire into
ther Men with more. Malice than
had been more than Man if he had
not

not made some Trips in so long a Race, and when there were so many Snares and Impediments that lay full in his way; and yet the greatest Faults that upon any Colour of Reason can be urg'd against him, seem rather the Effects of Human Infirmity than Perverseness of Will. His uxorious Temper gave his Wife *Theodora* a great Ascendant over him, who being her self a devoted *Eutychian* made use of her Interest and Authority in him to the Support of that Heresie, whereby the Church receiv'd no small Damage, and which created him some Enemies, who perhaps would otherwise have been more tender to his Memory. His interesting himself so zealously in the Factions of the *Circus* was a Fault not easily to be excus'd, any more than his frequent and severe Exactions; tho' the Mony rais'd by 'em was neither hoarded up, nor apply'd to the Gratification of any unlawful Pleasures, but employ'd in the Payment of his numerous Forces, and in publick Buildings, so that in a manner it may be said to return back to the Publick like Fountains whose continu'd Streams hasten back to the Sea, from whence they had their Original. In all his Exactions, with which he is so heavily charg'd, he took care to abstain from Sacrilege; as appears in his Behaviour to *Juliana*, his near Relation, a Widow, very old and extreamly rich: For being at a great Expence in his Preparations against the *Persians*, he desir'd her to lend him a good Sum of Mony to assist him towards carrying on the War; she, upon just Grounds thinking the Emperor intended never to pay what he now pretended only to borrow, answer'd, *That it requir'd some time to raise so considerable a Sum*, and promis'd upon a certain Day *to give him Satisfaction*. In the mean time she deliver'd all the Gold and Silver she had either in Mony or Plate, to an Artist, with Orders to form it into Utensils for a Church dedicated to one of the Martyrs in *Constantinople,* and when it was finish'd she carry'd *Justinian* to see it, telling him *She had apply'd all her Wealth to that Use, and if he thought fit 'twas now at his Service;* tho' the Emperor knew this had been done on purpose to disappoint him yet he never touch'd it, but seem'd so well pleas'd with the Lady's generous Devotion that at his Departure she gave him an Emerauld, for its Value worthy to be presented to an Emperor. They who call him Unlearn'd have the least Grounds of any for the Calumny, as appears from his constant Conversation with the most Learned Men in his Dominions, and a Book own'd by those who had no great Kindness for him to be written by him in Defence of the Council of *Chalcedon,* and his Epistle to *Vigilius,* Pope of *Rome.* Tho' perhaps he was not so great a Proficient in Learning as those who made it their Business, yet he was a great Lover of Learned Men, and govern'd his Subjects with Justice, and a truly pious Zeal for the Christian Religion. At least, one Part of the Learned World are highly oblig'd to him for the *Code,* which goes under his Name, and which he order'd to be Publish'd on the Sixteenth of *April* in the Second Year of his Reign, in which he not only abridg'd the Law, which through a long Succession of Ages was grown too bulky and voluminous, and in many Respects obsolete and useless, but chang'd the very Tenour and Genius of it. This *Code,* in the Compiling of which he employ'd the greatest Lawyers in the Empire, was compos'd out of the *Gregorian, Hermogenian,* and *Theodosian,* in retrenching what was thought superfluous, and omitting all that was useless and impertinent. The

P   Year

Year following he commanded the same Men to collect all the Laws and Odinances of Use, which lay diffus'd in the innumerable Writings of the most celebrated Lawyers for Twelve Hundred Years before, and to reduce 'em to a certain Order, and under such Titles as Recourse might readily be had to 'em upon all Occasions. This they industriously undertook, and in Three Years time they Publish'd no less than Fifty Books, which, because they comprehended every Thing relating to the Law, were call'd the *Pandects*. After these follow'd his *Institutes*, so useful for the Instruction of those who apply themselves to the Study of the Civil Law. At last, finding that all these Laws thus collected and digested could not afford proper Remedies for new Matters which arose every Day, he added some new Constitutions, which, from the Design of 'em, were call'd *Novellæ*. Of how much Use these Collections have since been to the World may easily be determin'd, since *Justinian*'s Law, as it's now call'd, continues to be that in general of the greatest Part of Christendom, who look on it as the most exact Form of that Nature. And as in this Particular he has deserv'd well of Posterity, so did he deserve no less from that State he govern'd, and the Age wherein he liv'd, for his Wisdom and Success, by which he recover'd to the Empire *Afric* from the *Vandals*, and *Italy* from the *Goths*. In Word, he may be said to have been the last Prince that shone with the genuin Lustre of the ancient *Roman* Majesty, which reviv'd a while in him, and flourish'd in the Variety of Affairs relating both to Peace and War, conducting great Armies, designing mighty Performances, and conversant in variety of Accidents. But as if it had been rais'd by some Charm, which forc'd it to act for a short time

contrary

contrary to the Law of Nature, it difappear'd again on a fudden, and vanifh'd into nothing: For we are now upon a mighty Precipice, to be hurry'd down from thence into low, obfcure and narrow Tracts, and the farther we pafs we fhall meet with little of Action, and lefs of Performance; fo that the Subftance of the remaining Part of this Hiftory will be a Subject fitter for our Contemplation than Curiofity.

CHAP.

CHAP. III.

From the Death of Justinian t[he]
the Usurpation of Phocas th[e]

Containing the Space of Thirty

JUSTIN II.
A. D.
566.

I. JUstinian had in his Life-time d[eclared]
his Sister's Son, for his Suc[cessor]
Consent as well of the Senate
Uncle dying about Midnight, *Callini*[cus Cham-]
berlain, raising him out of his Bed
of his Death, and advis'd him to p[resent himself]
to the Senate, at that time assemble[d]
the Fathers readily accepted him fo[r]
and accordingly desir'd him to tak[e the Govern-]
ment upon him. His Predecessor
with much Pomp and Solemnity, h[e caused him-]
self to be Crown'd by the Hands of [the Pa-]
triarch, with an equal Magnificen[ce]
Care was by some Act of Favour to [ingratiate him-]
self with the People, who made gr[eat Complaints]
of the Debts owing 'em by his Un[cle, which he]
immediately gave Order should be [paid out of the]
Publick Treasury; after which he a[bolished the A-]
ctions of the *Circus*, which had gi[ven occasion to]
many Disorders, as has been observ'[d. But as the]
People were in general displeas'd wit[h Justinian for]
abolishing the Office of Consul,
from 'em the Power of chusing th[eir own Magi-]
strates, the only Mark they had left [of their Anci-]
ent Liberty; *Justin* therefore pron[ounced .....]
that Office, and accordingly took t[he ..... upon]
him the First of *January*, and gave [.....]

a Donative as was usual upon that Solemnity; notwithstanding which this Office was again laid aside, almost as soon as reviv'd. Seeing some new Troubles had crept into the Church towards the latter End of *Justinian*'s Reign, he endeavour'd to recompose it by an Edict Publish'd to that Purpose, wherein he exhorted every one to embrace and persevere in the Purity of Faith. At the same time he sent *Photinus, Belisarius* his Son-in-Law, to *Alexandria*, to appease some Differences which troubled the Repose of the Church there.

Such was the Beginning of *Justin*'s Administration, in which he gave the World a Promise of a vigilant and virtuous Prince; but he quickly grew weary of doing well, and gave himself up to the Power of Lust, and the Satisfaction of his brutish Appetite, raising great Sums of Mony by unlawful Means, and squandering it away again upon profligate Pleasures. All the Offices in the Empire were set to sale, and the very Preferments of the Church sold to the most unworthy and vilest sort of People; who had Wealth enough to purchase 'em, thereby impiously affronting that God which at first he pretended so much to honour.

Not long after his Entrance upon the Consulship, *Chagan*, King of the *Avari* or *Asiatick Scythians*, sent his Embassadors to demand the Tribute, or Pension, *Justinian* had formerly paid 'em, to purchase the Quiet of his Provinces, and prevent their Irruptions into the Territories of the Empire. *Justin* gave 'em a peremptory Refusal, and threaten'd *to chastise their Insolence, if they presum'd to offer any Violence to his Subjects, or attempt any thing prejudicial to his Service.* This resolute Answer proceeded from some Negotiation which was then on Foot between him and the *Turks*, call'd heretofore the *Massagetes*, a People inhabiting those Parts that

border

border upon the *Tanais*, towards the East, who began then to be known by that Name to the World, and by their Embassadors had made him several rich Presents, desiring him not to enter into any Alliance with the *Avari*, their declar'd Enemies. As *Justin* by this Courage and Confidence highly oblig'd the People, who abominated the Name of Tribute, so the Year following he disgusted all sober, judicious Persons by his bloody Actions. Being entangl'd with two contrary Vices, Cruelty and Cowardice, he gave the World several Instances both of the one and the other. He had a near Kinsman call'd *Justin*, in great Honour and Esteem with the People, who then resided near the *Danube* to restrain the Incursions of the Barbarians. Being equal in Birth and Expectation, they had formerly Covenanted with each other, that which so ever of the two should be in time advanc'd to the Imperial Dignity, should Treat the other as the First and most Honourable Person, after himself, in the Empire. But *Justin*, who had now obtain'd the Purple, grew fearful and jealous of his Cousin's Virtues, so that instead of being just to the Promise he had formerly made him, he resolv'd to destroy him; in order to which he invited him, with Letters full of Friendship, to come to *Constantinople*, where he receiv'd him with open Hands, but a treacherous, deceitful Heart. He had not been long in Court before the Emperor forg'd several pretended Crimes against him, as if he had entertain'd Councils dangerous to the State, and the Dignity of his Person; tho' the People, who had a thorough sense of *Justin*'s Merit, and the great Service he had done his Country, were very well satisfy'd of his Innocence, yet the Emperor took from him his Guard, confin'd him to his House, and at length order'd

Marginal note: Justin turns Cruel.

order'd him to be convey'd away to *Alexandria*, where one Night he was cruelly murder'd as he lay asleep in his Bed, and the Emperor's jealous Fears for the present were remov'd; tho' neither his, nor his Wife *Sophia*'s barbarous Curiosity could be satisfy'd 'till they had beheld his Head, and in a scornful insulting manner spurn'd it with their Feet upon the Ground. This *Sophia* was Neice to *Theodora* the late Empress, as Haughty, Insolent and Imperious as her Aunt, but a Woman more capable of managing Publick Affairs, and better affected to the State, as we shall have occasion to remember in its proper Place.

Not long after this the Emperor did a peice of Justice upon the Persons of *Ætherius* and *Addæus*, two Senators of great Authority in the Reign of *Justinian*, and who were now accus'd of High-Treason. *Ætherius* confess'd he had a Design to poison the Emperor, and that *Addæus* was privy to it. *Addæus*, with solemn Oaths, and most dreadful Imprecations, protested himself altogether innocent, but confess'd at his Execution, *That tho' he was guiltless of the Crime for which he suffer'd, yet his Punishment was the Effect of God's just Judgments upon him for his wicked Practices against* Theodorus, *Præfect of the Palace, who lost his Life by his Inchantments.* The People were not more offended at his Cruelty towards *Justinus*, than pleas'd with his Proceedings against these two Persons, for whether they were guilty of the Crime with which they were charg'd or no, they were undoubtedly very wicked Persons; for *Addæus* was addicted to unnatural Pleasures, and *Ætherius*, in the Reign of *Justinian*, had robb'd both the Innocent and Guilty, the Living and the Dead, by his Calumnies and malicious Informations.

A. D. 568.

This Act was follow'd by another the next Year, no less agreeable to the People, and beneficial to the State. The Emperor was subject to a Vertigo, or Dizziness in his Head, which hinder'd him from appearing often in Publick, or giving Audience to the People; and when he did they flock'd to him with Petitions, and Complaints against many of the Senators and Great Persons in the Court, who grievously burden'd and oppress'd 'em. The Emperor, observing that after several Redresses of that kind the People still complain'd of their hard Usage, severely reproach'd the Senate for countenancing such Tyrannical Practices; threatning, unless they restor'd to every Man his own, he would see 'em punish'd without any regard had to their Quality, or Relation to his Person. When all this prov'd ineffectual one of the Senators undertook, at the hazard of his Life, to prevent the like Violence for the future, provided the Emperor would make him Præfect of the City, and support him with his Authority. *Justin* readily accepted of his Terms, and establish'd him in the Office. It happen'd one Day, whilst the new Præfect was hearing Causes upon the Bench, a poor Woman came to complain of one of the Principal Magistrates, who had robb'd her of all she was worth; whereupon the Præfect sent her with a Warrant to the Offender, requiring him to appear, and make his Defence in Court; but he, instead of obeying the Order, sent her back after he had most outragiously abus'd her. After which the Præfect sent one of his Officers with a Citation, which, in Defiance to the Præfect, he disdainfully refus'd to obey, and went to wait upon *Justin*, who had invited him to Dinner. The Præfect follow'd him immediately to the Palace, and requir'd the Emperor to deliver him up into his Hands,

LVII. Juſtin II.

g him of the Promiſe he had given
n with his Authority in the Exe-
)ffice; which, when the Emperor
condemn'd the Magiſtrate to be
ving order'd him to be Whipp'd,
him to be ſet naked upon an Aſs,
ſted through the Publick Streets of
which he confiſcated all his Eſtate,
to the Woman he had injur'd.
Example of Severity upon the Per-
nt a Magiſtrate kept all the reſt in
more Complaints were brought to
ho made the Præfect a Patrician,
e Office for his Life. About the *A popular*
perſuaded her Husband to pay the *Act of the*
poor Priſoners, as were inſolvent, *Empreſs.*
ck Treaſury, to the great Eaſe and
ie People.

as not only remarkable for theſe
ns at home, but for new Commo-
)arians abroad, that at firſt fill'd the
rror and Amazement, and at length
l Revolution in the Weſt; for the
now preparing for an Expedition
ince, in Proceſs of Time, they grew
in that Country, Part of which re-
e to this Day, 'tis hop'd an Ac-
)riginal will not be judg'd impro-
:.

Iabitation is by the concurrent A- *The Origi-*
oſt Writers allow'd to be *Scanzia,* *nal of the*
a large *Peninſula* in the Kingdom *Lombards.*
and that as the *Goths, Vandals* and
e ſame in their Original, tho' di-
on ſeveral Occaſions, by different
ſ moſt certain, that theſe *Lombards*
d from the *Gepidæ,* who were ſo
call'd

call'd becaufe, when the *Goths* made an Expedition out of *Scanzia* in three Ships, they fail'd flower than the reft, and fettl'd, for the prefent, in an Ifland upon the *Viftula*, which, when their Multitudes encreas'd, was too little to contain and nourifh 'em all; whereupon a third Part, call'd afterwards *Lombards*, was by Lot compell'd to leave their Native Country, and feek out new Habitations. After feveral Adventures and Changes of Fortune they fettl'd in *Rugia*, where they continu'd for fome time under the Government of *Lamiffio*, and his Succeffors, 'till at length *Godohoc* the Third, according to fome, but as others will have it *Audoin*, the Ninth King in Order from *Lamiffio*, led 'em into *Pannonia*, where their Name firft began to be known to the World, and where they grew confpicuous for their many Victories obtain'd over their Neighbours, and Alliances with Foreign Princes; for *Alboin*, who fucceeded his Father *Audoin* in the Government, was thought confiderable enough to marry the Daughter of *Clotaire*, King of the *Franks*. He was a very warlike and prudent Prince, not only well skill'd in the Arts of Government, but happy in the Invention of fuch Weapons, as from his Time were much us'd in the Wars. Having conquer'd the *Gepidæ*, whofe King, *Cunimundus*, he flew in the Battel, the Emperor *Juftinian* thought fit to enter into Alliance with him. Accordingly he affifted *Narfes* in his Wars againft the *Goths*, and, whilft that Great Man continu'd in Favour at Court, they were ready to ferve the *Romans* upon all Occafions. *Narfes* had for Thirteen Years together govern'd *Italy*, as the Emperor's Lieutenant, with much Reputation, in which time it was improv'd beyond Imagination; the late Peace, which upon the final Conqueft of the *Goths* was firmly eftablifh'd, made

room

room for a just and regular Execution of the Laws, and that gave Encouragement to Trade and Commerce, by which the Inhabitants grew exceedingly enrich'd; the Towns were opulent, and the Country fruitful, so that there was nothing wanting to make 'em compleatly happy, but a just and grateful Sense of their Happiness; instead of which the Common People grew Wanton and Luxurious, the Great ones Proud and Ungrateful. Tho' there was nothing they had just Reason to envy in others, which they had not abundantly in themselves, they look'd, with a malicious Eye, upon the Wealth and Authority of *Narses*, of whom they complain'd to the Emperor, as of a Tyrant, who, by his Arbitrary Proceedings, made 'em wish the Dominion of the *Goths* restor'd among 'em; so much happier were they under them, than under the Government of that Eunuch, who tyranis'd over them with an unbounded Pride, whilst their most virtuous and pious Prince was kept in ignorance of their Sufferings. For this Reason the Emperor recall'd him out of *Italy*, sent for him to *Constantinople*, and appointed *Longinus*, a Patrician, to succeed him in the Government of the West. *Narses*, who well knew what powerful Enemies he had at Court, resolv'd not to venture himself at *Constantinople*, but retir'd from *Rome* to *Naples*, as a Place of greater Security, where he was very much belov'd and esteem'd. Here he seriously consulted with his Friends about his own Safety, especially when he was inform'd that the Empress, by way of Derision, threaten'd *to send for that Eunuch home, and set him a Spinning among her Women.* Inrag'd at this Insolent Reflection, he reply'd, *He was ready to undergo any Punishment he had justly deserv'd, but would not put it in the Power of his Enemies to use him ill, after*

Narses recall'd out of Italy.

he

he had so eminently signaliz'd himself in his Service to the Empire; concluding, That he would have the Empress know he was going to Spin her such Thread, as neither She nor any of her Minions should be able to unravel whilst she liv'd: And so mov'd both by Fear and Disdain, he sent immediately and invited the *Lombards* into *Italy*, promising *Alboin*, with whom he was well acquainted, to open him a Passage into the Country. With these Messengers he sent several Presents to *Alboin* and his Chief Favorites, amongst the rest some of the best Fruits the Country afforded, as Baits to allure 'em. *Baronius*, and several others of his Followers, reject this Account as fabulous, alledging that *Narses* had been recall'd the Year before by *Justin*, at whose Inauguration he assisted, and continu'd in great Credit at *Constantinople*; and this they assert upon the Authority of *Chorippus*, a Poet and Grammarian of *Africk*, who flourish'd in that Age, and was then living in the Imperial City. This Objection Father *Petau*, the Jesuit, has very learnedly remov'd, proving that what *Chorippus* spoke was of another *Narses* much younger than this General, and that there were three of that Name living at that time; the first was the renown'd Deliverer of *Italy*, who dy'd, and was bury'd at *Rome* some time after he had call'd in the *Lombards*; the second was the Brother of *Aratius* and the third that *Narses* of whom *Chorippus* makes mention in his Poem, who was young, and handsome to a Miracle, who bore Arms for the Emperor *Justin* in the second Year of his Reign, and who was burnt alive by the Command of *Phocas* in the Year 605.

Invites the Lombards into it.

The Lombards prepare to Invade Italy.

Whatever the Inducements were, the *Lombards* made all necessary Preparations for their intended Invasion, calling the *Saxons* in to their Assistance, whom they promis'd a share in the Conquest; who, upon those Conditions, join'd with 'em to the Number of above Twenty Thousand Men, together with their Wives and Children. *Alboin*, before his Expedition, enter'd into a strict Alliance with the *Hunns*, the most powerful of his Neighbours, to whom he left *Pannonia*, with this Reserve, That if the *Lombards* should be forc'd back, they should have free Liberty to re-enter upon their former Possessions. Having concerted such Measures as he thought necessary for so great an Undertaking, he set forward with all his Nation, their Wives and Children, and what ever else of value they had in *Pannonia*, out of which they remov'd after a continuance of Forty Two Years in it. He began his March about the beginning of *April*, in the Third Year of *Justin* the younger, the Ninth of *John* the third Pope of *Rome*, in the first Indiction, *A. D.* 568.

Alboin enter'd into *Italy* by the way of *Istria*, and the Country of *Venetia*, without meeting any one in his March that offer'd to oppose him; for his Army, being chiefly compos'd of Pagans and *Arians*, drove the whole World with Terror before it. *Paulinus*, Patriarch of *Aquileia*, retir'd into an Island adjoining with the most valuable Utensils of his Church; and the greatest part of the Inhabitants sav'd themselves in the *Venetian* Islands, so that *Aquileia*, being almost totally abandon'd, open'd the Gates and receiv'd the King, as did likewise *Friuli*, where *Alboin* consider'd whom he could safely trust with those Territories, which, in a manner, were the Gates of *Italy*, and through which every Invader was first to force his Passage. After some Debate with himself he conferr'd the Charge on *Gisulphus*, his Nephew, and Master of the Horse, a Person in every Respect

spect fit for the Imployment. By this means *Friuli* was erected into a Dutchy, and has continu'd as such ever since. Here *Alboin* dispers'd his Forces into Winter Quarters, where they found all sorts of Provisions in great Abundance, for the preceding Summer had afforded such a Plenty of all Things as no Age could ever equal.

The Winter being over *Alboin* mov'd forward with his Army, through which he had establish'd an exact Discipline, forbidding 'em under the severest Penalties to affront or disoblige the Inhabitants, whose Friendship and good Will he was very desirous to purchase. As he drew near to *Treviso*, *Felix*, Bishop of the Place, came out and demanded an Exemption for his Church and Diocess, which he very bountifully granted. After he had taken the City, which yielded without any Resistance, and put a Garrison into it, he march'd on to *Vincentia*, *Verona*, and *Trent*, both which readily surrender'd to him, so that he was now possess'd of all the considerable Towns in that Quarter, except *Padua*, *Mantua* and *Cremona*, which he thought not fit to attack, either because they lay too much out of the Way, or for that he knew they were supply'd with sufficient Garrisons, and would take up too much of his Time if he stay'd to besiege 'em.

A. D. 570.

Thus ended the Second Year of his Expedition, and he had now got a good Footing in *Italy*, being become Master of the greatest Part of *Venetia*, which comprehended much more than what we at present assign to *Venice*, making one of the Eleven Regions into which *Augustus* divided *Italy*. *Alboin*, upon the first Return of the Spring, enter'd with his Army into *Liguria*, where the People were so terrify'd at his Approach that they left their Habitations, and hid themselves, with such of their Effects as they could carry off, in the he most remote and inaccessible Parts of the Mountains, so that he enter'd *Brescia, Bergamo, Lodi, Como,* and all the Towns thereabouts, up as far as the *Alps,* without any Opposition, and at last advanc'd towards *Milan,* the Capital of the Country. *Honoratus,* who was at that time Bishop of the Place, seeing there were not Forces in the Town sufficient for its Defence, retir'd with the principal Inhabitants to *Genoa,* and *Alboin* had the Gates open'd to him at the first Summons, for he had threaten'd to destroy all with Fire and Sword, if they forc'd him to make a Breach in the Wall. Here he was first proclaim'd King of *Italy,* as well by the Inhabitants as Soldiers; and from this time Historians give Date to the Kingdom of the *Lombards* in *Italy,* which continu'd for the space of Two Hundred Years and upwards. *Alboin* being thus invested with the Royalty march'd from *Milan* to *Pavia,* which was well fortify'd, and furnish'd with a very strong Garrison, and all sorts of Provision and Ammunition; for this Reason finding there was no Probability of its yielding he left a Part of his Army to block it up, and with the rest laid Siege to *Placentia, Parma, Modena,* and other Midland Cities, all which he enter'd with little or no Resistance: From thence he march'd into *Umbria,* where he took *Spoletto,* which he committed to the Custody of a Governor, dignify'd with the Title of a Duke. The same he did with the other Cities of any Consequence that submitted to his Obedience, most of which have retain'd the Title of Dutchies to this Day. *The Beginning of the Kingdom of the Lombards in Italy.*

Whilst this wonderful Progress of the Barbarians in the West threaten'd a Subversion to the Imperial Authority there, the Empire seem'd to receive some Recompence in the Submission of the *Armenians,* who subjected themselves to *Justin,* and implor'd *The Armenians revolt to the Emperor.*

implor'd his Protection. They had for a long time been Vassals to the *Persians*, who had us'd 'em with much Severity upon the Account of their Religion, which at length provok'd 'em to throw off the Yoke and apply themselves to the Emperor, who readily accepted of the Conditions, and swore solemnly to assist 'em. Upon which Encouragement they unanimously rose up, and cruelly murder'd all the *Persians* that were among 'em, renouncing at once their Duty to their lawful Soveraign, and all the Ties of Nature as well as Christianity, of which they made an outward Profession, but dishonour'd it by their Inhumanity and Disobedience.

A. D. 572.

Chosroes upon the first Alarm charg'd the Emperor with these clandestine and faithless Proceedings, to which *Justin* resolutely answer'd, That the Truce was expir'd, and that it did not become his Dignity or Profession to deny his Protection and Assistance to Christians, demanding it against those who cruelly oppress'd 'em upon the Account of their Faith. This Reply would have appear'd great and generous, had he arm'd himself by any timely Preparations against that Storm which he knew it must necessarily draw upon himself and those whose Cause he had espous'd: Instead of which he wallow'd in his wonted Sensualities and Delights. Upon a Report that *Chosroes* was raising a powerful Army in order to reduce the *Armenians*, he sent *Martianus*, one of the Captains of his Guards into the East, but without Soldiers, Arms, or any warlike Provisions, so that he was forc'd to enroll such Vagabonds and indigent Wretches as he met in his way; with whom having by chance defeated a small Body of *Persians*, on whom he fell before they were aware of his Coming, or prepar'd to receive 'em, he had the Confidence to sit down with his ragged Regiment before the City of *Nisibis*, the Gates of which the Inhabitants fcorn'd to fhut, reviling the *Roman* Army as a parcel of mercenary Slaves pofted there to watch Sheep, rather than befiege any defenfible Town. In the mean time *Chofroes* having mufter'd his Forces divided his Army into two Parts, committing one of 'em to the Conduct of *Artabanus*, his General, with Orders to wafte the *Roman* Territories near *Antioch*, and attempt that City; whilft he march'd with the other over the *Tigris*, in order to raife the Siege of *Vifibis*, which the *Romans* themfelves had done before his Arrival. For *Juftin*, who thought his Order fufficient to take the Town, without the Affiftance either of Men or Warlike Engines, was highly incens'd againft *Martianus* for prolonging the Siege, and fent *Acacius*, a proud, arrogant Man, to degrade him from his Martial Dignity, and deprive him of all his Military Employments. This was to be done upon the Confines unknown to the Army, but when the Officers underftood their Captain was cafhier'd they immediately threw away their Arms and quitted the Siege, rendring the Emperor exceedingly ridiculous to all Mankind for his extravagant Conceits, or rather fenfelefs Stupidity. *Artabanus* having e'er this pafs'd the *Euphrates* had been repuls'd from *Antioch*, lately re-built, by a handful of Men, who preferv'd the City beyond Expectation; after which he march'd to *Apamea*, which he pillag'd and burnt, contrary to his Faith given, for it furrender'd upon honourable Conditions. From thence he march'd to join the King, who was preparing to befiege *Daras*, which held out againft him for five Months, but was taken in the end, either through the Carelefnefs or Treachery of the Governor. The Emperor loft in this Siege the Flower of his Army, which, together

with

with the Loss of the Place, it being a Town of the greatest Importance, convinc'd him of his imprudent Management, and gave him a melancholy View of the Condition of his Affairs; the Consideration of which work'd so strongly with him, he being of a weak Constitution, that he often fell into Fits of Madness, and was thereby render'd unfit for any publick Business. This Misfortune happening at a time when the State was expos'd to so many Difficulties, as well from the Motions of the *Persians* in the East, as the Progress the *Lombards* made in the West, the whole Empire seem'd expos'd to unavoidable Ruin. In this Extremity, *Tiberius*, a *Thracian* by Birth, and one who had been long conversant in publick Business, undertook the chief Management of Affairs, to the great Satisfaction of the People in general, as well as by the Advice and Consent of the Empress *Sophia* and the great Men at Court. His first Advice was to redeem that by sober Councils which had been lost through Rashness and Folly, and accordingly sent *Trajan*, a Man of great Esteem for his Age and Wisdom, as Embassador to *Chosroes*, not from the Emperor nor Common-wealth, but from the Empress *Sophia*; in whose Name he was to represent to the King, that *It was not like a generous Prince, nor a Man of Honour, to insult an helpless Woman, to oppress an infirm Emperor, or make War against a weak, defenceless State, destitute of all Support and Succour; that it would become him to consider the Vanity and Uncertainty of Human Affairs, which he himself had formerly experienc'd, at which time the Emperor readily granted him the same Favour she now demanded,* and sent him the best Physicians the Empire could afford. *Trajan* enforc'd these Particulars so handsomly to *Chosroes*, that tho' he had resolv'd to invade the *Roman* Territories, yet he made a Truce

fo-

three Years, and confented *Armenia* fhould en-
 the Benefit of it.
During thefe Tranfactions in the Eaft *Pavia* was Pavia tak-
en by the *Lombards*, after it had held out with en by the
eat Refolution for three Years together. *Alboin*, Lombards.
o had not been fo oppos'd any where before,
 difdaining to meet with fo much Refiftance
re, had fworn to put all the Inhabitants to death;
t as he was entring the City on Horfeback his
rfe fell under him at the Gate, and all the Strength
 Art they had could not raife him again, tho'
y lafh'd him with their Whips, and the King
'd him deep with his Spurs: Whereupon a *Lom-
d* who ftood near him faid, *Sir, this City is full
Chriftians, fo that you muft firft revoke the cruel
w you have made before you will be permitted to
er.* Upon this he recall'd his Oath, and pro-
fing Imdemnity to the People his Horfe imme-
tely arofe, and he pafs'd on to the Palace built
Theodorich; where the People crowded to be-
ld him, and to fwear Allegiance to him; fo that
m this time forward the Kings of the *Lombards*
ided and kept their Court ufually in *Pavia*.
After this *Alboin* reign'd in his new Dominions
hout any or at leaft very little Difturbance, for
' his Succeffors had frequent Contefts with the
archs of *Ravenna*, yet the Exarchate was then
its Birth, and had not Strength fufficient to con-
d with fo powerful a Rival, the Emperor think-
 it enough if his Officers there put a Stop to
 further Progrefs of the *Lombards*, and fecur'd
much to the Empire as was not already conquer'd
 'em; and *Alboin*'s Care was firft to confirm
at he had lately acquir'd, before he pufh'd on
 frefh Conquefts: Accordingly he endeavour'd
 eftablifh Peace and good Order throughout his
minions, but was flain by the Treachery of his
Wife,

Wife, in the Fourth Year of his Reign, at *Veron*
This Princess, call'd *Rosamund*, was the Daught
of *Cunimond*, King of the *Gepidæ*, whom *Albo*
had overthrown before his Expedition into *Ita*
and, like an arrogant Conqueror, made a drinki

A. D. Cup of his Skull; notwithstanding which, havi
574. lately lost his first Wife, he marry'd *Cunimon*
Daughter, thinking by that Match to secure
Conquests. Being now feasting at *Verona* with
chief Favourites and principal Officers, in the E
travancy of his Mirth he commanded her to dr
out of that detested Cup; the Horror of whi
and her Husband's barbarous Triumph over
Misfortunes of her Family, so incens'd her, t
she resolv'd to be reveng'd, and immediately
scover'd her self to *Helmichild*, the King's Armo
bearer, promising to give him her self, and
Kingdom of *Lombardy* into the Bargain, if
would assist her in her Revenge. *Helmichild*
sten'd with a greedy Ear to what she propos'd,
readily embrac'd the Conditions: He knew he
unable to carry on a Design of that Conseque
alone, and therefore advis'd the Queen to eng
Peredeo, a Man of great Authority and Inte
with the King, to associate himself with the
Peredeo peremptorily refus'd to be consenting to
Death of his Prince, 'till the Queen by a sham
Stratagem forc'd him to a Compliance. She kn
ing he maintain'd an amorous Correspondence w
one of her Ladies plac'd her self in her Bed
Evening, when she knew he was expected, recei
and lay with him, whilst he imagin'd all the wh
he had his own Mistress in his Arms; before h
rose the Queen discover'd her self to him, and t
him after what he had done his own Security
pended entirely upon the Death of *Alboin*, and
that means engag'd him in a Treason which oth

erwife his Soul abhorr'd. One Day therefore
Alboin lay afleep in his Chamber after Dinner,
Queen introduc'd the Confpirators, by whom
was Affaffinated. *Rofamond*, having fecur'd Alboin
late King's moft valuable Jewels and Treafure, *Slain.*
with that, and *Albifvinda* her Daughter, and
nichild, who was now her Husband, to *Longi-*
Exarch of *Ravenna*, who receiv'd her very
urably, and affur'd her of his Protection; but
g a Man of an amorous Temper he fell in
e with her, and promis'd to marry her, pro-
d fhe would fend *Helmichild* out of the way.
mond, who had marry'd him for the fake of
Revenge, refolv'd now to kill him to fatisfie
Ambition, for fhe was highly pleas'd with the
ty of being Miftrefs of *Ravenna*, fo that without
Hefitation fhe prepar'd a Cup of ftrong Poi-
for him, which fhe prefented to him as he a-
out of the Bath and call'd for Drink. *Hel-
ild* having drunk half of it up quickly found,
he fudden and ftrange Operation, what it was,
with his Sword pointed at her Breaft com-
d her to drink up the reft; the Poifon had
ame effect in her that it had in her Husband,
hey both perifh'd the fame Moment, and fell
rible Inftance of God's Judgment upon Trai-
and Murderers. *Longinus* fent the Treafure
e *Lombards* and *Albifvinda*, the King's Daugh-
to *Conftantinople*, together with *Peredeo*, who
id to have follow'd *Rofamond* to *Ravenna*.
Queen, by this untimely Death, prevented
Fury of the *Lombards*, who were enrag'd at
for the Death of their King, under whofe
duct they had done fuch memorable things,
whom they attended to the Grave with fuch
ick Lamentations as the Occafion requir'd.
r which they proceeded carefully to the Choice
of

Clepho Elected King, A.D. 575. and murder'd.

of a Succeffor, and the Election fell upon o Clepho, a Man of the greateſt Nobility amoɪ them; who tho' he was a warlike, valiant Prin and extended the Kingdom of the *Lombards* the Gates of *Rome*, yet being of a cruel tyranni Difpofition, he was murder'd with his Wife *M fana*, after he had reign'd about a Year and hɛ He being thus remov'd the *Lombards*, who F fuffer'd much by his Tyranny, refolv'd to fubj themfelves no more to Kings, but divided th Conquefts in *Italy* amongft Thirty of their Pr cipal Captains. This Divifion continu'd for ɩ fpace of Ten Years and upwards, during wh they behav'd themfelves with all the Barbaɪ imaginable, without any regard had either to Churches or Monafteries, to the Perfons of Priɛ or Bifhops. The moſt remarkable of theſe Du were *Gifulfus*, of whom mention has been m already, *Alachis*, *Amo*, *Zaban* and *Rodan*; tɩ three laſt with united Forces invaded *France*, ɩ having pafs'd the *Alps*, rifl'd and deftroy'd where ever they came. *Gontran*, King of *Orleɑ* fent an Army againſt 'em under the Conduct *Amatus*, the Patrician, who gave 'em Battel, wh he loft together with his Life; after which tɩ rov'd with great Licence throughout *Burgundy*, ɩ return'd with ineftimable Spoils into *Italy*. Hav tafted the Sweetneſs of this Expedition, they m a fecond Attempt, but were defeated near *Ambr* a City in the higher *Dauphine*, by *Mummulus*, ɩ of *Gontran*'s Captains, a brave fagacious Comm der, who flew fuch Numbers of 'em, that aɪ this they never ventur'd to make any Irrupti into *France*, contenting themfelves with their C quefts in *Italy*, where they tyrannis'd with un rallel'd Cruelty, without receiving any effect

Op

Oppofition from the Emperors, who were wholly employ'd in the Affairs of the Eaft.

TIBERIUS. The Truce between *Juftin* and the King of *Perfia* being almoft expir'd, and the Emperor continuing ftill as uncapable for publick Affairs as ever, this Year created *Tiberius, Cæfar*, refigning up to him the publick Management, referving no more to himfelf than the meer Name of Emperor. Whilft *John*, the Patriarch, attended by the Princes and Chief Magiftrates of State, was invefting *Tiberius* with the Imperial Purple, *Juftin* is faid to have given him this Advice, *Let not the outward Pomp of Worldly Greatnefs mifs-lead thee, nor entangle thee in fuch Difficulties, into which I, who trufted too much to the Allurements of Senfe, have miferably plung'd my felf; nor do thou fuffer thy felf to be rul'd by thefe Men*, pointing to the Magiftrates, *for they are the Perfons who have reduc'd me to that wretched Condition in which thou feeft me*. Thefe Words, which he pronounc'd with an unufual Accent, ftruck the whole Affembly with great Wonder, and drew Tears from feveral of them, but wrought more with none than him to whom they were addrefs'd, who immediately apply'd himfelf with great Induftry to the Adminiftration of Affairs, and made all poffible Preparations for a War. For *Chofroes* before the Expiration of the Truce had over-ran all *Armenia*, and was marching with his Army to Befiege *Cæfarea*, the Metropolis of *Cappadocia*. Tho' *Tiberius* had rais'd a very powerful Army, confifting of near one Hundred and Fifty choice Troops of Horfe, befides Foot, and was in a Capacity to difpute it with the King of *Perfia* by Strength of Arms, he however chofe firft to try, by means of his Embaffadors, to prolong the Truce, and eftablifh a good Underftanding between the two Princes. But *Chofroes*, whom his late Success had render'd Haughty and Insolent, refus'd to give the Embassadors Audience, commanding 'em, with much Arrogance, to follow him to *Cæsarea*, *in which City perhaps he might vouchsafe to hear what they had to say;* but when he observ'd the *Roman* Army advancing under the Command of *Justinian*, the Son of that *Justin* who was murder'd at *Alexandria*, when he beheld their shining Armour, the Trumpets sounding to Battel, the Armies ready to join, but above all so vast a Body of Horse as no Emperor had ever before sent into the Field; he was surpriz'd at such an unexpected Sight, and endeavour'd by all means to decline fighting, and draw off. This was observ'd by a *Scythian*, who commanded the Right Wing of the *Roman* Forces, and who therefore charg'd the advanc'd Guard so briskly, that the *Persians* gave Ground, and the whole Army began to be in Confusion, upon which the *Romans* attack'd his Rear, where all the Baggage and Ammunition lay

Chosroes defeated. After a short Dispute the *Persians* were routed, leaving the Camp to their Enemies, who found in it great store of Provision, and the Royal Treasure, together with the Fire which *Chosroes* ador'd for his God; the King himself continu'd all this while in the Field with the main Body, not daring to engage 'till the Night drew on, at which time the *Romans* divided their Army into two Bodies *Chosroes* commanded great Fires to be kindl'd, and attack'd that Party which lay towards the North which giving Ground he pierc'd through and took *Melitina*, a City abandon'd by its Inhabitants, and destroy'd it, which when he had done he prepar'd to cross the *Euphrates*. In the mean time both Parties of the *Roman* Army being join'd, they pursu'd him so close that he was forc'd to save himself upon an Elephant, whilst the greatest part of his

Army

Army were either destroy'd by the Swords of their Enemies, or perish'd in the River. *Justinian*, after this Signal Victory, enter'd *Persia*, where he dispos'd his Army into Winter Quarters, whilst none of the *Persians* had either Strength or Courage enough to resist him; at which *Chosroes*, who now beheld his Victorious Enemies in the very Bowels of his Country, and from whence he found himself unable to remove 'em, was so nearly concern'd, that he fell sick and dy'd. During his Sickness he publish'd a Law, wherein he forbad his Successors at any time to War against the *Romans*, which Law was little observ'd by the *Persians*, who thought it gave too great an Honour to their Enemies. The Account *Agathias* has left us of this Prince's Death is something different from the former. He tells us, that whilst he was retir'd to the cool Refreshments of the *Carduchian* Mountains, in the heat of Summer, *Mauritius*, the General of the *Roman* Army, made an Irruption into the Neighbouring Parts, and advanc'd, in an Hostile manner, so near to the Place where he resided, burning all before him, that *Chosroes* himself beheld the Flames of the adjacent Towns, and was so surpriz'd at a Spectacle so very unusual within his own Dominions, that he fell sick suddenly, and was carry'd to *Ctesiphon*, where he dy'd after a long and victorious Reign of Forty Eight Years. The same Author makes him the most valiant and successful of all their Kings from the time of *Cambyses*, for which he deservedly acquir'd the Sirname of Great; and it must be acknowledg'd that he wanted nothing but a true Knowledge of the Faith of Christ to have been a compleat Prince, being otherwise adorn'd with all the Virtues Moral and Political that are requisite to a Crown'd Head. *Justinian* continu'd in *Persia*

Chosroes dies.

'till

'till towards the latter end of *June*, and then return'd triumphantly back into the Territories of the Empire, having lost but very few of his Men in the whole Expedition.

The Progress of the Lombards in Italy. The *Lombards* all this while lay not idle in *Italy*, but under the Conduct of *Faroald*, Duke of *Spoletto*, surpris'd a little Town call'd *Classi*, or *Chiassi*, situated upon an Arm of the Sea, into which they put a Garrison, designing it as a Curb upon *Ravenna*, near which it stood, and where *Longinus* the Exarch continually resided. About the same time they pour'd themselves with a numerous Army into *Tuscany*, where most of the Towns, being ill provided, submitted to 'em; after which they ravaged all the Country round *Rome*, the Territories of which they miserably wasted, seizing not only upon the Cattel, but the Inhabitants, whom they made Slaves, and tormented 'em with unspeakable Cruelty: *Longinus* in the mean time being unable to oppose 'em, for he found it a difficult matter to secure *Ravenna*, in which he was in a manner block'd up by the Garrison of *Classi*. This gave the *Lombards* an Opportunity of straitning *Rome*, which they did so closely that nothing could go in or out of the City, so that they thought of mastering it in a very short time, for it was neither provided with a Governor or Garrison, nor stor'd with any Ammunition or Provision, upon which Account the Famine began to rage with great Fury among the Inhabitants; but *Tiberius*, as soon as he was inform'd of the Condition the City was in, and how unable it was to hold out much longer, fitted out a handsom Fleet loaden with Men and Provisions, which arriv'd very happily at *Rome* by the way of *Ostia*, without meeting with the least Opposition from the Enemy. The Inhabitants were

Chap. III. LVIII. Tiberius II.

so encourag'd by these seasonable Supplies, that they forc'd the Enemy to raise the Blockade, and return home, after having made a Truce with the *Romans*, which however they observ'd no farther than as it conduc'd to their Benefit and Advantage.

About this time *Justin*, who had before that withdrawn himself from publick Affairs, resigning all up to the Management of *Tiberius*, left him the Empire too, after he had reign'd Sixteen Years, Nine Months and upwards. I know some have confin'd his Reign to a shorter term, cutting off from it the time during which *Tiberius* sat at Helm; but since all publick Affairs were manag'd in his Name, and his Authority was made use of in every thing relating to Peace or War, *Tiberius* his Reign cannot be said properly to begin 'till his Predecessor's Death. *Justin*, a little before his Death, call'd *Tiberius* to him, and in the Presence of the Senate and Patriarch gave him this Advice, Consider, said he, *these Imperial Ornaments conferr'd on thee by the secret Will and Pleasure of God, rather than by my Designation; this will teach thee to govern with Mercy, and to keep thy Hands unstain'd with innocent Blood. Honour thy Mother* (meaning *Sophia* the Empress) *to whom thou wert first a Servant, and art now her Son; behave thy self with as tender regard to the Publick, as thy own private Concerns. Consider what thou hast been, and what thou must be; for thou well knowest what I have been, and what now I am; avoid Pride, and then thou may'st be free from Sin. These thou here beholdest are not so much thy Servants as Children, when thou seest them think the Commonwealth is then in thy view, for in Confidence of thy good Qualities I have made thee Emperor, for the sake*

of

A. D. 578.

Justin dies.

of those who are as dear to me as my own Bowels. Be sure to have a particular Care of the Army, preferring none to any Command in it that are Effeminate or Imprudent; protect the Rich in their lawful Possessions, and relieve the Necessities of the Poor. What I now advise thee to is the Result of my own Experience, and therefore thou mayst with more safety follow it; and may that God, which made Heaven and Earth, put that into thy Heart which I have forgotten. After this, as he was proceeding in his Discourse to the same purpose, his Fit return'd, and carry'd him off. Tho' *Paulus Diaconus* tells us, that *Justin* was extreamly addicted to Covetousness, and all the other Writers of that Age set him forth as a sensual voluptuous Prince, from whose supine Negligence the State suffer'd as much as from the Cruelty and Tyranny of any of his Predecessors, yet we must either allow him to have acted all that while against the Dictates of his own Conscience, or else that he had some lucid Intervals, not only in respect of his Understanding, but Morality; for his two Discourses, at the Promotion of *Tiberius*, and the time of his Death, favour nothing of that Prince he is represented to us in the History of those Times.

II. *Tiberius* was no sooner advanc'd to the Imperial Dignity upon the Death of his Predecessor, before *Anastasia*, his Wife, was by his Order declar'd *Augusta*, to the great Regret and Indignation of *Sophia*, who had in a very great measure contributed to his Promotion, upon a Presumption that when once he was confirm'd in the Throne he would marry her; but when she saw, contrary to her Expectation, that *Anastasia*, to whom he had been secretly marry'd in his private State, was

saluted

saluted Empress, she grew his implacable Enemy, and attempted to promote *Justinian*, who did the Empire such great Service in the late *Persian* Wars, watching her Opportunity when *Tiberius*, according to a Custom of the Emperors, went to spend Thirty Days, during the Vintage, in the Country; but the Emperor being seasonably advertis'd of her Designs hasten'd back before she had time to put 'em in execution, and seizing on all her Treasures left her just enough to keep her from Want, which was all the Punishment he inflicted upon her: *Justinian* was likewise depriv'd of his Command, but it's uncertain whether it was upon the Account of *Sophia*'s Practices, or because he had not the same Success as formerly in the East, whither *Mauritius* was sent as General in his stead.

 Tiberius having thus secur'd himself against any Domestick Attempts began to provide for the publick Security of the Empire, and sent his Embassadors to *Hormisda*, King of *Persia*, with Propositions of a Peace between the two Crowns, which were with much Arrogance rejected by *Hormisda*, a young, tyrannical Prince; whereupon *Tiberius* sent a powerful Army against him, which, after an obstinate Fight, defeated the *Persians*, and took their Camp, the Spoil of which was given up to the Soldiers, excepting the Royal Plate and Treasure, which was carry'd upon twenty Elephants to *Constantinople*, together with great number of Prisoners, who, by the Emperor's Command, were richly cloth'd, and set at Liberty. *The Persians defeated.*

 Hormisda, notwithstanding this Defeat, continu'd averse to the Peace, and levying a greater Army than any of his Predecessors had rais'd for a long time before, he sent it towards the Borders under the Command of his two Generals, *Tamochosroes* and *Aduarmanes*; for by reason of his late Over-

Overthrow, and the Danger his Person was in, he made a Law that no King of *Persia* should be present in Person at any Battel for the future. *Tiberius* had, from the Beginning of his Power in the Empire, been purchasing great Numbers of Slaves from the *Hunns* and other Barbarians, whom he order'd carefully to be instructed in the Art of War; these he now form'd and divided into regular Troops, committing 'em to the Care of *Mauritius*, his General, who had Orders to join the rest of the Forces in *Mesopotamia*, and make Head against the *Persians*. *Mauritius* behav'd himself with much Valour and Conduct in this War, as may be gather'd from the Writings of *Evagrius*, who promis'd to leave Posterity a particular Account of it, which however was not perform'd by him or any other; at least, the Length of Time, or some unhappy Accident, have depriv'd us of it. He tells

Mauritius his Exploits in Persia.

us briefly that he took from the *Persians* such Towns and Forts as he judg'd stood most convenient for them, and got such great Booty that he peopled Islands and Countries, that had lain a long time uninhabited, with his Captives, of whom he had Numbers sufficient to form Armies, which fought couragiously against other Nations at Enmity with the Empire: That he defeated *Tamochosroes*, not by the Force of his Arms, but by his own most exemplary Piety, and Dependance upon God Almighty; that, on the other hand, *Aduarmanes* was overthrown purely by his Conduct, and the Courage of his Soldiers, and that at a time when *Alamandurus*, General of the *Arabians*, had betray'd him, and, contrary to a most solemn Promise, refus'd to assist him against other *Arabians* who had embrac'd his Enemies Cause; and *Theodorich*, King of the *Scythians*, had, at the first Onset, shamefully deserted him. This is the Substance of what is left us by

Eva-

Evagrius concerning this War, which, tho' it is thought to have begun in the Second Year of *Tiberius*, may reasonably be suppos'd to have continu'd 'till near his Death. And here *Baronius*, who for want of a true Information found himself unable to wait on *Mauritius* into the Field, is pleas'd to attend him back, after his Victory, to Court, whither he was recall'd by the Emperor; and entertains his Reader by the way with such wonderful Predictions concerning *Mauritius* his future Advancement to the Empire, as seem to require a stronger Authority than that upon which he delivers 'em. However, *Mauritius* being recall'd to Court was receiv'd with great Demonstrations of Affection by *Tiberius*, who marry'd him to his Daughter *Constantina*, and created him *Cæsar*. About the same time *Hormisda*, whose great Cruelty at home and ill Success abroad had drawn upon him the ill Will of his Subjects, sent his Embassadors to negotiate a Truce with the Emperor, which was at length concluded, tho' not long observ'd, as we shall see hereafter.

MAURITIUS.

Whilst *Tiberius* his Arms were thus employ'd for the Defence of the Empire in the East, he was no less follicitous for the Purity of the Faith and Protection of the Catholick Religion in the West, as appears from the Succours sent to *Hermenigild*, the Son of *Leuvigild*, King of the *Goths* in *Spain*. *Leuvigild* was a profess'd *Arian*, and a declar'd Enemy to the Orthodox Christians, notwithstanding which *Childebert*, King of *Austrasia*, was persuaded to marry his Sister *Ingonda* to *Hermenigild*, his Son, and accordingly sent her royally attended into *Spain*; where when she was arriv'd all Arts were us'd to make her renounce her Faith and turn *Arian*, in which she was so far from complying that she converted her Husband, who was entirely convinc'd

A. D. 582.

by

by the Strength of her Reason, and charm'd by her prudent Behaviour. His Father had, before the Marriage, settled upon him part of his Dominions and among other Cities that of *Seville,* where he usually resided, and where he first made a public Profession of the Catholick Faith, and which, according to *Gregory* of *Tours,* provok'd his Father to declare War against him; tho' the *Spanish* Writers affirm, that *Hermenigild* himself was forc'd to revolt, by the cruel Treatment he receiv'd from his Mother-in-law, who had gain'd an absolute Ascendant over the King, and that he surpriz'd and fortify'd *Seville,* and several other Places, for his own Security. Whatever the Provocation was it gave a Beginning to a bloody War between the *Goths* in *Spain,* and rais'd a cruel Persecution against the Faithful; insomuch that many Catholicks, terrify'd by the Sufferings of others, were forc'd to submit to an Abjuration, among whom were some Priests and even a Bishop of *Sarragossa,* call'd *Vincentius. Hermenigild,* who was unable to oppose his Father, sent *Leander,* Bishop of *Seville,* to demand Assistance from the Emperor at *Constantinople,* who accordingly sent him a Supply of Men, the Captain of which being upon his Arrival corrupted by Presents from the Father deserted the Son, who thus abandon'd fled for Refuge into a Church, whither his Brother came to him, by Order from the King, to assure him in his Name of Pardon upon an humble Submission, for a Confirmation of which himself came, and with open Arms embrac'd his Son, promising most solemnly to forget all that was past; but as soon as he had entic'd him out of his Sanctuary he loaded him with Chains and clapp'd him into Prison, where when he found he continu'd deaf to all his Threats and Promises, and that neither his Kindness could allure, nor his Severity terrify

him

him into a Recantation, he commanded him to be maſſacred, which cruel Sentence was executed accordingly.

The Year following, *Chagan*, King of the *Avari*, enter'd *Pannonia* at the Head of a powerful Army, and took *Sirmium*; from whence, by his Embaſſadors ſent to the Emperor, he demanded, not only a Sum of Mony which he had been promis'd to receive annually, but an Addition to it, together with an Elephant to be ſent him every Year, in Conſideration of which he promis'd no more to moleſt the *Roman* Borders. This the Emperor, who was unwilling to draw the Barbarians on that ſide againſt him, readily condeſcended to; but when he found *Chagan*, inſtead of being contented, enlarg'd his Demand, he ſent an Army againſt him and conſtrain'd him to retire out of the Counry.

A. D. 583.

From this time forward we meet with little or nothing in Hiſtory, worthy our Obſervation, 'till the Death of *Tiberius*, nor is it eaſie to determine in what Year he dy'd, ſo great a Difference is there between Writers in that Particular; for whereas ſome place his Death in the Year 586, others refer it to this very Year; and tho' the latter Aſſertion ſeems to be ſupported with the ſtrongeſt Reaſon I ſhall leave the Reader to his Choice, who perhaps may think the thing ſo indifferent in it ſelf as to deſerve no further Conſideration. Some time before his Death he order'd *Mauritius* to be inveſted with the Imperial Robes, at which Solemnity were preſent *John*, the Patriarch of *Conſtantinople*, and another *John*, an Orator, who, in the Emperor's Name, and by his Command, advis'd *Mauritius* to raiſe his Predeceſſor *a beautiful Monument by well governing the People he had left to his Charge, and adorn his Tomb with his Virtues; to reſtrain the Inſolence of Power*

Tiberius *Dies.*

by the Force of *Reason*, and *wisely steer the dubious Vessel of Authority by the steady Arts of Philosophy: Not to think he as far surpass'd others in Wisdom as he was advanc'd above 'em in Empire, but to listen to the wholesom Counsels of his Friends, and to prefer Plain-dealing to Flattery: To have no other Opinion of the Purple with which he was invested than of the vilest Rag, but to consider it rather, from the deepness of its Colour, as the Mourning Weeds of Monarchy, and that he was not call'd by it to the Exercise of any immoderate Power, but rather to undergo a splendid Servitude.* This Oration, pronounc'd in *Tiberius* his Name, drew Tears from the whole Assembly, who however applauded his Choice, in appointing so worthy a Person for his Successor.

His Character.   His Death was attended with the general Lamentations of the People: He was a Prince of a most beautiful Stature, and a Presence truly compos'd to Majesty: He was by Nature so courteous and engaging, that all Men were allur'd, at the very first Address, to love him: He thought it the great Duty of an Emperor to be munificent, and look'd on that Gold as Counterfeit which was rais'd by Extortion and Oppression: He was cautious in what he resolv'd, and zealous in the Execution of it: He met with no Enemies, during his Reign, but such as were Enemies to the Publick; and no Prince before him ever had more Friends: His Virtues and Abilities were as great as any of his Predecessors, tho' confin'd to a narrower Sphere: Whilst he liv'd he was the common Father of his People, to whom, in the Choice of a Successor at his Death, he may be said to have left a Legacy worthy the Greatness of his Mind and his Affection to his Subjects.

III. *Man*

s was, upon the Death of *Tiberi-*
Emperor by the Senate, the Peony; and tho' it was thought that
olute in Power he would pu-
) in his Predeceffor's Reign had
id provok'd him, especially *Ala-*
iin of the *Arabians*, who had be-
as before obferv'd, yet he fuffer'd
put to Death, but banifh'd *Ala-*
icily, and kept his Son in Prifon,
it Depredations committed upon
Empire had deferv'd to lofe his
peror, being Crown'd with great
e Patriarch of *Conftantinople*, ap-
h much Diligence to publick Af-
the Empire was threaten'd with
de he rais'd what Forces he could,
e that were already on foot, were
s Neceffity requir'd. The *Lom-*
s while with great Violence in *I-*
ere had been a Truce concluded
id the *Romans* they never truly
watching all Advantages con-
ftations in one Part or another;
ean time had not Strength suffici-
n, fo that *Rome* was in great dan-
clofely befieg'd than ever: Here-
e Second, at that time Pope of
regory the Great, his Succeffor,
l on his Behalf at *Conftantinople*,
Emperor the Neceffity there was
of Men into *Italy* to oppofe the
prevailing *Lombards*. Tho' the
t that time very hot, and requir'd
of the Empire, yet *Mauritius* re-
d fent *Smaragdus*, a Patrician, to

R 2 fuc-

Smaragdus sent into Italy. succeed him in the Exarchate of *Ravenna*. *Smaragdus* had from his Youth been bred up in the Wars, and upon his first Arrival in *Italy* gave a new face to Affairs in those Parts. He brought with him a new Army of chosen Soldiers, supply'd with all Necessaries for a War, to the great Encouragement not only of the Inhabitants of *Ravenna*, but of all *Italy*, which groan'd under the Yoke of the Barbarians. He prov'd very successful in several Engagements with the *Lombards*, and having restrain'd the Excursions of the Garrison of *Chiassi* he very much enlarg'd that of *Ravenna*. The *Lombards* had then in their Service an experienc'd Commander call'd *Droctulfus*, who being by Birth a *Sueve* had been taken in his Infancy, and forced from that time forward to follow the Fortunes of that Nation; him the Exarch manag'd with so much Address that he drew him over to his Party, to the great Detriment and Surprize of the *Lombards*, by whom he was entirely trusted, and against whom he secur'd *Vercelli*, a strong Town situate upon the *Po*, which he seiz'd and deliver'd up to *Smaragdus*, who furnish'd it with a sufficient Garrison. The taking of this Town prov'd of great Advantage to the *Romans*, for *Droctulfus* very much incommoded the Enemy by his continual Excursions upon 'em, and sent all sorts of Provisions down the *Po* to the Army of *Smaragdus* which was then employ'd in the Siege of *Chiassi*.

The *Lombards*, seeing themselves thus press'd by the *Romans*, thought they should never recover their former Reputation, and compleat their Conquest of *Italy*, 'till they restor'd their ancient and most natural Government by Kings; whereupon *Autharis chosen King of the Lombards.* they unanimously made choice of *Autharis*, the Son of *Clepho*, who being a forward and active Prince gave 'em great Hopes of a successful Reign

So soon as he was eftablifh'd in the Government he undertook the Recovery of *Vercelli*, which, being a Place of fo great Importance, he refolv'd, by all means, to force out of the Hands of the *Romans*. The Siege continu'd long, for *Droctulfus* was in the Town with a very ftrong Garrifon, and behav'd himfelf with much Caution and Courage; fo that during the Siege *Autharis* had leifure to Model the Affairs of his Kingdom; and firft he took upon him the Name of *Flavius*, and commanded it to be us'd as a Sirname by all his Succeffors in Imitation of the Ancient *Roman* Emperors. He confirm'd to the Thirty Dukes their Primitive Power and Authority, dependant of him, but ordain'd that every Three Years they fhould pay him a Moiety of their refpective Revenues, for the Maintenance and Support of his Royal Dignity. After this, being reinforc'd by frefh Troops drawn out of the Neighbouring Garrifons, he more clofely prefs'd the Siege, and in the end conftrain'd *Droctulfus* to Surrender upon Honourable Terms; for all his Men had Liberty to march out with their Arms and Baggage, and were conducted to *Ravenna*. *Autharis*, being thus Mafter of the Town, difmantl'd it, that he might make it unferviceable to his Enemies, if ever it fhould fall again into their Hands; after which he difpers'd his Troops into Winter Quarters, and then apply'd himfelf to the good Settlement of his Kingdom, which he fupply'd with wholefom and feafonable Laws, and enforc'd the Obfervance of them with fo much Vigour, that by degrees he reftrain'd his Subjects from their accuftom'd Rapine, Murder and Adultery, all which he punifh'd with Death. Being born a Heathen he had hitheito liv'd an Idolater, but now quitted the Errors in which he had been bred, and was Baptis'd. *Gregory*

Turns Chriftian.

the Great gives us a very particular Reason for his Conversion, which is, That a certain *Lombard* having found St. *Peter*'s Golden Key, drew out his Knife with a Design to cut it asunder, instead of which, being mov'd by some Secret and Divine Impulse, he cut his own Throat, and fell down dead upon the spot. This extraordinary Adventure happen'd in the Presence of *Autharis,* and several of his Nobility, who, being all surpriz'd at so unexpected a Tragedy, dar'd not for their Lives attempt to touch the Key, 'till a certain Catholick of the same Nation, who was accidentally present, approach'd boldly and took it up. Upon which the King, being convinc'd by the Miracle, commanded another Golden Key to be made like it, and sent 'em both as a Present to *Gregory*'s Predecessor of blessed Memory. Any Man that has not a Mind to be deceiv'd can't but laugh at so absurd and ill contriv'd a Fable; for where doth it appear in Scripture, that St. *Peter* ever wore material Keys: Those our Saviour entrusted him with are certainly to be understood in a Spiritual Sense, at least they could not be of Gold; for he himself tells us that *Gold and Silver he had none*; and yet with such Miracles as these has this Pope compos'd the greatest part of his Works. And after all, as if one Miracle was not sufficient for the thorough Conversion of this King of the *Lombards,* it is most certain he was instructed by an *Arian* Bishop in the Principles of Christianity, and was therefore ever after infected with that Heresie.

Smaragdus lay all this while with his Army before *Chiassi,* where he was join'd by *Droctulfus,* and the Forces under his Command. The Besieg'd had hitherto defended themselves with so much Courage, that the Exarch was as far from mastering

ng the Town, as when he first sate down before
t. *Droctulfus* observing that the Defendants had
only fortify'd themselves on that side that regarded
the Land, and that they lay naked towards the
Sea, from whence they never expected an Assault,
advis'd *Smaragdus* to Attack 'em from thence; he
suddenly put his Advice in Execution, and forc'd
'em to Surrender at Discretion. Some of the Gar- A. D.
rison, who had been most obstinate in the De- 586.
fence of the Place, were put to Death, and the
rest made Slaves.

Whilst *Smaragdus* the Exarch was thus employ'd
with various Successes against the *Lombards*, *Mauritius*, who knew what great Occasion he had for
the Forces of the Empire to carry on the War in
the East, sollicited *Childebert*, King of the *Franks*,
to assist him in *Italy*. *Childebert* listen'd to his
Embassadors, who brought him a good Sum of
Mony with 'em to Countenance the Negotiations, and made several fruitless Expeditions into *Italy*. The first time the *Lombards* out-bid the
Emperor, and brib'd him to return home; another
time his Army disagreed among themselves, and
separated before they were advanc'd far enough
to enter upon Action. Notwithstanding these
Disappointments the Emperor persuaded him to a
third Expedition, and *Childebert* thinking it highly
became his Honour at last to do some remarkable
Service for his Allie, rais'd a more numerous Army than he had before, which when he had mustered and supply'd with every thing necessary for
the Expedition, he order'd 'em to march once
more against the *Lombards*. *Autharis*, who had
formerly declin'd coming to a Battel, and secur'd
himself in his fortify'd Towns, resolv'd now to
fight 'em, thinking, if he could once give 'em an
absolute Defeat, they would have no great Inclination

nation to return hereafter. Accordingly he drew together all the Forces he had, and having, by a seasonable Speech, encourag'd his Army, presented the Enemy with Battel. The Fight was maintain'd with great Obstinacy on both sides, and the Victory, for a good while, continu'd dubious; but at lenth it declar'd for the *Lombards*, who routed the *French*, and slew great Numbers of their Men. Those who escap'd the Fight were in a great measure destroy'd by Hunger and Cold in their Return over the *Alps*, so that very few of 'em got safe home into their own Country. *Childebert*, being rather provok'd than disheartened by his ill Success, enter'd into a new Alliance with the Emperor, who undertook to act conjointly with him, and promis'd to have a strong Army ready in *Italy*, by that time *Childebert*'s should have made a Descent into the Country. Upon these Encouragements *Childebert* levy'd fresh Forces, with whom, having pierc'd into *Bavaria*, he subdu'd and pillag'd it. From thence he march'd into *Italy*, where he expected to be join'd by the Imperialists, who never came to the Rendezvous, so that *Childebert* was forc'd to be contented with taking a few Towns, in defeating the *Lombards* in some slight Engagements, and recovering *Gallia Cisalpina*, which they had taken from his Father *Sigebert*, and which at this Day is call'd *Lombardy* from the Name of the Conquerors. All this while *Autharis*, who thought himself too weak to contend with the Enemy in the open Field, retir'd into *Pavia*, and dispers'd his Forces into their Garrisons, concluding, upon good Grounds, that this Army of the *French* was no other than a casual Torrent, which would grow more impetuous by Resistance; but if suffer'd to roll on without Opposition, would by degrees spend it self, and come

to

to nothing. In short, after they had spent Three or Four Months in traversing the Country, and destroying the Fruits of the Earth, they were necessitated to return home, after their Army had been, in a great measure, diminish'd in that hot Climate, and those that remain'd were forc'd first to sell their Cloaths, and at last their Arms to purchase Provisions in their Passage. *Autharis*, being thus deliver'd for the present, thought it his safest way to conclude a Peace, if possible, with so importunate an Enemy, and sent his Embassadors to negotiate it accordingly, but never liv'd to see the Effects of their Negotiations, for he dy'd shortly after, and, as some say, by Poison, tho' it doth not appear by whose Hands it was prepar'd. And as after this the *French* had no Wars with the *Lombards* 'till the Reign of *Pepin*, so did the Emperor's Arms gain some Respite by his Death; for the Truce, which about this time was concluded, met with a more exact Observance than formerly, and *Mauritius* was more at leisure to attend the War, which rag'd with great Fury in the East.

Tho' *Hormisda* was the first that propos'd a Truce, as we observ'd before, he was the first that broke it; for finding the *Lombards* were too strong for the Emperor in *Italy*, and that the Barbarians were in Motion on every side, and having in some measure compos'd the Discontents of his Subjects, he rais'd a great Army, and advanc'd into the Territories of the Empire, destroying the Country about him, and putting all that came in his way to Death. Against him the Emperor first dispatch'd *John*, a *Thracian*, and made him General of his Forces in the East. *John* at first behav'd himself very gallantly, for he defeated an advanc'd Party of the *Persians*, and forc'd the main
Body

Body to retire; but whether he was by degrees corrupted by *Hormisda*, or had entertain'd some Dislike to the Emperor, by whom he thought he was not rewarded according to his Deserts, he in the end grew negligent and useless, and suffer'd the Enemy to gain so much upon him, that *Mauritius* found it necessary to remove him, and sent *Philippicus*, who had marry'd his Sister, to command in his stead. *Philippicus* was a Person generally belov'd by the People, whom he had oblig'd by his Liberality, so that he levy'd a considerable number of Forces in his Passage, with which, having join'd those that were already in the East, he made a very formidable Army. His principal Care, before he enter'd into Action, was to restore the ancient Military Discipline, restraining the Soldiers from that excessive Riot and Intemperance, to which they had been too long accustom'd. After this he made two Irruptions into *Persia*, in both which he show'd himself a General of good Courage, Conduct and Success. In the first of 'em he warily escap'd an Ambuscade, which *Cardariga*, the King of *Persia*'s General, had laid for him under the Mountains of *Media*, and return'd with great Booty which he had rais'd upon the Enemy's Country without any Control. In the second he encounter'd *Cardariga*, who trusting to the Numbers of his Men, and relying upon the Faith of his *Magi*, who had promis'd him an assur'd Victory, advanc'd, with so much Confidence, as if he was marching to a Triumph, rather than a Battel, and had prepar'd Chains for his Prisoners. *Philippicus*, being no ways terrify'd at the Multitude of his Enemies, prepar'd to receive him with a true *Roman* Courage, and Greatness of Mind. As both Armies were ready to engage he exhorted his Soldiers to rely upon the

Philippicus sent General into the East:

Protection of their Saviour, and to behave themselves like Men, whose Faith was founded in him; and then, having given the Word, he Charg'd the *Persians* with much Resolution, who receiv'd him with an equal Confidence ; but after they had stood their Ground for a considerable while they were forc'd to give way, and left the *Romans* Masters of the Field. The next Morning *Cardaga* rally'd his Forces, and renew'd the Fight, but was again defeated with a greater Loss than what he had sustain'd the Day before, he himself narrowly escaping the *Romans* in the Pursuit. Two Thousand of the *Persians* which were taken *Philippicus* sent to *Constantinople*, as Messengers of his signal Victory. *Philippicus*, having refresh'd his Army, prepar'd to march farther into the Country, sending *Heraclius*, his Lieutenant, with a detach'd Party before him. In the mean time *Carariga*, tho' he had been twice defeated, lost none of his Courage or Zeal for his Master's Service, but gathering all the Forces together that remain'd after his late Misfortunes, he stood upon his Guard, and designing to contend no more in the open Field, he lay prepar'd for any Opportunity, which he thought he might manage to his own Advantage. Some Deserters had inform'd him that the *Roman* Army was divided, and that those under the Command of *Philippicus* lay secure in the Confidence of their late Victories, and an Assurance that he was in no Condition to Assault 'em. Whereupon he pass'd secretly over the Mountains, and in the Night time fell so furiously upon the Rear of the *Roman* Army, that *Philippicus*, who little expected so sudden an Alarm, fled in great Consternation, being follow'd by the whole Army, who made such haste, that the *Persians*, fearing some Design, dar'd not pursue the Chace, 'till the

Put to Flight by the Persians.

Light

Light returning deliver'd the *Romans* from their Fear, and show'd their Enemies what an Advantage they had lost. *Heraclius* was all this while obeying the Orders he had receiv'd, with more Execution and better Success; for having pass'd the *Tigris* he took several Cities without any Opposition, the People being terrify'd more by the Fame of the late Victories than the Numbers of his Men, and return'd with the Spoils of the Country to *Philippicus*; who, asham'd of his late Miscarriage, was drawing all his Forces together, and prepar'd to revenge it upon his Enemies, when he receiv'd Orders from the Emperor to return to *Constantinople*, and resign the Command of the Army to *Priscus*, which occasion'd a great and dangerous Mutiny. For *Priscus*, tho' otherwise an old experienc'd Officer, was excessive Proud and Imperious: Being arriv'd at the Army he behav'd himself so arrogantly, and us'd the Soldiers with so much Rigour and Severity, that they rose up in a general Mutiny against him, pillag'd his Tents, and constrain'd him to fly for his Safety to *Edessa*, whither the most violent of the Mutineers follow'd him, and demanded him of the Inhabitants, who however resolutely refus'd to expose him to their Fury. The Soldiers seeing themselves without a Head, forc'd *Germanus* to take the Charge of the Army upon him; *Germanus* at first excus'd himself, alledging it was a thing not to be done without a Commission from the Emperor, whom he would by no means disoblige: Tho' this was a very reasonable Excuse, yet they persisted in their Demand, 'till by outragious Violences they oblig'd him to submit, and undertake to conduct 'em, or rather to be conducted by 'em; for they were grown headstrong and ungovernable, and broke out into all manner of Disorders. Those Officers that

A. D. 587.

A dangerous Mutiny.

would

would not suffer 'em to behave themselves as they pleas'd in their Quarters, where they were grown insolent and insupportable, they displac'd, and substituted others of a more complying Temper in their room. The Emperor, being inform'd of the Mutiny, sent *Philippicus* back into the East to reduce 'em to their Duty and a Military Discipline; but he found 'em furious, like wild Beasts, ready to tear those in pieces who presum'd to teach Obedience among 'em. This Disorder continu'd in the Army above a Year, during which the *Persians* were encourag'd to invade the adjoining Provinces, in hopes that the *Romans* were too busily employ'd among themselves to think of opposing them; notwithstanding which *Germanus* march'd against 'em, and gave 'em such a Defeat that there was scarce one left to carry an Account of it into *Persia*. The Emperor perceiving they still continu'd obstinate sent *Andreas*, the Captain of his Guard, to appease 'em, and persuade 'em to return to their Obedience; but when he found they gave no Ear to all they could say, he made choice of *Gregory*, Bishop of *Antioch*, to mediate the Matter between them. *Gregory* was the fittest Man in the Empire to be employ'd in that Conjuncture, for he was both a prudent Man, and had a great Influence over the Soldiers, whom he had frequently reliev'd, and supply'd with Meat, Drink and Apparel. The good Bishop readily accepted of the Employment, and procur'd the chiefest among 'em to give him a Meeting at *Litarbis*, a Town Three Hundred Furlongs distant from *Antioch*, where he made an excellent Discourse, in which he represented to 'em, *how much the Safety of their Country, and the Honour of the Empire, requir'd them to submit to the Emperor; that it was now in their Power entirely to break and ruin the Strength of the* Persian, *but that it would be a lasting*

ing

ing *Disgrace* to *Posterity* if they omitted the Opportunity; that *the Victory they had lately obtain'd under the Conduct of an illegal Commander, was an Earnest to 'em of the great Things they would perform, when led on by a lawful General.* This Discourse was attended with more efficacious Tears, which wrought *appeas'd by* so powerfully upon the Minds of the Soldiers that *the Bishop* they unanimously promis'd to do whatever he *of Antioch.* would have 'em; but when he mention'd *Philippicus* for their General they reply'd, that the whole Army had oblig'd themselves by Oath never to receive him as such again, from which however they at length departed at the Bishop's importunate Entreaties, and after he had absolv'd 'em from it. Having brought 'em to so good a Temper he invited the chief Officers, to the Number of Two Thousand, to Supper, and immediately upon *Philippicus* his Arrival they presented themselves to him, begging his Pardon for what was past, and promising an implicit Obedience for the future: *Philippicus* receiv'd 'em very civilly, and having muster'd his Forces he prepar'd for Action; for he was inform'd that *Murazas*, a new General, had taken the Field with a greater Army of *Persians* than any before, which is a great Argument of the Wealth and Power of that State; for tho' they had frequently been overthrown, and lost great Numbers of their Men, yet they still return'd with recruited Forces, and always had Peace from the Empire at the first asking, so unwilling were the Emperors to contend with them.

After several Towns had been lost and regain'd on either side, the two Armies came so near together that a Battel seem'd unavoidable, which *Philippicus* was unwilling to decline, tho' the Enemy far exceeded him in Numbers of Men: It was fought with great Obstinacy on both Hands for
some

some time, 'till at length Fortune declar'd for the Romans. The greatest Part of the *Persians* dy'd fighting upon the spot, and among the rest their General was kill'd by one of *Philippicus* his Guards; Three Thousand were taken Prisoners, the rest, to the number of Two and Twenty Hundred Men, secured themselves by Flight, and gave the King a melancholy Account of the Campaign, who however made great Preparations to repair his Losses and Dishonour the next Summer.

The Persians beaten.

The Joy the Emperor conceiv'd for this signal Victory was much lessen'd by a terrible Earthquake, which about the same time once more destroy'd the unfortunate City of *Antioch*, and Sixty Thousand of its Inhabitants; and the Year following there happen'd such an Inundation in *Italy* as had never been known since the Universal Deluge, destroying great Multitudes of Men, besides other living Creatures. The River *Athesis* flow'd as high as the Windows of St. *Zeno*'s Church near *Verona*, part of whose Walls were destroy'd by it. *Gregory* the Great, who succeeded *Pelagius* the Second in the Popedom shortly after, tells us, according to his usual Custom of recording improbable Miracles, that tho' the Waters were swoln as high as the Windows of the Church, and the Doors were left wide open, yet the Inside of the Church continu'd dry, and the People that had retir'd thither for their Safety drew Water out of the Porch as from a Cistern. At *Rome* the *Tiber* was so overcharg'd that it surmounted the very Walls of the City, and destroy'd a great Number of Publick Buildings, together with the Corn that was deposited in the Publick Magazines. A great quantity of Serpents, follow'd by a Dragon of a prodigious Bigness, were seen to pass down the River into the Sea, where the salt Water destroy'd 'em. This Inundation

A. D. 588.

undation left such a nauseous filthy Slime behind i[t] as infected the Air, and created the Plague, whic[h] spread it self throughout all *Italy*.

Notwithstanding these publick Calamities th[e] Emperor omitted nothing that was proper for car[r]ying on the War in *Persia*, whither he had sen[t] *Philippicus* fresh Supplies of Men and Mony, wit[h] Orders to recover *Martyropolis*, which had bee[n] lately betray'd to the *Persians*. *Philippicus* found i[t] impossible to take the City for want of warlike En[]gines, and therefore fortify'd the adjacent Castle to intercept whatever Succours the *Persians* shoul[d] attempt to send thither; notwithstanding which th[e] Garrison receiv'd considerable Supplies, and hel[d] out with very good Success: Whereupon *Philippi*[]*cus* was recall'd, and *Commentiolus* sent to comman[d] in his stead. *Commentiolus* fought the *Persians*, de[]feated them, and took the important Castle of *O*[c]*bas*, which being built on an high Rock over-again[st] *Martyropolis* very much incommoded the Garriso[n]. *Hormisda* was very much concern'd at these Lo[s]ses, which he attributed to *Barames*, his General[,] to whom he sent a disdainful Message and a Wo[]man's Habit, as the most proper Garb for one wh[o] he thought had behav'd himself so much unlike [a] Soldier, and order'd *Ferrochanes* to command in hi[s] stead. *Barames*, who imputed his ill Success t[o] Fortune, and not any neglect in his Office, wa[s] highly offended at so injurious a Resentment, and conspir'd against his Master. He poison'd the Ar[]my by several forg'd Letters produc'd amongst 'em[,] and drew *Ferrochanes* himself over to his Party[.] They found it no difficult Matter to put their De[]signs in Execution, for they knew *Hormisda* wa[s] generally odious to his Subjects for his Cruelty; s[o] that having depriv'd him of his Crown they ad[]vanc'd his Son *Chosroes* to the Throne, saw'd hi[m]

Hormisda depos'd by his Subjects.

Chap. III.   LIX. Mauritius.

Wife and other Son asunder before his Eyes, which then they pluck'd out, and threw him into Prison; where *Chosroes* treated him under-hand with much Civility, giving him a large Allowance of Provisions, which however the offended Prince so little acknowledg'd that he disdainfully trampled under Foot whatever was brought him; whereat his Son was so enrag'd, that, forgetting all Obligations of Nature, he commanded him to be beaten to Death with Cudgels. *and murder'd by his Son Chosroes;*

The *Persians* were very much displeas'd at this unnatural Action in their Prince, who shortly after gave the Nobility farther Provocations, in putting several of their Order to death, upon a bare Suspition that they were disaffected to him; so that a powerful Party was rais'd against him, and he forc'd to march at the Head of his Army to punish the Male-contents; but as he was ready to engage all his Men forsook him, and fled over to the Conspirators. In this abandon'd Condition he was forc'd to fly, uncertain whither to direct his melancholy Steps; having recommended himself to the Protection of the God of the Christians, he threw the Reins loose upon his Horse's Neck, and resolv'd to follow him whither ever he should go. Being arriv'd at *Circasium*, a *Roman* Town on the Frontiers, with his Wife and two small Children, attended by such of his Servants who were too just and faithful to leave him in his Misfortunes, he from thence writ in a very pathetick Style to the Emperor, beseeching him to commiserate his deplorable Condition. *Mauritius*, in a just Sense of the Uncertainty of Human Greatness, receiv'd him very affectionately, and having entertain'd him like a Prince at *Constantinople*, he sent him back with a powerful Army of *Romans*, and a prodigious Sum of Mony to augment it by new Levies of *Persians*. *who being dethron'd flies for Refuge to the Emperor,*

S   Chosroes

Chosroes being thus furnish'd march'd back to *Persia*, and was receiv'd into *Martyropolis*, where *Sittas*, who had formerly betray'd the City to the *Persians*, and had now sided with the Rebels, was put to Death: After this he had *Daras* deliver'd up to him, and pursuing *Barames*, who had been the principal Actor in the Rebellion, he defeated him, and constrain'd him to fly with great Infamy. This last Advantage quite broke the Power of the Rebels, and *Chosroes* was restor'd to his Throne with as much Ease as he had been driven from it. Tho' he was naturally a proud and arrogant Prince, yet in this Conjuncture he appear'd grateful and munificent; for he sent very rich Presents to *Gregory* of *Antioch*, and others, who had been zealous with the Emperor for his Restauration, and instrumental in it.

A.D. 591. and is restor'd by him.

IV. *Chosroes* being thus restor'd to the Throne of his Ancestors by the Emperor's Assistance a profound Peace ensu'd thereupon in the East, but the *Lombards* continu'd their Hostilities more or less from the Death of *Autharis* in *Italy*. Immediately upon his Decease the Chief of the Nation assembled at *Pavia* to elect a Successor, and when they could not agree among themselves in the Choice they remitted it to *Theudelinda*, the Widow of the Deceased, who for her Virtue was in much Esteem among them. She, upon the Advice of those who were in greatest Credit with her bestow'd her self and the Kingdom upon *Agilulf* or *Aigulf*, Duke of *Turin*; which Choice was universally approv'd by the rest of the *Lombards*, for he was a valiant Man, and had all the Qualities requisite in a compleat Governor. For Five Years together, during which *Romanus* had been Exarch of *Ravenna*, he had signaliz'd himself in no considerable

Aigulf, chosen King of the Lombards.

derable Action against the *Lombards*, who therefore oppress'd the Country almost as much by their Thefts and Robberies in times of Truce, as they could in an open legitimate War: At length, having by fair Words and a considerable Present perſuaded *Maurisio*, Duke of *Perouse*, to embrace the Emperor's Party, he made a formal Visit to *Rome*, and in his Return seiz'd on several Cities belonging to the *Lombards*, which were deliver'd up to him by the Authority and Assistance of *Maurisio*. *Aiulf*, enrag'd at this, march'd with a great Army from *Pavia* and sate down before *Perouse*, which, after a hot but short Resistance, he took, and in it *Maurisio*, whom he put to Death for his Treason, and having plac'd a Governor there of experienc'd Parts and Fidelity, he directed his Course towards *Rome*, taking several Towns in his Passage, and having destroy'd the Country all about he laid close Siege to the City, but was so vigorously repuls'd by the Inhabitants that at length he was glad to liſten to the Entreaties of Pope *Gregory*, who with the Queen's Intervention purchas'd a Peace for his *Romans*. *Aigulf* return'd home with the Prisoners he had taken, and having coupled them like Dogs he sent 'em into *France*, where they were sold for Slaves. *concludes a Truce with the Romans.*

A. D. 594.

It appears, from an Epistle of this Bishop's to *Constantina* the Empress, that the Inhabitants of those Parts were more oppress'd and afflicted by the Emperor's Officers there than by the *Lombards*; that their Impositions were so great and burdenſome, that several were forc'd to sell even their Children to raise Mony for the Collectors, who behav'd themselves in their Office with all the Rigour imaginable; and being at such a Distance from their Master they promis'd themselves all Impunity, and therefore labour'd to obstruct the Peace, which

S 2   would

would put an end to thofe extraordinary Taxes, and their cruel Exactions.

Shortly after the Conclufion of the Peace, in which *Gregory* had fo earneftly labour'd, *Romanus* the Exarch dy'd, and *Gallicanus* was fent to fucceed him by the Emperor. *Gallicanus* was a Man of Courage and Experience, who at firft religioufly obferv'd the Peace concluded by his Predeceffor, but finding fome time after that *Aigulf* was employ'd in fuppreffing Domeftick Infurrections he openly broke it, and feiz'd on *Parma*, wherein he took the King's Son-in-Law and Daughter; at which the King was fo highly provok'd, that he refolv'd to purfue the *Romans* with greater Fury than ever, and force thofe Towns from 'em which the Arms of the renown'd *Alboin* could not conquer. Accordingly he enter'd into a ftrict Alliance with *Cacanus*, or *Chagan*, King of the *Avari*, of whom we fhall hear more hereafter, and having rais'd a confiderable Army he laid clofe Siege to *Cremona*, which he took and demolifh'd; from thence he march'd to *Mantua*, which met with the fame Fate, as did likewife feveral other Cities which had revolted from him to the *Romans*. In the mean time *Gallicanus* dy'd at *Ravenna*, whither *Smaragdus* was fent once more to command, but with fuch fmall Forces that he found himfelf an unequal Match for the *Lombards*, and therefore labour'd earneftly to renew the Truce, which accordingly he effected, and prolong'd from Time to Time for a confiderable while after.

It is not unlikely but had the Emperor purfu'd the War with Vigour he might have much weaken'd the *Lombards* in *Italy*, who were divided into Factions amongft themfelves, and having tafted the Sweetnefs of an imaginary Liberty under the Government of their Dukes, they never after grew

ftedfaft

Chap. III.   LIX. Mauritius.

ſtedfaſt in their Obedience, nor contributed, as they might, to thoſe Deſigns which aim'd more at the aggrandiſing of their King, than the enriching of themſelves. But as on the one Hand the Emperor had been highly incens'd againſt the Pope, who he thought aſſum'd too much to himſelf, and uſurp'd too unlimited an Authority, ſo on the other the frequent Irruptions of the *Hunns* and *Avari* ſeem'd to require his utmoſt Application. *Chagan*, or *Cacanus*, their King, appear'd a declar'd Enemy to the Empire, which he had often infeſted by his Depredations, depopulating Towns, and impoveriſhing the Country. The Army, which had been ſent into the Eaſt to aſſiſt *Choſroes*, was recall'd to be employ'd againſt 'em, after ſeveral expenſive ways had been ſet on Foot to purchaſe their Friendſhip. The War for ſome time was carry'd on with various Succeſs; for tho' *Mauritius* had miſcarry'd in an Expedition, which he made in Perſon againſt them, yet they were often defeated by his Generals, and forc'd to return ingloriouſly home, whither *Mauritius*, having rigg'd out a very powerful Fleet, threaten'd to carry the War. Tho' ſome Authors are of Opinion that the Emperor made thoſe Preparations with no other Intent but to amuſe the Barbarians, and frighten 'em with a pretended Invaſion, yet *Evagrius* ſeems to think him in earneſt; and here we are to take leave of this Author, whoſe Hiſtory reaches down no farther than to the Twelfth Year of *Mauritius*. He divided it into Six Books, beginning there where *Theodoret* left off. Who ever has read it muſt allow him Superſtitious to a very high Degree, relating great numbers of Miracles, which very often appear ridiculous, abſurd and improbable; but Superſtition was a Weakneſs, which, about that time, began to gain very much upon the World, occaſion'd

Chagan's Succeſs againſt the Emperor.

occasion'd by the great number of Monks, who colour'd over their Ignorance and Irreligion with an outward appearance of a very extraordinary Sanctity. However, tho' this Fault is evident in all the Writings of this Author, yet he tells us they acquir'd him the Favour of the Emperors *Tiberius* and *Mauritius*, who conferr'd upon him many honourable and profitable Employments.

These Disappointments no way discourag'd *Chagan*, who return'd every Year with fresh Forces and still took Care to make the Territories of the Empire more than pay the Expence of his Expedition. He was excessive Proud and Arrogant, often declaring upon several Occasions, that *he would make himself Lord and Master of all Nations*; yet sometimes he knew how to behave himself with much Condescention and Generosity, as he did towards the latter end of this Emperor's Reign, at

A. D. 600.

what time the *Roman* Army Quarter'd at *Singeda* in *Mysia*, under the Command of *Priscus*, who was the most fortunate of all the Generals the Emperor had sent against him, was ready to starve for want of Subsistance; for he sent him Forty Waggons loaden with all manner of Provisions to refresh his Soldiers, and enable 'em to celebrate the high Festival of *Easter*, which was then at Hand with such a Chearfulness as became the Christian Profession, during which time he abstain'd from all Acts of Hostility, but as soon as it was over the Barbarians separated, and wasted the whole Country of *Thrace*, and approach'd without any Opposition towards *Constantinople*; at which the Inhabitants were seiz'd with so great Consternation that they thought of quitting *Europe*, and removing, with the best of their Effects, to *Chalcedon*, and other Places in *Asia*. But *Mauritius* who alone seem'd unmov'd at the Impendent Storm

made

Chap. III. LIX. Mauritius.

made the best Preparations he could for a Defence, fortifying the Walls, and arming the Citizens, who seem'd reviv'd at the Courage they observ'd in their Emperor. Notwithstanding which the Senate persuaded him to send an Embassy to *Chagan*, and try by fair Words and magnificent Presents to mollifie the Barbarian. These Preparations were worthy the Emperor's Care, and manifested the Affection he had for the State, but at this time prov'd unnecessary; for so great a Plague had seiz'd on the Barbarians, that *Chagan* lost no less than Seven of his own Sons in one Day, whereat being extreamly afflicted he prepar'd to return home, and offer'd to release his Captives, of whom he had Twelve Thousand, for a Crown a Head. Tho' this Offer seem'd very reasonable, and what *Mauritius* ought readily to have embrac'd, yet being, as he is generally reported, of a narrow parsimonious Temper, he refus'd to accept of it; at which *Chagan* was so incens'd, that in great Indignation he put all the Prisoners to the Sword. This Inhumanity exceedingly lost *Mauritius* the Love of his Subjects, and he himself grew so sensible of it shortly after, that he often awak'd in the Night time with great Anxiety, fancying some of those who had been Slain appear'd to him, and upbraided him for the loss of so many brave Men, who had been the Bulwark of his Empire. This, if it be true, will serve to instruct Princes how tender they ought to be of the Blood of their Subjects, if they would avoid drawing down the Divine Vengeance upon their Heads, which, after this, pursu'd *Mauritius*, and his whole Family to their utter Destruction, for from this time forward the Army grew very much disaffected to him, and even his Success seem'd to hasten on his Ruin. For *Priscus* had in several Encounters the

A great Plague destroys the Army of the Barbarians.

Advantage of the Barbarians, of whom he slew above Thirty Thousand, together with two of the King's Sons, and had taken above Five Thousand Prisoners; whereupon *Chagan* sent immediately to *Constantinople* to desire a Restitution of Captives, on both sides, and so surpriz'd the Emperor, who was ignorant what Multitudes he had in his Hands, that without any more Consideration he order'd 'em all to be dismiss'd, to the great Dissatisfaction of the Soldiers, who thought him too profuse of what they had purchas'd with so much hazard. After this he met with nothing but Crosses and Disappointments during the remaining part of his Reign. The General Officers in the Army became arrogant, the Soldiers mutinous, and the People in general discontented. The Emperor himself grew melancholy and uneasie, fancying his Fate approach'd, and that he had not long to live. He spent most of his Time in Prayer and Religious Retirements, in providing for his Children and settling his Family, in all which he behav'd himself with an entire Resignation to the Will of God, and prepar'd himself for the worst that could befal him. His Death is said to have been usher'd in by several things that portended his Ruin, which however did not render it more remarkable than his exemplary Behaviour in that last of Trials. Those who have written of it tell us, that a Lamp which for a long time had been kept continually burning in the Church, went out of it self, and tho' all ways imaginable were taken to restore it by the Monks that attended, yet it would by no means be rekindl'd. *Gregory* the Great saith, That at Noon Day, in the Market-place of *Constantinople*, a Person cloath'd like a Monk appear'd publickly to the Emperor with a Sword in his Hand, and cry'd out with a loud Voice, *By this shall the Emperor*

Several strange Accidents preceding the Death of Mauritius.

Emperor Mauritius *die,* after which he immediately difappear'd. Some foretold the Emperor that he fhould fall by the Hands of one whofe Name began with *Ph.* which made him fufpect *Philippicus,* his Sifter's Husband, and thereupon he threw him into Prifon; but being inform'd in a Dream that it was not *Philippicus,* but a Captain in his Army call'd *Phocas* was to do the Deed, he releas'd his Brother, and on his Knees befought him to forgive his Fears. After this he commanded Prayers to be made for him in all Churches, and apply'd himfelf, the beft he could, to Publick Bufinefs. His Brother *Peter* at that time commanded the Army upon the *Danube,* to whom he fent his Orders to pafs with the Forces over the River, and Winter in the Enemy's Country; the Soldiers, who thought it done on purpofe to expofe 'em to new Hardfhips, in a great Mutiny declar'd *Phocas,* a Centurion, Emperor, and lifting him up on a Target, with repeated Acclamations, as fuch faluted him: The News of which Revolution being divulg'd throughout *Conftantinople,* almoft as foon as the Intelligence of it was brought to Court, the Mob, for the moft part fond of Change, fell into great Tumults and Diforders; which when the unfortunate Emperor obferv'd, he in great Confternation Embark'd with his Wife and Children, with an intent to retire into fome Place of Safety, but met with contrary Winds, which drove him back, fo that he was forc'd to return into the City, where he took care to hide himfelf 'till he could meet with fome more convenient Seafon to efcape.

A.D. 602.

Phocas declar'd Emperor by the Soldiers.

In the mean time *Phocas,* being vefted with the Imperial Purple, advanc'd at the Head of his Army directly towards *Conftantinople,* where the Governor of the City, the Senate, and the Patriarch went out to meet him, and receiv'd him with the
general

general Applause of the People. After the Patriarch had receiv'd from him the Confession of his Faith, with a Promise to maintain the Rights of the Church, and preserve the Peace thereof, he was solemnly Crown'd in the Presence of the People in the Church of St. *John* Baptist, and, according to Custom, went in Procession to the *Circus* two Days after to be presented at the Publick Shows, where some hot Disputes arising between the two Factions formerly mention'd, *Phocas* sent his Guards to appease the Tumult, but the Soldiers dealt so roughly with some of the most obstinate, that their Friends cry'd out in a tumultuous manner, *that* Mauritius *was not yet dead*, and threaten'd to re-establish him, *who*, they said, *would do 'em Justice.* The Tyrant's Jealousie being awaken'd at this Reprehension he, in a great Passion, gave Order that diligent Search should be made for *Mauritius,* designing to establish his own Authority in the Death of his Competitor. As soon as he was found he commanded him to be dragg'd with his Children to *Chalcedon,* where first, by the Tyrant's Orders, Five of that Prince's Sons were murder'd before his Face, during which he behav'd himself with so much Courage and Submission to Providence, and was so far from repining or being impatient, that when a Nurse had hid one of his youngest Sons, and plac'd her own in his stead, the Emperor would not permit it, but discover'd him to the Executioner, frequently repeating these Words, *Just art thou, O Lord, and righteous in all thy Judgments.* Tho' this Circumstance, which is related with great assurance of him, appears something extraordinary at the first view, yet I believe the Reader, upon a farther Consideration, will conclude that it savours too little of natural Affection to be grounded upon the ust Motives of Christian Religion. After he had thus beheld the Death of his Children, he readily submitted his own Neck to the Executioner. Their Heads were cast on a Heap in the Fields near the *Forum* in *Constantinople*, where they lay 'till they putrify'd, and then the Tyrant suffer'd 'em to be bury'd with their Bodies. *Constantina,* the Wife of *Mauritius,* fled with her Daughters into a Church in *Constantinople,* from whence the Murderers prepar'd to force her, but were oppos'd by the Patriarch and the People, who would not suffer any Violence to be offer'd to 'em, insomuch that they continu'd there in Safety about Three Years, during which time the Tyrant could never get 'em into his Power, 'till by fair Words and mighty Promises he at length entic'd 'em out, and shut 'em up into a Monastery, where in the end they were all murder'd by *Phocas* his Order, tho' he had given 'em all imaginable Assurances of a civil Treatment. *Theodosius,* the eldest Son of *Mauritius,* had been sent by his Father at the beginning of his Troubles into *Persia,* with earnest Entreaties to *Chosroes* to take him into his Protection in return of the like Kindness he had formerly receiv'd from him; but *Phocas* his cruel Jealousie was not confin'd to *Constantinople* and the adjacent Parts, for his bloody Sentence o'retook him before he could reach the Confines, and murder'd him.

Mauritius and his Children murder'd.

The innumerable Miseries in which the Empire was shortly after involv'd, makes it evident to the World how great a Loss the Publick had in *Mauritius,* who was enrich'd with a great many Virtues, and subject to very few Vices; for he was Valiant, Prudent, Courteous, patient in Adversity, and in Prosperity moderate; he was eminent for the Purity of his Faith, and his Zeal for the Church, the Peace of which he labour'd with great Care to preserve

His Character.

serve and maintain; he was a great Lover of Virtuous and Learned Men, with whom he familiarly convers'd; and it's hard to determine which was most conspicuous in him, his Piety, for which he was exemplary remarkable, or his Felicity, which from a private State advanc'd him to the Imperial Throne, whereon he govern'd with so much Success, 'till his Covetousness destroy'd him, the only Vice of Note to which he was subject, in which he differ'd very much from his Predecessor, and which, of all others, is the most unworthy a Prince. *Mauritius* was murder'd in the Seventeenth Year of his Reign, according to some, but, according to others, in the Twentieth, *Gregory* the Great being then Pope of *Rome, A. D.* 602.

CHAP.

CHAP. IV.

From the Beginning of Phocas *his Reign to the Death of* Heraclius.

Containing about Thirty Seven Years.

I. M*Auritius* his untimely Death may serve as a Warning to all Princes, how they give way to that sordid Vice of Covetousness, as being the most dangerous and hateful wherewith a Prince can be infected: From hence spring Violence, Wrongs, Rapine, Bribery, Extortion, and intolerable Impositions; where this reigns Merit goes unrewarded, Guilt unpunish'd, Wars are often begun upon unjust Grounds, and Peace concluded upon dishonourable Condescensions. 'Tis a Vice pernicious in all Degrees of Men, but more especially in Kings, for it often renders their Reigns short and miserable, and their Deaths sudden and ignominious; whereas Liberality, that darling Idol of the People, has frequently prolong'd the Reigns even of wicked Princes. Of both these History can supply us with innumerable Instances, and particularly this Emperor *Mauritius* is a convincing Example of the first, whose Parsimony lost him both his Empire and Life; and yet so prone are the Minds of Men to it, that his immediate Successor, who could not but be convinc'd of the Truth of it, split afterwards upon the same Rock, as we shall have Occasion to shew hereafter.

Phocas, being thus own'd and crown'd Emperor in *Constantinople,* took Care to have his Election approv'd and Title acknowledg'd in *Rome,* and accordingly

cordingly gave Order to have his own Image, as the Custom was, and that of his Wife, to be sent thither; where the People, pleas'd with Novelty, and incens'd against the late Government by the violent Courses of *Mauritius* his Ministers in *Italy*, receiv'd 'em with joyful Acclamations, and *Gregory* the Pope commanded 'em to be reposited in the Oratory of St. *Cæsarius*, the Martyr; after which he writ Letters to *Phocas* full of fulsome Flatteries, unworthy a Person of his Character and Function, wherein having decry'd the precedent Administration, and exclaim'd against *Mauritius* as a Prince sordid and tyrannical, he in most exalted Terms extols *Phocas* and his Government, and congratulates him for his Advancement to the Throne, which was effected by the peculiar Designation of God, to relieve his People out of the Tribulation under which they had a long time groan'd. And certain it is, if History had convey'd down to us no other Account of *Phocas* than what we find in *Gregory*'s Letters, Posterity must have esteem'd him a very excellent Prince, but it will quickly appear to the Reader how far he fell short of that Character. But the Pope had a farther Design in these Encomiums, for being at ill Terms with the Patriarch of *Constantinople*, whom *Mauritius* still supported with his Authority against him, he was in hopes by this servile Compliance to preingage his Successor to his Interest. The Patriarchs of *Constantinople* had for some Ages before been distinguish'd with the Title of Oecumenic, or Bishops universal, and so likewise had the Bishops of *Rome*, *Alexandria*, and some other Patriarchs: This Title, which in its proper and most extensive Sense imply'd no more than what the Popes of *Rome* arrogate to themselves at this Day, was so highly displeasing to *Gregory* that he could not find Terms bad

[marginal note:] Gregory the Great flatters Phocas.

bad enough to exprefs it in, and was not only for having the Patriarch of *Conftantinople* lay it afide, but renounc'd it himfelf as Proud, Prophane and Diabolical; on the other hand, the Patriarch, concluding it a thing indifferently to be us'd by him and others of the fame Dignity, thought he fhould indeed be guilty of that Novelty of which the Pope accus'd him, if he fhould defignedly quit a Name his Predeceffors had enjoy'd fucceffively for fo many Years together. Upon this grew a great Divifion between him and the Pope, who enter'd into the Conteft not fo much out of an Abomination to the Title, as becaufe he had a Mind to deprefs the See of *Conftantinople,* which he found grew more Auguft every Day through the Refidence of the Emperors; whereas, on the contrary, that of *Rome* was much diminifh'd and impair'd by the continual Wars that deftroy'd *Italy,* and kept the City almoft in a perpetual Captivity. He knew that for the moft part the Patriarchs of *Conftantinople* were as ambitious as the Bifhops of *Rome,* and therefore, unlefs prevented, would in time affume a Precedency over 'em, amidft thofe publick Confufions with which the Weft was diftracted. He had been all along a zealous Afferter of the Power and Prerogative of the Popedom, tho' it was not then fwoln up to that high Pitch to which it is fince arriv'd; and confidering of what Service his Intereft in *Italy* might be to the Emperor, he thought he might fo far engage *Mauritius,* in the Difpute as to gain by the Quarrel; and tho' he ftrenuoufly inveigh'd againft the Title of *Univerfal Bifhop,* which rather than fhare with a Rival, at that time fo potent, he was contented to renounce himfelf, yet he ftill maintain'd with much Heat the Priviledge his Predeceffors had arrogantly ufurp'd, that of being the firft in Order and

Dignity

Dignity of all the Prelates and Patriarchs throughout the Church of Chrift. *Mauritius* was fo far from adhering to him in the Controverfie, that he very zealoufly oppos'd him, as well in that as in whatever elfe he groundlefly affum'd to himfelf and his Succeffors; for this Reafon he made his Court with fo much Application to *Phocas*, who being offended at the unfhaken Conftancy and Integrity of *Cyriacus*, Patriarch of *Conftantinople*, Three Years after declar'd the Pope of *Rome* Univerfal Bifhop, or Head of the Church, a Title fit for a Tyrant to beftow, and the Pope of *Rome* to embrace. *Cedrenus* obferves, that *Phocas*, being a wicked Prince, had a Reign fuitable to his Qualities, full of Misfortunes and Calamities, publick and private; infinite Numbers of Men and Beafts dy'd after an extraordinary manner; the Earth refus'd her Fruits in Seafon, and deform'd the Year with a barren Face, fo that whole Provinces were deftroy'd with Famine and Peftilence, whilft the War on every fide, like prevailing Flames, broke out upon the Empire. *Narfes*, who had been one of *Mauritius* his Generals in the Eaft, revolted upon the Death

A.D. 603.
of that Emperor, and feizing on the City of *Edeffa* fent for Affiftance to *Chofroes*, King of *Perfia*, who with a great Army invaded the Territories of the Empire. *Phocas* hereupon fent *Germanus* with a good Body of Troops againft *Narfes*, by whom he was defeated, and flain in Battel; nor could *Leontius*, who was fent to fucceed him, do much more for his Service, but was fo often baffled and overthrown by the Courage and Conduct of *Narfes* that the Tyrant in a great Rage recall'd him, and order'd him to be led about in Chains; and *Phocas* finding by Experience that *Narfes* was by no means to be overpower'd, endeavour'd to effect that by Craft which he could not accomplifh

by

by open Force, and accordingly left no ways unattempted to withdraw *Narses* from his Confederacy, and never gave over 'till by many Oaths and repeated Asseverations of Indemnity and Favour he persuaded him to desert the Barbarians, and return to his Country; but as soon as he had him in his Power, without any Regard to his former Promises and Engagements, he cruelly order'd him to be burnt alive, to the great Dissatisfaction of the People, who had a high Veneration for the Merits of *Narses*, and began to repent of their late Change. These Discontents at home made the Enemies of the Empire more successful abroad, for *Chosroes* ravag'd the Upper and Lower *Syria* at Discretion, meeting with none that were able or willing to oppose him; so that during the Reign of *Phocas* he took from the Empire all *Syria, Armenia, Cappadocia, Galatia* and *Paphlagonia*, whilst the Tyrant, instead of providing for the Security of the State, as he ought, employ'd his Time in Jealousie and bloody Inquisitions, or drunken Festivals, behaving himself sometimes like a sensual Beast, at others like a cruel and inexorable Monster. His Debauchery render'd him despicable, and his Cruelty odious, so that he led his Life like other Tyrants, under continual Anxieties and doubtful Apprehensions. In the Second Year of his Reign *Gregory*, Pope of *Rome*, dy'd of the Gout, after having sate in the Chair Thirteen Years and an half. He was undoubtedly a Man of extraordinary Qualifications, for which Reason he was sirnam'd *The Great* after his Decease. His Enemies must allow him to have been in most Respects a vigilant, active, and tractable Person, and one who had a peculiar Care of his Church and Diocess. He was devout and sober, an exact Observer of Church Discipline, and a great Foe to Simony; so that he may justly

Narses burnt alive

be

be esteem'd the greatest Bishop of those Times, and it evidently appears, throughout his Writings, in how many Things, relating both to the Doctrine and Discipline of the Church, his Successors have differ'd from him. He has not without Reason been call'd *The last Bishop of* Rome, for he was the last that took Care to acquit himself as he ought in his Episcopal Charge, by inspecting into his Church, as well as the growing Corruptions of the Age he liv'd in would permit him; the rest that have hitherto succeeded him for the most part have been ignorant, vitious, intriguing Prelates, who, abandoning the Care of their Flock, have regarded nothing but the Satisfaction of their Avarice, Ambition, and sensual Appetites; Upon which account it's no wonder if in the following Ages Superstition and mortal Errors infested the Church, and God in just Indignation suffer'd *Mahomet*'s Impiety to gain upon the World, to the great Scandal and Hazard of Christianity, of which the Histories of those Times give us too melancholy Accounts. After the Death of *Gregory* the Competitors for the Popedom manag'd the Dispute a long time with great Heats and Animosities, so that a Vacancy ensu'd for almost Six Months; at length *Sabinian*, born at *Volaterra* in *Tuscany*, was elected by the People, who were made to hope great Things of him, in all which he deceiv'd 'em after his Advancement, grinding the Poor by his excessive and unchristian Extortions, who therefore wounded him as he appear'd in Publick, of which he dy'd Six Months after his Election.

A. D. 607.
Phocas his Cruelty.

In the mean time *Phocas*, who was distracted by as many Fears as he was encumber'd with Vices, thought to strengthen and secure his Authority by Alliances with the Nobility, and marry'd his Daughter *Domitia* to *Priscus*, a Patrician, celebrating

ting the Nuptials with great Solemnity, and diverting the People with publick Shows and Entertainments. But the Masters of the Sports having expos'd the Images of the Bride and Bridegroom in the publick *Circus*, the People with a general Voice saluted them *Augusti*, whereat the distrustful Tyrant was so displeas'd that he commanded both the Masters to be immediately beheaded; at the same time his Son-in-Law had tasted of his Fury, had not the People interpos'd, and petition'd the Emperor in his behalf: Notwithstanding which he look'd upon him with a jealous Eye ever after, of which *Priscus* was sensible, and kept himself upon his Guard. *Phocas* his jealous Fears were hardly silenc'd before *Petronia*, who had been plac'd by his Order as a Spy upon *Constantina* and her Daughters, inform'd him of a private Correspondence maintain'd between that Princess and *Germanus*, a Man of great Authority in the former Reign, and what Hopes they conceiv'd that her Son *Theodosius* was still alive. Upon this the Tyrant commanded *Constantina* to be rack'd, who in the Height of her Torments confess'd that *Romanus*, a Patrician, who had been formerly Governor of *Rome*, was of the Conspiracy. He being tortur'd readily impeach'd several others, who he knew were inclinable and preparing to dethrone the Tyrant. Hereupon *Constantina* and her Daughters were put to Death, as we observ'd before, together with *Germanus* and his Sons, *John*, and *Ziza*, two Patricians, *Romanus*, and many more. And not contented with these Executions, he threw the most noble and deserving of the Citizens, of whom he had the least Suspicion, into Prisons, which were so crouded that several of 'em dy'd for want of Room, being suffocated with the Noisomness of the Place. However *Phocas* proceeded still in his inexorable Cruelty, and having remov'd all that were ally'd to *Mauritius*, he extended it farther, and swept off all that were in the least degree suspicious, or distasteful to him. Being inform'd that his Son-in-Law *Priscus* was offended at his barbarous Proceedings, he sent to have him seiz'd, but he narrowly escap'd the Tyrant's Ministers, and drew several among the principal of the Senate over to his Party, who hearing a Conspiracy was forming against him in *Africk* sent over their Deputies to *Heraclius*, Governor of that Province, by whom they desir'd him to dispatch with all Expedition his Son *Heraclius*, and *Nicetas* his Lieutenant, with an Army sufficient to oppose the Tyrant, who, ignorant of these Transactions, pursuant to his own Maxim, made choice of none but such as were as cruel as himself for his prime Officers, who were the ready Ministers of his bloody Passions. His extream Cruelty ought to have render'd him terrible to Mankind, and yet his sordid Covetousness and dissolute way of Life expos'd him to the Contempt of all the World, which in a great measure gave Ground to those many Designs form'd against him, and he scarce ever appear'd at the publick *Circus* but he met with some Affront from the People, his own Guards often reviling him for his Drunkenness and Luxury; at which he was once so incens'd that he commanded his Officers to seize a great Number of them, as well innocent as guilty, some of whom he beheaded, others he dismember'd, and binding 'em up in Sacks threw 'em into the Sea; notwithstanding which the Soldiers assembling in a great Body set Fire to the *Prætorium* and the Court, whereat *Phocas* was more terrify'd than enrag'd, and contented himself with no other Punishment than cashiering the most forward among 'em; for their Peremptoriness made him apprehend a general Insurrection:

surrection, of which growing every Day more and more in Fear, he requir'd the Prelates of the Church to agree to a Law, ordaining all those Soldiers to be honour'd as Martyrs, who dy'd couragiously fighting in the Service and Defence of their Prince, but never could prevail with them to consent to it.

Towards the latter end of his Reign the *Jews*, in hopes of an Impunity, which they thought to purchase with a great Sum of Mony, rais'd a most horrible Sedition at *Antioch*, in which they massacred incredible Numbers of Christians, and among the rest *Anastasius*, the renown'd Patriarch of the City. They ignominiously insulted his dead Corps, cutting off his Privy Parts, which they thrust into his Mouth, and then dragg'd him through the Publick Streets. *Phocas*, upon the first News of this Tumult, order'd *Bonosus*, his General in the East, to chastise 'em, who, arriving at the Head of a good Army before *Antioch*, found 'em still busied in their bloody Executions, so that most of 'em were put to the Sword, others dismember'd, and expell'd the City.

A.D. 609.

An Insurrection of the Jews at Antioch.

The same Year there happen'd so sharp a Winter that the Seas were frozen about *Constantinople*, and the Tyrant's own Court began at length to grow so weary of him, that several Designs were daily set on Foot to deliver the World from so great a Plague. *Theodorus*, Præfect of *Cappadocia*, *Helpidius*, General of the Artillery, and *Anastasius*, the *Comes Largitionum*, had about this time agreed with several others of great Authority near his Person, to kill him as he sate on his Throne in the *Hippodrome*, and to Proclaim *Theodorus* Emperor. But the thing being discover'd by *Anastasius*, all the Conspirators, both Principals and Accomplices, were put to Death. But, tho' he had escap'd escap'd this Danger, his Fate began to press hard upon him; for he being set against the World, and the World against him, the Controversie could not be long in Dispute. Those in *Africk* were now ripe for Action, where *Heraclius*, the Præfect, having rais'd a powerful Army embark'd it on Board a sufficient number of Ships, and committed it to the Conduct of his Son. At the same time *Nicetas*, the Son of *Gregoras*, *Heraclius* his Lieutenant, march'd with a Land Army by the way of *Alexandria* and *Pentapolis*. Some say there was an Agreement between these two Generals and their Friends, that he who first had the Fortune to defeat *Phocas*, and seize on the City of *Constantinople*, should be declar'd Emperor. *Heraclius* steer'd on his Course to *Abydos*, where he kindly receiv'd such Noblemen as had been banish'd by the Tyrant, after which he pursu'd his Voyage to *Heraclea*, and from thence to *Constantinople*, where, in the Haven of *Sophia*, he engag'd *Phocas* and defeated him. *Phocas*, being overthrown, fled to the Court, where an Officer, call'd *Photinus*, whose Wife the Tyrant had formerly ravish'd, assisted by a Party of Soldiers, pull'd him from his Throne, pluck'd the Imperial Robe over his Ears, and cloathing him in a black Vest led him bound to *Heraclius*, who ask'd him, with a grave Countenance, *If thus he had govern'd the Common-wealth?* To whom the Tyrant reply'd, *It was his Business, if he could, to govern it better*; whereupon he commanded first his Hands and Feet, then his Arms and Privy Parts, and at last his Head to be cut off, and then deliver'd his Trunk up to the Soldiers, who burnt it in the *Forum*. This in general is the Account Authors have left us concerning the Death of *Phocas*, tho' they disagree a little among themselves in the Particulars.

Heraclius sets out against Phocas,

who is Slain.

As to his Character they say he was of a mean *Stature*, Deform'd, and of a terrible Aspect; his Hair was red, and his Beard kept continually shav'd; his Eye-brows met, and his Cheek was mark'd with a Scar, which, when he was in a Passion, grew of a Colour like that of Lead. He was addicted both to Wine and Women, being a great Drunkard, and a notorious Adulterer; he was by Nature fierce, and in his Actions bloody, bold in Speech, free from all Compassion, furious in his Disposition, and in his Principles an Heretick, so that there was not so great a Monster throughout his Dominions, except his own Wife *Leontia*, who in all these Particulars was as bad as her Husband. *Phocas* was Slain in the Eighth Year of his Reign, *An. Dom.* 610.

<small>*His Character.*</small>

II. *Heraclius*, having been the Principal Instrument in delivering the World from the Tyranny of *Phocas*, was, as a Reward for so eminent a Service, with great Joy proclaim'd Emperor, and solemnly Crown'd at *Constantinople*; his Father, *Priscus*, and other Great Men, who had been the chief Actors in the late Revolution, assisting at his Inauguration. The same Day that he was Crown'd himself, he set the Imperial Crown on the Head of *Fabia*, the Daughter of *Rogatus*, an *African*, to whom he had been formerly contracted, and whose Name was now chang'd for that of *Eudocia*. Tho' the whole World, which had groan'd under the Tyranny of his Predecessor, thought themselves extreamly happy in so unexpected a Change, yet several remarkable Misfortunes fell upon the Empire during his Reign. At his first Advancement to the Throne he found the State in a very low Condition. In the East the successful Progress of the *Persians* render'd 'em exceeding

<small>HERACLIUS.</small>

<small>*The low Estate of the Empire at this time.*</small>

ceeding formidable; for having this Year travers'd *Syria* they took *Apamea* and *Edessa*, and came as far as *Antioch*, where they were oppos'd by a Party of *Romans*, who were all cut off; at the same time the *Scythians* and *Avari* broke into the Territories of the Empire, destroying all where ever they pass'd. These Calamities made the Crown sit uneasie upon the Head of *Heraclius*, who was scarce warm in his Imperial Robes before he felt the Cares with which, like *Hercules* his Shirt, they were poison'd. However he industriously apply'd himself to the Administration, and endeavour'd to make good the Expectation the World had conceiv'd of him. He knew he should be unable to oppose, as he ought, the Designs of his Enemies abroad, whilst he lay liable to any private Conspiracies at home; for which Reason he put all *Phocas* his Brothers and Relations to Death, and then, by several Acts of Grace, sought to endear himself to the People: After which, making as good Preparations as the weak Condition of the Empire would permit, he form'd an Army which consisted chiefly of new-rais'd Troops, for the old Legions were so entirely exhausted, that of those many Thousands, which had rebell'd against *Mau-* A. D. *ritius,* and advanc'd *Phocas,* there were but two 611. Soldiers remaining upon the Muster-Rolls, as if they had all fallen, by the avenging Hand of Providence, for their Perfidy to that Prince. Over this Army *Crispus* was declar'd General, and sent into *Cappadocia,* into which notwithstanding the *Persians* broke the Year following, where having kill'd an infinite number of Men, and laid all the Country waste before 'em, they seiz'd on the City of *Cæsarea,* which they sack'd, and then return'd back with all the Inhabitants, whom they kept as Slaves, or sold into Captivity. After this, finding

finding the sweetness of these successful Expeditions, they hardly ever lay still, but made continual Irruptions into the Territories of the Empire, taking what Cities they pleas'd, amongst the rest that of *Damascus,* in which they found a very rich Booty, besides great Numbers of Inhabitants, who shar'd the same Fate with those that had fallen into their Hands in their former Depredations. *Heraclius,* who was sensibly touch'd with the unexpressible Miseries of his Subjects, and saw how difficult a thing it was to restrain the *Persians* by force of Arms, in the Condition the Empire then was in, sent his Embassadors, furnish'd with very considerable Presents, to *Chosroes,* by whom he earnestly exhorted him to be guided by more moderate Councils, and putting a stop to that continu'd Flux of Blood, content himself with an annual Tribute. He reminded him of the great Favour and Protection he had receiv'd from *Mauritius,* and bid him propose his own Terms, upon which he would condescend to a Peace. *Chosroes,* being exalted by his great Success, dismiss'd the Embassadors without giving 'em Audience, aiming now at nothing less than making himself absolute Master of the Empire. Accordingly having rais'd a greater Army than any he sent before into the Field, he seiz'd on the Passages of the River *Jordan,* and passing that River he laid all *Palestine* waste, and took the City of *Jerusalem.* Here the *Persians* committed such outragious Acts, as the Horror of them is not to be express'd; they sold near Ninety Thousand Christians to the *Jews,* who did not buy 'em with an Intent to use 'em as the universal Consent of Nations requires Captives should be us'd, but inventing unheard of Torments, put 'em to most cruel Deaths. *Zacharias,* the Patriarch, was carry'd away into *Persia,*

Heraclius sends Embassadors to Chosroes,

who takes the City of Jerusalem.

fia, and with him vast Riches, which they found in the City and Parts adjacent, together with a peice of Wood, said to be part of the real Cross on which Christ suffer'd.

Great Numbers of miserable Christians fled from the Fury of these Inhuman Conquerors into *Egypt*, some leaving their dearest Friends and Relations, others their Wives and Children, and all of 'em what ever was necessary for the Comfort and Support of Life behind 'em: Whither notwithstanding they were shortly after pursu'd by their implacable Enemies, who, not content with their Devastations in *Asia*, roll'd on like an irresistible Stream, and overwhelm'd *Egypt*, pillaging *Alexandria*, the Metropolis of the Country, and at length return'd loaden with the Spoils of *Africk*, leaving a sufficient Force behind 'em to block up *Carthage*, which they took the Year following. These violent Irruptions of the *Persians*, in which they scatter'd Destruction all around, rous'd up the Emperor from his Domestick Shows and Triumphs, in which he had been too busily employ'd for some time before, and made him think of some Methods to obstruct or prevent 'em. Knowing the Forces of the Empire, at that time on Foot, were unable to stop their Impetuosity, he once more sent his Embassadors to *Chosroes*, who in most earnest Terms represented to him how highly he was engag'd to the Empire, and entreated him to accept of a Peace upon what ever Conditions he should think fit himself; but the Barbarian grew more Insolent from his Submission, and, grown intoxicated with his continu'd Success, affronted not only the Emperor and the Empire, but blasphem'd God himself; for he arrogantly reply'd, *That he would give Ear to no Terms of Accommodation, 'till he had solemnly renounc'd his crucify'd Saviour, and publickly*

A. D. 618.

His Insolence and Blasphemy.

publickly ador'd the *Sun*, the great God of the *Persians*. This barbarous Impiety provok'd the Almighty to raise, as from a Lethargy, the incens'd *Heraclius*, who two Years after having made Peace with *Chagan*, King of the *Avari*, he rais'd a very powerful Army, consisting not only of his own Subjects, but of *Hunns*, *Avari*, and other *European* Nations. Finding his own Treasures exhausted, and how dificult it was to raise Mony upon those who had been impoverish'd by the Wars, he had recourse to the Clergy, who were more immediately concern'd in this Quarrel, of whom therefore he borrow'd all the Vessels of Gold and Silver belonging to the Churches of *Constantinople*, which he Coin'd into Mony, wherewith to pay his Soldiers, who were marching to fight in defence of their Lives, their Liberties and Religion. This Example was follow'd by the other opulent Churches throughout his Dominions, where the Emperor had his Commissioners appointed to make the Collection.

Heraclius, before he began his Expedition, appointed his Son *Constantine* Governor of *Constantinople* in his Absence, under the Care and Assistance of *Sergius*, the Patriarch, and *Bonus*, a Patrician, a Man in great Reputation for his Wisdom and Experience. And having, by fresh Letters, adjur'd *Chagan* to be a strict Observer of the Articles between 'em, which heretofore he had treacherously violated, he set forward immediately after *Easter*, Training his Men as he march'd, and Disciplining such as were raw and unexperienc'd. In the mean time the *Persians*, under the Conduct of *Saes*, their General, continu'd their Ravages, piercing into *Galatia*, where they took by Storm the City of *Ancyra*, and wasted the Country without control *The Treachery of his General.*

as far as *Chalcedon*, where, hearing *Heraclius* was marching against him, he sent and demanded an Interview, in order, as he pretended, to set on Foot a Negotiation for a Peace. The Emperor, well pleas'd with the Proposal, readily consented, and was so ensnar'd by his fair Promises, that, according to his Desire, he sent Seventy of his Nobility with him to prepare and agree to the Articles in *Persia*; but the perfidious *Persian*, having gotten those Persons in his Power, threw 'em into Chains, and carry'd 'em bound with him to Court, where they were all cast into Prison, and severely treated by *Chosroes*'s Order, who however pull'd *Saes* his Skin over his Ears, for having once seen *Heraclius*, and not brought him away Prisoner with the rest. After which he sent a General, call'd *Sarbaras*, to Command in his stead, who at first did great Mischief in the Provinces; for the *Roman* Soldiers were at Variance among themselves, which *Heraclius* labour'd earnestly to compose, and then march'd with full Confidence against his Enemies, and at length arriv'd on the Confines of *Armenia*; and having defeated a Party of *Persians*, that pretended to dispute his Passage through the Straits, and Winter drawing on, he retir'd towards *Pontus*, as if he intended there to take up his Winter Quarters, by which means he deceiv'd the *Persians*, who thought him in earnest, and broke into their Territories, which he wasted in an Hostile manner, and drew the main Strength of the Enemies Army out of *Cilicia* for the Defence of their own Country, who pressing close upon his Rear, it came by consent to a pitch'd Battel, wherein the *Persians* were overthrown, and left the *Romans* Masters of their Camp and Baggage. This done *Heraclius* dispers'd his Forces to winter in

who is justly punish'd by his Master.

in *Armenia*, and he himself went to *Constantinople*, from whence he found himself oblig'd to return before the Spring was well advanc'd to oppose *Sarmanazar*, who at the Head of the *Persians* wasted the *Roman* Territories as usually. But before he open'd the Campaign he once more sent Letters to *Chosroes*, conjuring him *to incline to a firm and lasting Peace, and release those Seventy Embassadors which he injuriously retain'd contrary to the Law of Nations.* But *Chosroes* was so little concern'd at the Defeat his Army lately receiv'd, that he thought *Heraclius* his Message proceeded from a fearful unactive Temper, and therefore without vouchsafing to return an Answer he order'd his Forces to march into *Asia Minor*, with Orders to rove about the Country with their accustom'd Barbarity. On the other side *Heraclius*, seeing all Offers towards a Peace were rejected, mov'd with his Army out of *Armenia*, and arriv'd upon the *Persian* Frontiers towards the latter end of *April*, and advancing far into the Kingdom he took several Towns, and destroy'd all the flat Country. Upon this *Chosroes* commanded his Army to march back with all Expedition, joining to it another Body of equal Forces under the Conduct of *Sainus*, with Orders to fight the *Romans* wherever they found 'em. *Heraclius*, notwithstanding this, pursu'd his March, and having encourag'd his Army by Arguments drawn from Religious Considerations pierc'd into the Inner *Persia*, where he took several Towns and strong Holds, all which he levell'd with the Ground: Hearing the King himself lay at *Gazacotis*, in the Province of *Paropamisus*, with Forty Thousand stout Men, he resolv'd to march thither and attack him: Some of his Scouts fell upon *Chosroes*'s advanc'd Guards, part of which they defeated, and the rest fled in great Consternation and acquainted the

A. D. 623.

Heraclius's *great Success in the* Persian *Wars.*

the King with *Heraclius* his Approach. *Chosroes* who at first imagin'd the Emperor would not presume to pierce so far into his Country, but that he should find him work enough in his own, began now to perceive himself mistaken in his Account, and fled away in great Haste, burning and destroying all the Fruits of the Earth as he pass'd along. By this means the Emperor enter'd the City without any Trouble, in which was the Temple of the Sun, embellish'd with variety of Superstitions, together with the immense Treasure of *Chrysotidoras*, or, as others will have it, that of *Crœsus*, King of *Lydia*. Here likewise he found the Image of *Chosroes*, erected in the midst of a Palace arch'd like Heaven, enrich'd with the Sun, the Moon, and the Stars, before whom he bow'd and worshipp'd. *Heraclius*, having pillag'd the City, and secur'd all the Treasure, burnt the Temple and the Palace, in which were several other Rarities, at once expressing the Skill of the Workman and Vanity of the Prince. After this he pursu'd the King to *Thebatman*, in which City some Writers place the Treasure before mention'd, the Temple, and the Palace; however it be, he took all the Towns in those Parts, and follow'd *Chosroes* as far as the Frontiers of *Media*, raising vast Contributions in the Country as he march'd along: But the Summer being far spent he thought it time to provide for Winter Quarters, so that having set apart Three Days to return God publick Thanks in the Camp for his glorious Expedition, he retir'd back towards *Albania*. In his Return he was much incommoded by the *Persians*, who often way-laid him, with a Design rather to recover the rich Booty than weaken his Army, but in all those Encounters his Men had the Advantage. The greatest Inconvenience he labour'd under was the Frost, which

which began then to be very severe, and with which none were more bitterly pinch'd than his Prisoners, who therefore, to the Number of Fifty Thousand, were releas'd without Ransom by the Emperor's Order, and return'd into their Country highly affected at his generous Clemency, and privately praying for his Success against a Tyrant that kept his Country in Slavery.

The Year following *Chosroes* by fresh Recruits made good the Losses his Armies had receiv'd the preceding Campaign, and delivering the Flower of his Troops to *Sarablaca*, one of the prime Nobility, gave him Orders to fight the Emperor in *Alania*. *Heraclius*, hearing of his Approach, prepar'd to receive him and bring him to a Battel, before he should be join'd by *Sarbazanes*, who, at the Head of another Army, was following with Orders to join him; accordingly he began his March, which was unseasonably interrupted by a Mutiny in the Army, proceeding from an Apprehension they had of the Difficulty there was in the Enterprize. This Misfortune had almost broken all the Emperor's Measures, for whilst he was endeavouring to appease and pacifie his discontented Soldiers *Sarbazanes* approach'd, and was ready to join *Sarablaca*, which when the *Romans* observ'd they came with Tears in their Eyes and begg'd the Emperor's Pardon, desiring him to lead 'em against *Sarablaca*, before they had two Enemies to contend with at a time. Upon this *Heraclius* endeavour'd to draw *Sarablaca* to fight, but finding nothing would provoke him to a Battel, but that he waited for a Conjunction with *Sarbazanes*, he left both and march'd towards *Chosroes* himself. At the same time two *Romans* deserted to the Enemy, and assur'd 'em that *Heraclius* his Motion proceeded from a Fear he had of engaging;

A.D. 624.

which,

which, with the News that *Sain*, another *Persian* Commander, was at hand, made those two Captains resolve to engage *Heraclius*, before *Sain* could come up and take the Victory out of their Hands: Whereupon they march'd their whole Army and encamp'd near *Heraclius*, who perceiving they prepar'd to fight the next Morning remov'd farther in the Night, 'till he came to a piece of Ground more convenient for him to engage in, where he rested and refresh'd his Troops. The *Persians*, trusting to the Story of the Fugitives, interpreted this as a Flight, and fell with so disorderly a Fury upon him that he easily defeated 'em, killing great Numbers, and among the rest *Sarablaca*, one of their Generals.

Tho' the Loss on the side of the *Persians* was very considerable, yet being join'd by *Sain* and his Squadrons they prepar'd for another Battel, and follow'd the *Romans* through difficult and almost unpassible Ways, into the Territories of the *Hunns*. The *Roman* Army in general was under no small Consternation, but especially the *Lazians*, and some other of their Auxiliaries, quitted the Service and return'd home. Notwithstanding which the Emperor by very powerful and seasonable Arguments so encourag'd his Soldiers, that they desir'd him, with great Alacrity, to lead 'em on against the Enemy, upon which he immediately presented 'em with Battel. Both Armies stood in view of each other from Morning 'till Night without one Blow on either Side, after which *Heraclius* march'd in the Silence of the Night towards *Persia*, which when the Enemies observ'd they endeavour'd to get a Head of him, and intercept him, by marching through more compendious Ways, whereby they entangled themselves in the Woods and Marshes, and gave him time to gain Ground. The *Persians*,

imagining

imagining still that he was flying from 'em, pursu'd with so much Inadvertency, that *Heraclius*, spying his Advantage, turn'd about and entirely defeated 'em. After this he took their Camp, their Arms, and their Baggage, part of which was of inestimable Value, together with a great Number of Prisoners, both Men and Women. As a Consequence of this Victory he soon became Master of the whole Country, where he dispers'd his Army into Winter Quarters, resolving early in the Spring to pursue his Conquests; and accordingly began his March by Mount *Taurus* into *Syria*, and with much Labour and great Difficulty came at length to the River *Tigris*, and from thence to the Cities of *Martyropolis* and *Amida*, where he refresh'd his Troops, and by Letters inform'd the Inhabitants of *Constantinople* of his glorious Success, which created an incredible Joy throughout the City. After this he commanded the Horse to ford the River *Euphrates*, whilst he built a Bride for the Foot, and so pass'd his whole Army over, to the great Amazement of his Enemies. Shortly after the City of *Samosata* surrender'd to him, where having rested for some time he built a Bridge over the River *Sarus*, and secur'd it with several strong Forts. In the mean time *Sarabazas* the *Persian* pursuing him encamp'd on the other Side the River, on a piece of Ground that fac'd the Bridge, and several *Roman* Soldiers, being puff'd up with their late Victories, resum'd to venture over the Bridge in a tumultuous manner to attack the Enemy, and that contrary to the express Order of the Emperor: At first the *Persians* pretended to be overthrown, and counterfeited a Flight, 'till having betray'd the *Romans* into their Ambushes they fac'd about, and had cut 'em all off if the Emperor had not mov'd speedily to their Rescue, but upon his Approach

U the

the Enemy were so hardly press'd
those who had pursu'd the *Romans*
escap'd. The Emperor, in this A
Proofs of his Valour and Condu
him admir'd and rever'd by his ver
under the Covert of the Night th
tire. After this unexpected Victo
led his Army to *Sebastia*, in which
Parts adjacent, they winter'd.

Chosroes hearing how often and
his Troops had been defeated by t
in the Days of his Predecessors co
fore the prevailing *Persians*, grew n
Chosroes his Disgrace, and having seiz'd o
his Cruelty all the Churches within his Dom
against the pell'd the Christians that were his
Christians. brace the Heresie of *Nestorius*, t
means to vex and affront *Heracli*
time he prepar'd to take the Field
with a mighty Army, drawn ou
who were willing to serve him fo
a Prospect of Plunder. His chie
remove the War into the Territo
pire, and so compel *Heraclius* to
which purpose he sent his Embas
vari, the *Hunns* and *Sclavonians*, c
Sums of Gold, and Promises of m
on they would associate themselves
him, and falling into the *Roman*
their Quarters lay Siege to the Cit
ple. *Chagan*, King of the *Avari*,
beginning been a troublesome Nei
clius, treacherous in Peace, and un
He had often invaded *Thrace*, w
times he met with a Repulse, yet
bloody Marks of his Cruelty behir
quently proceeded so far in his In

threw *Constantinople* it self into the greatest Consternation. Whilst *Heraclius* was thus assaulted by him on the one side, and insulted by the *Persians* on the other, he was able to make Head against neither, and therefore often su'd for Peace from both, to which *Chosroes* his violent Temper would not let him condescend, but *Chagan* was more complaisant but no less dangerous, for he never made a Peace but with an Intent to break it, and had once so far deluded the Emperor by his fair Promises that he very narrowly escap'd his Hands, being glad to save himself with the Loss of his Baggage. Notwithstanding this, when *Heraclius* apply'd himself vigorously to the *Persian* War, he once more renew'd the Negotiations, and at length a Peace was concluded between 'em, *Chagan* appearing outwardly so sincere that *Heraclius* in a manner committed his Son and the Capital of his Empire into his Protection. And yet after all these Engagements and the Emperor's Reliance upon his Honour, he readily comply'd with the King of *Persia*'s Proposals, and appear'd the most vigorous of any in his Service; so vain a thing is it to depend upon the Oaths and Engagements of mercenary Princes, who desire to be Rich rather than Just, and are more ambitious of being Great than Honourable.

The Emperor was not ignorant of all these Negotiations, but made timely Preparations to encounter the Storm which he saw threaten'd him. He divided his Forces into three Armies, one of which was appointed for the Defence of *Constantinople*, the second was committed to the Conduct of *Theodorus*, his Brother, and with the third he himself advanc'd into the Province of the *Lazians*, where by powerful Presents he gain'd the Eastern *Turki*, otherwise called *Chazari*, to re-inforce his Army with

A. D. 626.

Heraclius *hires the* Turks *into his Service.*

with their Auxiliary Troops. These People, under the Conduct of *Ziebil*, to the number of Forty Thousand, broke through the *Caspian* Gates into *Persia*, ruining the Country, and destroying the Inhabitants as they pass'd along: As they were proceeding on in this hostile manner *Heraclius* met 'em in his March from *Lazica*; they approach'd him with the Reverence that was due to his Person and Character, and an Alliance was concluded between 'em, upon such Terms as were approv'd of by their Captain, who, highly satisfy'd with the Conditions *Heraclius* offer'd, return'd home himself, and left his Son to command the Forces in his Absence, and to attend upon the Person of the Emperor; who being now strengthen'd with so seasonable an Addition enter'd *Persia* in the Winter Season, to *Chosroes*'s his great Terror and Amazement. At first the *Turks* did *Heraclius* great Service, but growing at length dishearten'd by the Sharpness of the Weather, and frighten'd by the frequent Incursions of the *Persians*, they by degrees all left him and return'd home: Notwithstanding which he made use of several Religious Arguments to encourage his Men, who chearfully desir'd him to lead 'em where ever he pleas'd.

Chosroes by this time had receiv'd a melancholy Account of the Summer's Service: *Sarbarazes*, at the Head of a numerous Army, had advanc'd as far as *Chalcedon*, before which he sate down, and from thence straiten'd the City of *Constantinople*, whilst the *Avari* flocking in great Numbers out of *Thrace* besieg'd it both by Sea and Land, and for Ten Days together renew'd their Attacks with great Resolution; but having lost the best of their Men in the Service they were constrain'd to raise the Siege, and retire with Dishonour. *Baronius*, upon the Authority of *Cedrenus*, gives us a miraculous

Constantinople Besieg'd by the Avari.

culous Account of the raising of that Siege. He saith, the Besiegers beheld a Lady attended with a Train of Eunuchs issuing out at one of the Gates, and that concluding her, by her Port and Majesty, to be the Empress *Eudocia* coming in the Absence of her Husband to Treat of Peace with their General, they made way for her, suffering none in the Camp to follow after her: But when they observ'd she had pass'd the Trenches, and without going near the General's Tent, they then pursu'd her, and had almost overtaken her, when she suddenly disappear'd. Upon which the Pursuers, like Men infatuated, quarrell'd with one another, and from Words proceeding to Blows, great Numbers of 'em fell, 'till Night came and put an end to the Dispute. The next Morning when the Captain was inform'd of the great Slaughter that had been made, and how many Men he had lost, he rais'd the Siege, and made a dishonourable Retreat. At the same time the Fleet withdrew, and was overtaken with a Tempest in the *Euxine* Sea, where most of the Ships perish'd.

The Siege rais'd by a Miracle.

Another part of the *Persian* Forces, and the very Flower of their Army, call'd therefore *The Golden Company*, and committed to the Conduct of *Sain*, or *Sais*, was defeated by *Theodorus*, who obtain'd an absolute Victory with Loss of very few on his side. This Misfortune expos'd *Sais* so much to *Chosroes*'s Indignation, that through Grief he dy'd, with which the Tyrant was so little satisfy'd, that he committed several Indignities upon the dead Body.

These Losses, and the Progress of *Heraclius*, who continu'd in Arms even in the Winter Season, so amaz'd *Chosroes*, that he knew not what Measures to take. All the Forces he could raise were committed to the Care of *Razastes*, a Man of great Valour and Quality, who, presuming upon the Strength of his Arms, and late Diminution of the *Roman* Forces, thought to end the War at once in the Death of *Heraclius*, who, pursuing his Fortune, encamp'd on the First of *December* upon the River *Zabes*, near *Ninive*, whither *Razastes* immediately follow'd him. At first several Actions pass'd between the Parties sent out on both sides, in which the *Romans* for the most part had the Advantage. *Heraclius* was inform'd by some Prisoners, that *Razastes* waited only for the Arrival of Three Thousand fresh Men, who had Orders from *Chosroes* to join him, and then was resolv'd to fight, whereupon the Emperor was desirous to engage him before those Succours could come up. He never behav'd himself with more Gallantry in any Action than in this, for he kill'd Three of the *Persian* Officers with his own Hand, and had his Horse wounded under him. After an obstinate Dispute on both sides the *Persians* lost the Day, together with their General, and most of their Field Officers. The *Romans* on their side lost no more than Fifty Men, and had about as many wounded. The Body of *Razastes* was found in the Field of Battel, with a Shield and Armour all of Massie Gold.

The Persians defeated by Heraclius.

Heraclius suffer'd not his Men to grow cool, nor *Chosroes* to recover himself out of his Astonishment, before he mov'd forwards against him, and haunted him from one of his Palaces to another, 'till he forc'd him to fly at length to *Seleucia*, a strong City built upon the *Tigris*, where he lock'd up himself, his Wives and Children, with his most precious Moveables. At *Jesdemon*, one of the King's Houses of Pleasure, *Heraclius* kept his *Christmas*; at another, call'd *Dystagerda*, he found the Standards, which at several times had been

been taken from the *Romans*, with abundance of Spices, Hangings richly wrought, and much Silk, whereof, as much as could not be conveniently brought away, he burnt, as he did all his Houses of Pleasure, to make *Chosroes* feel in some measure, as he said, what Mischief he did when he destroy'd the *Roman* Cities. After this he releas'd several Captives that had been taken at *Edessa* and *Alexandria*, and distributed his Forces into Winter Quarters, prepar'd either to renew the War in the Spring, or conclude a Peace, if yet *Chosroes* his continu'd Misfortunes had inclin'd him to listen to it; but the Hand of God being against him for his abominable Impiety, and monstrous Barbarity, he was deaf to all those Councils that tended to his Safety, and hasten'd on his own Ruin.

All this while *Sarbarazes* lay before *Chalcedon*, without being able to do any considerable Service against the *Romans*, upon which some, who were near the King, persuaded him that he held Intelligence with the Enemy, and design'd to betray the Army up to 'em; whereupon *Chosroes*, who was now grown jealous, as well as revengeful, sent Orders to *Chardarigas*, another Commander in the Army, to kill the General, and return with the Forces into *Persia*. These Letters were intercepted by some *Romans* on the Borders of *Galatia*, and carry'd to the Emperor's Son at *Constantinople*, who sent it to *Sarbarazes*, and he show'd it to the chief Officers of the Army, whom he persuaded to throw off their Allegiance to *Chosroes*, and deprive him of the Crown, of which he was so unworthy. About the same time *Chosroes* had rejected new Proposals of Peace sent him by *Heraclius*, which increas'd his Subjects Aversion to him, and prepar'd 'em for any Innovation. But whilst *Chosroes* lay, as he thought securely, in the Castle of *Seleucia*, he was seiz'd by a Dysentery, which reduc'd him to the last extremity. Upon this occasion he thought to provide his Subjects with a Successor, and accordingly prepar'd to Crown his youngest Son *Mardesanes*, whom he had by *Syra*, the most belov'd of all his Wives. Of this when *Syroes* the eldest was advertis'd, he appeal'd to the Grandees of the Realm, the most considerable of whom declar'd in his behalf. Upon this Encouragement *Syroes* wrote to *Heraclius*, by whose Advice he set all the *Roman* Prisoners at Liberty; after which he seiz'd on his Father, and, having bound him in Chains, cast him into a Dungeon, which *Chosroes* had lately fortify'd for the Security of his Treasure. Here he was fed with nothing but Bread and Water, his Son declaring *he might feed on that Gold, for the sake of which he had made many innocent People perish with Hunger*; at the same time he sent several of the Nobles to insult him, to spit in his Face, and load him with Injuries more ignominious than the Chains he wore.

Chosroes murder'd by his own Son. After this he commanded *Mardesanes* and the rest of his Sons to be murder'd in his Sight, and then shot him to Death.

This was the deserv'd End of *Chosroes* the Second, a Proud, Cruel and Blasphemous Prince, after a long Reign of Thirty Five Years, during which time he took from *Heraclius* all that was left to the Empire of *Mesopotamia*, all *Syria*, and the Holy Land, with the City of *Jerusalem* it self; most of which he lost back again to the Emperor before his Death. *Syroes*, having thus accomplish'd his Designs, gave the Emperor an Account of

A Peace with the Persians. what had been done, and made a perpetual Peace with him, and that upon Conditions very advantagious to the Empire. For by Virtue of this Peace all the *Roman* Provinces, that had been lately seiz'd

by

by the *Perſians*, were reſtor'd, together with Three Hundred Enſigns, and what ever elſe had been taken from the *Romans*, among the reſt that Piece of Wood which was ſuppos'd to have been part of the Croſs, and which *Choſroes* had taken from *Jeruſalem*, and brought in Triumph into *Perſia*. All things being thus concerted, and agreed on both ſides, the Emperor prepar'd to return to *Conſtantinople*, giving Order in his Paſſage for the Settlement of Affairs in *Armenia*, and the other Provinces of the Empire. When he was arriv'd near to *Conſtantinople*, his Son *Conſtantius*, the Patriarch, and the People came forth to meet him with Songs of Triumph, and loud Acclamations. His Entry into the City was great and magnificent, and indeed he deſerv'd a Reception equal to the greateſt Captains, having, in the ſpace of Six Years, recover'd to the Empire all the Eaſtern Provinces which had been taken from it by the *Perſians*, puniſh'd that perfidious Nation for the many Indignities offer'd to the *Roman* Name, reſtor'd the diſtreſs'd People to their ancient Liberties, forc'd *Choſroes* ignominiouſly to fly, and in a great meaſure broke a State, which for ſeveral Years had been the moſt potent and formidable of all others; for the *Perſians* never after attempted any Noble Enterpriſe, but ſunk under the Subjection of the *Saracens*. All this was effected by *Heraclius*, at a time when the Empire was in a very low and helpleſs Condition; the Treaſure was exhauſted, the Militia decay'd, and the State threaten'd by the Barbarians on every ſide. So that had *Heraclius* dy'd here, or proceeded on in the ſame Tracts of Honour, he might have challeng'd a Place among the moſt renow'd Princes that ſhine in Hiſtory. But from the remaining part of his Reign we ſhall find he was more, by Nature, adapted to the

Heraclius his great Exploits.

the Hurry and Business of War, than the soft Retirements of Peace, and that nothing corrupts the Mind of Man sooner than Idleness and Inactivity. From a Soldier he grew a Disputant, and from a General in the Field, the Head of a Party in the Church, not only to the great Detriment of Christianity, but to the utter Ruin of the State, as we may have occasion to observe hereafter.

A. D. 629.
He takes a Progress to Jerusalem.

The Emperor having repos'd himself at *Constantinople*, where he spent the Winter, set out about the middle of *March* for *Jerusalem*, carrying thither the Piece of the Cross, which had been taken from thence about Fourteen Years before, together with *Zacharie* the Patriarch, who had been led into Captivity with it. Being arriv'd in the City he enter'd in great Pomp into the Chief Church, with the Cross in his Hand, and there, in a solemn manner, return'd God Thanks for the great Victories he had obtain'd, and for that it had pleas'd his infinite Wisdom to make choice of him to bring back the Cross to the Holy City. Upon this Occasion was instituted the Festival of the *Exaltation of the Holy Cross*, which is observ'd yearly by the Church of *Rome* on the Fourteenth of *September*. When this Ceremony was perform'd the Emperor banish'd all the *Jews* out of *Jerusalem*, forbidding 'em, under severe Penalties, to approach within Three Miles of the Place.

From *Jerusalem Heraclius* went into *Syria*, and spent some time at *Edessa*, where he receiv'd Ambassadors from the two extream Parts of the Continent, from *France* and the *Indies*, the Kings of which sent their Ambassadors with rich Presents to congratulate his Glorious Success, and desire to join in Confederacy with him. He expell'd all the *Nestorians* out of the City, who had been harbour'd

Chap. IV.   LXI. Heraclius.

pour'd a long time in it, and gave their Churches to the Catholicks. Here he found *Anastasius*, a Man of great Learning and Address, but an *Eutychian*; however he insinuated himself so far into the Emperor's good Opinion, that he promis'd to make him Patriarch of *Antioch*, upon Condition he renounc'd his Heresie, and subscrib'd to the Council of *Calcedon*. The Emperor having made good his Promise he openly renounc'd his Errors, but still retain'd 'em in his Heart, and the better to cover his Hypocrisie started a Question to *Heraclius*, *If it was lawful to affirm there were two Wills in Jesus Christ, or no more than one Will?* maintaining the latter by very plausible Arguments. To which when the Patriarchs of *Alexandria* and *Constantinople*, who were infected with the same Distemper, had readily subscrib'd, the Emperor, *He turns* who had more of Curiosity than Learning, was *Monothe-* prevail'd upon to espouse the same Opinion, which *lite.* created a dangerous Schism in the Church, and gave a beginning to the Heresie of the *Monothelites*, who tho' they did not openly declare for *Eutyches*, yet they press'd very close upon his Heels. In what Points they, the *Eutychians* and *Jacobites*, concurr'd and disagreed, and in what Numbers the latter prevail still in the East, as it is not the Business of this History to examine, so the Reader will find it already done to his Hands in several Authors, who have written upon that Subject.

This Heresie prov'd not more prejudicial to the Church, than fatal to the State; for whilst the Emperor busied himself with Opinions and Speculations, that were no way proper for him, the absurd and impious Doctrine of *Mahomet* was suf- *The Rise of* fer'd to spread abroad in the World, which Hera- *Mahome-* clius might have crush'd like a Cockatrice in the *tanism.* egg, before it had taken so deep a Root, and rais'd

its

its execrable Head to such a prodigious height, a[nd] to prove the greatest Plague that ever happen'd t[o] Christendom; which may teach us to be cautiou[s] how we enquire too busily into those Points o[f] Religion, which serve rather as a Subject for ou[r] Disputes, than a Motive to a truly Christian Life.

As *Mahomet* recommended his Doctrine by in[-]dulging his Proselytes in their sensual Desires, [so] he took Care to plant and propagate it by th[e] Power of the Sword, promising peculiar Recom[-]pences in his imaginary Paradise to those who a[p]pear'd the valiant Assertors of it, upon whic[h] account it gain'd incredible Ground in a sho[rt] time. He first spread it in his Native Countr[y] which was *Arabia the Happy*, where the People, fo[r] the generality, were bury'd in a profound Igno[-]rance, and divided into Twelve Sorts or Sects [of] Religion, and all of 'em Pagan and Idolatrou[s]. When he found his Doctrine almost universally r[e]ceiv'd there, he plac'd himself at the Head of [a] Company of Theives and Fugitive Slaves, who fle[d] from all Parts to him, allur'd by a Promise he ha[d] given of protecting 'em, and by a Law he ha[d] taught and publish'd, that *it was the Will a[nd] Command of God that all Men should be fre[e].* By the help of these Proselytes he assum'd a Sov[e]reign Power, and so by a double Usurpation d[e]clar'd himself both King and Prophet of the *Sar[a]cens*. His Successors prov'd the most fatal En[e]mies the Empire ever had, dismembring it [of] whole Provinces at once, and at length leading t[he]

<small>Persia con-</small>
<small>quer'd by</small>
<small>the Sara-</small>
<small>cens.</small>

Imperial City her self into Captivity. Having [o]vercome the *Persians* in the Year 632. under th[e] Conduct of *Othman*, or *Osman*, and slain *Ho[r]misda* the Second, the last *Persian* King, of th[e] Race of *Artaxerxes*, they seiz'd on the Kingdo[m,] and bury'd the Renown of that Nation in Capt[i]vity

...ty. The *Saracens*, seeing themselves Masters of ...at Country, made their Incursions into *Palestine*, A.D. ...e Governor of which they kill'd, and seiz'd on 633. ...*aza* with all the adjacent Country. About this ...me a Comet was seen in those Parts, form'd into ...e shape of a Sword, which was look'd on as a fa- ...l' Forerunner of the Wars which were to ensue. ...he Year following they laid Siege to *Bosra*, the ...apital City of *Arabia*, which in the end they ...ok, and so made themselves Masters of all that Coun- ...y; and improving their Conquests march'd from ...ence into *Syria*, where *Theodorus*, the Emperor's ...rother, prepar'd to oppose 'em, but was defeated, ...d forc'd to fly in great Disorder to *Heraclius*, ...ing then at *Edessa*. *Heraclius* considering the ill ...uccess of his Arms, and fearing the Issue of the ...Var, quitted *Syria* and went to *Jerusalem*, from ...hence he remov'd the Cross, with whatever else ...ere was of Value in the City, to *Constantinople*. ...n the mean time he order'd *Bohames*, whom he had ...ade General of his Armies, to join *Theodorus*, his ...hancellor, who lay with Forty Thousand Men at ...*messa*. Upon these the Infidels fell in such great *who defeat* ...Numbers that they entirely routed 'em, Heaven it *the Ro-* ...elf seeming to espouse their Cause; for a strong *mans,* ...North Wind arose full in the Face of the Christi- ...ns, and drove the Dust with so much Violence in- ...o their Eyes that they were forc'd to retire, and ...ere most of 'em lost in a River, which in that ...Confusion they attempted to pass. *Damascus* im- ...ediately fell into the Hands of the *Saracens*, as ...he Fruit of this Victory, from whence they ad- ...anc'd into *Phænicia*, which they seiz'd, and plan- ...ed with a Colony of their own. They were so ...ar from ruining *Damascus*, or suffering it to be ...illag'd, that they permitted most of the Inhabi- ...ants, especially the Christians, to continue in it,

where

where they were indulg'd with the free Exercise of their Religion; for *Aumar*, the Prince or Caliph of the *Saracens*, built a magnificent Temple in *Damascus*, which he appropriated to the peculiar Use of the Christians.

and conquer Egypt After this he divided his Army, which was grown very numerous, into two Parts; one of which he sent into *Egypt*, and with the other went in Person to besiege *Jerusalem*. The *Egyptians*, being sensible that they were unable to resist the Forces that were moving against them, and conceiving the Design of the *Saracens* was rather to plunder than conquer, employ'd *Cyrus* the Patriarch to treat with them, who paid 'em down a large Sum of Gold in Hand, and agreed upon an annual Pension of Two Hundred Thousand Crowns, upon Consideration they spar'd the Country. This Bargain was punctually observ'd for Three Years together, during which time the Infidels attempted nothing against *Egypt*. In the mean time the Patriarch was accus'd at *Constantinople* for having brib'd the Barbarians with the Gold of *Egypt*, and the Emperor was persuaded to renounce the Agreement; whereupon he sent one *Manuel*, an *Armenian*, Præfect into *Egypt*, where being supported by an Army he took the Government of the Country upon him in the Emperor's Name; and when the Commissioners for the *Saracens* came at the Year's End to demand the Sum the Inhabitants had oblig'd themselves to pay, *Manuel* receiv'd 'em with much Disdain, and told 'em *He was not a preaching Priest whom they had terrify'd into ignominious Conditions, but a Roman General at the Head of an Army.* Upon this the *Saracens* enter'd *Egypt* with a very powerful Army, and having forc'd *Manuel* to save himself in *Alexandria*, they seiz'd on the Country, and made it tributary to their Caliph. *Heraclius* finding

ing too late the ill Measures he had taken, sent *Cyrus* once more to the Infidels, who offer'd, in the Emperor's Name, that for the time to come the Articles should be religiously observ'd, provided they would forego their Conquest, and quit the Country: This the *Saracens* absolutely refus'd, so that *Egypt*, which had continu'd a considerable Member of the Empire ever since the Days of *Augustus*, was torn from it by the Hands of Infidels, who took care to plant their damnable Errors wherever they extended their Arms.

Whilst *Aumur*'s Captains were thus employ'd in *Egypt*, he was busied in the Siege of *Jerusalem*, whither he had march'd without receiving any Opposition, for the Emperor had not Forces sufficient in those Parts to make Head against him. Indeed it's a Subject of great Wonder, that he, who not many Years before had carry'd the *Roman* Eagle as far almost as any of his Predecessors, and by the Force of his Arms humbled a State which formerly made the Empire tremble, should not be able now to stop the Progress of an upstart Nation, hardly ever remember'd before for any notable Atchievements, but look'd on with a Contempt suitable to their Original. But we are to consider that *Heraclius* himself was busied in unseasonable Disputes about Religion, with which God was so justly offended, as to suffer the Empire in general to lye bury'd in a supine Security, regardless of the Dangers with which it was threaten'd. After a Conclusion of the *Persian* War several of the most deserving Officers had been dismiss'd unkindly, nor was any Care taken to reconcile 'em to the Court, with which they were upon good grounds offended. The Time the Emperor could spare from his religious War was employ'd in publick Pestivals and Entertainments,

tainments, with which the People were so diverted at *Constantinople*, that they had not leisure or were unwilling to think of the Condition of the Provinces; so that it was no difficult thing, in such a Conjuncture, for *Mahomet* to enforce his Absurdities upon the World by the Terror of his Arms, which were so wonderfully propagated by his Successors.

A.D. 637.
They take Jerusalem.

Jerusalem held out against *Aumar* for two Years together, but surrender'd at last, upon Condition the Inhabitants might continue in the peaceable Enjoyment of their Liberties and Estates, and the free Exercise of their Religion; to this *Aumar* readily consented, and as faithfully observ'd. From *Jerusalem* he march'd with his Forces against *Antioch*, the Capital of all the East, which was unfurnish'd with Men, or any Provisions fit to maintain a Siege, and was therefore forc'd to surrender, and receive a Garrison of *Saracens:* So that they were now absolute in *Syria* and the *Holy-Land*, and were Masters in *Persia*, *Mesopotamia* and *Egypt*, and had got firm Footing in *Africk*. So prodigious was the Encrease of Mahometism, and so suddenly did the Misfortunes of the Empire press her down.

This in Substance is the Account of those Wars, and the Beginning of the *Saracenical* Empire, left us by the *Grecian* Writers of that Age, who are justly to be accus'd for their Succinctness and Obscurity in a Subject that deserv'd to have been more copiously handled; for undoubtedly it must needs have been various as well as surprising in its Circumstances, containing no less than the subduing whole Nations, altering ancient Governments, and introducing a new Face of Affairs in the World.

Paulus Diaconus is more particular in his Account of *Italy*, especially so far as the Affairs thereof relate to his Countrymen the *Lombards*, who

seem'd

Chap. IV. LXI. Heraclius. 305

seem'd by a particular Favour of Fortune to have continu'd for the most part in Peace with the *Romans*, whilst the whole Strength of the Empire was employ'd elsewhere; notwithstanding which the Emperor was not free from his Cares in those Parts, for *John*, the Exarch of *Ravenna*, being kill'd by the Multitude in that City, and *Confinius*, Duke of *Naples*, having, contrary to his Faith given to *Heraclius*, seiz'd on that City and maintain'd it with a strong Garrison against him, *Eleutherius*, a Patrician and Chamberlain of the Houshold, was sent into *Italy*; where at first he made good the Opinion the World had conceiv'd of him for his great Wisdom and Virtue: For immediately upon his Arrival at *Ravenna* he made a diligent Inquisition after the Death of *John*, and punish'd those that were found guilty of the Murder; after which reasonable piece of Justice he went to *Naples*, which he took, and put *Confinius* to Death. This Success in the beginning of his Administration made him unhappily forget that Virtue and Moderation which till then had appear'd so eminent in him, and betray'd him to those Vices he had always condemn'd, and lately punish'd in other Men. The great Authority he had in those Parts, the Distance between that and the Emperor, together with the Wars in the East, presented him, as he thought with a fair Opportunity of setting up for himself, and he propos'd nothing less than the Sovereignty of all *Italy*: This he knew was not to be obtain'd without a firm Interest in the Army, upon which Consideration he took care to pay the Soldiers all their Arrears, and courted 'em by several other popular Acts and Condescentions. By that time he conceiv'd he had moulded the Army to his Will, he receiv'd new Encouragement by the Death of *Deusdedit*, Pope of *Rome*, for he thought whilst the

Eleutherius, aiming to make himself King in Italy.

X People

People were busied in the Election of a Successor he might easily seize upon that City, which would be a good Step to the Royalty, and having an Influence upon the Election he might make the succeeding Pope his Friend; whereupon having settled as he thought all things in good Order at *Ravenna*, he march'd at the Head of his Army towards *Rome*, in Order to take Possession of it, but was inform'd in his March that *Boniface* the Fifth was promoted to the Apostolick Chair, which threw him into a Suspence, and forc'd him to alter his Measures; for having commanded the Army to halt, he caress'd 'em in a very plausible Speech in which he inveigh'd against the Distempers of the Times, and made 'em large Promises of his Favour, Protection and Reformation; after which he assum'd the Title of King, the Soldiers rather permitting than consenting to it. For proceeding on towards *Rome*, where he intended to be invested with the Ensigns of Majesty, the Army consider'd better of the Matter by that time they came as far *is slain by* as *Luceoli*, and detesting the Treachery they slew *his Soldiers.* the Traitor, and sent his Head to the Emperor; who dispatch'd *Isaacius*, a Patrician, into *Italy*, to command as Exarch in his room. *Isaacius* met with little Disturbance in his Government for a long time, the *Lombards* being too much at variance among themselves to attempt any thing against the Empire, 'till *Rotharis* was elected King of that Nation upon the Death of *Ariold* his Successor.

A. D. 638. He, being a busie, active Prince, and zealous for the Honour of his Nation, whose Dominions he was ambitious of extending, broke the Peace which his Predecessors had made with the *Romans*, and took by Force the Cities of *Oderzo* and *Treviso*, with all the Territories dependant on them. The Exarch, being surpriz'd at this sudden and unexpected

pected Rupture, broke with all Violence into the Dominions of the *Lombards,* but was at length met by *Rotharis,* who fought him, and kill'd Eight Thousand of the *Romans,* which prov'd a Defeat of such Consequence, that from that Time forward, 'till the Reign of *Luitprand,* no Acts of Hostility pass'd betwixt the Exarchs and the *Lombards,* who were satisfy'd for the present with their new Conquests, and the Exarch was content to enjoy unmolested the Territories that remain'd under the Dominion of the Empire.

8000 Romans slain by the Lombards.

All this while the Errors of the *Monothelites* prevail'd very much in the East, where no Bishops were preferr'd by the Emperor but such as declar'd themselves to be of his Opinion; and *Severinus* being elected Pope of *Rome* upon the Death of *Honorius, Heraclius* refus'd to confirm the Election, as the Custom was, because the Pope would not sign an *Exposition* publish'd by *Sergius,* Patriarch of *Constantinople,* the great Patron of the *Monothelites;* which, together with some former Indisposition, wrought so effectually with the honest Pope that he dy'd shortly after, and then the Emperor thought none of his Successors would be so hardy as to dispute his Pleasure, but found a stronger Resolution in *John* the Fourth, who succeeded him; for he, immediately after his Election, summon'd a Synod, wherein he condemn'd the *Exposition* that had been sent to his Predecessor, and anathematis'd the Heresie of the *Monothelites*. The Emperor, surpriz'd at this resolute Proceeding, and finding that all the Western and *African* Churches were preparing to follow his Example, which he thought in the end would prove highly prejudicial to his Authority, began to retract, and laid all the Blame upon *Sergius,* who was lately dead, and who, he said, had made use of his Name without his

A.D. 640.

his Consent or Participation. But before he could convince the World that he was sincere in his Recantation he was call'd to give an Account of his Faith at another Place, for he dy'd of a Dropsie, on the Eleventh of *May* the Year following, after a Reign of Thirty Years and ten Months.

Heraclius Dies.

The Ecclesiastical Writers of those Times observe, that whilst he persever'd in the Maintenance of the true Religion he triumph'd over all his Enemies, and extended the Bounds of his Empire; as is evident from the History of the Eleventh to the Twentieth Year of his Reign: But as soon as he started aside from the Truth, and suffer'd himself to be seduc'd by the Teachers of Novelty and Error, the Hand of God was against him, and blasted all his Designs and Undertakings. The Distemper of which he dy'd was attended with strange and troublesome Symptoms, for he never attempted to make Water but his Urine would fly up in his Face; which some account a Judgment upon him, for his incestuous marrying his own Neece, after the Death of *Eudocia*, his first Wife; at whose Funeral the same Authors mention a very unfortunate Accident that happen'd: For as they were carrying her with Royal Pomp through the *Forum*, a Girl of some barbarous Nation, that was looking out at a Window to behold the Procession, by accident spate upon the Herse, for which the unhappy Offender was immediately seiz'd and cruelly burnt, and so added the Horror of a Parentation to the Solemnity of the Funeral. This Act of Barbarity shows us the Cruelty of *Heraclius* his Temper, and that his Resentment did not proceed from any extraordinary Respect to the deceas'd Empress appears from his marrying shortly after to *Martina*, his own Neece, to which incestuous Match the Ecclesiastical Writers ascribe all the Calamities that

His Character.

after-

afterwards befel the Empire during his Reign. A greater Contrariety was never obferv'd in any Man's Actions than in thofe of this Emperor, for if we view him in the Field at the Head of his Army, driving the *Perſians* before him, and hunting their King, a proud and arrogant Prince, from Place to Place, we may conclude no Man was fitter for the Imperial Dignity than himfelf; but if when the Bufinefs of the Field is over we obferve him, either wallowing in the fenfual Delights of the Court, or bufying himfelf in the Speculations of Religion, and thereby opening a Door in the Church for Herefie and Schifm, and fuffering the fworn Enemies of the Church and State to gain, by a ftupendous Progrefs, upon both, we can't but confefs he defil'd the Imperial Purple with which he was invefted. In a Word, it may be faid two Emperors were blended together in the Perfon of this Prince, one very good, and the other fcandaloufly ill.

CHAP. V.

From the Death of Heraclius *to the Re-establishment of the Empire in the West by* Charles *the Great.*

Containing about 161 Years.

A.D. 641.

I. HEraclius at his Death left the Empire of the East much decay'd; for all the Provinces of *Syria, Mesopotamia, Ægypt,* and *Arabia* were in the Power of the Infidels; the *Sclavi, Hunns,* and *Bavarians* were possess'd of those Countries, which to this Day are distinguish'd by their respective Names; the *Goths* reign'd in *Spain,* and the *French* prevail'd in *France,* and *Germany* was divided into several Principalities. So that the Dominions of the Empire consisted of *Thrace, Greece,* the Islands of *Sicily* and *Sardinia,* and great part of *Italy,* in *Europe*; in *Asia* it still retain'd *Asia* the less, *Cilicia, Pamphilia, Galatia, Bithynia,* and *Cappadocia*; and in *Africk* it had as yet lost nothing of what had been recover'd to it in the Reign of *Justinian.* This is convenient to observe here, that the Reader may better understand the remaining Part of this History.

Heraclius, before his Death, had declar'd his Son *Constantine, Cæsar,* and associated him in the Empire, so that he was readily receiv'd, and crown'd Emperor at his Father's Decease, but enjoy'd not the Dignity above Four Months, in which time he gave the World a Promise of a very hopeful and magnanimous Prince, being generally belov'd by the People, but detested by his

Step-mother *Martina*, by whose Practices he was poison'd to make way for her own Son *Heracleon*; but the God of Vengeance would not suffer her long to enjoy what she had purchas'd by the detested Sin of Parricide; for her Son had not been obey'd as Emperor Six Months together, before the Senate re-assum'd their Courage, and, joining with the Resentments of the People, depriv'd her and her Son of the Sovereignty, cutting off his Nose, and pulling her Tongue out of her Head, after which exemplary piece of Justice they were both banish'd. At the same time *Pyrrhus*, the Heretical Patriarch of *Constantinople*, who had been *Martina*'s Instrument in her Villanies, fearing he should be call'd to an Account for his wicked Practices, retir'd from his See, and secur'd himself by a voluntary Exile.

A. D. 642.

The Senate, having thus deliver'd the State from the Usurpation of *Heracleon* and his Mother, advanc'd *Constans*, the Son of *Constantine*, to the Throne, one which he sate Twenty Seven Years, and was the Heir of his Grandfather's Errors, as well as of his Dominions.

Constans II.

The great Progress of the Arms of the Infidels, which began in the Reign of *Heraclius*, was continu'd with wonderful Success in this of his Successor, upon which Account the World was fill'd with Desolations and Impiety; for where ever the *Saracens* carry'd their Victorious Arms they ruin'd the Country, and destroy'd the Faith: The Emperor for the present looking on as an idle Spectator, of what he had not the Power to prevent. These Distractions encourag'd *Mauritius*, who had been made Governor of *Rome* by *Heraclius*, to revolt, and set up for himself. The better to colour his Treason he pretended openly, that *Isaacius*, Exarch of *Ravenna*, had assum'd the Imperial Ornaments,

ments, and that therefore it was his
pose him before he had time to co
in his Usurpation. Upon which, ha
all the Forces he could raise, he exa
an Oath of Obedience, and prepar'c
gainst *Isaacius*, who, being inform
ceedings, and sensible how dangerou
motion might prove, sent an intir
his own, and a Person of great Auth
with a considerable Sum of Mony
Head of the choicest of his Troop
having led his Forces near to the W
ty, publish'd a Declaration, wher
was declar'd a Rebel, and those wl
the Traitor, and return to their O
not only promis'd a Pardon from the
a considerable Gratuity, which he
immediately to pay 'em. Upon tl
ment the Army totally deserted fr
who fled for Refuge into one of
from whence he was taken out by
his Head struck off by an Order fre
as they were leading him in Chain

The beginning of this Prince's
markable for nothing more than tl
ble Disputes in Religion, which l

A. D. unhappily began, and which he car
647. equal Impetuosity, and for the Suc
The Sara- *racens* in *Africk*, where in the
cens Con- themselves absolute. For one *Grego*
quer A- time Imperial Præfect in that Cou
frick. himself so odious to the Inhabitant
rannical Exactions, that the Infidc
Advantage of their Discontents, ar
acquainted with the Country by tl
ruptions, enter'd it this Year wir
Forces; and having defeated *Grege*

strain'd him to fly, and concluded a Peace with the Natives, who were to own them for their Lords, and pay 'em a certain Annual Tribute; and from this time forward the *Romans* laid no Claim to any Part of *Africk*, but left it in Possession of the *Saracens*, who, having thus render'd themselves Masters of that spacious Country, dispers'd part of their Forces up and down in Garisons to have an Eye upon the Inhabitants, and withdrew the rest to be employ'd in fresh Conquests.

In the mean time the Emperor was carrying on the War of Religion, which now grew more enlarg'd and violent than ever. For *Paul*, the Patriarch of *Constantinople*, finding that all the Bishops of the West, and those of *Africk*, strenuously oppos'd the Errror of the *Monothelites*, began to fear lest their Zeal for the Faith should cool that for the Emperor, and therefore persuaded *Constans* to publish an Edict, call'd the *Type*, wherein the Emperor declar'd, That in Order to preserve the Union of the Church he commanded all Bishops, Priests and Teachers, to observe an exact Silence upon the Point *touching the Will of Jesus Christ*, and not presume to maintain either that there was no more than one Will, or that there were two in God made Man. This Type, which the Emperor thought a proper Expedient to compose the present Differences, was so little approv'd by *Theodorus*, at that time Pope of *Rome*, that he condemn'd it as Impious and Heretical, in a Synod summon'd for that purpose, and Anathematiz'd *Paul*, who had been the Author of it. This rigorous Proceeding of the Pope has been justly condemn'd by latter Writers, who blame him for calling an Imperial Edict Impious, which had been chiefly design'd to abate the Severity shown in the De-

A. D. 648.

fence

fence of Monothelism, and by which no Man wa[s] oblig'd to believe it; and to Excommunicate [a] Man, who openly acknowledg'd the Five Genera[l] Councils, particularly that of *Chalcedon*, wherei[n] the Errors of *Eutyches* had been condemn'd, an[d] who forbad any one to assert there was no mor[e] than one Will in Jesus Christ, as *Paul* did in tha[t] Type. But we observ'd before the Jealousie an[d] Aversion the Popes of *Rome* express'd upon a[ll] Occasions towards the Patriarchs of *Constantinople*

A. D. 649.

and this seem'd a proper Season for *Theodorus* to e[x]ert himself against that See; which Animosity w[as] more vigorously pursu'd the Year following b[y] *Martin* the First, *Thoedorus* his Successor, in [a] Council celebrated at *Rome*, and call'd upon tha[t] Subject. Of which when the Emperor was adver[]tis'd, and how averse the Pope appear'd to his Typ[e] he sent *Olympius* to be his Exarch at *Ravenna* with express Order either to allure the Bishops b[y] Promises, or by Threats terrifie 'em into a Com[]pliance. But the Exarch found 'em all obstina[te] and untractable, whereupon perceiving he coul[d] not succeed in the principal Business for whic[h] he was sent into *Italy*, he retir'd by the Emperor[s] Order into *Sicily*, where he dy'd in Disconte[nt] shortly after, and *Theodorus Calliopas* was sent E[x]arch in his room, who, being a Man of a darin[g] Spirit, vigorously executed the Emperor's Order[s] which were by all means to bring *Martin* Prison[er] to *Constantinople*, where the obstinate Pope m[et] with a severe Treatment, and was at length ba[]nish'd into the Pontick *Chersonese*, and was mad[e] to undergo a great deal of Misery. These Pr[o]ceedings on the one side and the other put th[e] Church almost into a general Confusion; for th[e] Head being sick, the inferior Members were unab[le] to execute their Office as they ought.

It is not easily to be imagin'd how prejudicial these disputes prov'd to the Cause of Christianity, and destructive to the Empire. For *Constans* was so wholly taken up in 'em, that he was blind to several Advantages with which the Divisions of the *Saracens* presented him, occasion'd first by some controverted Points in their *Alchoran*, and afterwards by some Contests in the Succession, which in time grew so high between the Competitors, that they proceeded to Acts of Hostility; and *Mahuvias*, one of the Pretenders, fearing lest the Emperor should be persuaded to make a right use of their Divisions, and recover what they had unjustly torn from the Empire, sent Offers of a Peace between his Nation and the *Romans*, which the unwary Emperor readily condescended to, and it was agreed between 'em that each Party should peaceably enjoy what they had then in Possession, and *Mahuvias*, by way of acknowledgement, should send *Constans* every Year a Thousand Crowns of Gold, a fine Horse, and a Slave. Tho' this Treaty was propos'd by *Mahuvias*, and concluded at his desire, yet he maintain'd it no longer than the observance of it consisted with the Interest of his Nation, watching all Advantages to weaken the Empire, and make the Name of the *Saracens* terrible to Mankind. Before this Peace, and in the Twelfth Year of this Emperor's Reign, he seiz'd on *Rhodes*, and there he destroy'd the famous *Colossus*, founded by Rhodes. *Laches* or *Chares*, Thirteen Hundred and Sixty Years before, and esteem'd one of the World's Seven Wonders. It was compos'd of Brass, and cast in the Form of a Man, in height Seventy, some say Eighty Cubits. It stood with its Legs extended over the Haven, so that Ships with their Masts erect sail'd between 'em, said to be Twelve Years in building, and overturn'd Sixty Six Years after by

an

an Earthquake, which terribly shook the who[le] Island. The *Rhodians*, pretending a Prohibitio[n] from the Oracle, never presum'd to erect it agai[n] yet, esteeming the Brass and the other Materials [of] it in a manner sacred, they abstain'd from applyi[ng] it to any other use, 'till it was now sacrilegiousl[y] remov'd by *Mahuvias*, by whom it was sold to [a] *Jewish* Merchant of *Emessa*, who loaded Ni[ne] Hundred Camels with the Metal, which may ser[ve] to give us an Idea of its prodigious and almost i[n]credible Height and Bigness. Whilst *Mahuv[ias]* was thus employ'd in *Rhodes* his Countrymen bro[ke] into *Armenia*, which they pillag'd at Discretio[n] without meeting any from the Emperor, who we[re] able to oppose 'em, and put a stop to their Depr[e]-

A. D. 654. dations. This careless Deportment in the Emp[e]ror, who tamely suffer'd whole Provinces to [be] taken from him, encourag'd the *Saracens* to ma[ke] an Attempt upon *Constantinople* it self, and accor[d]ingly *Mahuvias* order'd a strong Fleet to be fitt[ed] out at *Tripolis* in *Phœnicia*, in which he might, [in] all probability, have very much incommoded t[he] Imperial City, had not two Christian Brothe[rs] the Sons of a *Grecian* Trumpeter, watch'd th[eir] Opportunity, and open'd the Prisons of *Tripol[is]* which were crouded with *Grecian* Captives, [by] whose Assistance they set Fire to the Fleet, d[e]stroy'd all the Naval Preparations, and afterwar[ds] escap'd in a Ship provided for that purpose into t[he] Emperor's Dominions. Notwithstanding whi[ch] the Infidels rigg'd out another Fleet, engag'd *Co[n]stans*, defeated his Navy, and forc'd him to fly [in] a borrow'd Dress to *Constantinople*; and they co[n]tinu'd to exercise their Barbarities upon the Lan[ds] of the Empire, 'till the Necessity of their own A[f]fairs made 'em sollicite the Truce before mention'[d] to which *Constans* unworthily condescended, a[nd]

LXII. Constans II.

[th]ey perfidiously broke, so soon as they had com[po]s'd their Domestick Contentions.

During this Truce, *Constans*, instead of uniting [th]e Minds of his Subjects, and preparing with all [hi]s Forces to oppose the sworn Enemies of the Em[pi]re, committed an Act which render'd him odious [bo]th to God and Man. He had a Brother call'd *[Th]eodosius*, whose Virtue and Integrity had ren[de]r'd him the Darling of the People, which made [th]e degenerate Emperor behold him with a jealous [E]ye: He was conscious how ill he had deserv'd the [A]ffections of his Subjects, and thought he had [jus]t Reason to apprehend some Innovations; to [pr]event which he forc'd his Brother, who was ca[pab]le of heading a Party against him, to be ordain'd [De]acon, and receiv'd the Cup in the Holy Sacra[me]nt from his Hands; as it was in those Days cu[sto]mary with the Deacons as well as Priests to admi[nis]ter the Eucharist. After which, thinking the [ho]ly Function an insufficient Security for him a[gai]nst his Fears, he order'd him to be murder'd; [Bu]t had no sooner committed the execrable Deed, [bef]ore he was most grievously terrify'd with the [Re]morse of Conscience, dreaming almost every [ni]ght that he beheld his Brother approaching him [wit]h a Cup of Blood in his Hand, and command[ing] him to slake his inhuman Thirst. Being perpe[tua]lly haunted and terrify'd with these Visions at [Con]*stantinople*, the Scene of his late Inhumanity, [he] thought by quitting that City to shake off the [Te]rrors of his Mind, and accordingly resolv'd for [Ita]*ly*, looking back with Scorn, Regret and In[dig]nation upon that Royal City, and Seat of his [Em]pire, where by his Obstinacy, Heresie and Par[tia]lity he had render'd himself odious to the Inha[bita]nts. From this time forward he rov'd up and [do]wn, like a Vagabond, with *Cain*'s Curse upon him,

Constans murders his Brother.
A.D. 659.

him, for wherever he wander'd his Guilt follow[ed] him, and he was every moment his own Judge a[nd] Executioner. The Account we have of the [re]maining Part of this Emperor's Reign is distract[ed] and broken, like the Temper of his Mind; for t[he] Authors that have written of him hardly agree [in] any thing more than this, that which way soev[er] he directed his Course he continu'd to oppress t[he] People, whom he pinch'd by new Imposts and E[x]actions. Whilst he lay in *Sicily*, where he ga[ve] himself up to superstitious Fancies and jealous I[n]quisitions, *Aripert*, at that time King of the *Lo*[m]*bards*, dy'd, leaving two Sons behind him, betwe[en] whom he most imprudently divided his Kingdo[m] *Pertharit*, the Eldest, kept his Court at *Milan*, a[nd] the Youngest, whose Name was *Gundebert*, resid[ed] at *Pavia*. This Prince, being dissatisfy'd with t[he] Partition his Father had made, quarrell'd with [his] Brother; and, as it is usual in such Contests, [his] Ambition at last would suffer him to be conte[nt] with nothing but the whole: The better to su[p]port his Pretensions he sent his Ambassador to *G*[ri]*moald*, Duke of *Beneventum*, to desire his Assi[st]ance against his Brother, and promis'd upon th[at] Consideration to give him his Sister in Marria[ge]. *Gundebert*'s Ambassador, instead of solliciting [his] Master's Cause, persuaded *Grimoald* to declare f[or] himself; he told him the two Brothers were your[g,] rash, and unexperienc'd; that the Nation of t[he] *Lombards* requir'd a Prince of Prudence, Pow[er] and Interest, and that they would never be able [to] preserve their Possessions in *Italy* unless he plac[ed]

A. D. 661. himself at the Helm. *Grimoald*, being natural[ly] of an active, ambitious Temper, readily listen'd [to] a Discourse strengthen'd in appearance with so mu[ch] Reason; so that without much Consideration [he] was persuaded instead of a Champion to become [a]
Comp[etitor]

Competitor, and accordingly having rais'd a very powerful Army he march'd towards *Pavia,* leaving his Son *Romoald* to command in *Beneventum* during his Absence. When he was arriv'd near the City the Ambassador was sent to acquaint *Gundebert* with his Approach, and concealing from him the true Intention of his Expedition persuaded the inconsiderate Prince to lodge him in his Palace, where at the first Enterview he was murder'd by *Grimoald,* who immediately seiz'd on his Treasure and Dominions. *Pertharit,* terrify'd at his Brother's Fate, and thinking himself unable to withstand so potent a Rival, fled from *Milan* to *Chagan,* King of the *Hunns,* demanding his Protection and Assistance. *Grimoald,* having thus kill'd one Brother and forc'd the other to fly his Country, marry'd their Sister, after which he was, by the universal Consent of the People, declar'd King of the *Lombards.* So soon as he saw himself confirm'd in his Power at home his first Care was to secure himself against any foreign Attempts, and therefore requir'd the *Hunns* to banish *Pertharit* out of their Dominions, otherwise he threaten'd to renounce the Peace that was at that time establish'd between the two Nations. Tho' *Chagan* express'd a great Affection to the unfortunate Prince, yet being averse to a War with the *Lombards* he commanded *Pertharit* to quit his Territories; who, not knowing where to direct his Course, resolv'd in that desperate Condition to try *Grimoald's* Honour and Generosity: To which purpose he remov'd to *Lodi,* from whence he dispatch'd *Unulfus,* his intimate Friend, to intercede in his behalf with *Grimoald,* and obtain a Permission to reside in Safety at *Pavia.* *Grimoald* appear'd at first exceeding glad of the Overture, he entertain'd *Unulfus* with much Friendship, and gave Order that *Pertharit* should be receiv'd with a

Respect

Respect due to his Quality; but when he observ'd the People attended his Entry with general Shouts and Acclamations, and that his Friends flock'd both by Day and Night in great Numbers to him, and attended his Person, he began to repent of the Kindness he had shown him, and apprehended left the People should be sorry for the Injuries had been done him, and endeavour to re-instate him. Tho' he was naturally just and generous, yet these Thoughts inclin'd him to Blood; for he plac'd a Guard upon him, and gave 'em private Orders the Night following to dispatch him. Of this *Pertharit* was inform'd by the Vigilancy of his Friend *Unulfus*, by whose Advice he chang'd Habits with him, and having by that means deceiv'd the Sentinels he escap'd into *France*; and *Grimoald* was so far from resenting this loyal Device in *Unulfus*, that he immediately gave him his Liberty, with high Commendations for his unshaken Fidelity, and left it to his Choice of staying there or following his Master. *Clotaire* the Third, at that time King of *France*, being sensibly touch'd with the Misfortunes of *Pertharit* and his Family, sent him back with a powerful Army into *Italy*; where *Grimoald*, who knew best how to contend with the Heat of the *French*, pretended at their Approach to fly with his whole Army, leaving his Camp well stor'd with all manner of Provisions behind him; whereupon the *French*, who thought they had effected their Design without Blows, broke into the Camp, where they eat and drank very plentifully and then fell fast asleep. But *Grimoald*, who had laid that Bait on purpose to ensnare 'em, return'd in the Dead of Night, and fell with so much Fury upon 'em that very few were left alive to carry home the News of their Defeat. The Emperor, seeing the *Lombards* engag'd in this War, thought he had now

A. D. 663.
The French defeated by the Lombards.

now a fair Opportunity prefented him of driving 'em out of *Italy*; fo that after he had wander'd up and down for a confiderable time with a difcontented Spirit, he fitted out a very powerful Fleet in *Sicily*, from whence fetting Sail he arriv'd at *Tarentum*, and march'd his Army immediately to *Beneventum*, taking *Luceria*, and feveral other Towns belonging to the *Lombards*, in his way. *Romoald*, as we obferv'd before, was left behind to command in his Father's Abfence; he, as foon as he was inform'd of the Emperor's Approach, fent *Sefuald*, who had been formerly his Governor, to give the King an Account of the Danger the Town was in. *Grimoald* inftantly prepar'd to march to his Relief, and difpatch'd back the Meffenger with News of his coming; but *Sefuald*, before he could recover the Town fell in with a Party of the *Romans*, by whom he was carry'd to the Emperor, who demanding what he was and whence he came, he reply'd without any Hefitation, that *he was fent by the King to inform his Son of his Approach at the Head of an Army to relieve him.* This put *Conftans* into a great Fright, who now thought of nothing but raifing the Siege, and retiring in the beft manner he could to *Naples*; and left the Enemy fhould moleft him in the Rear, he defir'd to frighten *Romoald* into fuch Conditions of Peace as would be moft for his Advantage: Accordingly he commanded *Sefuald* to go to the Walls, and advife the befieg'd Prince to deliver up the Place, upon an Affurance that there was no Poffibility of any Relief, threatning to fee him hewn in pieces if he refus'd to obey. *Sefuald* promis'd to do as he was required, but when upon his Summons *Romoald* appear'd upon the Walls, he encourag'd him to entertain no Thoughts of a Surrender or Accommodation, for that his Father was marching to his Affiftance with

Conftans his Expedition into Italy.

a very powerful Army; at the same time he desired him to take care of his Wife and Children, *For*, said he, *I am in the Enemies Hands, who this moment are beginning by a lingring, merciless Death to punish me for my Affection and Fidelity to my Prince.* Accordingly his Guard who attended fell upon him by the Emperor's Order, and murder'd him; after which *Constans* commanded his Head to be cut off, and by the Help of an Engine to be thrown into the Town, where it was taken up and carry'd to *Romoald*, who having kiss'd it with great Lamentations, very decently bury'd it. In the mean time the Emperor, hearing the *Lombards* were within a short March of him, rais'd the Siege in great Precipitation, and broke up for *Naples*, but was intercepted in his March by a Party of the *Lombards*, who fell upon the Rear, and cut off several of his Men, with little or no Loss sustain'd on their Side. To revenge which Disgrace, *Saburrus*, one of the Nobility, undertook with Twenty Thousand Men to defeat *Grimoald* himself, of whom the Court had so dreadful an Apprehension. With him *Romoald*, at his own earnest Request to his Father, engag'd; and tho' the Success for some time continu'd doubtful, yet the Victory at last inclin'd to the *Lombards*, who following the Chace flew a great Number of the *Romans*, and among the rest *Saburrus*, their vain-glorious Captain.

A.D. 664. These Misfortunes convinc'd the Emperor that it was in vain to contend any longer with them; yet that he might not be thought to have made a fruitless Expedition into *Italy*, he prepar'd to go and visit *Rome*, where when the News of his Intent was carry'd it was receiv'd with the great Satisfaction both of the Pope and the People, for *Rome* had not been honour'd with the Presence of an Emperor for a long time before, for which Reason they

Chap. V. LXII. Conſtans II.

they provided him a very magnificent Reception. In the Account *Paulus Diaconus* has left us of it we may obſerve, that the Pope pay'd the Emperor ſuch Honours as his Succeſſors have ſince diſdain'd to the Imperial Dignity, and that the Emperor was not in thoſe Days requir'd to kiſs the Pope's Toe; which Ceremony, had it been then perform'd, would not have been omitted by that Author. He tells us, the Emperor remov'd out of the City moſt of the richeſt and remarkable Rarities in it, which he order'd to be tranſported to *Conſtantinople*. After he had continu'd Twelve Days in *Rome* he return'd to *Naples*, and from thence into *Sicily*, ſettling his Court at *Syracuſe*, where he impoveriſh'd the Iſlanders by his heavy Taxes and unreaſonable Impoſitions.

By that time the Emperor was retir'd out of *Italy* that Country was threaten'd with a new Irruption of the barbarous Nations. *Lupus*, the Duke of *Forum Julii*, obſerving *Grimoald's* Forces were divided to defend him at once from the Emperor and the *French*, committed ſeveral Outrages, for which the King, who was now returning in a triumphant manner, threaten'd to call him to a ſevere Account; he, knowing he was unable to juſtifie what he had done, ſupported one Injury with another, and renounc'd his Allegiance to *Grimoald*, who was very deſirous to chaſtiſe him, but unwilling to lead his *Lombards* againſt him, left he ſhould bring 'em acquainted with Civil Wars. Upon which Conſideration he invited *Chagan*, the King of the *Hunns*, to fall upon him, promiſing to abandon him and all his Subſtance to him: *Chagan* (a Name common to all the Kings of that People) embrac'd ſo favourable an Opportunity of extending his Dominions, and fell the Year following with a very powerful Army into *Friuli*, where *Lupus* defended himſelf very vi-

Y 2 goroully

goroufly for four Days together, but was at length overthrown, and kill'd in Battel. This Victory made the *Hunns* look on the Country as their own, for which reafon they over-ran it, and wafted it at their Pleafure; whereupon *Grimoald* fent to the King, and demanded him to retire with his Forces, fince the Work was done for which they had been call'd in. *Chagan* anfwer'd plainly, that *he would not fo eafily quit a Country which he had conquer'd by the Force of his Arms, and at the Expence of fo many of his Subjects Lives.* *Grimoald*, provok'd at this refolute Reply, prepar'd to remove him by Force, and collected as good an Army as he could, which however was far fhort in Number to that of his Adverfary; for which Reafon he made ufe of a Stratagem to reprefent it more numerous than it was: For he mufter'd his Soldiers in the Prefence of *Chagan*'s Ambaffadors, and made the fame Troops march before him two or three Days together in a different Cloathing, by which means they appear'd to be treble the Number they really were, and as fuch the Ambaffadors reprefented them to their Mafter, with which he was fo terrify'd that he immediately retreated into his own Dominions.

Whilft *Conftans* was employing his Days in Extortions, and wafting his Nights in Terror, *Mahuvias*, who was now become Chief of the *Saracens* without any Competitor, began to contemn the unworthy Emperor, and fent his Son *Izod* into *Romania*, who proceeded as far as *Chalcedon*, and took *Armorium*, a City of *Phrygia*, wherein he left a ftrong Garrifon, and then retir'd home with extraordinary Spoils. *Conftans* recover'd the City the next Winter, and put all the Garrifon to the Sword, after which he return'd to his old Oppreffions, in which he grew infufferably troublefom to the Inhabitants

habitants of *Calabria, Sicily,* and *Sardinia,* sparing neither Churches nor the Holy Furniture of the Altar. From these enormous Courses he was shortly after diverted by *Saporius,* whom he had made Governor of *Armenia,* who, seeing him wholly employ'd in his Sacrilegious Violence, rebell'd, and sent *Sergius,* Master of the Horse, to require Assistance and Support from *Mahuvias*; at whose Court *Andreas,* one of the Bed-Chamber, arriv'd from the Emperor at the same Time, and upon the same Errand. Tho' the King gave Audience to both, yet he declar'd for *Saporius,* and promis'd to send him a very powerful Assistance; but before it could arrive the Usurper's Horse threw him, and he dy'd shortly after of the Fall. The same just Punishment befel his Embassador *Sergius,* who in his Return fell into *Andreas* his Hands, and was hang'd immediately.

A. D. 667.

For Four Years together the Emperor had resided at *Syracuse* in *Sicily,* from whence the most important Affairs of the Empire could not withdraw him, during which time he had render'd himself universally odious, and contemptible to all Mankind. This encourag'd some, who were the most implacably averse to him, to conspire against him, and they succeeded so luckily in their Measures, that he was knock'd on the Head by a Vessel in the Bath, after he had reign'd Twenty Seven Years, in the Fourteenth of *Vitalian,* Bishop of *Rome, A. D.* 668.

Constans Slain.

He left the Empire at his Death in as much a lower Condition than he found it, as he exceeded his Predecessor in his Corruptions and supine Negligence. He is not recommended to Posterity by One good Act throughout his long and unsuccessful Reign, but render'd himself odious to his Cotemporaries by a Thousand ill ones. He was neither

His Character.

ther a prudent Prince, a juſt Husband, a tender Father, loving Maſter, nor ſincere Chriſtian; ſo that in all the moſt conſiderable and indiſpenſible Duties of Life he was deficient. His extravagant Behaviour had render'd him ſo contemptible to the Inhabitants of *Conſtantinople*, that he is ſaid once to have reſolv'd to tranſlate the Seat of the Empire to *Rome*, and ſent accordingly for his Wife and Children; but the Citizens, being inform'd of his Deſign, reproach'd him with bitter Reflections, and would not let 'em go. He inherited his Grandfather's Zeal for the Hereſie of the *Monothelites* tho' he did not ſeem to act upon the ſame Principle; for *Heraclius* is thought really to have believ'd what he ſo zealouſly profeſs'd, whereas *Conſtans* his Profeſſion proceeded rather from the Perverſeneſs of his Will, than the Direction of his Underſtanding; and 'tis obſerv'd of him, that firſt or laſt he eſpous'd almoſt all Parties in Religion but the Orthodox. He never had an Enemy that really fear'd him, nor Friend that ſincerely lov'd him; and it may be truly ſaid of him, that during his Reign the Empire had no Enemy more pernicious than himſelf, and as ſuch he liv'd ſuch he dy'd, leaving a Son behind him that in ſome meaſure atton'd for his Father's Faults.

A. D. 668.

II. *Conſtans*, the late Emperor, had ſo generally diſoblig'd his Subjects, eſpecially the Army, that they readily receiv'd an Emperor from the Conſpirators, who proclaim'd one *Mezizius*, or *Melius*, an *Armenian*, who had no other Qualifications to recommend himſelf to 'em, but the Beauty of his Perſon. For ſome time this Man behav'd himſelf as Emperor in *Sicily*, whilſt *Conſtantine*, the Son of *Conſtans*, doubtful of the People's Affections, tho' his Father had aſſum'd him as his Collegue

Chap. V. LXIII. Constantine III.

egue in his Life time, was afraid, or unable to assert his Right. In the like manner *Theodorus*, Exarch of *Ravenna*, tho' he had a sufficient Army at Command, dar'd not resent, as he ought, the Usurpation of *Melius*, nor revenge the Death of his Master; for he found he was universally abhorr'd for his Covetousness, and the People for the present fond of the Change. Upon this Account he and other great Men sate silent for some time, and declin'd declaring themselves either for *Constantine* or the Usurper, 'till the Army at length discover'd the Inability of the Idol they had set up, and began to repent of his Promotion. This Disaffection in the Army in *Sicily* presently diffus'd it self into other Parts, so that a powerful Party began to appear for *Constantine*, who, having fitted out a strong Fleet, attack'd the Usurper, whom he defeated and put to Death, together with all those who had been the most active in his Behalf. Having settl'd all things according to his Desire in *Sicily*, where he was proclaim'd and acknowledg'd Emperor, he set Sail for *Constantinople*, where he was receiv'd with the general Satisfaction of his People, who gave him the Sirname of *Pogonatus*, because, being young when he left the City, he had no more than a little Down appearing upon his Chin, but now return'd to 'em with a mature Beard. At first he assum'd his two Brothers, *Tiberius* and *Heraclius*, as his Associates in the Empire with him, but finding the People pursu'd 'em with their Acclamations, and that some presum'd to demand they might be formally Crown'd as well as himself, he cut off their Noses, by which Mutilation he destroy'd their Hopes to the Sovereignty; and some add his Jealousie was not satisfy'd with that Remedy, but that he shortly after put 'em to Death. Notwithstanding

CONSTANTINE III.

withstanding this inhuman Action he always express'd a great Zeal for the Purity of Faith, and
appear'd much concern'd at the Divisions the *Monothelites* fomented in the Church, which he endeavour'd by all means possible to remove, for
which purpose he caus'd the Sixth General or
Oecumenical Council to be celebrated at *Constantinople* in the Thirteenth Year of his Reign.

This Year the *Saracens* made a new Irruption
into *Africk*, where some of the Natives had insulted their Garrisons, and after having committed
unspeakable Disorders they led away Eighty Thousand Prisoners. They were now grown so exceeding powerful, that there was hardly a Province in
the Empire into which they did not pierce the
Year following, destroying all in a most barbarous
manner where ever they pass'd with Fire and
Sword. Particularly, observing the unsettl'd Face
of Affairs at *Constantinople*, they made a Descent
into *Sicily*, taking *Syracuse*, the Capital City of the
Island, from whence they transported to *Alexandria* every thing of value, especially such Rarities
as the Emperor *Constans* had remov'd thither out
of *Italy*. This Success encourag'd 'em to greater
Attempts, for they shortly after rigg'd out a Fleet,
with which they pass'd into *Cilicia*, which they
wasted in a very Hostile manner, and winter'd at
Smyrna, from whence they prepar'd to Besiege
A. D. *Constantinople* it self, which they did by Sea and
671. Land the Year following.

But by this time *Constantine* had so firmly settled himself in the Throne, so throughly reform'd
the Court and the Army, and so effectually provided for the City and the Fleet, that he was very
little concern'd at their Motions. He receiv'd 'em
with so much Courage, and with an Army so well
appointed, that they were forc'd to retire with
great

great Loss towards the latter end of the Summer to *Cyzicus*, which they seiz'd, and there laid up their Fleet 'till the next Spring, and then they prepar'd to renew the Siege, which the *Grecian* Writers say continu'd for Seven Years together, tho' it appears from some of 'em that a Peace was concluded in the Fourth Year, to the great Satisfaction of the *Saracens*, and that for Reasons which will be shown hereafter. The Siege was carry'd on from Year to Year with various Success, during which *Constantine* gave the World remarkable Instances of his great Care and Conduct, and the *Saracens* found by Experience that their late successful Progress was rather owing to the senseless Stupidity, or the supine Negligence of the preceding Emperors, than their own Valour and Conduct. During this Siege *Callinicus*, a Mathematician of *Heliopolis* in *Egypt*, invented a Wild-fire, call'd by the *Saracens Græcus Ignis*, which was made to burn under the Water, and very much incommoded the Infidels, who in one Sea Fight lost Thirty Thousand of their Men, and shortly after had their whole Fleet burnt in the Port of *Cyzicus* by the means of that Wild-fire.

A Fleet of the Saracens destroy'd.

This Advantage over the Enemy was attended by another of as fatal a Consequence to the Infidels, for the Emperor's Lieutenants engag'd a great Body of the *Saracens* under the Conduct of *Suphianus*, the Son of *Aphus*, in *Syria*, where he was defeated, and lost the greatest part of his Forces. And as if these Losses were not sufficient to humble that proud Nation, which, like an irresistible Torrent, had with an unbounded Flood laid waste all before it, and had about this time fallen upon *Spain* with a Naval Army, compos'd of Two Hundred and Seventy Vessels; *Bamba*, a Captain, descended from the ancient and illustrious Race of the

A. D. 674.

the *Gothick* Princes, at that time King of *Spain*, watching an Advantage fell upon 'em and deſtroy'd their whole Fleet. Theſe concurring Misfortunes encourag'd the *Maronites*, or *Mardaites*, in great Numbers to ſeize upon Mount *Libanus*, the moſt ſerviceable Places whereof they ſo ſtrongly fortify'd, that they found themſelves ſecure againſt all Attacks, and were ſhortly after join'd with ſuch Multitudes of Slaves, made ſuch by the *Saracens* in the Courſe of their Wars, who fled thither for their Liberty, that they compos'd a very numerous Army, which deſcending in Bodies regularly form'd, cover'd the Plains of *Syria* and *Paleſtine*, and grew terrible to the *Saracens*. Hereupon *Mahuvias*, ſeeing himſelf thus aſſaulted on every ſide, and that Fate ſeem'd to threaten his Nation with an entire Diſſolution, thought a Peace with the Emperor the beſt Expedient at ſo dangerous a Conjuncture; accordingly he ſent his Ambaſſadors to Treat with *Conſtantine* upon that Subject. The Emperor, who thought it Prudence to embrace a Peace if to be obtain'd upon honourable Terms, and was zealouſly careful to compoſe the Differences in Religion, readily liſten'd to the Overture, and ſent *John*, Sirnam'd *Pitzigrandis*, a Patrician, famous for his Wiſdom and Nobility, as his Plenipotentiary into *Syria*, where he met with a Reception ſuitable to his Quality, and at length the Negotiations on both ſides were brought to this Iſſue, That for Thirty Years together a Truce ſhould inviolably be obſerv'd between the *Romans* and the *Saracens*, who, upon that Conſideration, were oblig'd to pay the Emperor and his Succeſſors every Year Thirty Thouſand Pounds of Gold, Five Hundred Slaves, and as many choice Horſes. Authors vary as to the Articles of this Treaty, but they all agree that in the ſubſtance of it,

A. D. 676.

A Peace with the Saracens.

, as Matters then stood, it was very much to the Honour of the Empire. For upon the Conclusion of it the King or *Chagan* of the *Avari*, the *Hunns, Bulgarians*, and other Nations bordering upon the Empire, sent to congratulate *Constantine*, and to renew their former Alliances confirm'd between 'em; by which means the Empire for some time enjoy'd a greater Tranquility than it had done many Years before.

The *Maronites*, who gave a beginning to this Peace, were, according to some Authors, Christians inhabiting the Mountain *Libanus*, so nam'd from a Monk call'd *Maron*, very much esteem'd by 'em for his extraordinary Learning and Holy Life. Others, upon more probable Grounds, derive their Name from the Country they inhabited, call'd *Maronia*, extending from the Sea near *Antioch* up to the Mountain *Libanus*. For it appears from some ancient Medals, that they were known by that Name to the World before the Days of Christianity, and for as much as their Country abounded with most excellent Wines they esteem'd *Bacchus* as their great Patron and Protector. For some time they were a great Check to the Conquests of the *Saracens*, but were in the end forc'd to submit, tho' upon reasonable Terms, securing to themselves, among other Privileges, the free Exercise of their Religion; and the better to keep their Country free from the intermixture of *Mahometans*, they are said at this Day to pay a great Annual Tribute to the Grand Seignior. At first they embrac'd the Errors of the *Monothelites*, but some say they have at length renounc'd 'em, and not many Years since submitted themselves to the Pope of *Rome*.

The Emperor, having thus concluded a Peace with the *Saracens*, and the rest of the Neighbouring

ing Nations, earneftly endeavour'd to find out fome Remedy for the Divifions of the Church, which every Day improv'd, and grew more incurable, and began to think of fummoning a general Council for that purpofe, in which he was earneftly feconded by *Agathon*, at that time Pope of *Rome*, but was a little diverted from his Defign by fome new Attempts of the *Bulgarians*, who to the number of One Hundred Thoufand Perfons came about this time out of *Scythia*, that inexhaufted Fountain of barbarous Nations, and leaving their Native Seats upon the Banks of the Rivers *Volga* or *Bulga*, from whence fome imagine they were call'd *Bulgarians*, they proceeded in a tumultuous manner 'till they came to the *Danube*, which they pafs'd, and exceedingly harafs'd the Territories of the Empire. *Conftantine* having rais'd a powerful Army fent it againft 'em, and the *Romans* though they fhould, with great eafe, mafter an undifciplin'd Multitude, who, being not poffefs'd of any fortify'd Towns, were Strangers to the Arts of Encampment, and lay, as they thought, liable to every Affault. In this Prefumption they march'd carelefsly, and without any Order, by which means they were the Inftruments of their own Difgrace and Ruin; for the Barbarians fell with fo much Vigour upon 'em that they were entirely defeated, of which when the Emperor was inform'd he chofe rather to embrace a difhonourable Peace, than continue a doubtful, but honourable War, and therefore appeas'd 'em with a great Sum of Mony, and fuffer'd 'em to fettle in the lower *Myfia*, from them afterwards call'd *Bulgaria* which they quietly inhabited for many Years, 'til they were finally fubdu'd by the *Turks*. I know fome Writers have plac'd this Settlement feveral Years backwards, but the generality of Authors, and

A. D. 679.

The Bulgarians pafs the Danube.

had indeed the Circumstances of History seem to refer it 'till this.

Tho' the Emperor had purchas'd this Peace upon mean dishonourable Conditions, he apply'd it to just and Christian Ends; for having thus secur'd the State, he labour'd earnestly for the Peace and Welfare of the Church. He had, the Year before, acquainted *Agathon*, Bishop of *Rome*, with his Resolution of summoning a General Council, there to have the Doctrine of the *Monothelites* debated and examin'd; in Order to which several National Synods were held, particularly in *France*, *Italy* and *England*, in all which some Articles of Faith relating to that Point were digested into Form, and were to be more particularly discuss'd at the following Council; which, after many Oppositions made by *Theodore*, Patriarch of *Constantinople*, who being a profess'd *Monothelite* endeavour'd by all his Artifices to frustrate the Emperor's good Intentions, and was therefore by his Authority depos'd, was opened at *Constantinople* on the Twenty Second of *November*, *A. D.* 680. In the Pope's Letters sent by his Legates to the Emperor the gross Ignorance of the *Roman* Bishops at that time evidently appears from his own Confession, for, after many Expressions full of Respect and Submission, he humbly beseeches the Emperor to excuse their Ignorance of the Languages and the Holy Scriptures, for he tells him *he was forc'd to send into* England *for a Divine, having no Person in* Italy *fit to appear in that Quality at the Council.* And this is written not only in Behalf of his own Legates, but the Deputies of the Synod. If this Ignorance prevail'd to so high a Degree among the Clergy of *Rome*, in what Darkness must the common People be involv'd? And yet such as these have been chosen to decide the most important Controversies relating to the

A. D. 680.

The Sixth General Council held at Constantinople.

Salva-

Salvation of Mankind, who were implicitly obslig'd to submit to their Decisions.

This Council was the most considerable thing relating to the Church that happen'd in that Age tho' it was remarkable for nothing more than that it anathematis'd *Honorius*, who had been Pope of *Rome* in the Year 626: From whence it is evident that the Pope is as liable to Errors as other Bishops and that a General Council is above him; which are Truths the great Champions for the Papacy have, in these latter Ages, very earnestly labour'd to overthrow. In the Sixteenth Session of the Council *Polychronius*, a Priest, was depos'd, as an obstinate Heretick and Seducer of the People. Being a profess'd *Monothelite* he had written his Confession of Faith on a large Paper, and laid it upon a dead Corps, declaring boldly, in the Presence of the Council and all the People of *Constantinople*, that he would confirm his Doctrine by a Miracle and by the Power, Purity and Efficacy of his Faith raise the Dead to Life; the whole World stood attentive for some time in Expectation of the Miracle which he had most blasphemously promis'd, but when they found it all Delusion they exclaim'd against him, and the Multitude were hardly restrain'd from falling upon him: So dreadful a thing is it for Men to give themselves up to Novelties or teach any thing for Truth but what is founded upon the undoubted Authority of the Scriptures. This Sixth General Council, celebrated at *Constantinople* under *Constantine* the Third, together with that which follow'd under his Successor *Justinian* did so far put a Stop to the Heresie of the *Monothelites* as to banish it out of *Constantinople*, tho' it could not entirely root it out in the East, for it still maintain'd its ground at *Antioch*, where the *Maronites* retain'd it for several Ages after: But
what

what is worse than all, the *Eutychians*, both of the East and *Egypt*, seeing the *Monothelites* had been condemn'd for no other Reason, but because they came up too near to their Errors, grew more obstinate and irreclaimable; and so carefully instill'd their poisonous Doctrine wherever they came, that even at this Day the Patriarchs of *Antioch* and *Alexandria* are said to be infected with that Heresie.

The Bishops were hardly dismiss'd from the Council, and the Pope's Legates return'd to *Rome*, before *Agathon* dy'd; whereupon there ensu'd a Vacancy in the See a full Year and Seven Months, occasion'd by the Intrigues and Dissention of those who aspir'd at the Papacy. However at this time the Emperor, in Behalf of himself and his Successors, remitted to the Bishops of *Rome* the Fine they were oblig'd to pay upon their Promotion, reserving still to himself the Right of Confirmation; and yet even that was renounc'd by him shortly after, when *Benedict* the Second was advanc'd to the Papacy. This Indulgence, as it was intended to prevent those Disorders upon Elections, which, as it appear'd afterwards, it could not remove, so was it a great Step to that Sovereign Authority, to which the Papacy in succeeding Ages attain'd.

A.D. 682.

Tho' *Italy* had for a long time enjoy'd a perfect Tranquility, and both the Exarchs and *Lombards* religiously observ'd the several Treaties concluded between 'em, yet was it not exempt from other Judgments, which appear'd more terrible and grievous than War it self: For about this time there happen'd such great Tempests and Convulsions in the Heavens, as if the Elements had conspir'd against Mankind; the Winds were so violent that many Buildings were overthrown, and Trees footed up; the Rains fell in such prodigious Quantities,

that

that all the Tillage was deftroy'd, and were attended with Thunders and Lightning, which flew great Numbers of People; and the Earth became fo corrupt, from thefe unufual and unnatural Alterations, that a deadly Plague enfu'd, which fwept off great Multitudes of the Inhabitants.

Conftantine's great Care and Zeal for the Peace of the Church preferv'd likewife that of the State, for he liv'd all the reft of his Reign in a Repofe and Tranquility which his Virtue had deferv'd. The *Saracens* religioufly obferv'd the Treaty concluded between them and the Empire, and the *Lombards* were too much at Variance among themfelves to attempt any thing againft his Officers in *Italy*, fo that he found himfelf at leifure to attend the Affairs of his own Family, and the Welfare of the Church, which he enrich'd with many magnificent Buildings and Royal Endowments. He had for a long time enjoy'd an uninterrupted Health, which now began to be impair'd, whereupon he declar'd his Son *Juftinian* his Collegue in the Empire, and took care to have his Choice approv'd by the Senate and the People. At length, when he perceiv'd the Hour of his Diffolution approaching, he fent for his Son, and in the Prefence of the Senate inftructed him in the Art of Government, and read him an excellent Lecture upon that Subject, in the Obfervance of which *Juftinian* might have made himfelf great, and his Subjects happy: After which, and fome private ferious Difcourfes with the Bifhops that attended, *Conftantine* dy'd in the Month of *December*, when he had reign'd Seventeen Years and fome Months, A. D. 685. *John* V. being then Pope of *Rome*.

JUSTINIAN II.

A. D. 685. Conftantine dies.

His Character. The Character of this Prince will beft appear from the Circumftances of his Reign, from which it is manifeft that he well deferves to be reckon'd among

mong the best of the Roman Emperors; he was Modest, Just, Cautious and Compassionate, and, unlike many of his Predecessors, apply'd the Peace, which he may be said to have purchas'd upon dishonourable Terms, to very honourable Ends, to the healing the Breaches of the Church, and removing the Distempers of the State. Two things he is justly to be tax'd with, his Cruelty to his Brethren, which however the Reasons of State seem'd to make necessary, and his little Care in appointing some proper Person before his Death to council and direct his Son, and provide for the Necessities of the State; but these are Faults his many other excellent Qualities have abundantly over-weigh'd.

III. The Inconstancy of Fortune, and Vicissitude of Human Affairs, appears so conspicuous no where as in those who are advanc'd in Dignity above the rest of Mankind; to prove which, the Emperor, of whose Reign we are now going to treat, is a most signal Instance; and the Reader will find him like an Actor, sometimes entring upon the Stage cloath'd in the glorious Ornaments of Imperial Majesty, at others desolate and forsaken, stripp'd of his Power, and expos'd to the Scorn and Contempt of the People.

Constantine, at his Death, had left the Sate in so good a Condition, and contracted such firm Alliances with his Neighbours, that his Son *Justinian*, tho' a Youth no more than Sixteen Years old, and degenerating from the Virtues of his Father, being rash, cholerick, fickle and intractable, yet was at first chearfully obey'd by all Men, and for some Time govern'd the Empire in that Tranquillity in which his Father had left it. *Abdelmelech*, Prince of the *Saracens*, sent and confirm'd the Peace made by his Predecessor, offering, among other Conditi-

ons,

ons, to restore to the Emperor whatever they of his Nation retain'd in *Africk*, together with other Annual Contributions of Men and Horses: In consideration of which *Justinian* undertook to repress the Inroads of the *Mardaites*, or *Maronites*, mention'd before, who by their frequent Excursions from Mount *Libanus* very much incommoded the *Saracens*. At the same time *Abdelmelech* engag'd himself to pay the Emperor a Thousand Crowns a Day, and provide every *Roman* employ'd in the Service with an Horse and a Slave. These Articles prov'd very prejudicial to the Empire, for there were at least Twelve Thousand experienc'd Soldiers of those *Maronites*, who continually harass'd all the Country held by the *Saracens* from *Mopsuestia* to *Armenia*, and, forcing the Inhabitants to desert it, render'd it barren and unserviceable. These People *Magistrianus* was sent by the Emperor to repress, to the utter Ruin and Destruction of the *Roman* Power and Authority in those Parts, as it afterwards appear'd, upon a Rupture between *Abdelmelech* and the Emperor, and brought unspeakable Calamities upon the Territories of the Empire.

A. D. 687.
Justinian, having by this means as he though secur'd himself against any Attempts of the *Saracens*, broke the League his Father had solemnly made with the *Bulgarians*; and having muster'd his Army he enter'd their Country in a very hostile manner, exacting unreasonable Contributions from the Inhabitants, and seizing on several Forts which had been abandon'd. This Success in the beginning of the War made him careless and presumptuous, which when the *Bulgarians* observ'd they recover'd Courage, and, drawing all the Forces they had together, press'd so closely upon the Emperor that he was oblig'd to restore most of his Prisoners.

Justinian overthrown by the Bulgarians.

Towns

Towns, and whatever else he had taken from 'em, to purchase a Retreat.

Notwithstanding this Miscarriage he return'd in a triumphant manner to *Constantinople*, and, as if his late imaginary Success had enabled him to give Law to the whole World, he renounc'd the League and Alliance lately concluded between him and *Abdelmelech*; who, having settled all his Matters in *Arabia*, was now grown able to contend with any foreign Opposition, and had therefore conniv'd at some of his Men who wasted the Borders and robb'd several of the Emperor's Subjects. At this *Justinian* was so highly offended that he resolv'd to proceed to an open Rupture, for which he laid hold of a very trivial Occasion; he refus'd to receive the Tribute of Gold which the *Saracens* had oblig'd themselves by the late Articles to pay him every Year, because it was not stamp'd with his Image: And tho' *Abdelmelech* promis'd to put a stop to the Depredations his Subjects committed upon the Borders, and to perform every thing else requir'd of him by the Treaty, yet he continu'd inflexible, and declar'd War against him. This Resolution, as it was inconsiderate and unnecessary, so in the Issue did it prove very prejudicial and fatal to the Empire, and gave Entrance to those innumerable Calamities which afterwards befel Christianity. *He declares War with the Saracens;*

Having thus resolv'd for the War he began with great Diligence to raise a very powerful Army, in which he made as false Steps as in any of his former Proceedings; for distrusting the Service of his *Roman* Legions, and the Forces already on Foot, he listed at a vast Expence Thirty Thousand *Sclavi*, distinguishing 'em from the rest of his Army by peculiar Marks of Honour and Favour. In the mean time the *Saracens*, with repeated Prayers and Com- A.D. 691.

Complaints, adjur'd him by the Living God, by the Interpoſition of whoſe Name the League was made, not to break it: But he, without giving Audience to any of their Meſſengers, drew down his Forces towards *Sebaſtopolis*, a Town in *Aſia Proconſularis*. Whereupon the *Saracens* march'd againſt him with all the Troops they were able to raiſe, and met him before he was got into the Bowels of their Country; there, advancing the Tables of the League upon the Top of a Spear, they engag'd him under the Conduct of *Moamed*, or *Mahomet*, *Abdelmelech*'s Lieutenant. The Emperor had the Advantage in the firſt Encounter, and in all probability had obtain'd an entire Victory, if *Moamed* had not ſupply'd his want of Men by the help of a Stratagem, always allowable, and frequently of great Uſe in the Management of a War. The *Sclavi* made up the ſtrongeſt Part of the Emperor's Army, theſe he knew follow'd *Juſtinian* from no other Conſideration than that of their Pay; he therefore ſent 'em a larger Sum than that they had been promis'd by the Emperor, to induce 'em to deſert over to him, or return into their own Country, whereupon Twenty Thouſand of 'em left the Emperor and join'd their Standards with thoſe of the *Saracens*.

This ſeaſonable Addition to *Moamed*'s Forces quite turn'd the Balance, for the *Saracens* fell inſtantly upon the *Romans*, whilſt they were amaz'd *and defeat-* at ſo unexpected a Deſertion, and forc'd 'em to fly, *ed by 'em.* the Emperor himſelf haſtening in great Precipitation to *Leucate*; where enrag'd at his Loſs, and affronted at the Treachery of the *Sclavi*, he in great Fury commanded thoſe that continu'd with him, together with their Wives and Children, to be ſlain, and their Bodies to be caſt into the Sea; after which barbarous Reſentment he return'd with

Shame

Shame and Dishonour to *Constantinople,* where he shortly lost the Memory of his late Disgrace in other Amusements.

In the mean time the *Saracens* grew so formidable by this important Victory, that *Sabbatius,* Governor of *Armenia,* being inform'd of the Emperor's Defeat, and knowing he had not Forces sufficient to make Head against the Victorious Enemy, deliver'd the Country instantly into their Hands, after which they subdu'd the inner Part of *Persia,* call'd *Chorosen.* At the same time *Moamed,* to be reveng'd on *Justinian,* and to make his Subjects feel the dismal Effects of that War his Obstinacy and Perfidiousness had brought upon 'em, invaded his Dominions, in which he was assisted by the *Sclavi,* his new Auxiliaries, by whose Direction he harass'd the Provinces that lay most expos'd; and after he had exercis'd as many Mischiefs and Cruelties as an enrag'd barbarous Enemy could desire, he return'd home with a vast number of Prisoners, who were all sold into Captivity.

In this manner were the Provinces exhausted and destroy'd, whilst *Justinian,* instead of providing for their Defence, was wholly employ'd in Buildings at *Constantinople,* where he erected a magnificent Banquetting-House, and encircled his Palace with a Wall. *Stephen,* a *Persian* by Nation, and chief of the Eunuchs, was appointed Surveyor of the Works; in which Office he behav'd himself with so much Cruelty, that he commanded several of the poor Labourers to be put to Death, and presum'd, in the Emperor's Absence, to beat *Anastasia, Justinian's* Mother, using with equal Barbarity and Impudence, the greatest Men of the City, many of whom he imprison'd, and loaded others with very scandalous Indignities, and that upon little

A. D. 693.

little or no Provocation; in all which he was seconded and assisted by *Theodotus*, a Monk, whom the Emperor had taken out of his Cell, and promoted to an honourable Employment in the Court. This Man persuaded *Justinian* to convert a Church, dedicated to the Virgin *Mary*, which stood near the Palace, into a Theater; and as the Labourers were going to demolish it for that purpose, the Emperor forc'd *Callinicus*, Patriarch of *Constantinople*, to sanctifie the ungodly Work by a Prayer; striving by this, and several other unchristian and inhuman Actions, to render himself odious to the People, and pull the Divine Vengeance down upon his Head. As a Prelude to his approaching Calamities there happen'd an Eclipse of the Sun on the Fifth of *October* this Year, which was so totally darken'd, that the Stars were plainly seen at Noon-day.

Justinian, having render'd himself odious to his Subjects.

Justinian's abominable Practices had exceedingly expos'd him to the Hatred of his Subjects, which by degrees grew so violent against him, as made him apprehend it would in a short time break out into some dangerous Effects; for this Reason he consider'd by what means he might provide for his own Safety, and anticipate their Resentments. After some Deliberation he gave Order to *Stephen* the Eunuch, and *Rufus*, an Officer in the Army, upon a set Night to Massacre all the Inhabitants of *Constantinople*, and to begin with *Callinicus* the Patriarch. *Leontius*, the Patrician, happen'd at that time to be in the City; he had formerly been General for the Emperor in the East, where his Conduct was so well approv'd that the Emperor grew jealous of him, and threw him into Prison; but some time before this he was releas'd, and made Governor of *Greece*, with Orders to Embark that very Day upon some Expedition,

pedition. As he was preparing for his Voyage several of his Friends came to him, and among the rest two Monks, one call'd *Gregory*, the Superior of a Monastery, and the other *Peter*, both very good Mathematicians, and who, whilst he lay in Prison in great Danger of his Life, had foretold him that he should be Emperor before he dy'd, notwithstanding the Condition he then was in. These Men represented to him, That *now was the time for him to make good their Predictions, if he would not be wanting to himself, but concur with the People, and save the Nobility from the Ruin which hung over their Heads:* That *he ought not to omit the Opportunity he now had of revenging himself upon* Justinian *for the Injuries he had receiv'd, and of rescuing his Country out of the Hands of a Tyrant:* That *the Minds of the People were totally alienated from their unworthy Prince, and that their Eyes were fix'd on him as on their Deliverer.* These Arguments so awaken'd and confirm'd *Leontius*, that being join'd by his most intimate Friends, and such Soldiers upon whose Fidelity he could depend, he got, by a Stratagem, into the Imperial Palace, where he seiz'd on *Justinian*, *is depos'd*, and, having cut off his Nose, led him in that Condition through the City, summoning, by Proclamation as he went, all those that were Christians to meet him at the Church of St. *Sophia*, whither the Multitude ran in great Crowds, to whom the Patriarch cry'd aloud, *This is the Day which the Lord hath made, therefore we will rejoice and be glad in it; this is the Lord's doing, and it is marvellous in our Eyes.* The next Morning *Justinian* was carry'd in an ignominious manner to the *Circus*, where the People attended and banish'd him by *and banish'd.* an unanimous Voice to the Pontick *Chersonesus.*

At the same time *Theodotus* and *Stephen* were dragg'd

dragg'd through the Publick Streets to the Ox Market, where they were burnt alive; after which publick Examples of Justice *Leontius* was saluted Emperor by the universal Acclamations of the People.

A. D. 694.

Thus fell *Justinian* from the height of Human Glory, down to the abject Condition of the meanest Slave, disfigur'd, banish'd, abandon'd and despis'd, glad to escape with Life, which was prolong'd to him by Providence, that he might remain to Posterity a perfect Example of the Inconstancy of Fortune, and the Mutability of Human Greatness. Almost all Ages can supply us with Instances of unfortunate Princes, who either through their own Mismanagement, or the Factions of State, have been forc'd to give way to popular Fury, and lose their Lives and Crowns together, or end their Days in a disconsolate Exile. But we rarely meet with those, who, like this *Justinian*, have out-liv'd their ill Fortune, and, after a stormy tempestuous Declension, risen again like the Sun with fresh Glories, and call'd the Authors of their Disgrace to a severe and fatal Account. From the Consideration of such Examples as these we are taught to have an humble Opinion of our selves; to pay a just Deference to those whom the Laws have set over us; to think no Man so high, but that there is a superior Power still presiding over, and able to control him; nor any so low, but the Hand of Providence can raise and restore him. This great Revolution happen'd in the Tenth Year of *Justinian*'s Reign, the Seventh of *Sergius*, Pope of *Rome*, A. D. 694.

IV. *Justinian* being thus banish'd *Leontius* was acknowledg'd and obey'd as Emperor, and he govern'd the State as such almost Three Years, but in the end met with the same Treatment he had given *Justinian*. The First Year of this new Emperor was discompos'd with no Commotions from abroad, so that he had more Opportunity to confirm his Authority at home. In his Second the *Saracens* made some Irruptions into the Territories of the Empire, from whence they return'd with great Booty; and having rais'd a powerful Army they once more Invaded *Africk*, in which they took *Carthage*, and over-ran all the Country: Whereupon *Leontius* sent *John*, the Patrician, a Man of great Valour and Reputation, with all the Ships he could rig out against 'em. *John* readily embrac'd the Service, and recover'd all the strong Holds and Castles they had taken, and drove the Infidels out of the Country, where he winter'd with his Army, and sent *Leontius* an Account of his Expedition. The *Saracens* Mann'd out a stronger Fleet than ever the Spring following, in order to repair the Losses they had sustain'd the preceding Campaign, and attack'd *John* with a powerful Army in the beginning of the Summer. *John* behav'd himself with a Courage answerable to his Reputation, but was betray'd by his Army, who shamefully forsook him, and thereby constrain'd him to fly to the Sea Coasts, where he took Ship and set Sail for *Constantinople*, leaving the *Saracens* to recover all that had been reconquer'd from 'em the Year before. In the mean time the Principal Officers of the *Roman* Army began to reflect on their late Conduct, for which they expected to be call'd to a severe Account by *Leontius*, and therefore prepar'd to divert the Punishment due to their Cowardice by Treason: Accordingly, after a short Consultation among themselves, they made choice of *Apsimar*, one of *Leontius* his Generals at

A. D. 697.

that

Apſimar declar'd Emperor by the Mutinous Army.

that time in the Army, and declar'd him Emperor. *Apſimar*, who, after his Promotion, exchang'd his Name for that of *Tiberius*, readily accepted of the Dignity, and maintain'd it almoſt Seven Years; for having been one of the firſt in the late Mutiny, he thought he could not better ſecure himſelf, than by being the foremoſt in the Revolt. So ſoon as he had aſſum'd the Imperial Ornaments he proceeded directly towards *Conſtantinople* to make ſure of the Imperial City. He held a cloſe Intelligence with ſome within the Town, who ſeiz'd on *Leontius*, and open'd the Gates to the Uſurper. *Tiberius*, having cut off *Leontius* his Noſe, confin'd him under a ſtrict Guard to a Monaſtery in *Dalmatia*, baniſh'd all his Friends and Relations, and ſeiz'd on their Eſtates.

A. D. 698.

After this he declar'd his Brother *Heraclius* General of all his Forces, and ſent him into *Cappadocia*, there to have an Eye upon the *Saracens*: He, taking his Advantage of ſome Diviſions which proceeded to Acts of Hoſtility among 'em, invaded their Territories, and pierc'd into *Syria* as far as *Samoſata*, which he took, and kill'd, according to the Hiſtorians, no leſs than Two Hundred Thouſand of their Men. Notwithſtanding which mighty Defeat that Nation ſtill improv'd in Strength and Power, as if ſo great a Loſs had hardly been felt among 'em: For *Abdalla*, one of their Generals, march'd the next Year with a numerous Army into *Armenia*, where he took *Mopſueſtia*, which he fortify'd, and ſecur'd with a good Garriſon, after which he recover'd the greateſt part of that Province. Thus the War was carry'd on with various Succeſs, in which however the *Romans* for the moſt part had the Advantage. For *Azar*, invading *Cilicia* with Ten Thouſand Men,

Cedrenus. Theophanes.

was

was overthrown by *Heraclius*, who kill'd a great number of the *Saracens*, and sent the rest in Chains to *Constantinople*. The News of this Defeat encourag'd the Nobility of *Armenia* to rise up against their new Masters, of whom they kill'd all they could find in that Country, and sent to *Apsimar*, demanding his Assistance against the Infidels; but *Moamed* came with seasonable Supplies, where, after some bloody Encounters on both sides, he repair'd the late Loss his Countrymen had sustain'd; and having seiz'd on the Authors of the Sedition, burnt 'em all alive. This encourag'd them once more to Invade *Cilicia*, which they did the Year following, and were once more overthrown by *Heraclius*, who forc'd 'em to retire with the loss of Twelve Thousand *Arabians*.

A.D. 701.

Whilst *Apsimar*'s Lieutenants were thus fighting in Defence of the Empire abroad, he was busily employ'd in securing his Authority at home; knowing how doubtful his Title was, he took care to remove all those who he imagin'd were ambitious of the Purple, and was so jealous in his Scrutiny, that he banish'd *Philippicus*, a Patrician, who had been very instrumental in his Promotion, for no other Reason but because he dreamt he was overshadow'd by an Eagle, which *Apsimar*'s Fears interpreted portended to him the Empire. Having, as he thought, sufficiently secur'd himself against any Pretenders at home, he began to cast his Eyes upon *Justinian*, who, tho' Defenceless and an Exile, presum'd to declare he was sure he should live once more to recover his former Dignity; whereupon *Apsimar* prevail'd with the Inhabitants of the Country either to kill him, or send him bound to him. *Justinian*, being inform'd of their Intentions, got out of the Monastery by the help of

his

his Friends, and fled to the *Chagan* or King of the *Avari*, who at first receiv'd him very honourably, and gave him his Sister *Theodora* in Marriage; but was in the end so corrupted by *Apsimar*'s great Presents, and larger Promises, that he undertook either to deliver him up to his Officers alive, or to send him his Head. This intended Treachery was reveal'd, by one of her Servants, to *Theodora*, and by her discover'd to her Husband, who kill'd those who had been instructed to destroy him, and fled by Sea to *Trebelin*, King of the *Bulgarians*, carrying with him, where ever he remov'd, a severe Sense of the Injuries he had receiv'd; for being seiz'd by a violent Storm in his Passage through the *Straits*, and in great Danger to be lost, some of his Friends advis'd and besought him to make a Vow to Almighty God to forgive his Enemies, if ever, in Mercy to his Sufferings, he should restore him to his Throne; he reply'd sternly, *Let God drown me this Moment, rather than oblige me to renounce my Revenge*. *Trebelin* receiv'd him with an unfeigned Friendship, and promis'd him, upon his first Request, to supply him with most powerful Assistance: Accordingly he rais'd a very great Army, with which *Justinian* seiz'd on *Thrace*, and laid close Siege to *Constantinople*; where at first he met with many Repulses, and more Indignities from the Inhabitants, who, presuming upon the Strength of the City, and that it would be impossible for him to take it, revil'd him from the Walls, and most arrogantly affronted him. But after he had been Three Days before the Town some of his Men got in by means of an Aquæduct, which the Besieg'd had forgot or neglected to secure; of which, as soon as *Apsimar* was inform'd, and that the City was lost, he fled with all his Treasure to *Apolloneas*, leaving *Justinian* to reap the

A. D. 704.

Fruits

Chap. V. LXIV. Juſtinian II.

Fruits of his Succeſs, which made him once more Maſter of the Imperial City and the Empire.

Juſtinian, being thus reſtor'd to his former Dignity, diſmiſs'd *Trebelin* with many Royal Gifts, and beſtow'd on him, in Return for his great Service, a Part of the *Roman* Dominions, call'd afterwards *Zagoria*; purſuing *Apſimar*, who fled with *Leontius*, once the Rival of his Power, but now the Companion of his Misfortunes, he overtook them, and *Heraclius*, *Apſimar*'s Brother: The two former he led in Triumph about the City, and ſet his Feet ignominiouſly upon their Necks in the *Circus*, whilſt the inconſtant Multitude repeated with loud Acclamations that Verſe of the *Pſalmiſt*, *Thou ſhalt tread upon the Lion and Adder, the young Lion and the Dragon ſhalt thou trample under Feet*; after which inſulting Pageantry he commanded their Heads, and that of *Heraclius*, to be cut off. As for *Callinicus*, the Patriarch, who had ſo vigorouſly oppos'd him, he pluck'd his Eyes out, and baniſh'd him to *Rome*; therein, as an Aggravation of his Miſery, conſtraining him to beg his Bread of the Pope, who he knew was his declar'd Enemy.

Thus was *Juſtinian* reſtor'd to his former Greatneſs by the particular Favour of Fortune; and it may be now expected, that having learn'd a new Leſſon from his Calamities, he would govern for the future like a Prince whom Experience had inſtructed to apply his Power to the Benefit of his Subjects: But we ſhall find him one of thoſe whoſe Perverſeneſs of the Will is too inveterate, either to be meliorated by the Sun-ſhine of Proſperity, or ſoften'd by the rough Hand of Adverſity. From bad he grew worſe, and tho' he inſolently bragg'd that he had deliver'd the State from the Bondage of Tyrants and Uſurpers, he was himſelf the greateſt Tyrant in it. So ſoon as he thought himſelf confirm'd

Juſtinian reſtor'd.

firm'd in the Throne he rag'd with an implacable Fury against great Multitudes of Citizens and Soldiers, depopulating, in the Heat of his Revenge, whole Provinces at once. Ungratefully forgetting how much beyond all Acknowledgment he had been oblig'd by *Trebelin*, King of the *Bulgarians*, he most shamefully broke the League concluded between 'em, in which his Success was answerable to his Ingratitude; for his Men presuming too much upon their Numbers grew confident and careless, thereby exposing themselves to the Attempts of their more cautious Enemies, who watching their Advantage fell with a regular Courage upon 'em, and totally routed 'em; after which they press'd the Emperor so closely in his Retrenchments, that after he had lost the greatest part of his Army he was forc'd to fly, with a few of his Followers, in a light Vessel to *Constantinople*, leaving his Camp and the Residue of his Soldiers to the Mercy of the *Bulgarians*.

A.D. 705.

This Miscarriage, instead of humbling the unworthy Emperor, made him more haughty and revengeful: He remember'd the Attempts some of the Inhabitants of the *Bosphorus* had form'd against his Life during his Exile, and that made him resolve upon the Ruin and Destruction of the whole Country at once: Accordingly he rigg'd out all the Ships he had that were fit for Service, on which he embark'd his Army, with express Orders to kill all the Inhabitants of those Parts, Women as well as Men, and the innocent as well as the guilty.

His Cruelty.

These Orders were executed with the same Barbarity they were given; for some of those miserable Wretches were roasted alive, others they cast into the Sea, and those who met with more Mercy at the Hands of their Butchers were put to the Sword, only the Children were spar'd in respect to their

A.D. 710.

their Age; at which the Emperor was exceedingly enrag'd, and in great Fury commanded 'em to be brought by Sea to *Conſtantinople*, there to be maſſacred in his Sight. Accordingly they were, to the Number of Seventy Three Thouſand, put on board ſeveral Ships prepar'd for that Purpoſe, but were all loſt in a Storm, to the great Diſpleaſure of the Tyrant, who thought his Vengeance imperfectly ſatisfy'd. Thoſe who ſtill ſurviv'd his cruel Reſentment, underſtanding he was preparing for a ſecond Expedition, and that he was reſolv'd to root out the Reſidue of their unhappy Nation, fled for Succour to their Neighbours the *Chazari*, by whoſe Aſſiſtance they deſtroy'd ſeveral of the Emperor's Troops; but ſeeing there was no end of their Miſeries, and deteſting *Juſtinian*'s execrable Inhumanity, they renounc'd their Allegiance to him, and ſaluted *Phi-* PHILIP-*lippicus* Emperor, who was at that time an Exile PICUS. in *Cephalenia*, whither he had been ſent by *Apſimar*, as we obſerv'd before. This Example was follow'd by the Tyrant's own Forces, who having in ſeveral Encounters been defeated by the *Chazari*, and knowing the implacable Humour of *Juſtinian*, thought they had no way left to juſtifie their Conduct, but by ſiding with thoſe againſt whom they had committed ſuch outragious Hoſtilities, upon no other account but to gratifie his brutiſh Paſſions.

Philippicus finding himſelf proclaim'd Emperor A.D. by the unanimous Conſent of two powerful Armies, 711. and having firſt receiv'd from 'em the Oath of Allegiance, march'd directly towards *Conſtantinople*; into which, after ſome Oppoſition, he was receiv'd. *Tiberius*, the Son of *Juſtinian* by the Empreſs *Theodora* lately deceas'd, was ſlain in the Preſence of *Anaſtaſia*, his Grandmother; and *Juſtinian* himſelf was ſeiz'd ſhortly after by *Elias*, a Prince of the

Cha-

Chazari, who cut off his Head and presented it to *Philippicus*, and *Philippicus* sent it to *Rome*. This was the deserv'd End of that furious implacable Monster, in the Eighth Year after his Restoration: And from the Account the Reader has had of him he must readily allow him to have been cruel and relentless to the last Degree, and so devoted to his Revenge, the Effects of a weak unmanly Temper, that he sacrific'd whole Nations in the Pursuit of it, and at length fell a Sacrifice to it himself. He left the Empire in a more distracted Condition than any of his Predecessors had done before him, which was owing wholly to his Heat and Intemperance; so that for some time hereafter we shall meet with Emperors that were more like Annual Magistrates in a Country Burrough, than the Sovereign Princes of a potent State. And yet so deluding a thing is Empire, that they were contented to sacrifice their Honour, their Consciences, and what is almost as extraordinary, the sincere Enjoyments of an innocent private Life, to be the first Man in a distracted Common-wealth, losing at the same time what with so much Earnestness they contended to gain, suffering the *Saracens* to gain insensibly upon 'em, and oppress the *Romans*, who by their own Divisions were render'd weak and defenceless.

The News of *Justinian*'s Death was receiv'd with great Consternation in *Rome*, especially by the Pope, to whom he had appear'd well inclin'd, and had done several Things in Behalf of that See; and he knew too well that he was not to expect the *Philippi-* like Favours from his Successor *Philippicus*, who *cus declares* was a declar'd *Monothelite*, and immediately upon *for the Mo-* his Promotion had expell'd *Cyrus*, Patriarch of *Con-* *nothelites.* *stantinople*, and advanc'd a Monk, who had formerly foretold him of his exalted State, and promis'd him now a long and happy Reign, upon Condition

he

he abolish'd the Sixth General Council held at *Constantinople*, and restor'd the *Monothelites*, to all which he readily consented; so that in a Council summon'd for that purpose all the Acts of the preceding Council were revok'd, one single Operation of the Will in Jesus Christ was inforc'd to be believ'd, and an Account of all that had pass'd in this new Council was sent to *Rome* for the Pope's Approbation, with Orders to oblige him to comply. *Constantine* was at that time Pope of *Rome*, who in a Synod of the *Italian* Bishops vehemently inveigh'd against *Philippicus*, who did not only endeavour to renew the ancient Heresies, with which the Church had been divided, but aim'd at farther Innovations; being so declar'd an Enemy to God and his Saints, that he had remov'd all Images not only out of *Constantinople*, and the Churches in the East, but commanded the like to be done in *Rome* it self. Upon this a Sentence of Condemnation was drawn up against all such Innovaters, who refus'd a Veneration to the Images of Saints; at the same time *Philippicus* was declar'd an Heretick, condemn'd, and adjudg'd unworthy and uncapable of the Imperial Dignity. *The Question relating to the Worship of Images.*

It will not be improper to observe in this Place, that 'till now, tho' Images had been permitted in several Churches, yet it was not done by the express Order of any Synod, much less was any Religious Service as yet requir'd to be paid to 'em. *Constantine* was the first who presum'd to ordain it in this Synod; and from this time forward the Bishops of *Rome* not only establish'd the Worship of Images, but, in Imitation of this Pope, took Advantage of this Opportunity to shake off their Obedience to the Emperor, and to advance themselves above him. From this time forward we find no more Proceedings form'd against the *Monothelites*, but the A. D. 713.

the Popes of *Rome* directed all their Force and Authority against those who were for removing all Images out of the Churches, and deny'd to pay 'em any Religious Veneration. These were branded with the Name of Hereticks, and as such declar'd uncapable of any Earthly Dignity, according to the Maxims which began then to be in use in the Church of *Rome*.

These Disputes between the Pope and the Emperor prov'd fatal not only to *Philippicus* but to his Successors, and in general to the whole Empire of the East; for the Popes had usually the Advantage in the Quarrel, which was continu'd more or less ever after, and serv'd to enlarge the Authority of the *Roman* See, and render'd the *Italians* less affected to the Emperor: All which made way for the Re-establishment of the Empire in the West, which was effected by the politick Popes, who thought they could more easily contend with a divided than united Power.

Whilst *Philippicus* was thus busying himself in Matters relating to Religion the *Bulgarians* invaded *Thrace*, and made an Irruption up as far as the Golden Gate of the City; and having kill'd and taken Captive great Numbers of People they return'd without any Opposition. These Calamities render'd *Philippicus* so disagreeable to the People, that several *Thracians* broke into the Palace one Day, whilst he was asleep after Dinner, and having pluck'd out his Eyes, before it was known abroad what they were doing, the next Morning, being *Easter-Day*, they inform'd the People, met together in the great Church, of what they had done, whereupon *Anastasius* was crown'd Emperor by the universal Consent of the Inhabitants.

V. II

V. If the Corruptions of the former Governments had not hung too heavy upon the State *Anastasius* the Second had prov'd an excellent Emperor, and in all probability have govern'd the Empire with much Prudence and Success; for he was a Learned Man, and had from his Youth been conversant in publick Business, and the Management of the greatest Affairs: But it happen'd at this time in the Body Politick as it often doth to particular Persons, where the malignant Humours are so predominant as to obstruct the Operation of Physick; Men had been so accustom'd to transgress, and escape with Impunity, that a due Execution of the Laws was look'd on as an Innovation, and a regular Administration esteem'd a Tyranny.

Anastasius, so soon as he was acknowledg'd and crown'd Emperor, made it his chiefest Care to avoid those Rocks on which his Predecessors had fatally split; he knew the Honour and Prosperity of the Empire depended upon the Peace and Unity of the Church, and therefore took care by his Letters to the Pope to assure him and all the World that he was well affected to the Catholick Faith, and that he was resolv'd to see all his Subjects pay the Obedience that was due to the preceding General Councils. He knew likewise the Frontiers were ill guarded, and the Army in general in great need of a thorough Reformation; for which Reason he sent such as he had great Cause to confide in to command upon the Frontiers, and having levy'd fresh Forces both of Horse and Foot he declar'd *Leo*, an *Isaurian* by Birth, a Man of great Capacity in Military Affairs, his General; commanding him to march to the Frontiers of *Syria*, from whence the *Saracens* made their Incursions, and infested *Asia* the less. At the same time he rigg'd out a very powerful Fleet, with which he propos'd to reconquer *Egypt*, and re-unite it to the Empire. The Fleet sail'd accordingly, attended with the Prayers of all those who wish'd well to their Country, and had an Esteem for the present Government. Their first Attempts were upon *Alexandria*, where the Consternation the Inhabitants were in by far exceeded the Damage they receiv'd; for the Imperialists were forc'd to raise the Siege for want of warlike Provisions, as they pretended, and after two or three fruitless Assaults retire to their Ships, and sailing to the Isle of *Rhodes* propos'd to prepare at that Place such Necessaries as were requisite for carrying on the Siege. The Emperor, being inform'd of their Retreat, was very much displeas'd, and sending 'em such Provisions of War as he thought were requisite commanded 'em to return to the Service, at the same time severely reproving the superior Officers for their ill Management: But Military Discipline declin'd in that Age, and grew as corrupt as the other Sciences; so that instead of obeying *Anastasius* they revolted against him, and forc'd *Theodosius*, a Receiver of the Revenue, to accept of the Purple. *Cedrenus* makes no mention of the *Alexandrian* Expedition, but saith, *Anastasius*, being inform'd the *Saracens* were making great Naval Preparations upon the Coasts of *Phœnicia*, and design'd from thence to besiege *Constantinople*, rigg'd out a strong Fleet, with Orders to sail and burn the Enemy's Navy; but that a Dissention arising among the Soldiers they kill'd the Admiral, and dreading the Punishment due to so horrible a Fact declar'd *Anastasius* unworthy of the Empire, and nam'd *Theodosius* for his Successor; that *Theodosius* being an honest Man, tho' of a mean Extraction, hid himself for some time, but was forc'd in the end to accept of the Sove-

A. D. 714.

The Army revolts, and declares Theodosius Emperor.

Chap. V. LXVII. Theodosius III.

Sovereignty. After which he return'd at the Head of his Army to Besiege *Constantinople*, where *Anastasius* defended himself for several Months with an extraordinary Valour, but was at length so straiten'd both by Sea and Land, that he was forc'd to fly to *Nice* in *Bithynia*, whither *Theodosius* pursu'd him, took him, and having order'd him to be Shav'd, sent him in the Habit of a Monk as an Exile to *Thessalonica*, after he had enjoy'd the Title of Emperor near Two Years.

A. D. 715.

Theodosius, the new Emperor, began his Administration with reforming several Abuses in Church and State, which had crept in during the Reign of his Predecessors, and by his Behaviour gave the World the Promise of a Just and Generous Prince; but the Corruptions of the Times were too strong for him to oppose 'em, and he miscarry'd in his Attempts, more to the Prejudice of the Empire than his own Dishonour. *Leo*, whom the late Emperor *Anastasius* had sent General of his Forces into the East, hearing of his Dethronement refus'd to submit to *Theodosius*, in which he was assisted by *Artavasdes*, an *Armenian*, and a Man of the greatest Interest in that Country, to whom he had promis'd his Daughter in Marriage. These two united their Forces, and march'd against *Theodosius*, pretending at first that it was to restore *Anastasius*, but *Leo* was shortly after persuaded to assume the Imperial Purple, having first defeated *Theodosius* his Son, near *Nicomedia*, where he took him and most of his Father's Friends Prisoners; after which he march'd on to *Chrysopolis*, being universally acknowledg'd Emperor in his March. *Theodosius*, seeing it in vain to contend, sent *Germanus*, the Patriarch of *Constantinople*, to *Leo* with an Offer to resign the Imperial Purple, which had been forc'd upon him against his Will, on Conditi-

Theodosius III.

Dethron'd by Leo.

on

on he would grant him his Life, which being agreed to, both he and his Son were Shav'd, and entered into Orders. So that now there were Three Emperors living at the same time, and all Three Depos'd, *Philippicus, Anastasius* and *Theodosius*; the last of which voluntarily resign'd, and therein may be said to have chosen the better part, and left the worse for *Leo*.

LEO II. *Leo* was Crown'd with much Solemnity at *Constantinople* on the Twenty Fifth of *March* the same Year, by the Hands of *Germanus* the Patriarch, having first made a Confession of his Faith, which was Orthodox, and in which he promis'd inviolably to persevere, and to defend it. He was scarce confirm'd in the Empire before *Masalmas*, or *Masalnias*, a Prince of the *Saracens*, who had been very instrumental in his Promotion, broke with great violence into *Thrace*, where he committed unspeakable Cruelties, and, having wasted the Country, sate down with his Army before *Constantinople* on the Fourteenth of *April*; and after he had block'd it up for several Months together he was join'd by *Solyman* the Sultan, who came with a very powerful Fleet from *Damascus*, promising nothing less to himself than the Spoils of the Imperial City, which was now assaulted on every side both by Sea and Land. *Leo*, unshaken at the Approach of so powerful an Army, prepar'd in the best manner he could for the Defence of the City: He rigg'd out all the Ships he had in his Arsenal, which he supply'd with the ablest Sea-men in his Dominions, and by means of the Wild-fire formerly invented destroy'd all the Ships of the *Saracens*: At the same time he sally'd out in a regular Order upon their Land Forces, and constrain'd 'em, after they had lost the Flower of their Army, to raise the Siege and return home.

A. D. 717.

Defeats the Saracens.

The

Chap. V.   LXVIII. Leo II.

A.D. 718.

The King of the *Saracens*, feeing himfelf thus defeated, and his Forces broken by the Arms of the Emperor, prepar'd, by way of Revenge, to perfecute all the Chriftians that were in his Dominions, forbidding 'em the Exercife of their Religion, interdicting 'em the Ufe of Wine, and taking from 'em the Liberty of Witneffing againft a *Saracen* in Matters of Law, and promifing great Rewards, Exemptions, and Indulgences to thofe who would blafpheme their Saviour, and embrace the Doctrine of *Mahomet*. This Edict, fupported by the Ignorance and Depravity of the Age in which it was publifh'd, feduc'd great Numbers of People who abandon'd the Faith, and fubfcrib'd to the Irreligion of their infulting Mafters.

The fame Year *Sergius*, Præfect of *Sicily*, obferving the great Preparations the *Saracens* were forming againft the Emperor, and conceiving it impoffible for him to refift 'em, declar'd one *Bafilius*, the Son of *Onomagulus*, Emperor, changing his Name into that of *Tiberius*. *Leo* fent *Paul*, an Officer of the Houfhold, againft the Ufurper, who coming into the Ifland readily reftor'd it to the Emperor's Obedience; and having cut off *Tiberius* his Head, he forc'd *Sergius* to fly for Safety into *Italy*, and throw himfelf into the Protection of the *Lombards*. About this time *Conftantine*, Sirnam'd *Copronymus*, for that he bewray'd the Font at his Baptifm, was born, to the great Joy of *Leo*, and Satisfaction of the Inhabitants of *Conftantinople*. *Paulus Diaconus*, who upon all Occafions expreffes a great Averfion to that Prince upon the Account of his Enmity to Images, tells us, That the Patriarch, obferving what the Infant had done at his Baptifm, foretold he would in time prove a great Plague and Enemy to the Church; tho' it

may

may easily be prov'd that this Tale was forg'd a long time after the Child had been Baptiz'd.

The Joy the Birth of this Prince occasion'd at *Constantinople* was hardly over before *Leo* was threaten'd with a fresh Invasion. For *Anastasius* the Second, who had been banish'd to *Thessalonica*, began to entertain some Hopes of his Restauration, being encourag'd to it by the Bishop of the Place. In order to which he escap'd to *Tribelin*, King of the *Bulgarians*, from whom he obtain'd a considerable Army, with which he march'd into *Thrace*, and approach'd the Imperial City upon a Presumption that the Inhabitants would open the Gates, and receive him in; instead of which, when the *Bulgarians* saw they defended themselves resolutely against him, and that *Leo* was raising a numerous Army, which it was impossible for 'em to resist, they seiz'd on the unfortunate *Anastasius*, and deliver'd him and the Bishop to *Leo*, who immediately order'd 'em both to be put to Death.

A. D. 720.
Leo, having thus diverted a Storm that threaten'd his Destruction, solemnly Crown'd his Son *Constantine*, and declar'd him Emperor with him, as the readiest means to prevent any such Attempts for the future, and secure the Empire to his Posterity. After which Solemnity he march'd once more with his Army against the *Saracens*, who, having been often repuls'd by the Emperor in the East, resolv'd now to try their Fortunes in the West, where they committed several Pyracies, and grievously infested the *Sicilian* and *Italian* Coasts; after which they seiz'd on *Sardinia*, where they rag'd with unspeakable Barbarity, abstaining neither from Churches, Monasteries, nor the Sepulchres of the Saints. Having restrain'd these Infidels, who shortly after broke out into Contentions among

mong themselves, *Leo* from this time forward labour'd with great Zeal to remove Images out of the Church, being justly scandaliz'd at the great Veneration that was paid 'em, and in all likelihood provok'd to it by *Gregory* the Second, Pope of *Rome*, who, suspecting the Emperor was disaffected to his Person, rebell'd against him, and entering into an Alliance with the *French*, stopp'd the Revenue that ordinarily was rais'd for the Emperor out of *Italy*. *The Pope rebels against the Emperor.* These Disputes, as they very much weaken'd the Emperor's Interest in the West, so they serv'd to exalt the Authority of the Popes, who on every Occasion took care to enlarge and extend their Power. *Leo* is said before this to have sent *Paul*, Exarch of *Ravenna*, into *Italy*, with express Orders to seize upon the Pope, and put him to Death; the Execution of which *Paul*, upon his Arrival in *Italy*, committed to *Basilius* and some others. But the Pope had so good Intelligence that the thing was seasonably discover'd, and *Basilius* and his Accomplices were put to Death. Shortly after this *Leo*, who was resolv'd, if possible, to destroy *Gregory*, sent fresh Instructions to *Paul*, with Orders at least to Depose him, and cause another to be Elected in his room, if he could not proceed so far as to take away his Life. But the Pope, being inform'd of these Practices against him, thought his Life and Liberty lay at Stake, and therefore call'd the *Lombards* in to his Assistance, who, marching with great Alacrity to his Aid, easily defeated the Army the Exarch had sent to secure *Rome* and seize on the Person of the Pope.

It is very likely that these Orders of the Emperor against the Person and Dignity of *Gregory* are forg'd by the great Champions for the Papacy, the better to colour over his Rebellion and unjust

Usurpa-

Usurpation. For as yet the Emperor had no reason to be incens'd, the Quarrel relating to Images being not begun between 'em 'till some time after, as appears from the Pope's own Letter written to *Ursus,* Duke of *Heraclia,* the Year following; so that without enquiring any farther for the Reasons which rais'd in the Pope so great an Aversion to *Leo,* we may conclude that the Pope began the War without any Provocation, and the better to carry it on drew *Luitprand,* King of the *Lombards,* into the Quarrel. For several Years before the Exarchs and *Lombards* had preserv'd a friendly Correspondence between each other. But *Luitprand* observing the Aversion the Pope and the *Romans* had for the Exarch, (who, in all probability, gave the first Grounds of Discontent,) and the Emperor, he thought he had now a favourable Opportunity of enlarging his Dominions, and adding to his Hereditary Honours the Glory of conquering the Exarchate. Upon which Considerations he very readily enter'd into the War; and having rais'd a very powerful Army, compos'd as well of *Romans* as *Lombards,* he laid close Siege to *Ravenna,* where the Exarch, *Paul,* who little expected such a Surprize, receiv'd him so couragiously that he forc'd him to retire. *Luitprand,* despairing of Success against the Town, and unwilling to hazard and weaken his Army in any fruitless Attempts, broke up and remov'd to *Chiassi,* which, being ill prepar'd for a Siege, he easily took and plunder'd. The Loss of this Place extreamly alarm'd the Inhabitants of *Ravenna,* whereupon *Luitprand* taking the Advantage of their Fears return'd back, and so tir'd the Garrison and Townsmen by his frequent Assaults, that *Paul,* in despair of any Succours, drew off privately, and left the Town to the Discretion of the Inhabitants, who

being

Chap. V.   LXVIII. Leo II.   363

being unable to defend it, it was taken by Aſſault, Ravenna and plunder'd. The *Lombards* found in it many *taken by the Lom-* Rarities of Antiquity, among the reſt the Brazen bards, Statue of an Emperor on Horſeback, which *Luitprand* remov'd to *Pavia,* where it continues to this Day.

Ravenna being thus taken the reſt of the Cities A. D. depending upon it fell of Courſe into the Hands 725. of the *Lombards,* ſo that *Luitprand,* being hereby become Maſter of the Exarchate, erected it into a Dutchy, and made his Grandſon *Hildebrand* Duke of it, who, being an Infant, had *Peredeus,* Duke of *Vicenza,* aſſign'd him for his Governor.

Gregory, having in this manner kindl'd up a War between *Paul* and the *Lombards,* ſate ſtill as an idle Spectator; he was willing to have the Exarch chaſtis'd, but not deſirous to ſee the Power and Dominion of the *Lombards* encreaſe; he had no great Kindneſs for the Emperor, and it was his Intereſt to wiſh both Sides weaken'd, that his own Authority, which already began to gain Ground every Day, might make a greater Progreſs in *Italy.* He began now to tremble at *Luitprand's* amazing Progreſs in the War, and thought it high time, if poſſible, to put a ſtop to his growing Greatneſs, leſt the Spirit he had rais'd ſhould fall upon him at laſt, and he ſhould be the Author of his own Deſtruction. Whereupon he writ a very preſſing Letter to *Urſus,* Duke of *Heraclia,* and the *Venetians,* in which he conjur'd 'em to aſſiſt his worthy Son, the Exarch, and endeavour to reſtore the Exarchate to the Imperial Service of the Lords his Sons, *Leo* and *Conſtantine* his Son, Emperors. *Urſus* and the *Venetians* had great Reaſon to be concern'd at the Growth of ſo potent a Neighbour, and therefore rais'd a very conſiderable Army, pretending it was deſign'd to ſerve the Em-

Emperor against the *Saracens*. *Paul* on the other side rais'd all the Forces he was able, and, having join'd the *Venetians*, they fell upon *Ravenna* both by Sea and Land. *Peredeus* defended the Town against all their Assaults for some time very couragiously, but being at length Slain the Town was taken, and *Hildebrand* made Prisoner by the *Venetians*; who, having thus recover'd the Exarchate to the Emperor, before *Luitprand* could march from *Pavia* to his Grandson's Assistance, return'd home, leaving *Paul* in the full Enjoyment of his Authority.

and recover'd.

These Wars, as we observ'd before, preceded the Emperor's Edict concerning Images, and very probably hasten'd the Publication of it; for shortly after it was publish'd by his Order throughout all his Dominions, enjoining his Subjects to break down and remove out of the Churches all the Images of the Saints. At the same time he commanded the Pope to see his Orders obey'd in all the Parts of his Diocess.

Those, who have been the great Defenders of Image Worship, have taken great Pains to find out the Motives which induc'd *Leo* to publish this Edict. Some of 'em affirming it was done at the Instigation of certain *Jews*, who promis'd him a long and prosperous Reign, provided he remov'd Images out of the Church. Others impute it to a Representation of *Aumar*, Caliph of *Damascus*, who accus'd the Christians in his Dominions of Idolatry, by reason of the Religious Worship paid to Images, and their Invocation of the Saints. But as neither the *Jews* or *Mahometans* entertain'd so friendly Thoughts of the Christians, as to be concern'd in what Religious Points they dissented from them, and in what Particulars they offended God Almighty, so on the other hand it is most certain

Chap. V. LXVIII. Leo II.

tain *Aumar* was dead Seven Years before the Publication of this Edict; and on the other side it's very unlikely *Leo* should listen to the *Jews*, a People he detested, and whom he was very zealous to extirpate, as it appear'd in several Instances of his Reign before the time of this Edict. However, since the Thing was so very conformable to the Law of God, *Leo* is to be commended for it, whether he did it freely of himself, or was induc'd to it by the *Jews* or *Saracens*.

Gregory, having receiv'd the Emperor's Letters, very industriously oppos'd the Edict, and in his Answer to *Leo* endeavours to convince him by such Arguments as could not but confirm him in his Design, concluding all with asserting that *Matters relating to Religion in no measure belong'd to the Emperor but him, who had the sole Power of maintaining and continuing the Faith, which had been left him by the Fathers.*

These Letters of *Gregory* to the Emperor were follow'd by other Circular ones, directed to the People of *Rome, Ravenna, Pentapolis,* and to the *Venetians,* in which he represented the Emperor as an Heretick, and declar'd that if he persisted in his Heresie he ought to be abandon'd by all Christian People, since he voluntarily separated himself from the Body of the Catholick Church.

In the mean time the Emperor did not only publish his Edict, but took care to have it put in Execution, beginning at *Constantinople,* where his Officers were employ'd to pull down the Images throughout the City; at which the Inhabitants, who had been accustom'd to Images in their Churches, were so offended that they ran in a tumultuous manner to the Palace, where they kill'd several of the Emperor's Houshold, and were hardly restrain'd from farther Mischief by the Guards of Leo,

A. D. 726.
A Tumult rais'd at Constantinople upon the account of Images.

Leo, who put several of the most forward among 'em to Death.

When the Pope was inform'd of these Proceedings at *Constantinople* he grew extremely enrag'd, and publish'd a Decree, in which he declar'd that *Leo ought not only to be excommunicated, but no longer to be acknowledg'd as Emperor;* for which Reason he absolv'd and releas'd all his Subjects from their Oath of Allegiance and Fidelity, and forbad 'em to pay him any farther Tribute: Whereupon the People of *Rome*, *Ravenna* and *Campania* threw off their Obedience, and seizing on the Magistrates that had been appointed over 'em by the Emperor in a cruel manner massacred 'em. At *Ravenna* they slew *Paul*, the Exarch, and pluck'd out the Eyes of *Peter*, the Governor of *Rome*; in *Campania* they put *Exhileratus* and his Son to Death, raging with equal Fury in other Places, and substituting others of their own Election in the room of those they had massacred or expell'd. This is a brief Account of the Pope's Measures in that Conjuncture, and what was done pursuant to 'em, as they are related by the great Friends of the Papacy themselves; which must of necessity raise the Indignation of every considerate unbiass'd Reader against this *Gregory*, who, upon the Pretence of Heresie, presum'd to divest an Emperor of his Right of Sovereignty, to absolve his Subjects from their Oath of Allegiance, and stir 'em up to Rebellion and most horrible unnatural Murders: By which it's evident the Pope laid hold of this Opportunity, and oppos'd the Emperor's Edict for no other purpose but to withdraw himself from his Obedience, and render himself Master of *Rome* and the Exarchate; for the *Romans* having kill'd their Governor, as we observ'd before, would acknowledge no other Soveraign but the Pope himself, which Example was fol-

The Pope usurps a Soveraign Power in Rome and other Places.

follow'd by almost Thirty other Cities, who revolted from the Emperor, and swore Allegiance to the Pope. Of this when *Leo* was inform'd he immediately sent away *Eutychius*, a Patrician, to be his Exarch in *Ravenna*, and provide in the best manner he could for the Disorders in *Italy*; where *Eutychius* being arriv'd at the Head of a powerful Army he earnestly courted the Friendship of *Luitprand*, King of the *Lombards*, as the most effectual way to reduce the Pope to Reason; who, in the mean time, thunder'd out his *Anathemas* against the Exarch, and prepar'd to oppose him.

Trasimond, Duke of *Spoleto,* had about this time revolted, and taken up Arms against *Luitprand,* which made the King the more inclinable to enter into an Alliance with the Exarch, that with their united Forces they might at once reduce the Pope and chastise the Duke: Accordingly they both began very vigorously to prepare for the War, at which *Trasimond* was so terrify'd that he sent a submissive Message to the King, declaring himself ready to obey his Orders, and to renew his Oath of Fidelity; which was perform'd to the entire Satisfaction of *Luitprand,* who receiv'd Hostages for his future Obedience, and then gave Orders for his Army to march towards *Rome*: But the Pope, who now found the whole Fury of the War directed against him, went accompany'd with some of his Clergy and the principal Inhabitants of the City to wait upon the King in his Camp, where he so effectually prevail'd upon him, in a pathetick Speech made for that purpose, that *Luitprand* commanded his Forces to retire from the Territories of *Rome*; and tho' the Exarch earnestly sollicited him to be just to his Promise, yet he contented himself with being a Mediator between him and the Pope, in which he was so succesful that *Eutychius*

A. D. 729.

shortly

shortly after enter'd peacably into *Rome*, where he was very honourably receiv'd.

Thus the Affairs of *Italy* were in some measure settled, tho' the Emperor's Authority was never restor'd in *Rome*, and *Leo* was more at leisure to apply himself to the Suppression of Images, and the Settlement of his own Family. *Germanus*, Patriarch of *Constantinople*, could not be brought to be of the same Sentiments with the Emperor, whereupon he was depos'd, and *Anastasius* was establish'd in his room; after which the Emperor proceeded with the like Severity against the other Bishops that oppos'd him, for which he is highly accus'd by the Papal Writers. At the same time *Leo* marry'd his Son *Constantine* to the *Chagan* or King of the *Chazari*'s Daughter, who had been first instructed in the Principles of the Christian Religion, receiving at her Baptism the Name of *Irene*, a Word signifying *Peace* in the *Greek* Tongue. In the mean time

A. D. 731.

Gregory the Pope of *Rome* dy'd, and was succeeded by another of the same Name, who carry'd on the same Design of usurping a Sovereign Authority independant of the Emperor, and made use of the same Means to attain and preserve it; for immediately after his Assumption to the Pontificate, he sent his Letters to *Leo* and his Son *Constantine*, in which he earnestly conjur'd 'em to continue the Worship of Images in the Church. These Letters were sent by a Priest, who being come to *Constantinople* was afraid to deliver 'em, and so return'd back with them to *Rome*, for which the Pope in great Rage excommunicated him; and in a Synod summon'd at *Rome* he ordain'd, That *whoever for the future, in Contempt of the ancient Customs of the Catholick Church, presum'd to abolish the Worship of Images, should be cut off, as an infected Member, from the Body of Christ, and remain excommunicat-*

Chap. V. LXVIII. Leo II.

ed. Whereupon the Emperor, who saw his Authority was quite abolish'd in *Rome* and the Territories belonging to it, that the Pope had usurp'd it, and put him under the Sentence of Excommunication, mann'd out a Fleet in order to make a Descent into *Italy*, but his Ships were all dispers'd by a Tempest which seiz'd 'em in the *Adriatick* Sea; so that he was forc'd to be satisfy'd with confiscating the Tribute rais'd to the Pope out of *Calabria* and in *Sicily*, which was usually call'd St. *Peter*'s Patrimony, and amounted to no more at that time than Half a Talent of Gold and Three Talents of Silver. These Contests between the Emperor and the Popes, in which the latter were always the Gainers, made *Leo*, towards the latter end of his Reign, grow morose and implacable, so that he burden'd the Provinces with intolerable Exactions, and laid a Tax upon every Male Child as soon as he was born; and tho' in the Beginning of his Reign he had often defeated the *Saracens* and weaken'd their Armies, yet now again they began to infest the Eastern Provinces, destroying whole Towns at once, and returning home with much Booty and great multitudes of Captives, meeting with none in their Incursions that were able to make Head against em, or put a Stop to their Depredations. After this, and in the last Year of *Leo*, a most dreadful Earthquake visited *Constantinople*, where many Churches, Monasteries and private Houses were overturn'd, and great Numbers of the Inhabitants bury'd in the Ruins, and the Statues of several of the ancient Emperors were remov'd from their Foundations. The same Calamity happen'd at *Nice* and *Nicomedia*, continuing for the Space of Eleven Months together, during which People labour'd under daily Apprehensions; the Sea was so much disturb'd that it forsook its usual Course, upon

A. D. 741.
A terrible Earthquake.

B b   which

which great Inundations follow'd. Not long after
Leo dies. this *Leo* dy'd, having reign'd Twenty Five Years,
Two Months and Twenty Days; in which time
he gave the World several remarkable Instances of
his great Moderation and Valour, having vigorously preserv'd the Empire from the Attempts of the
Saracens, whom he overcame in many signal Engagements. He was a zealous Professor of the
Christian Religion, an exact Observer of the General Councils, and a declar'd Enemy to Hereticks;
Towards the latter end of his Reign his Aversion
to Images render'd him odious to the ignorant and
superstitious, and gave the Popes of *Rome* an Opportunity of usurping his Authority in his Life-
time, and encourag'd them to wound his Reputation after his Death. The undutiful Opposition he
met with from them render'd him peevish and impatient; tho' an impartial Posterity must of necessity
commend him for that which made them and their
Partisans his profess'd Enemies, his earnest Desire
to suppress Idolatry.

Constan-   *Constantine,* the Son of *Leo,* had for several Years
tinus Co- before been associated with his Father in the Em-
pronymus. pire, so that he was acknowledg'd without any Difficulty as his Successor at his Death, and was
Crown'd accordingly on the Twenty Seventh of
June, reigning from that Day Thirty Four Years
and Three Months, tho' not without some Opposition even in the Beginning of his Reign, as we
shall have occasion to see hereafter. Immediately
after his Coronation at *Constantinople* he led an Army against the *Saracens,* who were advanc'd into
Asia, where he overthrew 'em in several Encounters, and drove 'em home. But whilst he was busily employ'd in this War, *Artabazdus,* who had
marry'd his Sister, and had been left behind as Governor of *Constantinople* in his Absence, perswaded
the

the meaner sort of People, who had a great Veneration for Images, to rise in Favour of him, and declare him Emperor. In this he was assisted by the Patriarch *Anastasius*, who had concurr'd with *Leo* in whatever he did relating to Religion, but now on a sudden chang'd his Sentiments and declar'd for the Usurper.

The News of this Insurrection was quickly carry'd to *Constantine* in *Asia*, notwithstanding which, and the great Danger his Authority was in at *Constantinople*, he was forc'd to continue in that Country with his Army all the Winter, which gave the Usurper an Opportunity of advancing his Designs, and strengthning himself in his Usurpation. He first endeavour'd to persuade the People that *Constantine* was dead, after which he seiz'd on his Sons, and having forc'd 'em to be shav'd he secur'd 'em in Prison; but knowing the Pretence of *Constantine*'s Death would quickly be detected, he persuaded the Patriarch most solemnly to swear that *Constantine* in his Presence had blasphem'd our Saviour, declaring that *he did not believe him to be the Son of God, but that he was born after the same manner of his Mother Mary as Mary his Mother had born him.* Tho' this Blasphemy was a mere Calumny, invented by the Patriarch to impose upon the People, and ingratiate himself with the Tyrant, yet the Multitude were so mov'd that they depos'd *Constantine*, and with general Acclamations saluted *Artabazdus* Emperor. This gave a Beginning to a Civil War in the East, the Particulars of which are not transmitted down by any Authors to Posterity; tho' they tell us in brief that it was more considerable than any that had ever happen'd before it. *Artabazdus*, hearing what great Preparations the Emperor made to chastise him, Crown'd *Nicephorus*, his Eldest Son, at *Constantinople*, and then march'd out to meet him. Having been defeated in several Encounters he was forc'd to retire back to the City, which he fortify'd in the best manner he could, and held it out with much Obstinacy for some time against the Emperor, tho' he besieg'd it closely both by Sea and Land: But in the end the Inhabitants, being reduc'd to the last Extremity, and ready to perish by Famine, were forc'd to surrender. *Artabazdus* and his two Sons were deliver'd up to the Emperor, who commanded their Eyes to be pull'd out, and to be closely imprison'd; after which he proceeded to punish those who had been the most forward in the Revolt, many of whom he put to Death, and suffer'd the City to be plunder'd for some Hours by his Soldiers. *Anastasius* the Patriarch he order'd to be whipp'd publickly, and then setting him upon an Ass, with his Face to the Tail, he was carry'd in an ignominious manner through the most frequented Streets of the City: Nowithstanding which this Man was afterwards continu'd in his Place; being, in all likelihood, a State Weather-cock, that knew how to temporise and comply with the most prevailing Party in all Changes and popular Commotions.

After *Constantine* had thus re-instated himself in the Sovereign Authority, he for some time endeavour'd by many Acts of Favour to ingratiate himself with the People, to whom he was not very acceptable for his late Cruelty and severe Inquisition; and this he did the rather because he observ'd that the *Saracens* were at Civil Wars among themselves, and he had a great mind to make his Advantage of their Divisions; and was willing to leave his Subjects well affected to him, and administer no Occasion for a Second Insurrection in his Absence.

A. D. 746. When he had muster'd his Army he fell upon *Syria*, and having overthrown the Infidels in several
Engagements,

Engagements he recover'd *Germanioia*, and several other Places of Importance, which for some time had been in the Hands of the *Saracens*; who, notwithstanding this great Loss, and tho' they were still threaten'd with greater, continu'd the Quarrels among themselves, besieging their Caliph in the Capital City of *Damascus*, and forcing him to fly into *Egypt*, where they kill'd him whilst he was at his Devotions, whereupon their Empire was divided into three Parts; for *Persia* was deliver'd to *Abubalas*, *Egypt* to *Salym*, and *Syria* to *Abdalla*. This Division very much weaken'd and endanger'd their Nation, 'till at length the Sovereign Authority became united in the Person of *Abdalla*.

The *Saracens* all this while were not more afflicted by the Civil Wars among themselves, and the Arms of the Empire, than the Empire it self was weaken'd and almost destroy'd by Earthquakes, which were more frequent and destructive about this time than had been known in any Age before. *Syria* and *Palestine* were most grievously shaken, innumerable Multitudes of Men perish'd, together with great Quantities of Buildings both publick and private; the same Provinces were visited with so extraordinary a Darkness, that for several Days together, in the Month of *August*, there was little or no Distinction between Day and Night. About the same time a furious Pestilence broke out in *Calabria*, and passing through *Sicily* proceeded as far as *Constantinople*, where it rag'd with an insatiate Thirst for Three Years together, insomuch that the Living were hardly sufficient to bury the Dead. It was observable that they who were seiz'd with this Contagion, and were doom'd to die, had little Crosses made as it were with Oil imprinted on their Cloaths, and by no

A strange Plague.

Art 'whatever to be remov'd. Tho' it was acknowledg'd by all to be the immediate Finger of God Almighty, yet it serv'd rather to terrifie, than reform Mankind. The World, for the most part, was grown too obstinate to be reclaim'd, tho' surrounded with Judgments, which in various Methods denounc'd the Divine Indignation.

A. D. 750.
Shortly after these publick Calamities, *Leo* the Third was born, who succeeded his Father in the Empire, by whom he was proclaim'd *Augustus* the Year following. *Constantine* had for several Years together been at Peace with his Neighbours, but having now, by some popular Acts, endear'd himself with the People, and strengthen'd his Interest by the Birth and Promotion of his Son, he rais'd an Army the next Year, and recover'd *Melitena*, the Metropolis of the lesser *Armenia*, and *Theodosioplis*; a City built by *Theodosius* in *Armenia* major; and observing that the Provinces which border'd upon the *Bulgarians* were in no good Posture of Defence, he rais'd several new Forts for their Security, at which the *Bulgarians* were so dissatisfy'd, that they sent their Ambassadors to complain of it to the Emperor, by whom they were ignominiously treated, and dismiss'd with a disdainful Answer; which so incens'd that People, that they made a sudden Irruption into the Provinces without any Declaration of War, and having wasted the Country for several Days together without any Resistance, they return'd home with an incredible Booty. At this the Emperor was highly provok'd, but being not then in a Condition of resenting it as he ought, he deferr'd his Revenge 'till some Years after, at which time being, as he thought, sufficiently prepar'd to chastise them, he march'd with a good Body of Forces against 'em, but was surpriz'd by the Enemy

in a narrow Paſſage, defeated, and forc'd to return home with a great Loſs of Men, but a greater of Reputation, which however he recover'd in a War with them, which broke out not long after, as we may have occaſion to ſhew in its proper place.

Conſtantine defeated by the Bulgarians.

About this time there happen'd a Revolution in *France*, which, for that it had ſo great an influence upon the Affairs of the Weſt, and ended in the Re-eſtabliſhment of the Empire there, it will not be thought Foreign to the Deſign of this preſent Hiſtory to give the Reader a brief, but clear Account of it.

We have had occaſion to obſerve before how *Gaul*, in the Declenſion of the Empire, was in a great meaſure divided among the *Goths*, the *Franks*, and the *Burgundians*. The *Franks* are allow'd by all, but ſome *French* Writers themſelves, to have been originally a *German* People, at firſt divided into ſeveral Tribes, which were all diſtinguiſh'd by particular Names, 'till in the end they united themſelves in a common Confederacy, the better to oppoſe the prevailing Power of the *Romans*, in Defiance of whom they call'd themſelves *Franks*, or *A free People*. Theſe *Franks* by degrees grew the moſt predominant of the Three Nations formerly mention'd in *Gaul*, and in the Year 424 choſe *Pharamond* for their King, who, to the Reputation his Subjects had already requir'd by their Arms, added the Strength and Beauty of wholſome Laws and Conſtitutions. For ſome time *Pharamond*'s Succeſſors greatly enlarg'd their Power and Dominions, ſo that the *French* began to make a conſiderable Figure in the World, eſpeciunder the Reigns of *Merovæus*, and *Clovis* the Firſt; the latter of which committed a fatal Overſight at his Death, in dividing his Territories among his Four Sons, which, tho' united by *Clotaire* the Second,

Second, were once more divided by his Son *Dagobert*; and from this time forward the *French* Kings degenerated from the Worth of their Progenitors, resigning themselves up to a luxurious, unactive Life, committing the Administration of Publick Affairs to the Majors of the Palace, who assum'd an unlimited Power, and govern'd in their Master's Name with an absolute Authority. Among these *Pepin* was the most remarkable, who was advanc'd to the Administration towards the latter end of the Seventh Century, in which, after he had govern'd Twenty Eight Years together, he was succeeded by his Son, *Charles Martel*, an active victorious Prince, who much augmented the Authority left him by his Father, and transmitted it down to his Sons, the youngest of which, call'd likewise *Pepin*, had from the beginning an Eye upon the Sovereignty, tho' at first he abstain'd from declaring himself openly, 'till finding at length that the Execution of the Sovereign Power resided solely in himself; that he was Master of the publick Treasure, and of the Hearts of the People; that there was but one remaining of the *Merovignian* Race, *viz. Chilperick* the Third, a stupid and senseless Prince; lastly, that the Pope had upon several Occasions been oblig'd by him, and would therefore, in all probability, approve of what he should do; he resolv'd to be that in Name, which he already was in Effect. To this purpose he summon'd an Assembly General of the Grandees of the Realm, in which some of his Creatures inveigh'd with much Art against the Sloth and Incapacity of *Chilperick*, insisting upon the great Disproportion there was between the great Character he wore, and the Abilities he had to discharge the Duties belonging to it. They added that *Pepin* was in the Flower of his Age, that

he

Chap. V. LXIX. Constant. Copronymus. 377

he was bless'd with an hopeful Issue, and was renown'd for his Personal Valour and Extraordinary Performances. These Considerations, urg'd in an Assembly consisting chiefly of such, who by reason of their Preferments, as well in Church as State, were engag'd to *Pepin*'s Family, had the Effect he and his Friends expected, so that he was universally desir'd to take the Royalty upon him, which however he declin'd a while: For, to render the matter more authentick and indisputable, he persuaded the Assembly to wait for the Advice and Consent of *Zachary*, at that time Bishop of *Rome*, who he knew was his intimate Friend, and whose Authority was but too great in the Church. Accordingly a Letter was sent in the Name of the Assembly to the Pope, in which they desir'd to know, *Whom he esteem'd most worthy the Title and Dignity of a King? One, who living at his Ease and Pleasure, contributed nothing to the Honour and Tranquility of the Publick, or him, who labour'd Night and Day for the Safety and Prosperity of the State?* The crafty Pope knew very well that *Pepin*'s Protection would be of great use to him in the Designs the Kings of the *Lombards* and the Exarchs were continually forming against him, and that no Disturbances could arise from his bribing him to it with the glorious Title of King, since he had already been desir'd to accept of it by the Assembly of the States; but on the other hand would give him and his Successors some sort of Authority above that of Kings, to which he had a long time aspir'd. Upon these Motives he readily declar'd for *Pepin*, and signify'd his Pleasure accordingly to the States assembled at *Soissons*, who, having receiv'd his Letters, degraded *Chilperick*, and confin'd him to a Monastery; after which *Pepin* was Crown'd with much Solemnity

nity by the Hands of *Boniface*, Bishop of *Mentz*, assign'd by the Pope's express Order to that Service.

<small>A. D. 752.

Pepin Crown'd King of France.</small>

Thus was *Pepin* acknowledg'd and crown'd King of *France*, and in all Respects appear'd worthy that eminent Dignity; for he was Prudent, Valiant, Vigilant and Liberal, particularly to the Church, to which, upon all Occasions, he express'd a profound Respect. These Qualifications made him highly esteem'd by his Subjects, nor were they less belov'd by him, but receiv'd repeated Testimonies of his Paternal Care and Affection towards 'em.

Shortly after this Revolution in *France*, *Zachary*, who had so large a Hand in it, dy'd at *Rome*, after he had sate in the Chair Ten Years and Three Months. He is remarkable for nothing more than his extravagant Desire of aggrandizing the Papal Authority, and his great Ignorance; for this is he who condemn'd the learn'd *Virgilius* as an Heretick, for asserting the *Antipodes*.

In his time *Rachis* was King of the *Lombards* in *Italy*, who at first confirm'd and prolong'd, for Twenty Years, the Treaty of Peace concluded between him and his Predecessor *Luitprand*; but at length observing the Emperor had, in a great measure, remov'd his Care from *Italy*, which he consider'd as a Country lost irrecoverably, and that there was not much Friendship between *Zachary* and the Exarch, who he knew was so far from assisting others, that he would find it a hard matter to defend himself, should he be attack'd, he enter'd suddenly with an Army into *Pentapolis*, a District in *Italy*, at that time comprehending *Rimini*, *Pezace*, *Ancona*, *Sinigallia*, and some other little Places of less Importance, several of which he surpriz'd; after which he Invaded the Dutchy

of

of *Rome* it self, seiz'd on part of those Territories to which the Pope pretended a Right, and laid Siege to *Perusa*. The Pope, finding he had not Forces sufficient to oppose the *Lombards*, went in Person to *Rachis*, as he lay before *Perusa*, where he remonstrated to him the Violence and Injustice he was doing, in so lively a manner, that he not only rais'd the Siege, and restor'd the Towns he had taken, but shortly after resign'd his Crown, and turn'd Monk; tho' in the Year 757 he repented of his Resignation, and would have re-assum'd it upon the Death of his Brother *Aistulphus*, but found, when it was too late, that it was much easier to quit a Crown than recover it.

Upon *Rachis* his Resignation, *Aistulphus*, his Brother, was chosen King of *Lombardy* in his room, and immediately upon his Establishment renew'd the Peace lately concluded between the Pope and his Predecessor, which he observ'd not long; for taking the Advantage of the Emperor's Wars with the *Saracens* and *Bulgarians* in the East, he rais'd a very potent Army, and sate down before *Ravenna*, in which *Eutychius*, the Exarch, defended himself like a Man of Honour, and a Valiant Soldier, for a long time, 'till despairing of any Succours from the Emperor he quitted the Place, and retir'd to *Constantinople*, leaving *Aistulphus* Master of *Ravenna*, and the Territories belonging to it; by which means the Office of Exarch, which had continu'd in *Italy* for about One Hundred and Eighty Two Years, was at length abolish'd by the *Lombards*, in the Eleventh Year of *Constantine* the Emperor, the First of *Pepin*, King of *France*, and the last of *Zachary*, Pope of *Rome*, *An. Dom.* 752. With the Exarchate the Emperor's Authority, in a great measure, expir'd in *Italy*; Divine Providence seeming, by the Con-

The Expiration of the Exarchate.

sequences

sequences that attended it, to prepare for the Reception of another Empire to be erected in the West.

For *Aistulphus* having thus render'd himself Master of *Ravenna*, all the Towns of *Pentapolis* submitted to him, upon which Success, growing elate and arrogant, he aim'd at nothing less than the entire Subjection of all *Italy*, and march'd accordingly with his Army towards *Rome*, the Inhabitants of which Place he demanded to acknowledge him for their Soveraign; alledging, in Justification of his Demands, that the Exarchate, which was his in Right of Conquest, gave him the same Power which the Emperor had 'till then in *Italy*, and consequently that the Pope and Inhabitants of *Rome* were his Vassals. Notwithstanding the Emperor, who from a Sovereign Prince in *Italy*, condescended now to be a Mediator, interceded by his Ambassadors in the Pope's behalf, yet *Aistulphus* pursu'd his Pretensions with so much Resolution, that the Pope found himself oblig'd to go in Person to *Pepin* to sollicite his Assistance. *Pepin* receiv'd him with very extraordinary Honours, and at his Request, and by the Advice of his Parliament, persuaded *Aistulphus* to come to an Accommodation with the Pope. *Aistulphus* receiv'd the King's Ambassadors with a Respect due to their Character, and promis'd to quit, for the future, his Pretensions to the Sovereignty of *Rome*, and the Territories belonging to it; which was all *Stephen* the Second, at that time Pope, desir'd at first: But when he found himself supported by so puissant a Prince as *Pepin*, he made more important Demands, requiring the *Lombards* to resign to him the Exarchate, and whatever else *Aistulphus* claim'd by Virtue of his late Conquests; all which he affirm'd belong'd in Right to him, *they being*

A. D. 754.

The Ambition of the Pope.

being the Spoils of an Heretick Prince, for such he term'd the Emperor. The Reader will easily observe upon what pernicious a Maxim the Pope's Pretensions were founded; for if the Dominions of Heretick Princes ought to devolve upon him, 'tis in his Power to condemn whom he thinks fit as such, when he has a Desire to seize upon his Territories; a thing which has been too often put in practice by *Stephen*'s Successors. In pursuance of his Pretensions he dealt so effectually with *Pepin* that he resolv'd, in Favour of the Pope, to declare War against the *Lombards,* and the Year following march'd over the *Alps* with a powerful Army, notwithstanding the Care the *Lombards* had taken to secure the Passes. *Aistulphus,* being terrify'd at so unexpected an Invasion retir'd in great Precipitation, and secur'd himself in *Pavia,* which *Pepin* invested, and was upon the Point of taking it, when *Aistulphus,* justly sensible of the great Danger he was in, had Recourse to *Stephen,* the grand Author of the War, whom he promis'd in a most solem manner to perform whatever he should require of him, upon Condition he prevail'd with *Pepin* to withdraw his Troops and return home. The Pope, who began at length to commiserate the Condition of *Italy,* which had been grievously harass'd by the *French*; and fearing lest *Pepin,* having taken *Pavia* and secur'd *Aistulphus,* who was in it, should render himself absolute in *Italy,* where he would suffer no one, if possible, to have a greater Authority than himself, persuaded the King to listen to Overtures of Peace, which was concluded between 'em, and *Aistulphus* oblig'd himself to surrender the Exarchate to the Pope, with whatever else he had belonging to it. But so soon as *Pepin* was return'd out of the Country, *Aistulphus,* finding he was freed from his Enemies, absolv'd himself from the

A. D. 755.

Obser-

Obfervance of the Articles, and fate down with the beſt of his Forces before *Rome*, having firſt ſpoil'd the Country about it.

Pepin thought this Breach of Faith in the King of the *Lombards* ſo nearly touch'd his Honour, that he return'd the Year following into *Italy*; where he forc'd the *Lombards* to riſe from before *Rome*, and once more block'd up *Aiſtulphus* in *Pavia*; where when he found himſelf reduc'd to the laſt Extremity, he ſent his Ambaſſadors to *Pepin*, imploring his Compaſſion, and deſiring him to be the Umpire of the Differences between him and *Stephen*. To this the King readily condeſcended, and Peace was concluded on all ſides, upon Condition *Aiſtulphus* punctually obſerv'd the former Treaty, and, over and above, ſurrender'd *Comachio* to the Pope, a Town of great Importance at that time in the *Ferrareze*.

This Agreement was concluded in the Preſence of the Emperor's Embaſſadors, who came to demand in their Maſter's Name ſuch Territories belonging to the Exarchate, as *Aiſtulphus* and his Predeceſſors had from time to time torn from the Empire; but had the Mortification to obſerve no Reſpect given to their Remonſtrances, and ſee the Pope, the Emperor's avow'd Enemy, declar'd Temporal Lord of *Rome*, of the Exarchate, and all the Cities belonging to it, and, in a word, of the beſt Part of what formerly belong'd to the Emperor in *Italy*. *Pepin* ſent the Abbot *Vollard*, his Chaplain, to receive from *Aiſtulphus*, in the Pope's Name, the Towns compris'd in the Agreement; the Keys of which were brought to *Rome*, and, together with the Articles of Peace, depoſited upon the Altar of St. *Peter* and St. *Paul*, as an Inſtance that King *Pepin* made a Donation of 'em to thoſe two Apoſtles.

Chap. V. LXIX. Constant. Copronymus.

Constantine was highly sensible of the Injustice A.D. done him, and the Dishonour he had receiv'd by 758. the late Treaty, but was in no capacity of vindicating himself by Force of Arms; for about this time the *Sclavi* had thrown themselves into *Macedonia*, where they wasted the Country and destroy'd the Inhabitants in a most barbarous manner, before he could raise Forces sufficient to remove 'em. The Imperial Authority was now contracted into very narrow Bounds, and grew every Day more unregarded. Tho' the *Saracens* for several Years before were not at open Wars with the Empire, and so could not be look'd on as declar'd Enemies, yet they liv'd like very ill Neighbours, and were more untractable and less to be trusted than those whose Dominions they usurp'd, and who, tho' they were not subject to the Empire, liv'd in Friendship with it, and upon all Occasions were ready to assist it. The Distractions in Religion weaken'd the State, and there were more Bigots in the Church than Soldiers in the Army: And the Accounts of the Wars which happen'd in those Times, whatever they were, are transmitted down to us with the same Negligence with which we may conclude they were manag'd; and Fortune was preparing to remove the Scene of Action into the West, forsaking the Majesty of the *Byzantine* Empire, which now grew languid and defenceless.

Despairing therefore of recovering that by Force which had been forcibly taken from him, unless *Pepin* would engage not to assist the Pope against him, he sent his Ambassadors with very rich Presents upon that Errand, but found *Pepin* deaf to any Proposals of that nature, and resolv'd to preserve the Pope in the Possession of what he had conferr'd upon him; in which he was encourag'd by the

Pope's

Pope's Legates sent to him upon that Occasion, and who by their Behaviour in their Negotiations afforded *Constantine* new grounds for his Displeasure; whereupon he exacted with more Rigour than ever a strict Observance of his Edicts concerning the Worship of Images, in which he was oppos'd by none so much as the Monks, who so far provok'd the Emperor by their Opposition, that he publish'd a Law forbidding any Person whatever to turn Monk, and was proceeding with much Severity against 'em, when he was diverted for the present from his intended purpose by the *Bulgarian* War, the Occasion and Circumstances of which are differently related by different Authors; the most probable is, That the Emperor was offended at the *Bulgarians* for that in a Sedition they had put all the Princes of the Blood Royal among 'em to Death, and advanc'd *Telesis*, a Man meanly descended, to the Throne. To revenge which Treason he rigg'd out a strong Fleet, and rais'd a good Army, which had Orders to march through *Thrace*, and meet the Fleet at *Anchialus*, a Town standing upon the Sea in *Cilicia*, where both Parties engag'd and continu'd fighting for Eight Hours together, 'till in the end the Imperialists got the Victory, and the *Bulgarians* put their King to Death, either for that they mistrusted he entertain'd a private Correspondence with the Emperor, or because he did not behave himself worthy of the Dignity to which they had advanc'd him. *Constantine*, after this Victory, return'd with his Prisoners to *Constantinople*, where he made a magnificent and triumphant Entry.

A.D. 763.

Constantine overthrows the Bulgarians.

The same Year the *Turks* descended in prodigious Multitudes through the *Caspian* Gates out of the *Asiatick Scythia*, in which cold but populous Country they were inform'd of the great Wealth

of

of *Asia*, which their own Poverty made 'em eager to enjoy. They first fell into *Armenia*, from thence into *Persia* and *Asia minor*, all which Countries they rifled, and return'd home with incredible Booty.

About the same time there happen'd so violent a Frost, which most Authors who have written of that Age have thought fit to mention, for the extraordinary Severity of it. It began on the First of *October*, or, according to some, about the Beginning of *November*, and continu'd to the End of *February* following. All the *Euxine* Sea was frozen over, and the Ice was cover'd with Snow Fifty Foot deep, which render'd it passable for Men and all sorts of Cattle. When the Thaw came the Ice and Snow were dissolv'd together into several Heaps, sufficient to hold and support above Fifty Persons each; these moving Mountains being driven by the Winds crouded through the Straits, and did great Mischief at *Constantinople*, several of 'em being so high that they appear'd above the Walls, which, together with the Castle, were very much shaken by 'em. The Month following, the same Year, several Prodigies appear'd in the Air; for the Stars seem'd to fall from Heaven, and terrify'd the World with the Apprehensions of Dooms-day, which was thought in that general Amazement to be at hand; this was attended with a wonderful Drought, during which divers Fountains were dry'd up, and many Rivers fail'd.

Strange Casualties about this time.

Notwithstanding these amazing Prodigies, *Constantine* renew'd his Severity against those who appear'd the most forward and zealous for the Worship of Images, in which no Persons had a larger share than the Monks, who very industriously oppos'd him, and thereby provok'd him so far that he had a Design of driving 'em out of his Dominions,

nions, and accordingly sold all their Monasteries at *Ephesus*, bestowing the Mony rais'd by 'em upon his Soldiers. In many other Places, particularly at *Constantinople*, he constrain'd 'em to marry, and forc'd 'em to lead their Brides publickly through the Streets; condemning, at the same time, by his publick Edicts, the Intercession of the Saints and the Virgin *Mary*: And proceeded so far as to banish *Constantine*, Patriarch of *Constantinople*, who with much Heat defended the Worship of Images, for which Reason he was recall'd a Year or two afterwards and publickly beheaded.

A Sedition at Rome.

Whilst the Emperor was proceeding with so much Rigour against the Clergy in the East, *Rome* was shaken with a violent Sedition, which happen'd upon the Death of *Paul* the First, who succeeded *Stephen* in the Popedom, and the Election of *Constantine*, who was advanc'd to the Papacy by the Power and Artifices of his Brother *Toton*, Duke of *Nepi*. For *Toton* understanding the Condition in which *Paul* lay, and how impossible it was for him to recover, gather'd all the Forces he was able to raise, to which he join'd those of his Friends, and entring *Rome* by Force seiz'd on the City, where he presented his Brother to succeed *Paul*, who was by that time in the last Extremity; but forasmuch as *Constantine* was qualify'd with no Ecclesiastical Orders, he was first made a Clerk, the Day following he was ordain'd Sub-Deacon, and on the Third Deacon: After which he was conducted by main Force to the *Lateran*, where Three Bishops consecrated him Pope of *Rome*, to the great Scandal and Indignation of the People and the Clergy, who were farther provok'd by the Insolence with which he behav'd himself; whereupon, in a private Assembly summon'd for that purpose, consisting of the principal Citizens and most eminent of the Clergy,

A. D. 768.

it

it was refolv'd to expel *Conftantine,* and advance a Prieft call'd *Philippus,* whom they conducted in great Pomp to the fame Church, and folemnly declar'd him Pope, rendring him fuch Acknowledgments as are ufual upon the like Occafions. In the mean time *Chriftopher,* who, after the Præfect, was a Man of the greateft Authority in the City, and his Son *Sergius,* the next in Dignity to him, prefented themfelves to *Conftantine,* who was not as yet depriv'd, and, the better to conceal their villainous Defigns againft him, defir'd Leave in a fubmiffive manner to be difmifs'd out of the City, with an Intent, as they pretended, to become Monks; but as foon as they were got out of the Gates they fled to *Defiderius,* King of the *Lombards,* defiring him to afift 'em in their Defign, which was to depofe both *Conftantine* and *Philip,* and advance a Creature of their own to the Papacy. *Defiderius* gave 'em a Body of *Lombards* to affift 'em, with whom entring fecretly into the City they rais'd a terrible Sedition, in which *Toton,* his Brother *Paffinus,* and a great number of their Party were murder'd; and then commanding *Philip* to return to the Monaftery from whence they had taken him, in an Affembly of the Chief Officers of the Militia, and Principal of the Citizens and Clergy, they made Choice of *Stephen,* Prieft of St. *Cæcilia,* and confecrated him Pope, with the publick Acclamations of the People, on the Seventh of *Auguft.* After which they exercis'd all manner of Cruelties upon *Conftantine's* Officers and Domefticks; for they pluck'd out the Eyes and the Tongue of *Theodore,* a Bifhop, who was Mafter of his Houfhold, and proceeded with equal Barbarity againft the reft. *Conftantine* was fhut up in a Monaftery, where he was loaden with Irons, 'till they could form his Procefs, and bring him to his Trial, which was

C c 2   done

done the Year following, and he had a formal Sentence pronounc'd upon him; in Execution of which he was degraded from Sacred Orders, thrown out of the Church, had his Eyes pluck'd out, and some add that he was burnt alive, after he had been moſt cruelly buffetted. By theſe inhuman Means *Stephen* the Third obtain'd and confirm'd himſelf in the Popedome, which his Friends would perſuade the World he was no Actor in himſelf, nor that he ſought the Dignity, but receiv'd it as a voluntary Offer from the Hands of thoſe bloody Reformers. Yet if he was not himſelf the Author of theſe Cruelties, he at leaſt favour'd thoſe that were; for he employ'd *Sergius*, the Son of *Chriſtopher*, in an Embaſſy into *France*, ſhortly after his Promotion, and advanc'd others of mean Degree, who had been *Chriſtopher*'s chief Inſtruments, to the higheſt Dignities both of Church and State; but more eſpecially his Proceedings againſt *Conſtantine*, ſufficiently declare how well he approv'd of what had been done.

Marianus Hiſ. Sæcl. undec.

Pepin dies. The ſame Year that *Stephen* the Third was advanc'd to the Papacy in *Italy Pepin* dy'd at St. *Denys* in *France*, after he had liv'd about Fifty Four Years, and reign'd Sixteen and an half. His Wife's Name was *Bertha*, Daughter of *Charibert*, Earl of *Laon*, by whom he had Four Sons, *Charles*, *Carloman*, *Pepin* and *Giles*, of which *Pepin* dy'd very young, and *Giles* was ſent in his Youth into a Monaſtery upon Mount *Soracte* in *Italy*, ſo that *Charles* and *Carloman* were left Joint-Heirs of their Father's Dominions; in the Partition of which they at firſt differ'd with much Contention, 'till in the end it was agreed between 'em, that *Charles* ſhould have *Neuſtria* for his Share, comprehending the Southern and Weſtern Parts of *France*, and ſhould quit *Auſtraſia*, or the Oriental Part, to *Carloman*. Accordingly

cordingly *Charles* was Crown'd at *Noyon*, in the Thirtieth Year of his Age, and *Carloman* at *Soissons*, when he was about Two and Twenty. Besides these Sons *Pepin* left a Daughter, call'd *Gisella*, behind him, whom *Constantine*, the Emperor, demanded of her Brothers in Marriage, at which *Stephen* the Third was so alarm'd, that he made use of all his Artifices to prevent the Match; for he dreaded an Alliance between those Princes, which, considering the Emperor's Inclinations to him, could not but prove very prejudicial to his Affairs. For this Reason he endeavour'd to persuade *Charles* and *Carloman*, that it was not permitted to the Princes of *France* to contract Marriage with Strangers, without the Consent and Approbation of the Pope; and made use of the same Arguments the next Year, when a Match was propos'd between *Charles* and *Theodora*, the King of the *Lombards* Daughter; for he imagin'd, upon good Grounds, that if those two Kings, by Virtue of so strict an Alliance, should come to have a good Understanding with each other, they would in time demand a Restitution from him of what he and his Predecessors had unjustly usurp'd in *Italy*; and therefore, in a long Letter, which he writ to *Charles* and his Brother upon that Subject, he call'd the propos'd Match *a Develish Suggestion*, adding, That *it appear'd in the Holy Scriptures, that many Princes were led aside from the Worship of the true God, by the Artifices of strange Women whom they had marry'd*; by which it is evident he did not know, or rather would not understand, what the Scripture meant by *Strange Women*, who were not esteem'd such upon the Account of their Birth, but their Religion, which was Idolatry. Now he and all the World knew that the Kings of *Lombardy* held the same Faith with

with those of *France*, and *Charles* afterwards marry'd *Hildegard*, a Daughter of *Childebrand*, King of the *Suevi*, who was in every respect as much a Stranger as the Daughter of *Lombardy*; but it was the Pope's Interest to oppose the latter, and to abuse and pervert the Sense of the Holy Scriptures themselves, the better to accomplish his Designs. However, notwithstanding all the Opposition the Pope could make, *Charles* was in conclusion marry'd to *Theodora*, tho' he Divorc'd her Two Years after, either to please the angry Pope, or for some particular Dislike to her Person, she being an infirm sickly Princess.

Desiderius, King of the *Lombards*, was highly incens'd against the Pope for his endeavouring to obstruct the Match; however he conceal'd his Resentments for the present, and, under the Pretence of Devotion, made a Progress to *Rome*, where he renew'd his Promises of observing the Peace concluded between the Pope and his Predecessors, and of suffering him to enjoy, without any Molestation, whatever had been granted to him by the late Treaty, and behav'd himself so cunningly in every Respect, that he left the Pope no room to entertain any Suspicions of the ill Designs he had contriv'd against him; but, during his Residence at *Rome*, he grew acquainted with *Affiarta*, the Governor of the City, and, by his many Presents and powerful Persuasions, made him undertake to form a Process against *Christopher* and his Son for the late Tumults, and the Promotion of *Stephen* to the Papacy, and that he would Banish or Imprison the chiefest of the Citizens, who approv'd not of his Designs, all which *Affiarta* perform'd with too much Rigour, tho' it turn'd not to the Advantage *Desiderius* had propos'd, but rather prov'd the Occasion of his Ruin. He had

A. D. 770.

marry'd

marry'd both his Daughters into *France*, one to *Charles*, and the other to *Carloman*, who, dying about the latter end of this Year, left a Widow and two Sons behind him, who fled to *Tabillon*, Duke of *Bavaria*, upon an Apprehenſion that *Charles* intended to ſeize and confine 'em, and from thence fled to their Grandfather in *Italy*, who was vehemently incens'd againſt *Charles* for Divorcing his other Daughter, as we obſerv'd before. So that now he had a Quarrel to the Pope and *Charles*, and reſolv'd, if poſſible, to be reveng'd upon 'em both. In the mean time *Stephen* dy'd, and was ſucceeded by *Adrian*, a *Roman* Citizen, who, immediately upon his Promotion, releas'd and recall'd from Exile all thoſe who had been impriſon'd or baniſh'd by *Affiarta*, and prepar'd to oppoſe himſelf with all his Power againſt the King of the *Lombards*. Notwithſtanding which *Deſiderius* conceal'd his Reſentments for the preſent, and ſent an Embaſſy to *Rome* to congratulate him upon his Election, and renew the former Treaty concluded with *Stephen*. His Ambaſſadors were inſtructed to inform the Pope, that their Maſter intended to ſend his Grandſons by *Carloman* to *Rome*, where he deſir'd the Pope to Crown 'em, that they might be duly qualify'd to enjoy the Inheritance left 'em by their Father. He knew, if the Pope conſented to his Demands, he would thereby make *Charles* his Enemy, and raiſe ſome Commotions in *France*, which would give him an Opportunity of revenging himſelf upon the Pope, and conquering *Rome* and all *Italy*; but if he refus'd he thought he might then reaſonably endeavour to obtain that by Force, which he could not procure by a Treaty. *Adrian* would willingly have condeſcended to his Demands, and therein have given an Inſtance of the Authority he arrogated

A. D. 772.

A. D. 773.

gated to himself over Kings; but being of a piercing Judgment, he quickly found that *Desiderius* his sole Ambition was to set him at Variance with the King of *France*. For this Reason he return'd the Ambassadors a civil but ambiguous Answer, with which *Desiderius* being in no measure satisfy'd, he enter'd with a strong Army into the Exarchate, where he surpriz'd *Ferrara* and some other Places, and prepar'd to Besiege *Ravenna* it self. The Pope, highly incens'd at this Rupture, sent to demand Assistance from *Charles*, who very readily promis'd him his Protection; and having by two repeated Embassies requir'd *Desiderius* to evacuate those Towns belonging to the Pope, which, in Breach of the Treaty, he had already seiz'd; and finding the King, notwithstanding his fair Promises, resolv'd to retain 'em, he made such Preparations for the War, as appear'd design'd not only to assist the Pope, but to make an entire Conquest of the Kingdom of *Lombardy*.

Charles, King of France, prepares to conquer Italy.

His whole Army met at the general Rendezvous near *Geneva*, where he divided it into two Bodies, one of which he committed to the Conduct of his Uncle *Bernard*; and the other he led himself another way. *Desiderius*, having certain Intelligence of his Motions, sent some Troops to make good the *Straits*, and then rais'd all the Forces of his whole Kingdom, which, having form'd into a mighty Army, prepar'd to give *Charles* Battel, in case he forc'd the *Straits*, and descended from the Mountains. Some say that both Armies came to an Engagement, in which, after an obstinate Dispute, *Desiderius* was defeated; others less affected to the *Lombards* say, they fled in great Consternation, without daring to look in the Face of their Enemies. However it were, the *French* surmounted all the Difficulties they met with in their

their March, and enter'd in an orderly manner into *Italy*, at which *Desiderius* was so terrify'd, that he retir'd and shut himself up in *Pavia*, where, expecting to be Besieg'd, he made all necessary Provisions for a Defence. At the same time he sent his Son *Adalgise*, with his Daughter, the Widow of *Carloman*, and her two Children to *Verona*, the strongest and most commodious Town in his Dominions, next to *Pavia*.

In the mean time the Inhabitants of *Spoleto*, and the *Reatines*, observing that *Desiderius* was unable to keep the Field, and that he was securing himself and his Family in his fortify'd Towns, revolted from him, and submitted themselves to the Pope, who took 'em into his Protection, and in a most solemn manner receiv'd the Oath of Allegiance from 'em. This Example was follow'd by the Marche of *Ancona*, and several other Places. During which Solemnity *Pavia* was very closely Besieg'd by *Charles*, who sate down before it with one Part of his Army, and sent the other to Invest *Verona*; and that the Besieg'd might know how little he was dispos'd to dislodge 'till those Two Towns were in his Power, he sent for his Wife into the Camp, where he continu'd and celebrated the Festival of *Christmas*; after which, leaving the Siege of *Pavia* to his Uncle's Conduct, he went to push on that of *Verona* more vigorously. *Adalgise* defended the Town with much Bravery for some time, but, finding *Charles* was resolv'd to take it, he fled to *Constantinople*, where he was kindly receiv'd by the Emperor; and the Inhabitants, despairing to make good the Place after his Departure, surrender'd it to *Charles*, who found *Carloman*'s Widow and Children in it, whom he sent into *France*, where they were very honourably

Verona surrender'd to Charles,

bly Treated, tho' we have no Account from History what became of 'em afterwards.

Pavia held out hitherto with great Constancy, whereupon *Charles* resolv'd to go and keep his *Easter* at *Rome*, where *Adrian*, the Pope, gave him a most magnificent Reception, and all the People follow'd him with Acclamations, frequently repeating that Saying in the Gospel, *Blessed is he that cometh in the Name of the Lord.* In the midst of these triumphant Shows *Charles* arriv'd at the Church of the *Vatican*, where he devoutly kiss'd every Step as he mounted, and where the Pope, seated on high, waited to receive him, and where, when they met, they embrac'd each other with many Tokens of a mutual Friendship.

A. D. 774. *and* Pavia. *Charles*, having spent a Week at *Rome*, return'd to his Army lying before *Pavia*, which began now to suffer as much from the Famine and Pestilence that rag'd within, as from the Enemy without, so that after a Siege of Ten Months it was constrain'd to surrender. The People before this had been so tir'd with this War, that they massacred the Duke of *Aquitain*, because they imagin'd he had fomented, and did still prolong it. *Desiderius*, apprehending the like Danger from the popular Fury, deliver'd himself up with his Wife and Children to *Charles*, who sent him into *France*, where he was Shav'd and made a Monk, dying not long after at *Liege*. With him ended the Kingdom of the *Lombards* in *Italy*, in the Two Hundred and Sixth Year after its Establishment, during which they made a considerable Figure in the World; and tho' their Dissolution is describ'd with Pens partial in Behalf of *Charles* and the Pope, yet we must allow 'em to have been a People warlike and considerable. Their Government at first was severe and cruel, but when they had embrac'd the Christian

The End of the Lombardian Kingdom in Italy.

Chap. V. LXIX. Conſtant. Copronymus.

Chriſtian Religion it grew gentle and equitable, as appears by the many good Laws made for the Peace and Security of their Subjects; their magnificent Churches, ſtately Monaſteries, and other publick Buildings. The Church is indebted to 'em for many renown'd Confeſſors, and the See of *Rome* owes 'em no leſs for ſeveral of her moſt liberal Benefactors; ſo that it would be hard to conceive why the Pope ſo induſtriouſly procur'd to ruin them, if we did not remember that his Ambition out-weigh'd all other Conſiderations whatever. After he had driven the Emperor in a manner out of all *Italy*, and ſeiz'd on what of Right belong'd to him, he could not ſuffer a Neighbouring Prince ſhould preſume to control or contend with him, and therefore was never eaſie 'till he had remov'd him out of the way, that he might ſafely enjoy what he had moſt ſhamefully uſurp'd, and add to his former Extortions ſuch Parts of *Lombardy* as lay moſt convenient for him.

Paul, the Deacon and Hiſtorian, was carry'd Priſoner with *Deſiderius* into *France*, where he was accus'd of ſome indirect Practices in Favour of his Prince, whom he attempted to releaſe; whereupon *Charles* order'd his Hand to be cut off, but recalling his Sentence before it could be executed, he only confin'd him to *Capraria*, an Iſland in the *Tuſcan* Seas, from whence he retir'd to the Abby of Mount *Caſſin*, where he became a Monk. He left ſeveral Writings behind him, the chief of which is his Hiſtory of the *Lombards*, compris'd in Six Books, wherein he appears very much addicted to the Superſtitions of that Age, and zealous for the Honour of his Prince and Nation.

Paulus Diaconus.

Charles, having ſettl'd his Authority in *Pavia*, return'd to *Rome*, where the Pope receiv'd him at the Head of Fifty Biſhops, and conferr'd upon him

him the Dignity of a Patrician, which was the first Degree in Honour after that of Emperor, to whom of Right it belong'd to confer it; but his Authority being now extinct in *Italy*, the Pope arrogated it to himself, as he did by degrees all the Imperial Honours and Ornaments.

Before *Charles* departed for *France* he was Crown'd King of *Lombardy* by *Thomas*, Arch-Bishop of *Milan*, at *Monza*, a little Town near that City, and then took care to settle the Affairs of those Parts, in order to his Return into *France*. He resign'd to the Pope the Dutchies of *Rome* and *Perouse*, with some other Towns and Territories, retaining however to himself and his Successors the Right of Sovereignty, and an Acknowledgement by way of Homage. The Dutchies of *Beneventum*, *Spoleto* and *Friuli*, he gave to some of the Chief among the *Lombards*, who had not been busie against him in the late War, retaining to himself *Liguria*, *Tuscany* and *Emilia*, which comprehended the Dutchies of *Parma*, *Placentia*, and *Modena*, *Bologna*, *Venetia*, *Trent*, *Mantua*, and the *Cottian Alps*; and from this time forward these Territories were call'd the Kingdom of *Italy*, which extended to the River of *Ofanto*; but *Apulia*, *Calabria* and *Sicily* continu'd still in the Possession of the Emperor. These remarkable Transactions happen'd in *Italy* in the Thirty Fifth Year of *Constantine*, the Sixth of *Charles* the Great, King of *France*, the Third of Pope *Adrian* the First, An. Dom. 774.

All this while *Constantine* was employ'd in Prosecuting the Image Worshippers in the East, or in his Wars with the *Bulgarians*, which were intermitted by frequent Treaties, and renew'd with various Success. Some time before this a Peace was concluded between 'em, the Articles of which
were

were so dislik'd by the *Bulgarians*, that they intended to observe it no longer than 'till they could find a covenient time to break it. For which Reason Twelve Thousand of their Men fell this Year into the Territories of the Empire, but met with a Success their Perfidy deserv'd, for *Constantine* fell upon 'em and cut 'em all in pieces; after which great Victory he return'd in Triumph to *Constantinople*. This he afterwards call'd his *Noble War*, because there was not one Christian lost in it; tho' it seems the Victory was obtain'd by Treachery, he being secretly inform'd by some *Bulgarians* of the Designs of their Countrymen against him. *E-lerich*, Prince of the Country, knew he had been betray'd, and made use of a Device to discover the Traitors. He wrote to *Constantine*, and told him he was willing to quit his Dignity, and lead a private Life in *Constantinople*; for which purpose he desir'd his Letters of safe Conduct, and to know what Friends he had amongst the *Bulgarians*, that he might commit his Person to their Trust, and repair with them to his Presence. *Constantine*, who thought *Elerich* sincere in his Pretensions, sent him the Names of those who held Intelligence with him, who were all put to Death by the crafty Prince, to the great Shame and Indignation of the Emperor, who in the Extravagance of his Passion pluck'd his Beard up by the Roots, and prepar'd to be sufficiently reveng'd upon *Elerich* the Spring following; but in his March against him he was seiz'd with a contagious Feaver, of which he dy'd the Fourteenth of *September*, after he had reign'd Thirty Four Years and Three Months.

Constantine deluded by the King of the Bulgarians.

A. D. 775. *Constantine dies.*

He left the State almost in the same Condition in which he found it; tho' it's very probable, if he had liv'd at a time when the Vigour of the Empire had not been quite decay'd, he had rul'd with more

His Character.

more Honour, and dy'd in greater Reputation; for he was naturally Sober, Chaste, and Valiant, and at least restrain'd the growing Distempers of the Body Politick, which it was not in his Power to remove: And this may be said of him, That he knew very well how to manage an ill Hand. He defended the aged Body of the Empire against the frequent Attempts of the *Saracens, Bulgarians,* and other insulting Neighbours, and in that respect deferr'd the Calamities he was not able to avert. He was cordially affected to the Purity of the Christian Religion, and maintain'd the Catholick Faith against all those Hereticks who had been condemn'd by the several Oecumenical Councils. He was a great Enemy to Images, and to all those who labour'd to establish the Worship of 'em in the Church; by which he contracted the ill Will of those who were zealous for it, and who for that Reason omitted no Opportunity of wounding his Reputation. This afforded the Bishop of *Rome* an Opportunity of withdrawing himself from his Subjection to the Empire, and erecting his own Authority in *Italy*; which, being founded upon the Principles of Idolatry and Rebellion, gave a Beginning to the Kingdom of Antichrist.

LEO III.   VI. *Constantine* was succeeded in the Empire by his Son *Leo*, who had been proclaim'd *Augustus* in the Tenth Year of his Father's Reign, as was observ'd before; and in the Year 770 marry'd *Irene,* Daughter to the King of *Bulgaria,* by whom he had another *Constantine,* whom shortly after his Coronation he associated with him in the Empire. At first he appear'd moderate in his Temper, and remitted the Rigour his Father had express'd towards the Worship of Images; but it appear'd, by his Proceedings afterwards, that he only temporis'd

'till

Chap. V.   LXX. Leo III.

'till he had settled himself in the Government, and secur'd it to his Son *Constantine*; in the Description of whose Coronation *Theophanes* is very particular. He tells us, *Leo* by his Moderation had so universally oblig'd the Inhabitants of *Constantinople*, that they came with a general Petition to him to make his Son *Constantine* Emperor; to prevent, in case of his Death, a Civil War, which would of necessity arise between his Brothers, in Contention for the Succession. *Leo*, who well knew the Game he had to manage, reply'd, That *he was ready to comply with their Request, but was willing first by a solemn Oath to oblige 'em to adhere to his Son, at that time an Infant, after his Decease, and defend him against all Competitors whatever.* This they readily consented to, and for a Week together the *Hippodrome* was crouded with such as with great Earnestness desir'd his Son's Promotion, concluding all with an Oath of Allegiance to him, and obliging themselves by a Paper, subscrib'd by the Army, the Senate, and all sorts of People, never to admit of any but *Leo*, or *Constantine*, or their Issue, to reign over them. The next Day, being *Easter* Eve, the Emperor ascended a Throne rais'd to an extraordinary Eminence for that purpose, where he conferr'd the Title of *Nobilissimi* on his Brothers *Anthimius* and *Eudoxius*, and from thence carry'd young *Constantine* in a solemn Procession to the Church, where changing his Habit, as his Predecessors us'd to do, he, with his Son and the Patriarch, mounted the Place proper to such Solemnities, whilst the People laid their subscrib'd Papers upon the Holy Altar. When this was done, the Emperor address'd himself in this manner to the Assembly, *Behold, my Brethren, how ready I have been to grant your Petition; receive, according to your own Demands, my Son for your Emperor; take him*

A.D.
776.

him in the Presence of the Almighty, from the Hands of his only begotten Son *Jesus Christ*. To which the People with loud Acclamations reply'd, *Be thou our Surety, thou Eternal Son of God; from thy Hand we receive our Lord* Constantine *for Emperor, and stand engag'd to defend him with our Lives and Fortunes.* The Day following, being *Easter*-Day, the Patriarch Crown'd young *Constantine* in the Presence of all the People in the *Hippodrome*, after which they return'd in great Pomp to the Palace.

A. D. 778.
The Pomp of this Solemnity seem'd to raise an Appetite in *Nicephorus*, *Leo*'s Brother, to the Sovereignty, who therefore form'd a Conspiracy against his Brother; but being discover'd and convicted, he was banish'd, together with his Accomplices, into the *Chersonese*. Shortly after which *Elerich*, King of the *Bulgarians*, who had so often contended in the preceding Wars with *Constantine*, the late Emperor, being in some popular Tumult driven out of his Country, made a right use of his Misfortunes, and retir'd for Safety to *Constantinople*; where *Leo* receiv'd him with much Honour, and, according to his own Request, order'd him to be instructed in the Principles of the Christian Religion, which he embrac'd, created him a Patrician, and marry'd him to a Relation of the Empress *Irene*.

A. D. 779.
These Popular Acts in the Beginning of his Reign render'd *Leo* very gracious to the People, by whose Encouragement he prepar'd an Army to be sent against the *Saracens*, who had lately been very troublesome upon the Borders. This Expedition prov'd very fortunate to the Empire, for both Armies engag'd in the Month of *February* in *Syria*, where the *Saracens* were defeated, and lost Eleven Thousand of their Men upon the Place. To repair

repair which Lofs *Mahdy*, or *Mahady*, rais'd a very powerful Army, with which he pierc'd into the Territories of the Empire. *Leo*, perceiving he had not Troops sufficient to oppose him in the open Field, took care to have the Towns and fortify'd Places well provided, and destroy'd all the Forage that was in the open Country; and this Design succeeded so well, that the Caliph, finding no manner of Subsistence for his Army, was forc'd to retire without doing any thing considerable against the Emperor: But he was so much concern'd at this unfortunate Expedition that he punish'd all the Christians in his Dominions for it. He publish'd an Edict, which subjected all those who had forsaken Mahometism and embrac'd Christianity to the severest Punishments, and order'd all the Churches of the Christians to be destroy'd, which was executed with much Rigour at *Emessa*, and in other Parts of *Syria*.

This Persecution rais'd against Christianity abroad made *Leo* more zealous for the Purity of it at home; for now he appear'd an open Enemy to Images, and, following the Steps of his Father, very severely punish'd those who asserted the Lawfulness of the Worship that was paid to 'em. Nor would he in this respect decline reprehending the Empress *Irene* his Wife, whom, in Defiance to the solemn Oaths she had made his Father to the contrary, he accus'd of favouring those who adher'd to it. She made such an Apology in her own behalf as appear'd afterwards to be no more than a mere Excuse, when she authoriz'd and established the Veneration paid to 'em. This Excuse did not appear so plausible to the Emperor, but he thought he had just grounds to mistrust too intimate a Familiarity between her and some of his Domesticks, who therefore were put to Death, and *Irene* was forbid-

Leo an Enemy to Images.

forbidden his Bed for some time after. These are the most remarkable Transactions during this Emperor's Reign, which exceeded Five Years no more than Ten Days. *Theophanes*, and some others, who were zealous in the behalf of Images, have given us a very odd Account of his Death. They say that *Leo*, being a great Admirer of precious Stones, would needs wear the Crown of *Heraclius*, which being embellish'd with inestimable Jewels was deposited in the great Church, from whence it was never taken but upon a Coronation; this Crown *Leo* presum'd to wear whenever he appear'd in publick, but as one Day he had it on a Carbuncle arose in his Head, and he was seiz'd with a violent Feaver, of which he dy'd on the Sixteenth of *September, An. Dom.* 780. after he had reign'd Five Years and Ten Days; leaving the World little of moment to discourse of him after his Death, except his Aversion to Images, which rais'd him Enemies enow among those who were addicted to the See of *Rome*.

CONSTAN-
TINUS POR-
PHYROGE-
NETUS.

A. D.
780.

Leo, in the Twenty-Ninth Year of his Father's Reign, had been espous'd to *Irene*, Daughter to the King of *Bulgaria*, by whom he had a Son call'd *Constantine*, and sirnam'd *Porphyrogenetus*, because born at a time when his Father and Grandfather were both Emperors. *Constantine*, at his Father's Death was no more than Nine or Ten Years of Age, for which Reason his Mother *Irene* procur'd her self to be declar'd Regent during her Son's Minority. She, being a cunning ambitious Princess, and a Woman that would stick at no Villany which could promote her Designs, made several think that she hasten'd her Husband's Death, that she might have the sole Administration of Affairs in her own Hands during her Son's Nonage: And this Conjecture is made more than probable,

by

by the ill Underſtanding there was between her and *Leo* ſome time before his Death. Before ſhe had been eſtabliſh'd in the Management Forty Days, ſeveral of the Senators and principal Citizens, grown weary of her Government, met together, and conſulted how they might advance *Nicephorus*, *Conſtantine*'s Uncle, to the Imperial Dignity; this rais'd a great Sedition in the City, inſomuch that *Irene* was forc'd to preſent her ſelf to the Multitude, whom ſhe reminded of the ſolemn Oath given to *Leo*, never to acknowledge any other for Emperor but his Son *Conſtantine*; and this ſhe apply'd to 'em in ſuch ſeaſonable Terms that the Tumult was inſtantly appeas'd: After which ſhe arreſted and impriſon'd all thoſe who had been the moſt forward in the Sedition, moſt of whom ſhe ſhav'd, and then baniſh'd into ſeveral little uninhabited Iſlands, where they all periſh'd for want of Suſtenance; *Nicephorus*, and *Chriſtopher*, another of *Conſtantine*'s Uncles, were thruſt into Holy Orders, and ſome others ſecur'd, in whoſe Power it was to raiſe any Diviſions in the State. This Danger being over ſhe endeavour'd to ingratiate her ſelf with the People, and procure the Favour of the Pope, by reſtoring Images, to whom ſhe commanded a Religious Worſhip to be render'd in all the Churches of her Dominions.

Having by theſe Means, as ſhe thought, ſecur'd her ſelf in the Government at home, ſhe ſent an Army againſt *Helpidius*, Governor of *Sicily*, who ſhe was inform'd privately favour'd *Nicephorus*, and incited the *Saracens* to invade the Territories of the Empire. *Helpidius* defended himſelf for ſome time with good Succeſs, but was at length forc'd to fly into *Africk*, whither he carry'd all his Treaſure with him, and liv'd in great Security in *Egypt*; where the *Saracens*, in Oppoſition to *Conſtantine*,

A. D. 782.

ſtantine, declar'd and own'd him Emperor. Taking the Advantage of this Opportunity they fell with great Fury upon the Eaſtern Provinces, which *Aaron*, the Son of *Mahadi* the Caliph, waſted in a terrible manner, and oblig'd *Irene*, for the Preſervation of the Empire, to make it tributary to the Infidels, whom ſhe appeas'd with an Annual Penſion. So ſoon as ſhe had put an end to this War ſhe ſent *Stauracius*, a Patrician, againſt the *Sclavi*, who entring *Greece* and the *Peloponneſus* had ravag'd all the Country. *Stauracius* engag'd them at ſeveral Times, in all which he had the Advantage, and reduc'd them to Obedience; after which, and when he had impos'd a Tribute upon them, to which they were forc'd to ſubmit, he return'd in great Triumph to *Conſtantinople*.

The Empire made tributary to the Saracens.

During theſe Wars on each ſide a Negotiation was ſet on foot between *Irene* and *Charles*, of whom ſhe demanded his Daughter in Marriage for her Son *Conſtantine*, being then about Twelve Years of Age. This ſhe propos'd, that ſhe might be the better able to ſupport her ſelf againſt her Enemies by the Power of *France*; and the Propoſal was ſo well approv'd of, that Ambaſſadors were ſent into *France* to conclude the Treaty, and *Eliſæus*, an Eunuch, left behind, to inſtruct the young Princeſs in the Language and Cuſtoms of the *Roman* Empire. Tho' both Parties ſeem'd fond of the Match the Accompliſhment of it was deferr'd at preſent, becauſe the young Princes were under Age, and was at laſt totally laid aſide by the Artifices of *Irene*, who being unwilling to reſign the Government to her Son, when he began to be qualify'd in Years for it, was afraid ſo powerful an Alliance and the Friendſhip of *Charles* would make him too conſiderable for her Management; upon which account ſhe highly offended *Charles*, and diſob-

disoblig'd her Son, who had entertain'd an Inclination for the Lady, and was never after truly reconcil'd to his Mother; who aggravated all by forcing him to marry a Virgin of obscure Parentage, and one whose Person and Education made her in every respect unfit for the Imperial Dignity. This gave a beginning to the many Troubles that ensu'd afterwards.

In the mean time *Irene* persisted in her Zeal for the Worship of Images, which she was desirous to establish by the Authority of a Council, to which purpose having made *Therasius*, contrary to the Ecclesiastical Canons, Patriarch of *Constantinople*, and being assur'd of the Pope's Assistance, who she knew as earnestly desir'd the same thing, she summon'd a Council to be celebrated at *Constantinople* on the Seventh of *August*, *An. Dom.* 786. but as they were all ready to form the Assembly, a great Number of the Inhabitants, and the Soldiers Garrison'd in that City, knowing what the Business of the Council was to be, rose in a tumultuous manner, and oblig'd all the Deputies that were arriv'd to retire, to the great Indignation of *Irene*, who for that Reason remov'd the Council the Year following to *Nice*, where every thing was done according to the Purposes for which it was summon'd. And tho' by the *Romans* it is esteem'd a General Council, it was not acknowledg'd as such by the several National Synods held after it in the East and the West. *The Second Council of Nice summon'd in the behalf of Images.*

Hitherto *Irene* had govern'd in the Empire with an unlimited Authority, tho' her Son was now Twenty Years of Age; whereupon several Courtiers, who were grown weary of his Mother's imperious Administration, encourag'd him to take the Government into his own Hands, to which he was easily persuaded, especially when he observ'd that A. D. 789.

her great Favourite, *Stauracius*, who govern'd all under *Irene* at his Pleasure, was more follow'd and respected than the Emperor himself, so that he prepar'd, by the Advice and Assistance of his intimate Friends, to throw off the Bonds of Pupillage, and seize on that Inheritance by Force, which he thought would not voluntarily be resign'd to him. Of this *Stauracius* was inform'd before their Design was ripe for Execution, and by *Irene*'s Order Arrested the Conspirators, who were first whipp'd and shav'd, and then sent into Exile. Her Son she chastis'd in an outragious manner with her own Hands, and confin'd him to his Apartment for a considerable time after. *Stauracius*, being an experienc'd successful General, had a great Interest in the Army, the Principal Officers of which were at his Devotion, and therefore at his Instigation took an Oath of Fidelity to *Irene*, exclusive of her Son, who, by Virtue of that Oath, was not permitted to Reign so long as she liv'd. The same Oath was impos'd upon the Senate, and the Forces Quarter'd in the Provinces, who all took it except some Legions in *Armenia*, who declar'd resolutely for *Constantine*, whom their Duty and Allegiance oblig'd them to obey.

This Resolution of the Army in *Armenia* being known to the rest of the Forces quarter'd upon the Borders, had such an Effect upon 'em, notwithstanding the Oath they had lately taken, that they follow'd their Example, and requir'd unanimously to have the Government vested in *Constantine*. *Irene*, who had just reason to fear the Violence of the incens'd Multitude, releas'd her Son from his honourable Restraint, who, being receiv'd by the repeated Acclamations of the Citizens and Soldiers, took the Reins of the Empire into his own Hands. Those who had been banish'd

A. D. 790.

nish'd upon his Account he recall'd, and advanc'd 'em to Employments of Honour and Profit. *Stauracius,* and such others as had been his Mother's Favourites, he banish'd, but suffer'd *Irene* to live at a Palace of her own, which she had built in *Eleutherium,* and where she had laid up an immense Treasure. Whilst the State was thus shaken with these Commotions, *Constantinople* was thrown into so violent a Convulsion by a furious Earthquake, that the Inhabitants were forc'd to quit their Dwellings, and retire into the Fields 'till the Fury was abated.

The Emperor being thus restor'd to his Liberty, and the free Exercise of his Imperial Authority, rais'd an Army against the *Bulgarians,* whom he fought, but with what Success is uncertain; for some say he had the Victory, others that it was a drawn Battel, and the rest affirm he had the worst in the Engagement, wherein he lost the Flower of his Army. His Success against the *Saracens* is as variously reported; so dark are the Accounts left us of that Age, as if the State of the Empire was so low, as not to deserve to be remember'd in an ingenuous disinterested History.

But, whilst he was busily employ'd in these Wars abroad, *Irene* and her Party were as busie at home. They were sensible how dangerous it was to attempt her Restauration by Force, and therefore they labour'd to effect it by submissive Entreaties and plausible Remonstrances; they endeavour'd to persuade him by Arguments drawn from filial Duty and Obedience, and to terrifie him by suggesting to him the Dangers to which he was expos'd from the Designs of his Enemies. These Considerations made him recal his Mother, with whom he was contented to Act in Conjunction. Having, as he thought, strengthen'd his Authori-

A.D. 792.

ty, which he was persuaded in this manner to divide, he once more fell upon the *Bulgarians*, encourag'd to it by some Mathematicians, who made him so confident of the Victory, that he omitted the proper Means to obtain it; so that the Enemy, taking the Advantage of his ill grounded Security, gave him a very remarkable Defeat, in which, besides great Numbers of common Soldiers, he lost the best Officers of his Army, and the most considerable Men in the Empire, together with *Pancratius*, the Astronomer, who, upon the Presumption of his Knowledge, had given him all the Assurances of a glorious Success, but now experienc'd in Death the Vanity of his treacherous Art. The *Bulgarians*, having thus gain'd the Battel, forc'd the Camp, seiz'd on all the Emperor's Baggage, and sent the dishonourable Prince naked home to *Constantinople*.

The Emperor overthrown by the Bulgarians.

These Misfortunes open'd his Adversaries Mouths against him, whilst he, being conscious to himself of his own Unworthiness, grew jealous and distrustful, which some, who were near his Person, endeavour'd to improve, by insinuating to him that the Soldiers then quarter'd in *Constantinople*, grown weary of his Government, had a Design to promote *Nicephorus*; at which he was so enrag'd, that he commanded his Uncle's Eyes to be pluck'd out, and proceeded with the same Severity against *Alexius*, a Man in great Credit with the Army in *Armenia*, and against his other Uncles, and most of his near Relations, tho' it did not appear they were any ways concern'd in the Conspiracy. These Barbarities are said to be acted at the Instigation of *Irene*, who Five Years after upon the same Month, and the same Day of the Month, did as much by her Son *Constantine*, as we shall have occasion to show hereafter.

For tho' that Princess seem'd satisfy'd with the Title of Empress without the Power, yet in secret she was continually contriving how to make her self Mistress of both. Her greatest Adversaries were the *Armenian* Legions, whom the Emperor's Cruelty to *Alexius* had driven into a Mutiny, in which they had seiz'd on *Constantianus*, and some others, who were sent into that Province at the Head of a strong Party to reduce 'em; whereupon *Constantine* march'd against 'em himself, and gain'd an entire Victory over 'em, killing great Numbers of 'em in the Field, and taking the rest Prisoners, who were dispers'd into *Sicily* and other Islands. Tho' they had justly drawn the Emperor's Indignation upon 'em for their Disobedience, yet in destroying them he provok'd his own Destruction; for he had now lost those who had been always ready to assist him against the ambitious Designs of his Mother, who rejoic'd secretly at all his Misfortunes, and was pleas'd to see him expose himself to the Resentments of the People. She privately encourag'd him in all Attempts tending to his Dishonour, and knowing he had no great Affection for the Empress *Mary*, whom she had forc'd him to marry contrary to his Inclination, she persuaded him to divorce her, and marry *Theodecta*, one of the Maids of her Chamber, who was Crown'd Empress with much Solemnity at *Constantinople*, where the Nuptials were solemnis'd with publick Festivals for Four Days together.

A. D. 795.

This unequal Match contributed to *Irene*'s Designs, for it created great Contests among the Clergy concerning the Lawfulness of it, in all which she countenanc'd those who were against her Son, and privately caress'd such as she knew would upon occasion be ready to oppose him.

The

The Solemnity of the Nuptials were hardly over before *Constantine* was call'd from the Arms of his new Bride to oppose the *Saracens*, who, by way of Revenge for some Advantages he had lately gain'd over 'em, made an Irruption into *Cilicia*, which they wasted with Fire and Sword, and upon the Emperor's Approach return'd home with great Booty. After this he turn'd his Arms against the *Bulgarians*, whose King *Cardanes* sent to demand a Tribute from him, and threaten'd to come as far as the *Golden Gate* of *Constantinople* to force it, if it was refus'd him. *Constantine* reply'd, *That since he was an old Man he would not give him the Trouble of so long a Journey, but come with it in Person, and wait upon him.* Accordingly he march'd against him with a considerable Army, upon sight of which the Barbarians fled away in great Consternation, and *Constantine* return'd to *Constantinople*, where the Disputes among the Ecclesiasticks relating to his late Marriage were grown so high, that the Abbot *Plato* had Excommunicated *Tharasius*, the Patriarch, for having confin'd *Mary*, the Emperor's Divorc'd Wife, to a Monastery, and consented to his espousing another. Whereupon *Constantine* threw *Plato* into Prison, and banish'd all his Monks, which encreas'd the Displeasure the generality of the People had conceiv'd against him, and encourag'd his unnatural Mother to hasten the Execution of her Designs.

A. D. 796.

In the Month of *October* he waited on her to the Baths of *Prusa*, where he had not been long before an Express from *Constantinople* inform'd him that his Empress was deliver'd of a Son, at which he was so overjoy'd, that he return'd in great haste to the Imperial City, and his Impatience was such, that it would not suffer him to stay and take a decent leave of his Mother, who interpreted it as

an

an Indignity offer'd to her Person; and taking the *Irene's De-*
Advantage of his Absence, so dispos'd the chief *signs a-*
Officers of the Army to her Service, that they *gainst her*
promis'd to Depose her Son with the first Oppor- *Son.*
tunity, and confirm her solely in the Government.

Whilst these things were in Agitation the Emperor undertook another Expedition against the *Saracens*, in which he was attended by *Stauracius*, and other of his Mother's Creatures, who, at her Request, had lately been recall'd home. *Stauracius,* observing the Emperor, and the greatest part of the Army were grown confident of Success, dreaded the Consequences of a Victory, which might render him too great for all their Designs; he therefore hir'd the Scouts to report to the Emperor that the *Saracens,* having wasted the Country, were return'd home, and left no Employment for his Arms in those Parts. Whereupon being disappointed, as he thought, of a glorious Victory, he return'd to *Constantinople* in much Discontent, which was aggravated by the Loss of his young Son, who dy'd on the First of *May.* The Conspirators, being quicken'd by repeated Letters from his Mother, were now prepar'd for Execution; and as he was returning one Day from the *Circus* he was privately inform'd, that some People were hir'd by his Mother to seize on him, and carry him bound to her. Thinking to be secure in *Armenia,* he committed himself to the care of some, who he thought had great Reason to be faithful to him, but on the contrary they carry'd him, by *Irene's* Order, to the Palace, and there in the Chamber wherein his Eyes first saw the Light, he lost it by the Hands of Inhuman Traitors, who most barbarously digg'd his Eyes *Constan-* out of his Head, with the insupportable Pain of *murder'd.* which

A. D. 797.

which he dy'd shortly after. The Heavens, saith the Historian, beheld with so much Horror the excessive Cruelty of this unnatural Mother, that for Seventeen Days together the Sun withdrew his Beams, insomuch that several Ships at Sea lost their Course for want of Light, and fell foul on each other. Tho' the Reader may observe, in the Death of this Prince, the visible Footsteps of Divine Justice, and the Punishment he deserv'd for the innocent Blood he had spilt during his Reign, particularly that of his Uncles, who lost their Eyes by his Order Five Years before upon the same Day of the same Month, and in the same Chamber; yet doth it by no means excuse the Inhuman Treason of his inexorable Mother, who Sacrific'd her only Son to her Ambition and Revenge. So soon as she saw her self confirm'd without a Rival in the Imperial Authority, she sent *Nicephorus* and *Christopher*, her late Husband's Brothers, to *Athens*, where they were murder'd by her Order shortly after; so that now the whole Race of *Leo Isauricus* was totally extinct, and no one left to dispute the Title with her. Wherefore she order'd her self to be drawn into the City by Four Horses in a gilt Chariot, attended by some of the Patricians, who waited as her Slaves on either side, whilst she distributed Mony amongst the People, as it was usual at the Solemnity of a Coronation; which was hardly finish'd before the *Saracens* wasted the Eastern Provinces of the Empire, and having defeated the Forces *Irene* sent out against 'em, and destroy'd all the Cavalry she had Quarter'd in *Thrace*, pillag'd the whole Country, and made their Excursions almost as far as the Gates of *Constantinople*, after which they return'd with a very rich Booty home.

Being deliver'd from these Foreign Dangers she fell into greater at home; for *Stauracius*, who had hitherto

A.D. 798.
The Saracens insult the Empire.

hitherto behav'd himself like the Slave of her Ambition, began now to envy her the Crown which his Villanies had help'd to put upon her Head, and therefore consulted with his most intimate Friends the Means to deprive her of it. His Designs were prevented by a seasonable Discovery to *Irene*, who, in consideration of his former Services, punish'd him no otherwise than by forbidding all Men to keep him Company; which moderate Carriage towards him made him so asham'd of his Offence, that he dy'd for Grief shortly after.

From this time forward, like other Tyrants and Usurpers, she enjoy'd that in continual Fears and Jealousies which she had obtain'd by Treason and Paricide, and was in the end dethron'd by her Subjects, after she had endeavour'd by several Acts of Grace and popular Condescensions to purchase their Favour; and had the Mortification to see an Emperor created in the West, in Defiance, as it were, of her Dignity, and that by the Pope of *Rome*, whom, during her Authority, she had so many ways study'd to oblige.

For about this time *Charles*, the King of *France*, who had deservedly acquir'd the Sirname of Great, was call'd into *Italy*, to remove some Disorders that had prevail'd there during his Wars with the *Saxons*, (whom he finally conquer'd, and converted to the Christian Faith) and vindicate *Leo* the Third, at that time Pope of *Rome*, who came to follicite his Assistance against some *Roman* Citizens who had most grievously insulted him. For by this time the *Romans* had forgot the Fear and Awe in which the *Lombards* had kept 'em, and, grown wanton in Idleness and Luxury, began to dislike their Subjection to the Pope, and were ambitious of recovering their ancient Liberty. This encourag'd the
Gover-

A.D. 799.

Governor of the City, and some principal Officers related to the late Pope *Adrian*, to accuse *Leo* of several enormous Crimes, and raise a seditious Party against him. As he was assisting in a Procession upon a solemn Festival they fell upon him, beat him, and endeavour'd to pull out his Eyes and his Tongue, after which they threw him, when he was half dead, into a Dungeon; from whence however *Albinus*, his Chamberlain, found an Opportunity of delivering him, and committed him to the Protection of *Winigise*, Duke of *Spoleto*, at that time in *Rome*, by whose Assistance he was convey'd to *Charles*, who was then at *Paderbonne* in *Saxony*, to whom he complain'd of the Injuries had been done him. *Charles* receiv'd him with much Honour, and gave a favourable Ear to his Complaints, and after he had entertain'd him for some time with much Magnificence he sent him back under a strong Guard, and promis'd to come in Person to *Rome* so soon as his Affairs would give him leave, there to do him Justice; in the mean he sent his Commissioners with him, to try the Merits of his Cause before his Arrival. These Commissioners having heard what the Conspirators could urge against *Leo*, or offer in their own Behalf, found all they said so trivial, that they were sent in Chains into *France*.

Charles the Great goes into Italy.

Shortly after *Charles*, having prepar'd all things requisite for his Expedition, set out for *Italy*, giving his Orders and reforming such Things as were done amiss in all Places as he pass'd. At *Rome* he was receiv'd with all the Magnificence the Pope could express to a Soveraign Prince, who was his great Patron and Protector. After he had been there some Days he acquainted the People with the Cause of his Coming, and appointed a Day to hear their

their Bishop's Cause. When the Accusers had deliver'd in their Charge, and *Leo* was preparing to make his Defence, the Bishops, as well *French* as *Italian*, who sate upon the Bench, would not suffer him to answer formally, as other Criminals were us'd to do; so that he was acquitted by his Judges, when he had declar'd solemnly upon Oath that he was innocent of the Crimes they had objected against him.

Charles having done this piece of Service for *Leo*, there remain'd something for him to do by way of Acknowledgment; which some imagine to have been the principal Motive to this Expedition. *Charles* his large Territories and mighty Dominions made him deserve the Title of Emperor, and *Leo* knew his Predecessor had been notoriously persecuted by the Heretical Emperor of *Constantinople*, who was of late grown no less unable than unwilling to protect him, and that it was the general Opinion some other Prince ought to take the Defence of the Church upon him, and to that purpose be dignify'd with the Imperial Title, which he knew no one deserv'd so well as *Charles*.

Accordingly on *Christmass*-Day *Charles* went early in the Morning to the Church of the *Vatican*, where the Pope, after he had finish'd his Devotions, vested him with an Imperial Robe, and set a Crown of Gold upon his Head, the People in the mean time with reiterated Shouts acclaiming *To Charles Augustus, Crown'd of God, the most mighty and most Pious Emperor of the* Romans, *Long Life, and Perpetual Victory*. After which he anointed him with the Sacred Oil, and *Charles* undertook the Defence of the *Roman* Church. When this was done the Pope fell down upon his Knees before the Emperor, acknowledging him for his Soveraign,

A.D. 800. *and is made Emperor.*

veraign, whilst his Images were expos'd in publick, as it had been customary with the Emperors of *Rome*, to the intent all the People might render him Subjection and Obedience. *Eginhard*, who was Secretary to *Charles* the Great, and therefore might reasonably be thought to know more of the Matter than some later Writers, saith his Master was not ambitious of the Title, nor would have accepted of it, if he had not been supriz'd in it by the Pope; and 'tis very likely he thought nothing of it when he first set out upon this Expedition, for in effect he gain'd nothing by it; and, if he had thought it convenient, he might have assum'd it without the Intervention of the Pope.

His Character. However it were, his exalted Virtues and Heroick Actions made him truly deserving of the Dignity and Title of Emperor, being undoubtedly one of the most excellent Princes that ever was in the World; for besides those other Accomplishments as well Civil as Military, which rais'd him above all his Cotemporaries, he surpass'd all the Men of that Age in the Knowledge of the Tongues and Sciences, and was equall'd by none in Eloquence; he had a fervent Zeal for the Propagation of the Christian Religion, and for the Support of the Honour and Discipline of the Church. If he was guilty of some Superstitions, which can't be deny'd, it is to be imputed to the Corruptions of the Times in which he liv'd, and the Ignorance of the Clergy. His greatest Faults were, his being too much addicted to the Love of Women, and his profuse Favours to the See of *Rome*.

This new Empire comprehended all *Italy* as far as the Rivers *Ofanto* and *Volturno*, with *Bavaria*, *Hungary*, *Croatia*, *Austria*, *Dalmatia*, *Sclavonia*, *Germany*, *Gaul*, and a considerable Part of *Spain*; whilst

whilst the Emperors of *Constantinople* retain'd no more in the West than the Residue of *Italy*, *Sicily*, and such Countries of *Europe* as border upon the East, with the Lands beyond the *Bosphorus*.

Thus have we endeavour'd to continue this History down to a new Period, which neither puts an end to the *Constantinopolitan* Empire, nor in reality introduces a Division of it; but rather the Erection of a new one, that bears no Relation to the former, unless in this Respect, that it ow'd its Beginning to the Power of the Sword, and a just Regard to Military Discipline: Tho' if the Strength of both had been united together, it would have fallen as far short of the ancient *Roman* Majesty, as does the imperfect Resemblances of a Person taken after his Decease fall short of his living Lineaments. The mighty Body of the Empire had, like a prodigious Mountain Oak, been long since hewn down by the Sword of the Barbarians; and if the Root was left still remaining, it brought forth nothing but a tender Scion, which was too weak to contend with the Storms that continually assaulted it, or over-top the Weeds and Brambles with which it was encumber'd. The *Romans*, contrary to an old Maxim, had in Process of Time, by their perpetual Wars, taught their Enemies not only their manner of Fighting, but their Ambition of Glory and Thirst of Empire; and thereby contracted a Debt larger than their Posterity was able to pay. The Reasons of the Rise, Progress, and Dissolution of this State, which have been occasionally hinted at in these Volumes, are so well known, and have been summ'd up by so many abler Hands, that a Repetition of 'em here would be superfluous. We shall only add this useful Observation, That it is with States as with particular Persons, none are so Strong, so

Powerful and Mighty, but sooner or later they come to a Period: From their Birth they creep gradually up to their utmost Strength and Vigour, and then first descend to a Decay, and after that drop into nothing; nor ought we to wonder at it, since the World it self must expect a Dissolution.

INDEX.

A

Acacius, *Bishop of Amida, his extraordinary Charity,* Vol. 3. Pag. 309
Actium, *see* Battel.
Adaulfus, *Brother to* Alarich, *defeated in* Italy, Vol. 3. p. 289. *made King of the* Goths, 297. *marries* Placidia, *Sister to* Honorius, ibid. *makes* Attalus *Emperor a second time,* 301. *slain by his own Subjects,* 302
Adrian *made Emperor,* Vol. 2. p. 303. *his great Moderation,* 307. *persecutes the Christians,* 308. *his Journey,* 309. *his Exploits in* Britain, 310. *his Death,* 320
Æmilian *proclaim'd Emperor by the Soldiers,* Vol. 2. p. 391. *his Death,* 392
Æmilius Paulus *his Actions in the second* Macedonian *War,* Vol. 1. p. 228, 229
Æneas *his Arrival, and Settlement in* Italy, Vol. 1. p. 3
Ætius *espouses the Interest of* John *the Usurper,* Vol. 3. p. 313. *Reconcil'd to* Placidia, 315. *imposes upon her,* 316. *fights* Boniface, 319. *his Services in* Gaul, 326, 332. *frustrates the Designs of* Attila, 339. *relieves* Orleance, 341. *slain by* Valentinian's *Order,* 348
Africk *conquer'd by the* Vandals, Vol. 3. p. 318
Afranius *and* Petreius, *their Wars against* Julius Cæsar, *and their Losses,* Vol. 1. p. 329, 330. *their Deaths,* 358
Agricola *his Exploits in* Britain, Vol. 2. p. 240, 241, 251. *his dishonourable Reception by* Domitian, *and Retirement to a private Life,* 255
Agrippa Menenius, *see* Menenius.
Agrippa Vipsanius *beats young* Pompey, Vol. 1. p. 410. *and* Antony's *Forces at* Actium, 424. *his Speech to* Octavius *about laying down the Empire,* 440. *marries* Julia,

INDEX.

Julia, Augustus's *Daughter*, Vol. 2. p. 16. *compleats the Conquest of* Spain, 19. *refuses a Triumph*, 25. *his Death*, 26

Agrippina *marry'd to the Emperor* Claudius, Vol. 2. p. 123. *her Designs for her Son* Nero, 127. *poisons her Husband*, 129. *in Disgrace with her Son*, 133. *she is murder'd by his Order*, ibid.

Aigulf *chosen King of the* Lombards, Vol. 4. p. 258

Alani *make an Irruption into the Empire*, Vol. 2. p. 223. *fix in* Spain, Vol. 3. p. 277

Alarich *prepares to invade* Italy, Vol. 3. p. 257. *besieges* Honorius, 260. *defeated by* Stilicho, 261, 262. *makes a Peace with* Honorius, 263. *raises new Trouble*, 279. *Lays Siege to* Rome, 287. *enters it*, 291. *takes* Rome *by Force*, 294. *dies at* Consentia, 297

Alavivus *leads the* Goths *into* Thrace, Vol. 3. p. 167. *begins a War with the Empire*, 173

Albinus *created* Cæsar, Vol. 2. p. 396. *his Overthrow and Death*, 401

Alboin, *King of the* Lombards, *enters* Italy, Vol. 4. p. 221. *where he is proclaim'd King*, 223. *takes* Pavia, 227. *assinated*, 229

Alexander *created* Cæsar, Vol. 2. p. 441. *declar'd Emperor*, 444. *his Expedition into the East*, 451. *his Conquests*, 453. *his Death*, 456

Allobrogick *War*, Vol. 1. p. 251, 252

Ambrose, *Bishop of* Milan, *his Embassy to the Usurper* Maximus, Vol. 3. p. 201. *his Death*, 244. *his doctrinal Errors*, ibid.

Amalasont *declar'd Regent by the* Goths *in* Italy, Vol. 4. p. 53. *murder'd by* Theodatus, 94

Amida *besieg'd by* Sapor, Vol. 3. p. 46. *taken* 48. *restor'd to the* Roman *Army for Money*, Vol. 4. p. 33

Ammianus Marcellinus, *the Historian, his narrow Escape out of* Amida, Vol. 3. p. 49

Amphilochius, *Bishop of* Iconium, *his seasonable Answer to* Theodosius *the Great*, Vol. 3. p. 202

Anastasius *declar'd Emperor*, Vol. 4. p. 16. *Reigns well at first*, 17. *a profess'd Heretick and impious Persecutor*, 23, 27. *his Cruelty*, 29. *excommunicated by the Pope*, 30. *his Death*, 43

Andra-

INDEX.

Andragathius *murders* Gratian, Vol. 3. p. 199. *is made Admiral of the Usurper* Maximus *his Fleet*, 210. *drowns himself*, 211

Ancus Marcius, *the fourth King of* Rome, *his Reign*, Vol. 1. p. 30 *to* 34

Annibal, *the Carthaginian General, see* Hannibal.

Annibal, *the Carthaginian Admiral, his ill Successes and Death*, Vol. 1. p. 184, 185

Annibalianus *made Governor of* Cappadocia *and* Armenia *the Less*, Vol. 3. p. 5. *slain by* Constantius, 8

Anthemius, *Emperor of the West*, Vol. 3. p. 359. *his Death*, 366

Antiochian War, *or the War of* Antiochus, *King of* Syria, Vol. 1. p. 221, 224

Antiochians *offend* Julian, Vol. 3. p. 74. *raise a Sedition*, 205

Antoninus Pius *made Emperor*, Vol. 2. p. 321. *his Clemency*, 328. *his Death*, 331

Antonini Philosophus, *and* Verus, *Emperors*, Vol. 2. p. 332. Verus *his Expedition into the East*, 337. *marries the Daughter of* Philosophus, 338. *his Death*, 342. Philosophus *obtains a miraculous Victory*, 347. *his Speech and Death*, 357, 358

Antonius Caius, *the Consul, defeats* Cataline, Vol. 1. p. 288

Antonius Marcus *his Management upon* Julius Cæsar's *Death*. Vol. 1. p. 375 *to* 378. *his Attempts of raising himself*, 379, 380, 381. *beaten at* Mutina, 382. *joins in the second Triumvirate*, 384, 385. *his Acts against* Brutus *and* Cassius, 391, 392. *his Eastern Journey*, 396, 397. *falls in Love with* Cleopatra, 399. *his Luxurious and Prodigal Life with her*, 403, 404, 416, 419. *his Marriage with* Octavia, 405. *his ill Success against the* Parthians, 414. *falls out with* Octavius, 417, &c. *challengeth* Octavius *twice*, 421, 429. *beaten by him at* Actium, 424, 425. *treats with* Octavius, 427. *his Despair, Death and Character*, 430, 431, 432.

Antonius Lucius, *his Brother, raises a War against* Octavius, *and is worsted*, Vol. 1. p. 401, 402, 403

Apodemius *instrumental in the*

INDEX.

the Death of Gallus, Vol. 3. p. 24. *put to Death by* Julian, 67

Appius, *one of the Decemvirate, his ambitious Designs,* Vol. 1. p. 111, 112. *his Tyranny, Lust and Death,* 116 to 119

Arbetio *sent against the* Germans, Vol. 3. p. 27. *defeated by 'em,* 28. *a corrupt Judge,* 49. *provok'd by* Procopius, 113. *declares for* Valens, 114

Arbogastes *procures* Valentinian II. *to be murder'd,* Vol. 3. p. 220. *kills himself,* 226

Arcadius *declar'd Emperor,* Vol. 3. p. 196. *marries* Eudoxia, 235. *his Remissness,* 426. *persecutes St.* Chrysostome, 264. *his Death,* 274

Archimedes *his famous Works and Death,* Vol. 1. p. 209

Aristobulus, *King of* Judæa, *conquer'd by* Ptolemy, Vol. 1. p. 282, 283

Arsaces, *King of* Armenia, *assists* Julian *in his Wars against the* Persians, Vol. 3. p. 79. *deserted by* Jovian, 93. *murder'd by* Sapor, 130

Arsenius *made Tutor to* Arcadius, Vol. 3. p. 196. *retires into* Egypt, 197

Artabanes *his great Service to* Justinian *in* Africk, Vol. 4. p. 89. *against whom he conspires, and is pardon'd,* 165

Aspar *seizes on the Usurper* John, Vol. 3. p. 314. *defeated in* Africk, 319. *slain with his Sons,* 363

Athalarick, *King of the* Goths *in* Italy, Vol. 4. p. 13. *disobedient to his Mother,* 91. *his Death,* 93

Athanasius, *Bishop of* Alexandria, *banish'd,* Vol. 3. p. 3. *highly esteem'd by* Jovian, 100

Attalus *made Emperor by* Alarich, Vol. 3. p. 291. *degraded,* 293. *once more made Emperor by* Adolph, 301. *taken and confin'd to the Island of* Liparc, 302, 303

Attila *invades the Empire,* Vol. 3. p. 328. *sells a Peace to* Theodosius, 331. *breaks out again,* 335. *invades* Gaul, 339. *overthrown by* Ætius, 341. *enters* Italy, 343. *his Death,* 346

Augustus Cæsar, *see* Octavius.

Augustulus *proclaim'd Emperor,* Vol. 3. p. 375. *dethron'd,* 379

Avitus

INDEX.

Avitus *made Emperor in* Gaul, Vol. 3. p. 353. *dethron'd*, 354
Aurelian *made Emperor*, Vol. 2. p. 514. *kill'd*, 524
Autharis *chosen King of the* Lombards, Vol. 4. p. 244, *and turns Christian*, 245

B

Barbatio *sent to dispatch* Gallus, Vol. 3. p. 24. *opposes* Julian, 38. *beheaded*, 44
Belisarius *appeases a Mutiny at* Constantinople, Vol. 4. p. 68. *lands with an Army in* Africk, 70. *defeats* Gelimer, 71. *enters* Carthage, 72. *triumphs at* Constantinople, 79. *reduces* Sicily, *besieges* Naples, *and takes it*, 98, 99. *enters* Rome, 102. *which he valiantly defends against the* Goths, 111, &c. *to* 120. *refuses the Empire of the West*, 134. *recall'd out of* Italy, 135. *sent into* Persia, 139. *he returns into* Italy, 154. *his ill Success there*, 156, &c. *recovers* Rome, 164. *being envy'd at Court he falls into Disgrace*, 202, 203
Boetius *in Disgrace with* Theodorick, Vol. 4. p. 49. *is put to Death*, 51

Boniface, *Governor of* Africk, Vol. 3. p. 310. *calls in the* Vandals, 317. *and endeavours, when it's too late, to send 'em back*, 318. *returns into* Italy, *and challenges* Ætius, 319. *dies*, 320
Britain *reduc'd by the* Romans, Vol. 2. p. 254. *the* Britains *rebel, and set up a new Emperor*, Vol. 3. p. 272
Britannicus *poison'd by* Nero, Vol. 2. p. 134
Brutus Decimus, *one of the Conspirators with* M. Brutus *against* Cæsar, *his Actions and Death*, Vol. 1. p. 381, 382
Brutus Lucius Junius *his politick Designs*, Vol. 1. p. 49, 50. *he overthrows the Kingdom of* Rome, p. 52 *to* 55. *causes the Execution of his own Sons*, 62, 63. *his Death*, 64
Brutus Marcus *joins with* Pompey, Vol. 1. p. 332. *conspires with* Cassius *against* Cæsar, *and kills him*, 370 *to* 373. *his Success in the East*, 389, 390. *sees a Ghost, and his Discourse with* Cassius *concerning it*, 390, 391. *another Discourse with him before the*

Battel

INDEX.

Battel of Philippi, 391, 392. *both their Defeats and Deaths,* 392, 393, 394

C

Cæsar, *see* Julius *and* Octavius,

Caligula *made Emperor,* Vol. 2. p. 85. *his Expedition,* 103. *his exceeding Cruelty,* 101. *his Death,* 108

Calocerus *sets up for himself in* Cyprus, Vol. 3. p. 4. *taken and burnt alive, ibid.*

Calpurnia, *Wife to* Julius Cæsar, *her Dream,* Vol. 1. p. 372

Calpurnius Flemma *his great Valour,* Vol. 1. p. 185

Camillus Furius *takes the City of* Veii, Vol. 1. p. 132, 133. *his extraordinary Generosity at* Falerii, 134. *his Banishment,* 135. *he saves his Country,* 141, 142. *his after Acts both at home and abroad,* 142 *to* 149

Capitolinus, *see* Manlius.

Caracalla *made* Cæsar, Vol. 2. p. 400. *made Emperor with his Brother* Geta, 412. *kills his Brother,* 416. *and marries his Mother,* 413. *his Death,* 414

Carus *made Emperor,* Vol. 2. p. 536. *his Death,* 538

Carthaginian *War, see* Punick War.

Cassius, *the Consul, his ambitious Designs and Death,* Vol. 1. p. 95, 96

Cassius, *the Prætor, surrenders his Fleet to* Julius Cæsar, Vol. 1. p. 350. *For his other Actions see* Brutus Marcus.

Castinus *sent into* Spain, Vol. 3. p. 310. *defeated by the* Vandals, 311. *made General by* John *the Usurper,* 313. *taken Prisoner in* Africk, 315

Cataline *his Conspiracy against the State,* Vol. 1. p. 283, 284. *is reprimanded by* Cicero, *and leaves the City.* 285. *defeated and slain,* 288

Cato Porcius *the elder, his Behaviour towards the Women and his Soldiers,* Vol. 1. p. 221. *and towards* Scipio Africanus, 225. *his great Enmity to* Carthage, 230

Cato Porcius *the younger, his Grandson, his Management in* Cataline's *Conspiracy,* Vol. 1. p. 287, 288. *opposes* Pompey, 291. *and* Julius Cæsar, 292. *his Opinion concerning Bribery,* 296. *he is sent from* Rome *by* Clodius *his means,* 300. *his nice Advice in* Pompey's

INDEX.

pey's *Camp*, 332, 333. *his remarkable Death*, 358, 359

Caudium, *the dishonourable Treaty, and its Effects*, Vol. 1. p. 164, 165

Censors, *the last private Persons that bore that Office*, Vol. 2. p. 14

Chæreas *conspires against* Caligula, Vol. 2. p. 107. *put to Death by* Claudius, 111

Charles *the Great, King of France*, Vol. 4. p. 388. *prepares to conquer* Italy, 392. *where he abolishes the* Lombardian *Kingdom*, 394. *declar'd Emperor by the Pope*, 415

Chosroes I. *invades the* Roman *Territories*, Vol. 4. p. 137. *his second Invasion*, 140. *lays Siege to* Edessa, *which he is forc'd to raise*, 172, 173. *defeated by the* Romans, *and dies*, 232, 233

Chosroes II. *murders his Father*, Vol 4. p. 256. *is dethron'd, and flies to the Emperor*, 257. *by whom he is restor'd*, 258. *he takes the City of* Jerusalem, 281. *his Insolence and Blasphemy*, 282. *his Cruelty towards the Christians*, 290. *murder'd by his Son*, 296

Christ, *when born*, Vol. 2. p. 36. *when crucify'd*, 78

Chrysostome, St. *his Christian Courage*, Vol. 3. p. 253. *persecuted*, 263, *dies*, 266

Church, *the State of it in* Constantius *his Reign*, Vol. 3. p. 56. *in that of* Valens, 119. *oppress'd by the* Donatists *in* Africk, 270. *depress'd by the* Goths, 368. *a Schism in it*, Vol. 4. p. 22. *the State of it under* Justinian, 103. *persecuted, see* Persecution.

Cicero, *the renown'd Orator, procures* Pompey *his first great Authority*, Vol. 1. p. 277. *his skilful Management in* Cataline's *Conspiracy*, 284 to 288. *his Banishment*, 299, 300. *his Restoration*, 303, 304. *pleads for* Milo *in vain*, 314. *desires a Triumph without Success*, 319, 320. *procures* Anthony *to be declar'd Enemy to the State*, 381. *his Death by the second Triumvirate and Character*, 385, 386

Cimbrian *War*, Vol. 1. p. 251, 252

Cincinnatus Quintius *is chosen Consul and Dictator, both times from the Plough*, Vol. 1. p. 105, 106

Cinna,

INDEX.

Cinna, *the Conful, joins with* Marius, *and acts in the firſt Civil War,* Vol. 1. p. 259, &c. *his Death,* 263

Cinna, Pompey's Grandſon, *engages in a Conſpiracy againſt* Auguſtus, *by whom he is pardon'd, and declar'd Conſul,* Vol. 2. p. 42, 43

Ciſalpine Gallick War, Vol. 1. p. 195, 196

Civil Wars in Rome; *the firſt was between* Marius *and* Sylla, Vol. 1. p. 258 to 271. *the ſecond between* Julius Cæſar *and* Pompey, 321 *to* 348. *continu'd by* Cato *and* Pompey's Sons, 357 *to* 364. *the third between the ſecond Triumvirate, and* Brutus *and* Caſſius, 389 *to* 394. *the fourth between* Octavius Cæſar *and* M. Anthony, 420 *to* 432

Claudius *made Emperor,* Vol. 2. p. 111. *governs well at firſt,* 112. *his Expedition,* 114. *and Triumph,* 115. *his great Fear,* 118. *marries his Neece* Agrippina, 123. *by whom he is poiſon'd,* 129

Clelia *her great Bravery,* Vol. 1. p. 68, 69

Cleopatra, *Queen of* Egypt, *her Enterview with* Julius Cæſar, Vol. 1. p. 325. *the Favours ſhe receiv'd from him,* 355. *her Character and famous Enterview with* M. Anthony, 397, 398, 399. *her Management of him,* 403, 404, 415. *treats with* Octavius, 427. *ſhe retires to the Temple of* Iſis, 428. *her Carriage towards* Octavius, 434, 435. *her Lamentations over* Anthony's *Tomb, and Death,* 436, 437

Clodius *his Attempts upon* Julius Cæſar's *Wife,* Vol. 1. p. 289. *his Tribuneſhip,* 298, 299, 300. *his Death by* Milo, 358, 359

Cocles Horatius, *his extraordinary Valour,* Vol. 1. p. 67

Commodus *made Emperor,* Vol. 2. p. 360. *narrowly eſcapes a Conſpiracy form'd againſt him,* 365. *his Cruelties,* 367. *and Luxury,* &c. 369, 370, *& ſequ. his Death,* 372

Conſtans I. *created* Cæſar, Vol. 3. p. 4. *his ſhare at the Diviſion of the Empire.* 8. *his Wars in* Gaul, 9. *murder'd by* Gaiſo, 10

Conſtans II. *declar'd Emperor,* Vol. 4. p. 311. *murders his Brother,* 317. *his Expedition into* Italy, 321. *ſlain at* Syracuſe, 325

Con-

INDEX.

Constantine *the Great made Emperor,* Vol. 2. p. 557. *his Expedition against* Maxentius, 562. *whom he defeats,* 564. *summons the first General Council at* Nice, 571. *puts his Son* Crispus, *and the Empress* Fausta *to Death,* 572. *removes the Imperial Seat to* Byzantium, 574. *which he repairs, and calls* Constantinople, Vol. 3. p. 2. *divides the Government of the Empire,* 4. *is Baptis'd,* 5. *his Death and Character,* 6

Constantine, jun. *made Governor in* Gaul, &c. Vol. 3. p. 4. *slain near* Aquileia, 8

Constantine III. *succeeds in the Empire,* Vol. 4. p. 327. *concludes a Peace with the* Saracens. 330. *calls the sixth General Council at* Constantinople, 333. *his Death and Character,* 336

Constantius Copronymus *declar'd Emperor,* Vol. 2. p. 370. *overthrows the* Bulgarians, 384. *dies,* 397

Constantine V. *is made Emperor,* Vol. 4. p. 402. *confin'd by his Mother* Irene, 406. *whom he thrusts out of the Government,* 407. *and recalls her,* ibid. *he is overthrown by the* Bulgarians, 408. *and murder'd by his Mother's Orders,* 411

Constantine *Usurps in* Britain, Vol. 3. p. 272. *his Progress in* Gaul, 277. *made Partner in the Empire by* Honorius, 288. *but acts against him,* 298. *and is put to Death,* 299

Constantius Chlorus *made* Cæsar, Vol. 2. p. 543. *his Expedition,* ibid. *made Emperor with* Galerius, 553. *with whom he divides the Empire,* 554. *his Death,* 557

Constantina *marry'd to* Gallus, Vol. 3. p. 14. *her extravagant Behaviour,* 19. *her Death,* 23

Constantius *marry'd to* Eusebia, Vol. 3. p. 4. *murders his Relations,* 8. *creates* Gallus, Cæsar, 14. *overthrows* Magnentius, 15. *resolves to destroy* Gallus, 23. *grows Cruel and Jealous,* 25. *his Vanity,* 27. *he Defeats the* Germans, 28. *his Ingratitude,* 31. *makes* Julian, Cæsar, 33. *takes a Progress to* Rome, 36. *suppresses the* Quadi, 41. *grows jealous of* Julian,

INDEX.

lian, 50. *protects the A-rians*, 57. *his Death*, 64

Conſtantius, *a Noble* Roman, Vol. 3. p. 298. *made Lieutenant General by* Honorius, ibid. *grants a Peace to the* Burgundians, 301. *marries* Placidia, 303. *declar'd* Auguſtus, 306. *dies at* Ravenna, ibid.

Coriolanus Marcius, *his great Valour*, Vol. 1. p. 86, 87. *his Behaviour exaſperates the People*, 88. *his Trial and Baniſhment*, 89, 90. *turns againſt his Country with great Succeſs*, 91, 92, 93. *is perſuaded by his Mother to deſiſt, and is afterwards ſlain*, 94

Corvus, *or* Corvinus, *ſee* Valerius Corvus.

Craſſus *ſuppreſſes* Spartacus, Vol. 1. p. 272. *joins in the firſt Triumvirate*, 293. *gains the Conſulſhip with* Pompey *by Force*, 305. *his Eaſtern Expedition, Overthrow and Death*, 311, 312

Curiatii, *ſee* Horatii *and* Curiatii.

Curio *his ſerviceable Aſſiſtance to* Julius Cæſar, Vol. 1. p. 318, 319. *his Death*, 331

Curius Dentatus *Overthrows*

Pyrrhus, Vol. 1. p. 177, 178

Curſor, *ſee* Papyrius Curſor.

Curtius *his incredible Bravery*, Vol. 1. p. 150

Cyrill, *Biſhop of* Alexandria, Vol. 3. p. 304. *juſtly condemn'd*, 305. *procures the third General Council to be ſummon'd at* Epheſus, 322. *accus'd to the Emperor, impriſon'd and releas'd*, 323, 324

D

Dacia *conquer'd by* Trajan, *and made a Province*, Vol. 2. p. 286

Dagalaiphus *his bold Anſwer to* Valentinian, Vol. 3. p. 103. *ſent againſt the* Germans, 105

Decabalus, *King of* Dacia, *ſubdu'd by* Trajan, Vol. 2. p. 283

Decius *made Emperor by the Army againſt his Will*, Vol. 2. p. 482. *raiſes the ſeventh general Perſecution*, 485. *the manner of his Death*, 488

Decius Mus, *the Father and the Son, die for their Country*, Vol. 1. p. 158 *and* 168

Dentatus, *ſee* Curius Dentatus, *and* Siccius Dentatus.

Diocleſian *choſen Emperor*, Vol.

INDEX.

Vol. 2. p. 539. *makes* Maximian *his Companion in the Empire*, 542. *his Expedition*, 544. *and Resignation of the Empire*, 551

Domitian *made Emperor*, Vol. 2. p. 285. *his extravagant Pride*, 257. *and Cruelty*, 258. *murder'd*, 267

Drusus, *the Tribune, his unfortunate Attempts, and Death*, Vol. 1. p. 254

Drusus, *the Brother of* Tiberius, *saluted by the Army with the Title of* Imperator, Vol. 2. p. 27. *suppress'd the* Germans, 28. *his Death*, 29.

Drusus, *the Son of* Tiberius, *quiets a Mutiny in* Pannonia, Vol. 2. p. 57. *poison'd by his Wife's means*, 73

E

Encounter, *a strange one near* Rome, Vol. 4. p. 109

Erarick *chosen King, and slain by the* Goths, Vol. 4. p. 145

Eudocia *marry'd to* Theodosius II. Vol. 3. p. 307. *her Ingratitude*, 332. *she retires to* Jerusalem, 336

Eudoxia *calls* Genserich *into* Italy, Vol. 3. p. 351. *who leads her Captive into* Africk, 352

Eugenius *usurps*, Vol. 3. p. 221. *turns Heathen*, 223.

engages Theodosius, 224. *defeated*, 225. *and beheaded*, 226

Eutropius *opposes* Rufinus, Vol. 3. p. 233. *succeeds him in his Power*, 239. *his treacherous Practices*, 241. *put to Death*, 250

Eutyches *his Heresie*, Vol. 3. p. 334

F

Fabii, *their Generosity, Valour, and Destruction*, Vol. 1. p. 98, 99

Fabius Maximus *his cautious Proceedings against* Hannibal, Vol. 1. p. 203, 204, 205

Fabricius *his great Steadiness and Generosity*, Vol. 1. p. 173, 174, 175

Firmus *revolts in* Africk, Vol. 3. p. 124. *submits himself to the* Roman *General*, 143. *his Treachery*, 144. *he flies, and hangs himself*, 146, 147

Flemma, *see* Calpurnius Flemma.

Fritigern, *a* Goth, *his Exploits against the Empire*, Vol. 3. p. 171, &c.

Fulvia, Mark Anthony's *Wife, her Hatred to* Cicero, Vol. 1. p. 386. *raises a Civil War against* Octavius, 401. *her Death*, 405

Gabi-

G

Gabinius, *King of the* Quadi, *treacherously murder'd by the* Romans, Vol. 3. p. 131

Gaines *procures* Rufinus *to be slain,* Vol. 3. p. 238. *turns Male-content,* 245. *made General in the East,* 246. *his Treachery,* 248. *and Insolence,* 252. *reprov'd by* St. Chrysostome, 253. *his Designs upon* Constantinople *frustrated,* 254. *his Death,* 256

Galba *declar'd Emperor by the Soldiers in* Spain, Vol. 2. p. 152. *confirm'd Emperor,* 158. *slain* 169

Gallienus *made* Cæsar, Vol. 2. p. 492. *and Emperor,* 496. *oppos'd by the Thirty Tyrants,* 497. *slain with his Brother* Valerian, 508

Gallus Trebonianus *his Treachery,* Vol. 2. p. 487. *made Emperor,* 489. *revives the Seventh General Persecution,* 490. *is slain with his Son,* 491

Gallus, *the Son of* Constantius, *created* Cæsar, Vol. 3. p. 14. *his extravagant Behaviour,* 18. *and Cruelty,* 21. *put to Death,* 25

Gauls, *their principal Wars with the* Romans, Vol. 1. p. 135 *to* 142

Gelimer *makes himself King of the* Vandals *in* Africk, Vol. 4. p. 69. *defeated by* Belisarius, 71. *flies,* 75. *surrenders himself,* 77. *his Behaviour at* Constantinople, 79

Genserich *call'd by* Boniface *into* Africk, Vol. 3. p. 317. *conquers the Country,* 318. *takes* Hippo, 319. *breaks the Peace,* 326. *his Cruelties,* 327. *sacks* Rome, 351. *his piratical Excursions,* 359

George, *the Arian Bishop, his Character,* Vol. 3. p. 75

Germanicus *adopted by his Uncle* Tiberius, Vol. 2. p. 41. *refuses the Empire offer'd him by the Soldiers in* Germany, 57. *envy'd by* Tiberius, 61. *who recalls him out of* Germany, 63. *his Triumph,* 64. *he is sent into the East,* 65. *where he is poison'd,* 66

Germanus *declar'd General against the* Goths *in* Italy, Vol. 4. p. 168. *his Death,* 169

Gildo *serves the* Romans *against his Brother,* Vol. 3. p. 142. *Revolts,* 242. *Murders his Brother's Sons,* 243. *Overthrown,* 250. *strangles himself,* 251

Godegisil, *King of the* Vandals,

INDEX.

dals, *invades the Empire,* Vol. 3. p. 271. *settles in Spain,* 277

Gordian *with his Son made Emperor in* Africk, Vol. 2. p. 463. *the Father and the Son both slain,* 465, 466

Gordian, junior, *made Emperor,* Vol. 2. p. 472. *his Expedition into the East,* 475. *murder'd,* 477

Goths *admitted into* Thrace, Vol. 3. p. 167. *defeat the* Romans, 172. *besiege* Adrianople, 173. *cut off a* Roman *Legion,* 175. *Overthrow* Valens, 181. *great numbers of 'em destroy'd in the East,* 188. *settle in* Italy, Vol. 4. p. 26. *their Wars with the Emperor there* 98 & deinceps. *finally conquer'd by* Narses, 195

Gracchus Tiberius *his Laws, seditious Attempts, and Death,* Vol. 1. p. 237 to 240

Gracchus Caius *his many Attempts and Alterations in the State, and Death,* Vol. 1. p. 241 to 246

Gratian, *Son of* Valentinian, *declar'd* Augustus, Vol. 3. p. 125. *sends his Forces to the Assistance of* Valens, 174. *defeats the* Germans, 176. *marches into the East,* 177. *makes* Theodosius *his* *Partner in the Empire,* 190. *slain by* And agathius, 199

H

Hannibal, *the* Carthaginian *General, his March over the* Alps, Vol. 1. p. 199, 200. *beats the* Romans *at* Ticenum, *and at* Trebia, 200, 201. *at* Thrasymene, 202, 203. *and at* Cannæ, 205, 206. *he declines,* 207 *to* 213. *is entirely beaten by* Scipio, 216, 217. *his after Acts,* 222, 223. *his Death, and Reflections upon the* Romans, 226

Heliogabalus *sets up for Emperor,* Vol. 2. p. 430. *overthrows* Macrinus *and his Son,* 431. *confirm'd Emperor,* 432. *his Effeminacy,* 434, &c. *slain by the Soldiers,* 443

Heraclian *commands for* Honorius, *in* Africk, Vol. 3. p. 291. *defeats the Enemy,* 292. *usurps, and is kill'd,* 300

Heraclius *his Expedition against* Phocas, Vol. 4. p. 278. *he is declar'd Emperor,* 279. *sends Ambassadors to* Chosroes, 281. *his Success in the* Persian *Wars,* 285 *to* 296. *his great Exploits,* 297. *his Progress to* Jerusalem, 298. *turns* Monothelite, 299.

his

INDEX.

his Death and Character, 308

Herod, *King of* Judæa, *his Submission to* Octavius, *and Cruelty to his Wife*, Vol. 1. p. 426, 427. *his Death*, Vol. 2. p. 39

Hersilia *her generous Behaviour*, Vol. 1. p. 14

Honorius *declared Emperor*, Vol. 3. p. 222. *marry'd to* Stilicho's *Daughter*, 235. *besieg'd by* Alarich *in* Hasta, 269. *reliev'd by* Stilicho, 261. *makes Peace with* Alarich, 263. *marries his first Wife's Sister*, 278. *grows jealous of* Stilicho, 281. *orders him to be put to Death*, 283. *rejects* Alarich's *Proposals of a Peace*, 285. *makes* Constantine *his Associate in the Empire*, 288. *besieg'd in* Ravenna, 291. *his Wars with the Barbarians in* Spain, 310. *his Death*, 312

Horatii, *and* Curiatii, *their Combat for their Country*, Vol. 1. p. 27, 28

Horatius Cocles, *see* Cocles Horatius.

Hormisda, *King of* Persia, *depos'd by his Subjects*, Vol. 4. p. 256. *and murder'd by his Son*, 257

Hortensia, *her Speech and Behaviour to the second Triumvirate*, Vol. 1. p. 387, 388

Hunns *invade the Empire*, Vol. 3. p. 328. *their second Invasion*, Vol. 4. p. 201.

Hypatia, *Daughter of* Theon *the Philosopher, massacred in an Uproar*, Vol. 3. p. 305

I

James, *a Syrian, his great Sanctity*, Vol. 4. p. 31

Janus, *its Temple built, and shut the first time by* Numa Pompilius, Vol. 1. p. 21. *a second time*, 193. *a third time by* Octavius, 437, 438. *a fourth time by him*, Vol. 2. p. 11. *a fifth time by the same*, 36. *shut the sixth time by* Nero, 143. *the seventh by* Vespasian, 217

Jerusalem, *its total Destruction by* Titus, Vol. 2. p. 215. *rebuilt by* Adrian, 316

Jews, *their great Misery*, Vol. 2. p. 206. *their Rebellion, and Calamities under* Trajan, 299. *their last great Dispersion by* Adrian, 317. *their Insurrection and Barbarity at* Antioch, Vol. 4. p. 277

Ildebald *chosen King of the* Lombards, Vol. 4. p. 143. *and murder'd*, 144

Illyrian *War*, Vol. 1. p. 437, 438

John

INDEX.

John *usurps in the West*, Vol. 3. p. 312. *taken Prisoner, and beheaded*, 314, 315

John, *the Pope, his famous Miracles*, Vol. 4. p. 50

Josephus, *the Historian, taken Prisoner by* Vespasian, *to whom he foretels his future Advancement*, Vol. 2. p. 149

Jovian *elected Emperor*, Vol. 3. p. 90. *Concludes a Peace with the* Persians, 93. *found dead in his Chamber*, 99

Isauri, *their Inroads into the Empire*, Vol. 3. p. 20. *their Depredations*, 567

Isdegerdes *made Guardian to* Theodosius II. V. 3. p. 274

Italian *War, see Social War.*

Jugurthin War, Vol. 1. p. 248 to 251

Julia, Augustus's *Daughter, her first Marriage with* Marcellus, Vol. 2. p. 11. *he second with* Agrippa, 16. *her third with* Tiberius, 26. *her Banishment*, 35. *and Death*, 58

Julian, *the Apostate, created Cæsar*, Vol. 3. p. 33. *his Exploits in* Gaul, 34. *his Victory*, 39. *declar'd Emperor by the mutinous Army*, 52. *enters* Sirmium, 61. *his Reformations after the Death of* Constantius, 68. *he opens the Heathen Temples*, 69. *oppresses the Christians*, 70. *his Expedition against the* Persians, 72. *his Endeavours to rebuild the Temple of* Jerusalem, 77. *his great Danger*, 83. *his Obstinacy and Rashness*, 84. *he defeats the* Persians, 85. *is wounded and dies*, 86, 87

Julius Cæsar, *his Danger in* Sylla's *Proscription*, Vol. 1. p. 266. *he favours* Pompey's *first great Authority*, 277. *his Behaviour in relation to* Cataline's *Conspiracy*, 286, 287. *his Rise and Acts in* Spain, 288, 289, 290. *he quits his Triumph, and joins with* Pompey *and* Crassus *in the first Triumvirate*, 292, 293. *his Consulship*, 296, 297, 298. *his Expeditions against the* Gauls, Germans, Britains, &c. 300 to 304. & 306 to 310. & 315, 316. *falls out with* Pompey, *and the Senate, and becomes Master of all* Italy, 320 to 327. *his Expedion against* Afranius *and* Petreius *in* Spain, 328 to 331. *against* Pompey *in* Illyricum, 333 to 341. *and in* Thessaly, 342 to 348. *his Wars in* Ægypt *and Love to* Cleopatra, 351 to 355. *against* Pharnaces

INDEX.

in Asia, 356, 357. *against* Cato *and others in* Africa, 357, 358, 359. *his magnificent Triumph,* 360, 361. *he regulates the* Roman Year, 361, 362. *his Expedition against* Pompey's *Sons in* Spain, 362, 363, 364. *his great Honours and Acts at* Rome, 365 *to* 370. *his Death and Character,* 371 *to* 374. *his remarkable Funeral,* 377, 378, 379

Justin I. *advanc'd to the Empire,* Vol. 4. p. 45. *his Death,* 57

Justin II. *declar'd Emperor,* Vol. 4. p. 212. *recalls* Narses *out of* Italy, 219. *declares* Tiberius, Cæsar, 231. *Dies,* 234

Justin, *Martyr, his Apology for the Christians,* Vol. 2. p. 325

Justinian *succeeds* Justin I. *in the Empire,* Vol. 4. p. 59. *Overthrows the* Persians, 61. *resolves upon the* African *War,* 69. *and the* Italian, 95. *ill serv'd by his Officers in* Italy, 146. *makes a Truce with the* Persians, 199. *makes an ignominious Bargain with the* Hunns, 202. *escapes a Conspiracy,* 203. *his Inclinations to Building,* 204. *he embraces some Heretical Opinions in his Old Age,* 205. *his Death and Character,* 207

L

Lampadius *his bold Saying in the Senate,* Vol. 3. p. 279

Leo I. *elected Emperor at* Constantinople, Vol. 3. p. 355. *puts* Aspar *and his Sons to Death,* 363. *marries his Daughter to* Zeno Isauricus, 369. *his Death,* 370

Leo II. *crown'd Emperor,* Vol. 4. p. 358. *defeats the* Saracens, *ibid. an Enemy to Images,* 361. *upon which account a Tumult is rais'd at* Constantinople, 365. *his Taxes,* 369. *his Death,* 370

Leo II. *made Emperor,* Vol. 4. p. 398. *crowns his Son* Constantine, 399. *defeats the* Saracens, 400

Lepidus *joins in the second Triumvirate with* Octavius *and* M. Anthony, Vol. 1. p. 384, 385. *confin'd to* Africk *by* Octavius, 406. *and banish'd by him,* 411

Libanius, *the Sophist,* Julian's *Instructor in the Pagan Superstition,* Vol. 3. p. 70. *his Blasphemy,* 88

Licinius *created* Cæsar *by* Galerius, Vol. 2. p. 560. *whom he succeeds in the Empire,* 561. *his wicked Practices,*

INDEX.

Practices, 568. *put to Death*, 570

Limigantes Sarmatæ, *their Obstinacy*, Vol. 3. p. 42. *punish'd by the Emperor* Constantius, 43

Livia, *the Empress, her prudent Advice to* Augustus, Vol. 2. p. 42. *persuades him to adopt her Son* Tiberius, 41. *her Death*, 77

Lombards, *their Original*, Vol. 4. p. 217. *invited by* Narses *into* Italy, 220. *where they erect a Kingdom*, 223. *they take* Pavia, 227. *the Progress of their Arms*, 234. *they take* Ravenna, 363. *the End of their Kingdom in* Italy, 394

Lucius Junius Brutus, *see* Brutus Junius Lucius.

Lucretia, *her Rape, and voluntary Death*, Vol. 1. p. 51, 52

Lucullus *his Acts, and Success against* Mithridates, Vol. 1. p. 271, &c. *is stopp'd in his Progress by the Senate*, 274. *falls out with* Pompey, 278

Lupicinus *his corrupt Practices in* Thrace *pernicious to the Empire*, Vol. 3. p. 171

M

Macedonian *War, the first*, Vol. 1. p. 218 *to* 222. *the second*, 226 *to* 229

Macrinus *made Emperor*, Vol. 2. p. 425. *his Death*, 431

Mætius *his popular Design and Death*, Vol. 1. p. 125, 126

Magnentius *rebels in* Gaul, Vol. 3. p. 10. *his Cruelty*, 11. *Overthrow and Death*, 15, 17

Majorianus *declar'd Emperor of the West*, Vol. 3. p. 355. *defeats the* Vandals, 356. *murder'd by* Ricimer, 358

Manlius Capitolinus *his Valour in saving the Capitol*, Vol. 1. p. 141. *his Designs, Trial, and Execution*, 143, 144

Manlius Torquatus *his Combat with a* Gaul, Vol. 1. p. 151. *his severe Justice*, 158

Marcellus *his Success against* Hannibal, Vol. 1. p. 207. *his Acts in* Sicily, 208, 209. *his Death*, 212

Marcellus, *the Son of* Octavia, *marry'd to* Julia, Vol. 2. p. 11. *his Death*, 13

Mariamne, *Wife to* Herod *King of* Judæa, *her Death*, Vol. 1. p. 426, 427

Marinus *proclaim'd Emperor, and slain*, Vol. 2. p. 481, 482

Marius *his first Rise, and Acts against* Jugurtha, *King of* Numidia, Vol. 1. p. 250, 251. *against the* Cimbrians, 251, 252. *in the Social War,*

INDEX.

War, 256. *occasions the first Civil War, and his Danger*, 257, 258, 259. *his Acts and Cruelties in this War, with his Death*, 259, 260, 261

Marius *the Younger, his ill Success in the first Civil War, and his Death*, Vol. 1. p. 264, 265

Martian *declar'd Emperor in the East*, Vol. 3. p. 337. *summons the Fourth General Council*, 338. *his Death*, 355

Martian, *the Son of* Anthemius, *rebels against* Zeno, *and is made a Priest*, Vol. 4. p. 6, 7

Masanissa *his remarkable Passion*, Vol. 1. p. 215

Mauritius *his Exploits in* Persia, Vol. 4. p. 238. *advanced to the Empire*, 239. *enters into an Alliance with* Childebert, *King of the* Franks, 247. *protects* Chosroes, *King of* Persia, 257. *his great Covetousness*, 264. *his Death and Character*, 267

Maximian *made* Dioclesian's *Collegue in the Empire*, Vol. 2. p. 542. *his Expedition*, 544. *his Resignation*, 551. *attempts to recover his Authority, and is hang'd*, 559

Maximinus *made Emperor*, Vol. 2. p. 457. *his Success and Cruelties*, 462. *his passionate Behaviour*, 464. *his Death*, 468

Maximus, *the Philosopher and Magician*, Vol. 3. p. 72. *put to Death*, 139

Maximus *usurps in* Britain, Vol. 3. p. 197. *his Cruelty*, 200. *and Policy*, 208. *enters* Italy, 209. *defeated and beheaded*, 211

Maximus, *see* Petronius.

Mazezil *opposes his Brother* Gildo *in* Africk, Vol. 3. p. 243. *drown'd by* Stilicho's *Procurement*, 251

Mecænas *his Speech and Advice to* Octavius, *in relation to his holding the Empire*, Vol. 1. p. 441, 442, 443. *his further Advice to him*, Vol. 2. p. 4. *his politick Suggestion*, 16. *his Death and Character*, 31, 32

Menenius Agrippa *his skilful Management of the seditious Commons*, Vol. 1. p. 81, 82

Messalina *her cruel Artifices*, Vol. 2. p. 118. *her Lewdness*, 119. *and Death*, 122

Metullus Numidicus *his Acts against King* Jugurtha, Vol. 1. p. 249, 250. *his Troubles and Recovery*, 252, 253

Milo,

Milo, *the Tribune, opposes* Clodius, Vol. 1. p. 303, 304. *at last kills him,* 313. *and is banish'd,* 314

Mithridatick *War, the first,* Vo.1.p.257,262. *the second,* 268. *the third,* 271 *to* 274, *and* 277 *to* 281. Mithridates *his Death,* 281, 282

Mutiny *in the East by the* Goths, Vol. 3. p. 91. *at* Tricinum, 281. *at* Constantinople, Vol. 4. p. 65. *in* Africk, 82. *by the whole Army in the East,* 252

Mus, *see* Decius Mus.

Mutius Scævola, *see* Scævola Mutius.

N

Nævius, *his Augury,* Vol. 1. p. 38

Narses *sent into* Italy, Vol. 4. p. 122. *opposes* Belisarius *his Designs,* 124. *declar'd General in the West,* 171. *his great Success against the* Goths, 183 *to* 195. *recall'd out of* Italy, 219. *he invites the* Lombards *into* Italy, 220

Nepos Julius *declar'd Emperor in the West,* Vol. 3. p. 371. *expell'd by* Orestes, 375. *murder'd,* Vol. 4. p. 5

Nepotianus *sets up for himself, and is slain,* Vol. 3. p. 11

Nero *made Emperor,* Vol. 2. p. 131. *reigns well at first,* 132. *offended at his Mother,* 133. *poisons* Britannicus, 134. *his beastly Extravagancies,* 135. *murders his Mother,* 138. *marries* Poppæa, *and kills his first Wife* Octavia, 142. *sets* Rome *on Fire,* 144. *raises the first general Persecution,* ibid. *puts* Lucan *and* Seneca *to Death,* 147. *and* Petronius, 148. *and kills himself,* 156

Nerva *made Emperor,* Vol. 2. p. 272. *favours the Christians,* 274. *his great Clemency,* 275. *his wholesom Laws,* 276. *adopts* Trajan, 278, *and dies,* 279

Nestorius, *Bishop of* Constantinople, *his Heresie,* Vol. 3. p. 321. *condemn'd in the Council at* Ephesus, 323. *his miserable End,* 324

Niger *proclaim'd Emperor in* Syria, Vol. 2. p. 398. *his Overthrow and Death,* 238

Nigrinus *his Loyalty to* Constantius, Vol. 3. p. 62. *for which he is put to Death by* Julian, 67

Numa Pompilius, *the second King of* Rome, *his backwardness to accept of the King-*

INDEX.

Kingdom, Vol. 1. p. 19, 20. *his Reign,* 21 to 24

Numantia, *its Siege,* Vol. 1. p. 235, 236

O

Octavia, *Sister to Augustus Cæsar, her Worth and Marriage to* M. Anthony, Vol. 1. p. 405. *reconciles her Husband and Brother,* 409. *her generous Speech in relation to both Parties,* 417. *her Compliance,* 419, 420. *her Death,* Vol. 2. p. 28

Octavia, Claudius *his Daughter, marry'd to* Nero, Vol. 2. p. 123. *by whom she is kill'd,* 142

Octavius Cæsar *declares himself Heir to* Julius Cæsar, *with his Success,* Vol. 1. p. 379, 380, 381. *marches against* M. Anthony, 381, 382. *falls out with the Senate,* 383. *joins with* Anthony *and* Lepidus *in the second Triumvirate,* 384, 385. *marches against* Brutus *and* Cassius, *and by* Anthony's *Assistance overthrows 'em,* 393, 394, 395. *his Cruelties after their Deaths,* 396. *his troublesome Division of Lands,* 400. *his War with* L. Antonius, *and Success,* 401, 402, 403. *and with* Pompey *the younger,* 408, 410. *his Marriage with* Livia, 408. *chosen perpetual Tribune,* 413. *falls out with* Anthony, 417, &c. *proclaims War against him,* 420. *beats him at* Actium, 424, 425. *visits* Cleopatra, 434, 435. *reduces* Egypt, *and shuts the Temple of* Janus, 437. 438. *his Grand Consultation with* Agrippa *and* Mecænas, 439 to 443. *his Ordinances,* 444, 445, 446. *his Speech to the Senate,* 446, 447. *he establishes the* Roman *Empire, and takes upon him the Title of* Augustus, 448, 449, 450. *the extraordinary Honours decreed him by the Senate,* Vol. 2. p. 2. *shuts the Temple of* Janus, 11 *and* 36. *falls dangerously ill,* 12. *refuses the Dictatorship,* 14. *made Consul for Life,* 19. *succeeds* Lepidus *in the Office of* Pontifex Maximus, 25. *reforms the* Roman *Year,* 40. *adopts* Tiberius, 41. *his Speech to the* Equites, 46. *his Death and Character,* 50, 51, 52

Odoacer *invited into* Italy, Vol.

Vol. 3. p. 376. *slays O-reſtes,* 377. *declar'd King of* Italy, 379. *overthrown by* Theodorich, Vol. 4. p. 13, 14, *and* 18. *he is murder'd,* 20

Olybrius, *Emperor in the Weſt,* Vol. 3. p. 366

Olympius *practices againſt* Stilicho, Vol. 3. p. 281. *after ſome Services diſmiſs'd from Court,* 289

Oreſtes *rebels in the Weſt,* Vol. 3. p. 375. *ſlain by* Odoacer, 377

Oſtorius Publius, *his Actions in* Britain, Vol. 2. p. 124

Otho, *his Deſigns upon the Empire,* Vol. 2. p. 167. *made Emperor,* 170. *gains the Affections of the People,* 171. *his Army overthrown,* 177. *he kills himſelf,* 179

Ovid *baniſh'd by* Auguſtus, Vol. 2. p. 47

P

Papirius Curſor, *his Acts againſt the* Samnites, Vol. 1. p. 163, 165

Paras, *King of* Armenia, Vol. 3. p. 132. *deſtroys his two Friends at the Inſtigation of* Sapor, *King of* Perſia, 133. *detain'd Priſoner by the* Romans, 151. *eſcapes into* Armenia, *and is treacherouſly murder'd,* 152, 153

St. Paul *brought Priſoner to* Rome, Vol. 2. p. 135. *put to Death together with St.* Peter, 145

Paulus Æmilius, *ſee* Æmilius Paulus.

Pepin *Crown'd King of* France, Vol. 4. p. 378. *his Death,* 388

Perſecution, *the ſeveral Perſecutions of the Chriſtians,* Vol. 2. p. 144, 261, 290, 340, 406, 460, 485, 490, 493, 523, 549

Pertinax *made Emperor,* Vol. 2. p. 375. *his great Danger in* Britain *and* Africk, 377. *hated by the Soldiers for his ſtrict Diſcipline and Regulations,* 379. *his Clemency,* 380. *his Death,* 383

Peruſian *War,* Vol. 1. p. 401, 402, 403

Peter, *Sirnam'd the Fuller, his Hereſie and Inſolence,* Vol. 3. p. 369, & ſequ.

Petreius, *ſee* Afranius.

Petronius Caius, *his Behaviour at his Death,* Vol. 2. p. 148

Petronius Maximus *murders* Valentinian III. Vol. 2. p. 348. *uſurps the Empire,*

INDEX.

pire, 349. *he is slain,* 351
Philip, *the* Arabian, *made General,* Vol. 2. p. 476. *puts* Gordian *to Death,* 477. *declar'd Emperor,* 479. *and slain,* 483
Phocas *declar'd Emperor by the Soldiers,* Vol. 4. p. 265. *his perfidious Cruelty,* 273, 274. *his Death and Character,* 278, 279
Piso Lucinianus, *adopted by* Galba, Vol. 2. p. 165. *and slain,* 170
Placidia, Honorius *his Sister, marry'd to* Adolph, *King of the* Goths, Vol. 3. p. 297. *and to* Constantine, 303. *retires to* Constantinople, 311. *made Regent of the Empire,* 315. *her Death,* 335
Plutarch *his Advice to* Trajan, Vol. 2. p. 280
Pompey *the Great, his Acts in the first Civil War,* Vol. 1. p. 164, 165. *in* Africk, 265. *against* Sertorius *in* Spain, 269, 270. *against the Pyrates,* 275, 276. *against* Tigranes, Mithridates, *and other Eastern Kings,* 278 *to* 283. *his magnificent Triumph,* 290, 291. *he is oppos'd by the Senate,* 292. *and joins in the first Triumvirate,* 293.

assists Julius Cæsar *in his Consulship,* 297. *procures* Cicero's *Restoration,* 303, 304. *gains the Consulship with* Crassus *by force,* 305. *his sole Consulship,* 314. *falls out with* Julius Cæsar, 320. *abandons* Rome, 323. *and also* Italy, 326, 327. *his Wars with* Julius Cæsar, 332, 347. *his Misfortunes, Death and Funeral,* 347 *to* 350
Pompeius, Sextus *his Son, joins with his elder Brother* Cneius *against* Julius Cæsar, Vol. 1. p. 362, 363, 364. *the great Authority procur'd him by* M. Anthony, 380. *relieves many proscrib'd Persons,* 387. *he severely molests* Italy, *and comes to a Treaty with* Octavius Cæsar, 405, 406. *his Wars with him after that, and his Death,* 408 *to* 411
Pontius Comimus *his bold Attempt,* Vol. 1. p. 140
Pontius Pilate *kills himself at* Vienna *in* Gaul, Vol. 2. p. 88
Poplicola Valerius *his several Acts and Death,* Vol. 1. p. 61 *to* 70
Poppæa Sabina *her insolent Advice to* Nero, Vol. 2. p. 137.

INDEX.

p. 137. *marry'd to* Nero, 142

Porcia, *Daughter to* Cato *the younger, her Courage,* Vol. 1. p. 371. *her strange Death,* 396

Porsena, *King of* Hetruria, *Besieges* Rome, *and shows a great Generosity to the* Romans, Vol. 1. p. 66 *to* 69

Probus *made Emperor,* Vol. 2. p. 528. *his Expedition,* 529. *he suppresses* Saturninus Bonosus, *and* Proculus, 531, 532. *a remarkable Saying concerning him,* 532

Procopius *conceals himself after the Death of* Julian, Vol. 3. p. 98. *usurps,* 105. *grows insolent,* 113. *taken and beheaded,* 115

Proscription, *the first by* Sylla, *and its Effects,* Vol. 1. p. 266, 267. *the second, by the second Triumvirate, and its Effects,* 385 *to* 389

Pulcheria *persuades* Theodosius *to marry,* Vol. 3. p. 307. *forc'd to retire from Court,* 333. *marry'd to* Martian, 337

Punick, *or Carthaginian War, the first,* Vol. 1. p. 181 *to* 191. *the second,* 198 *to* 217. *the third,* 230 *to* 233

Pyrrhus, *King of* Epirus, *his Successes against the* Romans, *and Civility,* Vol. 1. p. 171 *to* 176. *he is at last worsted, and abandons* Italy, 177, 178, 179

Q

Quadi *invade the Empire,* Vol. 3. p. 41. *suppress'd by* Constantius, 42. *insult the Empire,* 148. *cut off two Roman Legions,* 150. *waste* Illyricum, 155. *sue for a Peace,* 157

Quintius Cincinnatus, *see* Cincinnatus Quintius.

Quintius Flaminius, *his Success against King* Philip *in the first Macedonian War,* Vol. 1. p. 219, 220

R

Radagaisus *invades* Italy, Vol. 3. p. 268. *defeated and slain,* 269, 270

Regulus *his Acts against the* Carthaginians, *and Defeat,* Vol. 1. p. 186. *his extraordinary Bravery, and Death,* 189, 190

Remus *falls out with his Brother* Romulus, *and is slain,* Vol. 1. p. 6, 7

Revolution, *the first great Revolution in the* Roman Empire,

Empire, Vol. 2. p. 150

Rhætians, *their Cruelty and barbarous Manners,* Vol. 2. p. 24

Ricimer, *a Goth, made General of the* Roman *Army,* Vol. 3. p. 355. *kills* Majorianus, *the Emperor,* 357. *besieges* Rome, 365. *kills* Anthemius, 366, *and dies,* ibid.

Romanus *his Tyrannical Government in* Africk, Vol. 3. p. 126. *his Policy,* 129

Rome *incredibly Populous,* Vol. 2. p. 112. *sack'd by her own Subjects,* 196. *overflown by the* Tiber, Vol. 3. p. 151. *her Inhabitants imitate the* Gothick *Fashions,* 243, *besieg'd by* Alarich, 287. *taken by him,* 293. *and by* Genserich, 351

Romulus *his Birth,* Vol. 1. p. 5. *reinthrones his Grandfather* Numitor, 6. *founds the City of* Rome, 7. *his Reign,* 8 to 18

Rufinus *made Tutor to* Arcadius, Vol. 3. p. 223. *his Ambition,* 232. *renders himself odious to the People,* 233. *his Cruelty,* 234. *Treachery,* 235. *and Death,* 238

S

Sabinianus, *a decrepit old Man, made General of the* Roman *Army,* Vol. 3. p. 44

Sabinus *his bold Reflection,* Vol. 3. p. 97

Salust *made Præfect of* Gaul, Vol. 3. p. 60. *his good Advice to* Julian, 79. *refuses the Empire,* 89

Sapor, *King of* Persia, *his Wars with* Constantius, Vol. 3. p. 44. *takes* Amida, 48. *concludes a Peace with* Jovian, 93. *invades* Armenia, 130. *his Artifice,* 132

Saracens *converted to the Christian Faith,* Vol. 3. p. 186. *a strange Action of a* Saracen, 187. *they embrace the Doctrines of* Mahomet, *and conquer* Persia, Vol. 4. p. 300. *defeat the* Romans, 301. *conquer* Egypt, 302. *their Success in* Africk, 312, 313. *they make the Empire tributary to them,* 404

Sarmatæ, *their first Irruption into the Empire,* Vol. 2. p. 204. *overthrown by the* Romans, 256

Saturninus *his Sedition and Death,* Vol. 1. p. 252, 253

Scævola,

INDEX.

Scævola Mutius *his extraordinary Courage and Boldness*, Vol. 1. p. 67, 68

Sceva *his great Valour*, Vol. 1. p. 338

Scipio Africanus *his first Rise*, Vol. 1. p. 211. *his great Success in* Spain, 213. *and* Africk, 214, 215. *where he at last overthrows* Hannibal, 216, 217. *goes Lieutenant under his Brother into* Asia, 223, 224. *his noble Carriage to his Accusers, with his Retirement and Death*, 225, 226

Scipio Africanus *the younger, or* Æmilianus, *his Encouragement of Learning*, Vol. 1. p. 229. *his Acts against* Carthage *in the third Punick War*, 231, 232, 233. *and in* Spain, 236. *his Death*, 241, 242

Scipio Asiaticus, *Brother to the Senior* Africanus, *his Success against* Antiochus, Vol. 1. p. 223, 224. *his Disgrace*, 226

Seditions, *the Principal, besides those which caus'd a Separation, were that about Marriages*, Vol. 1. p. 121. *that concerning Honours and Dignities*, 145, 146, 147. *that of the elder* Gracchus, 237 *to* 240. *that of the younger* Gracchus, 241 *to* 246. *that of* Saturninus, 252, 253. *that of* Drusus, 254. *a Sedition at* Rome, Vol. 3. p. 120. *at* Constantinople, 194. Vol. 4. p. 38, 365. *at* Antioch, 205. *at* Alexandria, 213, 303

Sejanus *his Rise*, Vol. 2. p. 72. *his vile Practices*, 74. *his Execution*, 79

Separations *between the Patricians, and Plebeians the first*, Vol. 1. p. 80. *the second*, 119. *the third*, 196

Sertorius *his valiant Acts in* Spain, *and Death*, Vol. 1. p. 269, 270

Servius Tullius, *the sixth King of* Rome, *obtain'd the Kingdom by Policy*, Vol. 1. p. 39, 40. *his Reign*, 41 *to* 46

Severus *proclaim'd Emperor by the Soldiers in* Germany, Vol. 2. p. 390. *confirm'd in the Empire*, 393. *his Expedition against* Niger, 397. *against* Albinus, 401. *into the East*, 404. *into* Britain, 409. *his Death, and Apotheosis*, 411, 413

Sextus, *Son to the last* Tarquin, *his Stratagem*, Vol. 1. p. 48, 49. *ravishes* Lucretia, 51, 52

Sibyll's

Sibyll's *Books, the Story,* Vol. 1. p. 49, 50

Siccius Dentalus *his bold Speech,* Vol. 1. p. 108. *his great Valour, and Death,* 116

Social *War, or* Italian *War,* Vol. 1. p. 254 *to* 257

Sophonisba, *her Tragical Story,* Vol. 1. p. 215

Spartacus *his Rebellion and Superstition,* Vol. 1. p. 271

Stilicho *his Ambition,* Vol. 3. p. 232. *his Exploits in* Rhætia, 260. *defeats* Alarich, *and procures a Peace between him and* Honorius, 261, 262, 263. *defeats* Radagaisus, 269. *rewarded by the* Romans, 270. *his Power in the Senate,* ibid. *his Death,* 283

Suevi *settle in* Spain, Vol. 3. p. 277

Sylla *his first Skill in War,* Vol. 1. p. 251. *his Acts in the* Social *War,* 256, 257. *against* Mithridates, 261, 262. *in the Civil War,* 263, 264, 265. *his great Cruelties,* 266. *his perpetual Dictatorship,* 267, 268. *his Death,* 269

Syracuse, *its Siege,* Vol. 1. p. 208, 209

T

Tacitus *made Emperor,* Vol. 2. p. 526. *his Death,* 527

Tarpeia *betrays the Capitol, and is slain,* Vol. 1. p. 13

Tarquinius Priscus, *the fifth King of* Rome, *his first Settlement in the City,* Vol. 1. p. 33. *his Reign,* 41 *to* 46

Tarquinius Superbus, *the seventh and last King of* Rome, *he murders his Prince, and obtains the Kingdom by Force,* Vol. 1. p. 45, 46. *his Reign,* 46 *to* 54. *his Banishment,* 54 *to* 55. *his first Effort to regain his Kingdom,* 60, 61. *his second,* 64. *his third,* 65, &c. *his fourth and last,* 73, &c. *his Death,* 78

Tatius, *King of the* Sabines, *his War against* Rome, Vol. 1. p. 13. *is made King of* Rome *with* Romulus, 14. *his Death,* 15

Theodatus *made King of the* Goths, Vol. 4. p. 93. *murders* Amalasont, 94. *his timorous Submission,* 96. *he is depos'd,* 100

Theodora, *the Empress, the great*

INDEX.

great *Patroness of the* Eutychian *Hereticks,* Vol. 4. p. 103, &c.

Theodorick, *King of the* Goths, *his Expedition into* Italy, Vol. 4. p. 12. *sirnam'd* Veronensis, 14. *besieges* Ravenna, 18. *declared King of* Italy, 20. *his prudent Administration,* 25. *his Reception and Behaviour at* Rome, 28. *he overthrows the* Bulgarians, 34. *his Death and Character,* 52

Theodosius, *senior, sent into* Britain, Vol. 3. p. 123. *his Success against the* Moors *in* Africk, 142. *he is put to Death,* 147

Theodosius *the Great declar'd Emperor by* Gratian, Vol. 3. p. 190. *summons the Second General Council,* 196. *concludes a Peace with the* Persians, 202. *his Clemency,* 207. *and Moderation,* 212. *he shuts up the Heathen Temples in* Rome, 213. *he defeats* Eugenius, 225. *his Death, and Character,* 228, 229, 230

Theodosius, *junior, declar'd* Augustus *by his Father,* Vol. 3. p. 263. *his Wars in* Persia, 308. *he buys a Peace with the* Hunns, 331. *his Death,* 336

Tiberius I. *marries* Julia, Augustus *his Daughter,* Vol. 2. p. 26. *his Retirement,* 34. *his Return to* Rome, 38. *Adopted by* Augustus, 41. *his Exploits against the* Germans, 44. *made perpetual Tribune,* 49. *takes upon him the Empire,* 56. *his profound Dissimulation,* 58. *he grows jealous of* Germanicus, 61, &c. *whom he procures to be poison'd,* 66. *his State Politicks,* 71. *his Answer to the* Trojan *Ambassadors,* 73. *his second Retirement,* 75. *his great Favour to the* Christians, 78. *his Cruelty,* 80. *and Death,* 83

Tiberius II. *created* Cæsar, Vol. 4. p. 231. *advanc'd to the Empire,* 236. *his Death,* 241

Tigranes, *King of* Armenia, *his Pride, and ill Success against the* Romans, Vol. 1. p. 273, 274. *refuses to receive* Mithridates *after his Defeat, and makes a Peace with the* Romans, 279, 280

Titus *his Expedition against the* Jews, Vol. 2. p. 206. *his Acts in that War,* 209

to

INDEX.

to 215. *his great Authority during his Father's Reign,* 218. *his Expedition against the Barbarians,* 224. *made Emperor,* 233. *the Calumnies rais'd against him,* 234. *turn to his Praise and Advantage,* 235. *his memorable Apothegm,* 238. *the Calamities during his Reign,* 239. *his Death,* 244

Torquatus, *see* Manlius Torquatus.

Totilas *elected King of the Goths in* Italy, Vol. 4. p. 145. *his prudent Conduct,* 152. *besieges* Rome, 156. *which is taken and pillag'd,* 160. *his Embassy to the Emperor,* 161. *he recovers* Rome *from* Belisarius, 167. *his Progress in* Sicily, 170. *his Death and Character,* 185

Trajan *adopted by* Nerva, Vol. 2. p. 278. *made Emperor,* 279. *his worthy Administration,* 281, &c. *his famous Bridge over the* Danube, 285. *his Conquest of* Dacia, 286. *his great Assurance founded upon his Innocence and Integrity,* 288. *he raises the Third general Persecution,* 290. *his great Expedition into the* East, *and Conquests,* 291 to 299. *his Death,* 301

Tullus Hostilius, *the Third King of* Rome, *his Reign,* Vol. 1. p. 25 to 30

V

Valens *declar'd Emperor by his Brother* Valentinian, Vol. 3. p. 103. *his Cowardice,* 110. *and great Severity,* 116. *a Friend to the* Arians, 120. *his Tyranny,* 136. *he admits the* Goths *into* Thrace, 168. *with whom he engages in Battel, and is defeated and slain,* 181, 182. *his Character,* 183

Valentinian I. *elected Emperor,* Vol. 3. p. 101. *his Speech to the Army,* 102. *makes his Son* Gratian, *Augustus,* 125. *his Cruelty,* 126. *his Exploits in* Germany, 134, 135. *his Expedition against the* Quadi, 155. *his Death and Character,* 158, 159

Valentinian II. *declar'd Emperoor,* Vol. 3. p. 162. *flies to* Theodosius, 209. *murder'd,* 221

Valentinian III. *made Emperor,* Vol. 3. 315. *ravishes the Wife of* Maximus, *and is slain,* 347, 348

Va-

INDEX.

Valerius Corvus *his remarkable Combat with a* Gaul, Vol. 1. p. 153.

Valerian *declar'd Emperor,* Vol. 2. p. 492. *led into Captivity by* Sapor, 495

Veii *besieg'd, and taken after Ten Years,* Vol. 1. p. 130 to 133

Venice, *when founded,* Vol. 3. p. 343

Vespasian *his Expedition against the* Jews, Vol. 2. p. 149. *created Emperor by the Eastern Legions,* 188. *confirm'd in the Empire,* 199. *he builds a Temple to Peace, and shuts up that of* Janus, 217. *his Regulations in the Army,* 218. *his Moderation,* 225. *a great Enemy to vicious Persons,* 228. *justly accus'd of Avarice,* 229. *his Death,* 232

Veturia, *Mother to* Coriolanus, *her generous Care for her Country, and Success,* Vol. 1. p. 93, 94

Virgil *his Death,* Vol. 2. p. 18.

Virginia *her Tragical Story,* Vol. 1. p. 116, 117, 118

Vitellius *his Endeavours to make himself Emperor,* Vol. 2. p. 164. *declar'd Emperor by the* German *Legions,* 172. *confirm'd in the Empire,* 181. *his formidable Entry into* Rome, 182. *his prodigious Gluttony,* 184. *he offers to resign the Empire,* 193. *he is slain,* 197

Vitiges *proclaim'd King of the* Goths, Vol. 4. p. 100. *marches towards* Rome, 108. *which he besieges,* 111. *his Stratagems defeated,* 118. *forc'd to raise the Siege,* 120. *taken Prisoner, and sent to* Constantinople, 134, 135

Ursicinus *sent into* Gaul, Vol. 3. p. 29. *procures* Sylvanus *to be murder'd,* 31. *Recall'd from his Command,* 44. *oppos'd by* Sabinianus, 47. *Accus'd at Court,* 49. *his generous Defence,* 50

X

Xantippus *overthrows the* Romans, *and is murder'd,* Vol. 1. p. 186

Z

Zeno *kills* Aspar *and his Sons,* Vol. 3. p. 363. *marry'd to* Leo's *Daughter,* 369. *made Emperor in the East,* 372. *flies into* Isauria, 374. *he is restor'd,* Vol. 4. p. 4.

his

INDEX.

his Death and Character, 15

Zenobia *her masculine Conrage and Conduct*, Vol. 2. p. 502. *her extraordinary Virtues*, ibid. *overthrows the Romans*, 503. *is overthrown by Aurelian*, 517. *her haughty Answer to him*, 518. *she is at length conquer'd by him*, 519. *and led in Triumph*, 522

Zozimus *his great Partiality*, Vol. 3. p. 191

FINIS.

www.ingramcontent.com/pod-product-compliance
Lightning Source LLC
Chambersburg PA
CBHW032007300426
44117CB00008B/926